The Burt Affair

The Burt Affair

Robert B. Joynson

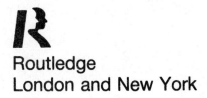

Routledge
London and New York

First published 1989 by Routledge
11 New Fetter Lane, London EC4P 4EE
29 West 35th Street, New York, NY 10001

© 1989 Robert B. Joynson

Typeset by Photoprint, Torquay, Devon
Printed and bound in Great Britain by
Billings & Sons Limited, Worcester

British Library Cataloguing in Publication Data

Joynson, Robert B., *1922–*
    The Burt affair.
    1. Psychology. Burt, Sir, Cyril
    I. Title
    150′.92′4

Library of Congress Cataloging in Publication Data

Joynson, Robert B. (Robert Billington), 1922–
    The Burt affair / Robert B. Joynson.
        p.   cm.
    Bibliography: p.
    Includes index.
    1. Burt, Cyril Lodowic, Sir. 1883–1971. 2. Hearnshaw, L.S.,
(Leslie Spencer).   Cyril Burt, psychologist.   3. Psychologists–
–England—Biography.   I. Title
BF109.B88J68   1989
150′.92′4—dc19   88-27098
                                                        CIP

ISBN 0–415–01039–X

Contents

Contents

Preface

Few reputations have undergone so dramatic a reversal as that of the late Professor Sir Cyril Burt. At his death in 1971, he was acclaimed as a founding father of British psychology and a commanding figure in the world of education. Five years later, he was accused of having committed gross scientific fraud.

The charge was directed primarily against Burt's published data on the inheritance of intelligence, much of which was alleged to have been fabricated. The question of inheritance is not only of great scientific interest; it also bears heavily upon the controversial social and political question of educational provision. If there are large natural differences in human ability, it follows – so many argue – that different children need different schooling; whereas equality of natural endowment is held to require similar schooling. Burt was accused of fabricating evidence for the inheritance of intelligence in order to support his own preference for selective education.

The bitter dispute which followed these accusations continued until the publication in 1979 of Professor Hearnshaw's biography of Burt. This tipped the balance decisively against him. Hearnshaw not only accepted many of the charges already made; he also alleged numerous additional deceptions. The Council of the British Psychological Society, in February 1980, endorsed Hearnshaw's conclusions; and at the annual conference of the society, held at Aberdeen in April 1980, his guilt was generally accepted. A few of Burt's old associates remained unconvinced, but to the world in general Burt's name became a byword for scientific deceit.

Today, many psychologists would perhaps consider that no good can come from raking over this regrettable episode. I must therefore briefly explain how I have become concerned, and why I ask for my colleagues' attention.

When the accusations against Burt first broke in 1976, I was not especially interested, nor did it occur to me that I should ever be. I had never known Burt; I had never worked in the field of educational psychology; and I had no position to defend on the question of the inheritance of intelligence. Hence I did not become involved in any of the controversy which erupted at that time. Indeed, so slight was my interest that I did not read Hearnshaw's biography when it appeared in 1979, and although I was present at the Aberdeen conference in 1980 I did not attend any of the papers about Burt which were given there.

It was only in the autumn of 1980, when general interest in the matter was rapidly subsiding, that I read the biography and began, for the first time, to acquire some detailed knowledge of the accusations and the evidence. My motive for studying the book was not a concern with Burt's conduct or character. It came from a long-standing interest in the history of psychology. I happened at that time to be studying the origins of intelligence testing, and the biography was an obvious reference. It did not occur to me that I was embarking upon anything other than a relatively short and routine task. How this became transformed into the present work is described more fully below (Chapter 3). Here I need only mention the initial impetus.

According to Hearnshaw, one of Burt's major deceptions concerned the early history of research on intelligence. It was claimed that he had in his later years given false accounts both of his own early contributions, and of those of his great predecessor Spearman, in such a way as to enhance his own achievements and diminish those of Spearman. Hearnshaw placed great emphasis upon this alleged distortion. It was 'entirely at variance with the evidence'. Indeed, it was such a travesty of the truth that Burt must have been mentally unbalanced to imagine that it could ever be accepted.

I found these assertions puzzling. It was not merely that the distortions seemed to have attracted remarkably little critical comment during Burt's lifetime. There also seemed to be very little evidence that, while he was alive, anyone had seriously supposed that he was mentally ill, and certainly not to the extent of perpetrating such extensive inaccuracies. Yet how else could they be explained? After much fruitless reflection, another possibility occurred to me. Was Burt's account really as inaccurate as Hearnshaw claimed? If it was not, the problem would disappear. It seemed, indeed, unlikely that Hearnshaw could be entirely mistaken. But the accusations against Burt were immensely damaging. They ought in any case to be checked.

To my surprise, the first check I made seemed to indicate very clearly that Burt's account was in fact correct. A second check produced the same answer, and a third and a fourth. As the inquiry proceeded, it gradually became evident that Hearnshaw's allegations were ill-founded.

When I became convinced that Burt had not been guilty of any deliberate historical falsification, it was unthinkable that I should not go on to examine the further allegations against him, especially those concerning the inheritance of intelligence. So I found myself involved, quite unexpectedly, in an examination of the whole case against Burt. I have come to the conclusion that the evidence which has so far been presented is insufficient to support the accusations which have been made. It does not follow that Burt's behaviour was invariably commendable, and that he possessed no weaknesses of character. But the gross misbehaviour of which he has been so widely accused has not, in my opinion, been established. A grave injustice has been done.

Those who believe that Burt was guilty have focused their attention on Burt as an individual, and have asked why he did it. Two main answers have been given: that of Hearnshaw, who suggests that Burt suffered from 'incipient paranoia'; and that of Burt's less charitable critics, who suppose that he had been a 'confidence-trickster' all his life. Either way, the 'Burt affair' becomes the story of a flawed individual. The only question is how far he may be granted the excuse of 'mental illness'.

But if Burt was innocent, different questions have to be asked. Why did the evidence seem adequate? Did those who accused him also have other reasons for their actions? Why did Hearnshaw accept their charges, and why were his conclusions so rapidly and widely accepted? In short, how was it that psychologists made such a mistake? Our attention is turned towards the character of contemporary psychology, and the Burt affair is found to have much graver implications for a scientific psychology than could ever be raised by doubts about the integrity of a single man, however eminent. I am far from thinking that Burt's own personality and behaviour are irrelevant. They must inevitably play their part, and colour the pattern of events as it unfolds. But they are not the only, or even the main, factor underlying the affair. We must look to the nature of psychology, and to the attitudes, beliefs, and desires of those around him.

This book also touches upon such closely related questions as the general reliability of Burt's findings, his place in British psychology, and his character and relations with his colleagues. But it is not intended to offer any definitive answer to those further issues. It does not purport to be a biography of Burt, or to provide an assessment of his contribution to psychometrics. Nor does it claim to deal with every aspect of the affair. It is concerned first to examine the evidence, and second to explore the consequences of concluding that he was innocent.

From the above account, it will be seen that the writer may fairly claim to have been unbiased at the outset. But it should be added that it is extremely hard to remain so. If examination of the evidence suggests that Burt was guilty, it is easy to become incensed by his behaviour. If it suggests that he was innocent, one may become enraged by the behaviour of others. In addition, one becomes committed to one's own interpretations, and blind to evidence which undermines them. Nobody can guarantee that they will remain without prejudice throughout the inquiry. The reader's only defence is constant vigilance.

Finally, in order to avoid misunderstanding, my position on the question of the relative importance of heredity and environment should be stated. It is similar to that recently expressed by Bouchard and McGue (1981). After reviewing 111 separate studies, giving 526 IQ correlations drawn from some 55,000 pairings of relatives, they conclude that IQ has both a genetic and an environmental component, in proportions unknown.

Robert B. Joynson

Acknowledgements

I am indebted to the many colleagues and friends who have generously responded to my queries or have provided me with copies of their correspondence with, or other material relating to, Burt, and especially to the following: Dr C. Brotherton, for his correspondence with the late Mr D. F. Vincent; Sir Halford Cook, for his recollections of Burt and his comments on the allegations against him; Dr Alan Gauld, for correspondence with Burt about F. W. H. Myers; Miss Rosemary Graham of Trinity College Library, Cambridge, for searching relevant records; Professor D. W. Harding, for many illuminating comments on Burt's character; Professor L. S. Hearnshaw, for sending me copies of Vincent's correspondence with Burt, and of his 'critical study' of Burt's statistical papers; Miss Sarah Joynson, for enquiries at London University; Miss Shirley Lander, of the Science Library, University of Nottingham, for invaluable assistance in pursuing elusive references; Dr M. McAskie, for throwing light on the origin of his own suspicions of Burt; Dr Elizabeth Newson, for her recollections of life at University College during Burt's final years there; and to the immigration departments of the Canadian and Australian Embassies for answering queries. I am especially indebted to Dr Charlotte Banks. She was closely associated with Burt during the last thirty years of his life, and her knowledge of his work is extensive. It is unfortunate that her own contribution to the subject (Banks, 1983) was published in a journal of restricted circulation, and has not received the attention which it deserves. Dr Banks has kindly read the historical sections of this book, and I have benefited greatly from her critical comments. She has also generously answered numerous questions on other aspects of Burt's life and work. None of those who have helped me is responsible for the conclusions and opinions expressed.

I have also to thank the following for permission to use their material: Mrs Heywood, for her correspondence with Burt discussing the use of pseudonyms; Mrs Geoffrey Merton, for her photographs of Burt; the University of Liverpool Library, for access to the Burt Archives; Mrs Vincent, for her late husband's correspondence concerning Burt, and especially for correspondence between Vincent and William Brown and Godfrey Thomson, not included in the Liverpool collection; the British Psychological Society, for permission to quote extensively from the Society's journals, and from the records of meetings of Council; the Association of Educational Psychologists, for permission to quote from their journals; and especially Hodder & Stoughton, and the Cornell University Press, for permission to quote extensively from *Cyril Burt: Psychologist*, copyright © 1979 by L.S. Hearnshaw. Professors Clarke, Eysenck, Harding, and Hearnshaw have also given permission to include extracts from their letters. Finally I must apologize to anyone who may have been inadvertently overlooked, or whom I have been unable to contact.

In reading what others have written on this topic, and still more in preparing my own manuscript for publication, I have become acutely aware how often we all make mistakes and errors which, though usually trivial, can also sometimes lead us to give inaccurate, and even downright false, accounts of the findings, opinions, and motives of our colleagues. I apologize to those who may find themselves unfairly treated in consequence of all the errors which, I am only too sure, must remain in my own work.

List of tables

Chapter one

Pioneer

Cyril Lodowic Burt was born on 3 March 1883. He died in his eighty-ninth year on 10 October 1971. His life coincided with a period of outstanding interest in the history of psychology. In 1875 psychological enquiry as we know it today did not exist. Psychology was still generally regarded as a branch of philosophy, of little scientific interest and less practical significance. But the last quarter of the nineteenth century saw the beginnings of a concerted attempt to establish this sphere of knowledge as a branch of natural science, which would have both theoretical and practical value; and Burt was a leading figure in Great Britain in this undertaking.

His career was a brilliant microcosm of the major trends and influences of the period. In the first decade of the century, as McDougall's first student at Oxford, Burt helped to conduct Galton's anthropological survey of the British population, devising and adapting for this purpose some of the earliest tests of intelligence. After a period of teaching and research at Liverpool, where he worked in the department of the great physiologist Sherrington, he accepted in 1913 an appointment as educational psychologist to the London County Council, the first such appointment made in Britain. Here he pioneered the methods and principles upon which the new profession of educational psychology was to be built. In 1933 he succeeded to the chair of Psychology at University College, London, then the leading position in British psychology; and there he wrote his major theoretical contribution, *The Factors of the Mind* (1940). In 1946 he was knighted, the first psychologist to be so honoured; and in 1950, the year of his retirement, he was elected a Fellow of the British Academy. After retiring, he remained for more than twenty years a prolific writer and pungent critic, abreast of current thought but embodying the historic roots of the subject.

Burt's life falls squarely in the period when psychology was struggling to attain the status of an independent science. This is not a tale of steady progress, of the gradual accumulation of agreed principles, established by generally accepted methods. It is a far more turbulent and uncertain business. It is comparable to the pioneering days of the exploration of new territory, rather than to the peaceful years of orderly development which may follow. It is a process of trial and error, in which various methods are attempted, and various solutions proposed, with no guarantee of a successful outcome. Critics are sometimes quick to condemn the rough and ready methods, the bombastic claims, and the fruitless arguments which have so often disfigured twentieth-century psychology. But perhaps these are the inevitable accompaniments of a would-be science, with all its opportunities, its difficulties, and its dangers.

Origins

Burt was born in London, the elder child of a general practitioner. In 1892, when he was nine years old, his father moved to a country practice at Snitterfield in Warwickshire. At first Burt went to King's School, Warwick; but in 1895 he returned to London to attend Christ's Hospital, a traditional boarding school. There he remained until 1902, when he entered Jesus College, Oxford. During his school holidays young Cyril would often accompany his father on his rounds, so he soon acquired a nodding acquaintance with the scientific study of man. It was during his schooldays, too, that Burt first became interested in psychology. In an autobiographical study (Burt, 1952a), he records the two famous works which set him going. The first was James Ward's article on 'Psychology' (1886) which he came across when he was fifteen years old in the *Encyclopaedia Britannica* in his grandfather's study. The second was Sir Francis Galton's *Inquiries into Human Faculty* (1883). The Galtons' family home happened to be in the village of Claverdon, only three miles from Snitterfield. So Burt heard a good deal about Galton from his father, and got the *Inquiries* from his school library. 'And I still recollect a superstitious thrill,' he wrote (1952a: 58–9), 'when I noticed on the title-page that it first saw daylight in the same year that I was born.'

 Burt was fortunate. It would have been hard to find two works which together provided a better introduction to British psychology in the late nineteenth century. Ward was among the most distinguished contemporary exponents of the traditional philosophical approach; while Galton was a brilliant representative of the newer empirical movements. These two men were to exercise a profound and permanent influence over Burt's outlook; and it is here that a study of his thinking should begin.

In the last quarter of the nineteenth century the traditional *philosophical approach* still exerted a powerful influence. As late as 1900 James was recommending introspection as the method of psychology 'first and foremost and always' (James 1890, I: 185). But there were already numerous signs that philosophy's long monopoly of psychological enquiry was ending. Much earlier in the century Herbart in Germany and John

Stuart Mill in Britain, themselves both philosophers, had urged the need to establish an independent mental science; and as the years passed the progress of the natural sciences made such a venture increasingly plausible.

The philosophical approach is sometimes treated as if it were necessarily hostile to the newer scientific developments, and had to be swept aside before psychology could advance. This interpretation is not wholly false, since there were often tensions between the older and the newer methods and conceptions. But as a general statement it is far from accurate, for the philosophical tradition played an important part in stimulating the rise of an independent science of psychology, as may be seen in a number of ways.

We have just noted that philosophers were among the first to advocate the formation of an independent mental science. Ward himself attempted, though unsuccessfully, to establish a laboratory at Cambridge in 1877 (Hearnshaw 1964: 171). Philosophers also contributed notably to the introspective analysis of mental life, and they continued to fill a prominent role right down to the end of the century, as when Henry Sidgwick, Professor of Moral Philosophy at Cambridge, became president of the second International Congress of Psychology, held at London in 1892. The pioneers of the newer empirical movements also often derived their hypotheses from the theories of the philosophers. Ebbinghaus undertook his epoch-making experiments on memory in order to check the suggestions of the associationists, a dominant school in the older tradition; and Wundt's experiments on the perception of distance were designed in part to explore the cues to distance proposed much earlier by Berkeley.

Such instances display a co-operative rather than a competitive relationship between the old and the new. This was expressed by the Frenchman Ribot, in his opening address to the first International Congress of Psychology, held at Paris in 1889, when he declared that 'psychology advances by combining physiological and pathological observation and experiment with the older introspective method' (see James 1889). The rationale of such a relationship is not far to seek. The use of relatively sophisticated scientific methods, such as experiment, presupposes that the phenomena to be studied have been sufficiently well described and analysed for an appropriate control of relevant factors to be undertaken. Such a preliminary analysis, using the method of self-observation, was a primary function of the philosophical tradition. In his *Analytic Psychology* of 1896, for instance, Stout described the 'time-honoured procedure' as providing a 'chart of the coast' which served as a preliminary guide to the 'inland explorers' with their more specialized methods. William James's classic, *Principles of Psychology* of 1890, owed much of its success to its masterly combination of the older and the newer approaches.

James Ward (1843–1925), an eminent exponent of the philosophical approach, was also the prime mover in a revolt from within British philosophical psychology against the long-continued dominance of the associationists. In a famous phrase of the historian Brett, Ward 'challenged the associationists to show cause why they should continue to exist' (Peters 1962: 675). Ward – to oversimplify greatly – favoured a psychology based on 'purpose' where the associationists had preferred 'habit'. Ward soon found powerful supporters in his British colleagues Stout and McDougall. When Burt became interested in psychology, this was the exciting and radical thinking of the day; and Ward's ideas left a strong impress on him, not only because the encyclopedia article was the first thing he ever read on psychology, but also because at Oxford his tutor in psychology was McDougall.

Throughout his life Burt believed that a study of the introspective tradition provided the best introduction to psychology, and within that tradition he always adhered to the standpoint of Ward and McDougall. Inevitably this has meant that some other psychologists, reared in other traditions, have found themselves out of sympathy with much that Burt stood for, just as Burt found himself out of sympathy with them. This was especially marked in the case of behaviourism, an objective revival of the associationist emphasis on 'habit', which McDougall repeatedly attacked. It is intriguing to note that in his old age Burt is to be found criticizing the contemporary spread of behaviourist ideas among the younger generation of British psychologists (Burt 1962b). To Burt this was nothing new. It was only one more shot in a campaign which he had been familiar with for more than sixty years, since he first read Ward's revolutionary article.

Darwin's *Origin of the Species* (1859) was a major stimulus to the newer *empirical movements*. Darwin placed the occurrence of evolution beyond question, and directly or indirectly inaugurated many subsidiary developments of great importance for psychology. Most important, from our point of view, was the increased attention given to individual differences, for it was in this field that Burt was to make his contribution. Individual differences were essential to the theory of evolution, for without variation natural selection would have nothing to act on.

The study of individual differences was taken up with great imagination and energy by Sir Francis Galton (1822–1911), a cousin of Darwin. Galton devoted much of his long life to exploring the implications of evolutionary theory for the understanding of human nature. His first important work, *Hereditary Genius* (1869), attempted to grade eminent men into classes according to the frequency with which their degree of eminence appeared. Galton argued, from the tendency for such abilities to recur in successive generations of particular families, that genius is primarily a matter of inheritance. In this he probably underestimated the influence which might be exerted in such cases by superior environment – as many would argue today. However this may be, in Galton's writings there are two closely related themes which were to exert a profound influence upon psychology, and especially British psychology, in the first half of the twentieth century: the study of individual differences, and the belief that such differences are strongly influenced by heredity. In his later books, such as the *Inquiries into Human Faculty* (1883) and *Natural Inheritance* (1889), Galton developed these themes and contributed many refinements of method. He introduced some of the earliest mental tests and pioneered their application in his anthropometric laboratory at the South Kensington Museum. The laboratory was eventually moved to University College, London.

Galton amassed a great deal of data about human differences, physical and mental, and he soon became aware of the need for systematic statistical treatment, both for economical description of the data and for their reliable interpretation. Although not by training a mathematician, he was a pioneer in the discovery and application of many of the basic concepts of the emerging discipline of statistics. Already in *Hereditary Genius* he had suggested that people could be graded for ability in accordance with the normal distribution, and it was in this work that the famous bell-shaped curve was first applied to individual differences. His major statistical contribution came some twenty years later. A French criminologist, Alphonse Bertillon, had recently introduced a method of classifying and identifying criminals on the basis of only twelve bodily measurements, together with some photographs and distinguishing marks. His proposals raised, in a very practical form, the question of how many physical measurements are actually needed to characterize a particular physique uniquely. Are so many as twelve really necessary? If a man's height is known, for example, is it also necessary to measure the length of the arm or the leg, or the size of the head? Galton believed that there was so little variation in the ratios among the twelve that little fresh information was added by measuring more than one or two of them. Many could be discarded. But reliable conclusions depended upon the accurate measurement of the degree of concomitant variation among the dimensions involved, and a suitable method remained to be discovered.

Galton found the key to the problem in a formula which he presented to the Royal Society in 1888, and published the following year in a paper entitled 'Co-relations and their measurements chiefly from anthropometric data' (Galton 1888–9). Galton records that the solution came to him while he was sheltering from a shower at Naworth Castle, near Carlisle; and his biographer, Karl Pearson, remarks that the spot deserves to be commemorated as the birthplace of the far-reaching conception of correlation (Pearson 1914–30, 2: 393). Galton set out this conception more fully in his *Natural Inheritance* of 1889. From the standpoint of psychology, the chief interest of the episode lies in the possibility of applying similar methods to the analogous problem of classifying individuals according to their mental characteristics.

Galton's ideas were taken up with great flair and enthusiasm by Karl

Pearson (1857–1936). Appointed in 1884, when still in his twenties, to the chair of Applied Mathematics at University College, London, Pearson was among the first to appreciate the potential of the statistical techniques which Galton was exploring. Pearson records that in 1894 Galton gave the first academic lecture on variation and correlation at University College, marking the inauguration of Pearson's 'Biometric Laboratory', as he called it. In the following years Pearson, together with a number of able colleagues, devised and perfected a remarkable number of the basic statistical methods which are taken for granted today in the biological and social sciences. London University became the headquarters of the biometric movement.

Galton, now approaching the end of his long life, took a great interest in Pearson's work and did much to help him. In 1901 they jointly founded the journal *Biometrika* to encourage the spread of their new methods – and Burt records that he bought a copy of the first number (Burt 1952a: 60). Both Galton and Pearson continued to attach great importance to heredity, believing that in the human as in the animal world selective breeding could dramatically improve the stock. *Punch* (20 March 1880) poked fun at the belief in a cartoon depicting an earl in his coronet gazing from behind a five-barred gate at his prize bull. 'Well, you are a fine fellow, and no mistake', he says. The bull replies, 'And so would you be, my lord, if they'd taken as much pains in choosing your ancestry as you did in choosing mine'. But Galton and Pearson took it very seriously. Galton's *Inquiries*, for example, shows an underlying preoccupation with the dangers of racial degeneration. In 1907 the Eugenics Society was formed, and in 1911 Galton endowed a new chair of Eugenics at University College, to which Pearson transferred. In terms of contemporary politics, such ventures are readily seen as 'racist' and 'elitist', a theme to which we shall return.

Opinions differ as to the ultimate value of the biometric movement, whether for biology in general or psychology in particular. In Pearson's view, Galton had inaugurated a new method which for psychology was comparable in its importance to the method of experiment itself, introduced by Wundt in 1879. Certainly, for Burt, Galton's work – and everything which it led to – was the great intellectual stimulus of his life. When still a schoolboy, accompanying his father on his rounds, he had met Galton, and Galton always remained his guiding spirit. Burt's own tribute to him was unqualified:

> if we try to sum up his life's work in a single phrase, it is . . . as the founder of individual psychology that Galton is to be remembered. When he left it . . . he had transformed it into a reputable branch of natural science – perhaps for mankind the most important branch there is.
>
> (Burt 1961a: 20; see also Burt 1962a).

Burt's enthusiasm is infectious. But Galton was not the last who would be credited with transforming this field into a reputable branch of natural science; only the first.

Burt at Oxford

In October 1902, when Burt entered Jesus College, Oxford, it was not yet possible to take a degree in psychology there, nor at any other British university. Burt at first wanted to take a scientific course, but he held a scholarship in classics, and his tutors insisted that he take the traditional Oxford Greats course in classics and philosophy. As it happened, this was the only course which included any psychology at all. A private benefactor had recently endowed a post in 'mental philosophy' – the Wilde Readership – whose holder taught an optional paper in psychology for the later stages of the Greats course. The first holder of the post was Stout, but he left in 1903 and does not seem to have influenced Burt at this stage. Stout was succeeded in 1904 by McDougall, and Burt was among his first pupils.

William McDougall (1871–1938) is best known for his theories of instinct and sentiment, which brought him into conflict with the behaviourists. In 1904 he was still in the process of acquiring his encyclopedic knowledge of psychology, which must have made him an exceptionally effective tutor. Many of Burt's permanent interests and emphases may be traced, at least in part, to McDougall's influence: his sympathy with the standpoint of Ward and Stout; his rejection of behaviourism; his studies of emotion and feeling; his interest in the hierarchy of nervous centres; his realization of the importance of Pearson's biometric work; and, most important of all perhaps, his early involvement in Galton's survey. This last came about in the following way.

McDougall liked the German system of university education, where the student learned by attempting some research of his own; and a suitable topic soon turned up. In 1905, the British Association decided to sponsor an anthropological survey of the British population, under the chairmanship of Galton, which was to cover both mental and physical qualities. Galton set up a sub-committee under McDougall to handle the mental side; and McDougall, knowing of Burt's interest in Galton's ideas, recruited him to assist in the devising of methods and the collection of data. And so at this very early stage, before he had even taken his first degree, Burt found himself embarking upon research in his favourite topic, with the aim of helping Galton himself. It was in this way that Burt began to collect the material which was to form the basis of his first paper, entitled 'Experimental tests of general intelligence' (Burt 1909). Once launched upon this theme, he never looked back.

Before he came to Oxford, McDougall had held a post at University

College, London, and while there he had naturally become acquainted with the statistical work of Galton and Pearson. Though not a mathematician himself, he appreciated its potential, and welcomed the opportunity of supervising the psychological side of Galton's survey. Burt records that 'Galton had suggested that the efficiency of the tests should first be checked by the correlation techniques which he and Karl Pearson had worked out; and accordingly McDougall invited Pearson to Oxford to give a brief exposition of his new methods of statistical analysis' (Burt 1952b: xi). It was in this way, according to Burt, that he met Pearson while he was still an undergraduate; and Pearson's interest in the testing which they were conducting was enhanced, apparently, by the circumstance that Pearson's son happened to be among the group of schoolboys whom Burt was assessing (Burt 1952a: 60); the school in question was the Dragon School in north Oxford, a popular establishment then as now for the children of academics. As we shall see in detail later (Chapter 5), Burt subsequently claimed that, from the talk which Pearson gave on this occasion, he gathered some important hints for the development of his own work. Thus he stated that, at a meeting of a college club called the Delian Society, he gave a talk which 'outlined a method of factorizing correlations (modified from Pearson's) which I subsequently used in my 1909 and 1917 articles' (Burt 1952a: 61). The talk, Burt added, was full of 'adolescent affectations'. Burt does not date either Pearson's visit or his own talk, but these events – if they occurred – must have happened before 1907, when Burt graduated. It is a question of some moment in 'the Burt affair' what truth, if any, there may be in Burt's assertions.

It was also through McDougall that Burt became acquainted with another important figure, Charles Spearman (1863–1945). Spearman had embarked in his youth upon a career in the army, and saw service in India in the great days of the British raj. It was not until 1897, at the age of thirty-four, that he transferred his allegiance to the academic life, and specifically to psychology. After a lengthy training in Germany, then the Mecca of all budding psychologists, he became interested in the nature and assessment of intelligence; and in 1904 he published two papers in the *American Journal of Psychology* which were destined to exert great influence. The first, entitled 'The proof and measurement of association between two things', drew attention to the statistical methods of correlation being developed by the biometric school. 'Psychologists never seem to have become acquainted,' he wrote (Spearman 1904a: 96), 'with the brilliant work being carried out since 1886 by the Galton–Pearson school.' The second, and better-known, paper was entitled 'General intelligence: objectively determined and measured', and proposed the development of what he called a 'Correlation Psychology' (Spearman 1904b). This adumbrated his well-known theory of ability as a general power.

Spearman was eager to obtain an academic post, but it was not until

1907, when he was forty-four, that he was able with McDougall's support to secure an appointment at University College, London. This was the beginning of the long association of the Department of Psychology there with the analysis of ability by statistical methods, which eventually came to be known as 'factor analysis'. After the First World War, in 1920, McDougall emigrated to America, and Spearman was left with few rivals in the small world of British psychology. He was able to make the psychometric movement a dominating influence at University College, and after his retirement in 1932, the tradition was carried on by Burt.

Spearman's arrival at University College brought him to work in the same institution as Pearson; and it might have been expected that the two men, sharing a number of interests, would soon form an amicable relationship. But unfortunately this was not to be. In his first paper, Spearman had ventured to criticize certain aspects of the biometric method, and Pearson, a peppery person, took umbrage. Relations between the two men never recovered. Banks (1983: 31) records a University College story that if either saw the other approaching, he would beat a hasty retreat and wait until the coast was clear. Their rivalry is a circumstance to be borne in mind as our simple tale of academic folk unfolds.

The precise nature and extent of the influence which Pearson and Spearman exerted over Burt in these early years is a key question. Here it may be emphasized that Burt was never a pupil of Pearson (as Rose, Kamin and Lewontin 1984: 26, state), nor a pupil of Spearman (as Oléron 1957: 72, supposes), nor a pupil of Galton (as Gillie 1976a: 179, has it). Nor was Burt ever a student at University College, either undergraduate or postgraduate. Burt was a pupil of McDougall at Oxford; and it was McDougall who gave Burt the chance of working on Galton's survey, who first encouraged his interest in intelligence, who introduced him to Pearson and Spearman, and who moulded his intellectual outlook. Burt always acknowledged his debt with warm admiration, as in his obituary notice, 'William McDougall: an appreciation' (Burt, 1939a).

Burt graduated in 1907, and spent a further year studying for a teaching diploma. This marked his first practical experience in the educational field, and allowed him to continue with his research into intelligence. During this year, also, he was awarded the John Locke scholarship, which enabled him to spend the summer of 1908 studying at Wurzburg, then a major centre of psychological research in Germany. Brief as his stay there was, it had an important influence on his thinking, which deserves to be noted.

When Wundt had first introduced experimental psychology at Leipzig, nearly thirty years earlier, he had concentrated initially on such relatively simple functions as sensation and perception. In these areas, some of the more important conditions are fairly readily controlled. But Wundt always supposed that more complex functions, such as problem-solving and thinking, were likely to remain permanently beyond the scope of experiment. At Wurzburg, however, Kulpe and his followers created much interest in the first decade of the new century by their ingenious, if controversial, efforts to overcome the difficulties and incorporate the 'higher mental processes' in their experimental programme.

These developments were relevant to Burt's interests. The pioneers of mental testing in Britain and America, influenced in part by Wundt's beliefs, had shown a marked tendency to base their tests on sensory processes and other simple reactions. They had then been disappointed – somewhat unreasonably, as we might now think – to find that their measurements seemed to have little connection with academic success or other accepted criteria of ability. However, these failures suggested to some psychologists that perhaps a wider range of functions ought to be examined, rather as the Wurzburg group were attempting in the experimental field. In this way, a more realistic measure of the elusive faculty 'intelligence' might be gained; and Ebbinghaus and Meumann in Germany had already begun to extend their own tests in this direction. Burt took the hint, and these influences may be traced in his 1909 paper.

The Oxford of 1900 might seem an unpropitious place for a young psychologist to learn his trade. But a student who had been McDougall's pupil, who had collected data for Galton's survey, who had been introduced to Pearson and Spearman, and had been able to visit Wurzburg, had not been given a bad start in life.

Burt's career

Burt's first post was as Lecturer in Psychology at Liverpool University, which he took up in 1908 on his return from Wurzburg. Such opportunities were extremely rare in those days, and Burt's appointment was actually in the Department of Physiology. This was due to the interest of the great physiologist Sir Charles Sherrington, who was Holt Professor at Liverpool from 1895 to 1913. Sherrington was author of a classic study, *The Integrative Action of the Nervous System* (1906), which gave a systematic exposition of the major findings of nineteenth-century neurology. Sherrington favoured the conception of a nervous system organized through a hierarchy of control centres, subserving successively more complex forms of behaviour. It was an idea which had appealed to James, and also McDougall, and Burt himself was frequently to employ it in discussing the physiological counterpart of intelligence.

Burt's paper entitled 'Experimental tests of general intelligence' (Burt 1909) described the work he had embarked upon at Oxford at McDougall's instigation, and provided some of the earliest evidence for Spearman's conception of a general ability. This paper was followed by others on the same theme: on higher mental processes (Burt 1911c), and on mental differences between the sexes (Burt and Moore 1912). By the time he was thirty, Burt was already beginning to make his mark in his chosen field.

In 1913, Burt left Liverpool to become a part-time educational psychologist for the London County Council. This was the first professional appointment in psychology to be made in Britain. The move, from the academic to the applied, was not so great a change in Burt's intellectual interests as has sometimes been represented. He continued to publish in the field of intelligence, notably in his *Distribution and Relations of Educational Abilities* (Burt 1917) and in *Mental and Scholastic Tests* (Burt 1921). The former, in particular, made notable theoretical contributions, which are relevant in the Burt affair. Burt was certainly deeply interested in the applications of psychology, and was committed to promoting the value he believed it possessed in helping the individual. But he did not see this as an alternative to, and certainly not as excluding, a continued interest in theoretical questions. For Burt, it was only on the basis of sound theory that psychology's practical potential could be realized. Those who label Burt as an applied psychologist, and intend to imply thereby that he lacked interest in general scientific questions, are therefore misguided. Like Freud, Burt found the data he needed in facing the challenges of everyday life, rather than in the laboratory; and his move from Liverpool to London was as much a quest for the most appropriate context in which to pursue his intellectual interests as it was a change of occupation.

Throughout Burt's career these two interests, the theoretical and the practical, go hand in hand, though sometimes the one and sometimes the other may be more obvious. The practical concern is to the fore in the part which Burt played in the twenties in the foundation of the National Institute of Industrial Psychology, and in the formation of Child Guidance Centres. Burt's theoretical concerns took pride of place in his magnum opus, *The Factors of the Mind* (1940), which was a comprehensive review of the various contrasting methods of analysing ability, together with an attempt to harmonize and combine their good points. There were also other very influential books in which Burt displayed the two interests in harness, such as *The Young Delinquent* (1925), *The Backward Child* (1937a), and the posthumous *Gifted Child* (1975).

In 1924 Burt was appointed Professor of Educational Psychology at the London Day Training Centre, which later became the University of London's Institute of Education. But the peak of his career came when, after Spearman's retirement, he succeeded him in the chair of Psychology at University College. Here from 1932 until his own retirement in 1950, Burt occupied what was then effectively the top job in British psychology. Burt was unlucky in that his time was disrupted by the Second World War. His department was evacuated to Aberystwyth, and much of his time taken up with war work, so that he never had a clear run to develop psychology at London as he might have wished. However, his services were publicly recognized in 1946 when he received a knighthood, the first psychologist to be so honoured – and still one of only two, the other being Sir Frederic Bartlett, Professor of Experimental Psychology at Cambridge from 1931 to 1952.

Burt enjoyed an exceptionally long and productive retirement. Some 200 of his publications date from this period (1950–71), and they covered a remarkably wide range: from the history of research on intelligence to psychical phenomena, and from the legibility of print to the philosophy of mind. He was also active in many other ways, whether lecturing, or examining, or reviewing books and manuscripts; but perhaps his most onerous task was as editor of the newly founded *British Journal of Statistical Psychology*, sometimes jointly and sometimes alone, from 1947 until 1963. Despite these wide – perhaps too wide – preoccupations, Burt's major interests recur again and again: the theory of intelligence; heredity and research with kinship groups; and the practical implications of these interests. It was in precisely these central areas that Burt was to be accused of deception; but during his lifetime his reputation remained high and unsullied to the end, as shown by his award in 1971 of the Thorndike Prize, an American distinction for outstanding contributions to educational psychology. Here again Burt was the first British recipient.

The analysis of ability

Questions about human intelligence, its varieties and individual differences, were never far from Burt's thoughts; and it is only through an understanding of his work in this field that we can appreciate his contribution to British psychology.

A fundamental problem, from which many other questions stem, concerns how far ability is specialized, how far general. Athletic ability presents a similar problem in a more concrete form. A number of observations might suggest that athletic ability is highly specialized: great sprinters do not distinguish themselves in the marathon, nor do outstanding hurdlers win the javelin. Again, there is a tendency for black men to dominate the sprint races, while in the middle distances white men seem to be to the fore. These considerations seem to point to the existence of several distinct kinds of athletic capacity, possibly related to genetic factors. But other observations suggest a different conclusion: some athletes, notably those who distinguish themselves in the pentathlon or decathlon, are remarkably versatile. This might mean that athletic ability is fundamentally general, and that specialized achievements result from individual preference and concentrated training.

Similar questions arise in the more abstract matter of intellectual pursuits. If a man shows a bent in one direction, how far does this mean that he will prove able in other directions too? If a man shows a flair for mathematics, is this a highly specialized gift, whose possession will distinguish him in the mathematical field alone, and leave him on a par with everyone else in other matters? Or is it, rather, an expression of a high general level of ability, so that he might equally distinguish himself in literary, or musical or philosophical pursuits, if he chose to apply himself? Plainly, this is a question of great theoretical and practical interest.

These problems were discussed long before psychologists appeared on the scene, as Burt (1967a: 265 and note 1) remarked when reviewing the history of ideas about intelligence:

> Robertson, the historian, had argued that it was by virtue of very different gifts that Newton had become a great scientist, Caesar a great commander, Shakespeare a great poet. 'No', replied Johnson, 'it is only that one man has more mind than another, though he may prefer this matter to that. Sir, the man who has vigour may walk to the North as well as to the South, to the East as well as to the West'. . . . Carlyle defends much the same conclusion: 'I have no notion of a truly great man who couldn't be all sorts of men – Poet, Prophet, Priest, King, or what you will'.

So far the argument has envisaged two main possibilities: either that intelligence is a single, unitary, power capable of application in any direction ('general ability'); or that it is a composite of varied powers of faculties, each especially suited to a particular range of tasks ('special aptitudes'). Galton, however, was inclined to prefer a third possibility. He believed that an exclusive emphasis on either 'general ability' or 'special aptitudes' was too simple, and that mankind in fact possessed both. But he also believed that 'general ability' was the more important of the two.

> People lay too much stress on apparent specialities, [he wrote (Galton 1869: 64)] thinking over-rashly that, because a man is devoted to some particular pursuit, he could not possibly have succeeded in anything else. They might just as well say that, because a youth had fallen desperately in love with a brunette, he could not possibly have fallen in love with a blonde. He may or may not have more natural liking for the former type of beauty than the latter, but it is as probable as not that the affair was mainly or wholly due to a general amorousness of disposition.

Perhaps Galton's conclusion about the greater importance of 'general ability' was influenced by his own prodigious versatility, which is one of the more remarkable historical examples of that capacity.

To the three possible analyses mentioned so far, a fourth may be added. It might be that the notion of ability or aptitude, whether general or special, is illusory, and has arisen merely from the chance combination of particular habits or responses, differently distributed in different people. There would then be no 'ability' expressing itself in some particular accumulation of habits, and the mind would have no 'structure' at all.

Burt (1955a: 163) summarized the whole matter by presenting an outline of the four possible views in the following passage:

At the beginning of the century the problem which chiefly exercised students of individual psychology was, in Bain's phrase, 'the classification of intellectual abilities or powers'. (i) Were there, as the faculty psychologists maintained, a number of specialized abilities, each independent of the rest – observation, practical ability, memory, language, reasoning and the like? (ii) Or was there, as Ward maintained, 'not a congeries of faculties, but only a single subjective activity' – a general capacity for cognition as such? (iii) Were there, as Galton believed, both a general ability and a number of more or less specialized capacities? (iv) Or, finally, might there be, as the earlier associationists and most of the later behaviourists alleged, no discernible structure in the mind at all?

In the course of the twentieth century, there have been distinguished exponents of each of these four main possibilities.

(*Position ii*). The most influential view in the earlier part of the century was that of Spearman. He argued powerfully for the conception of a unitary general intelligence, or 'g' as he called it. Spearman saw his work as overturning the traditional theory of faculties (position i). His views were adumbrated as early as 1904 (Spearman 1904b), and received their full exposition in his *Abilities of Man* (1927). His pre-eminence was recognized when Murchison invited him to contribute to *Psychologies of 1930*, one of a series of volumes depicting the major psychological systems of the period.

(*Position i*). The strongest challenge to Spearman came from Thurstone (1938), whose exposition of what he called 'primary mental abilities' began seriously to undermine Spearman's views in the thirties. Thurstone was proposing to dissolve 'general intelligence' into a number of unrelated 'special aptitudes'. As Vernon (1950: 19–20) put it, this was in effect a return to the nineteenth-century conception of faculties which Spearman had spent his life attacking. Thurstone's work was especially influential among American writers such as Guilford, whose *Nature of Human Intelligence* (1967) proposed an even larger number of specialized abilities.

(*Position iii*). A combination of 'general ability' and 'special aptitudes' was represented by Burt himself in his *Factors of the Mind* (1940), and was supported by Vernon in his *Structure of Human Abilities* (1950). This standpoint combines the positions of Spearman and Thurstone, considering 'general ability' and 'special aptitudes' as complementary, rather than incompatible as both Spearman and Thurstone tended to think. Burt had adumbrated this position as early as 1917 in his *Distribution and Relations of Educational Abilities*, where he summarized his conclusions in the following words: 'School achievements are due to mental qualities of two kinds: first, a general ability entering into all school work; secondly, special aptitudes for particular subjects' (Burt 1917: 64). Burt's claim that he had expressed this view even earlier is discussed later.

(*Position iv*). Throughout the period, there were exponents of the belief that 'ability' was no more than a structureless collection of specific responses. This was defended in the early part of the century, in opposition to Spearman, both by Thorndike (1909) and by William Brown in his *Essentials of Mental Measurement* (first edn, 1911). Later it reappeared in more sophisticated form in Godfrey Thomson's *Factorial Analysis of Human Ability* (1939). Thomson believed that the chance sampling of unrelated responses would give the superficial appearance of a general ability.

Even from this brief and oversimplified account, some of the historical ramifications involved may be appreciated. Ward's conception of a 'single subjective activity – position (ii) – was part of his rejection of association-ism, for which there was 'no discernible structure in the mind at all' – position (iv). Spearman's 'general ability' continues Ward's reaction against the associationist tradition, but then meets opposition from Thorndike, an American forerunner of behaviourism, which as we noted earlier is the objective form of associationism. Thurstone's 'multiple ability' – position (i) – recalls another nineteenth-century standpoint, that of faculty psychology. Finally, Burt's position, in echoing Galton's combination of 'general ability' and 'special aptitudes' – position (iii) – owes something to Ward and Spearman, but also attempts to do justice to Thurstone's views. It is important to stress these historical continuities and connections in order to see the twentieth-century contributions in perspective.

The methods of factorial analysis

If twentieth-century writers had done no more than expound their preferred solutions, with such support from logic or common observation as they could muster, they would have made little advance over the tradi-tional discussions. But they attempted to justify their views by reference to statistical evidence, based upon Galton's method of correlation. Different writers have recommended somewhat different versions of these statistical methods, which have come to be known as 'factorial analysis'. A full exposition is entirely beyond the scope of this book, especially as they are currently employed. However, for an understanding of the Burt affair, it is chiefly necessary to appreciate certain points which have been disputed in the past, and the essential matters may for our purposes be fairly simply set forth.

If a number of mental tests are administered to a number of people, the extent to which each test correlates with every other may be calculated. The correlation is expressed in a coefficient, varying from 0 for a complete absence of correlation to 1.0 for perfect correlation. When the calculations have been made, the whole collection of coefficients may be set out in a table, or matrix. An example is given in Table 1.1. This is a table of correlations drawn up by Spearman (1904b: 275). It was the only matrix given by Spearman in 1904, and was one of the earliest to appear. Factor analysis begins with tables such as this.

Table 1.1 Spearman's matrix of 1904 (Spearman 1904b: 275)

	Classics	French	English	Mathem.	Discrim.	Music
Classics	0.87	0.83	0.78	0.70	0.66	0.63
French	0.83	0.84	0.67	0.67	0.65	0.57
English	0.78	0.67	0.89	0.64	0.54	0.51
Mathem.	0.70	0.67	0.64	0.88	0.45	0.51
Discrim.	0.66	0.65	0.54	0.45	–	0.40
Music	0.63	0.57	0.51	0.51	0.40	–

(The coefficients in italics are 'self-correlations' and may be ignored; 'Discrim' means 'Discrimination'.)

In so far as two tests correlate, the coefficient may be regarded as indicating the extent to which the tests are measuring the same ability or function, or what they have in common. But what conclusions can be drawn from a matrix of coefficients? Can we deduce what abilities are common to the whole range of tests, and how they are related? This is the aim of factor analysis – and it rapidly becomes a highly complex and controversial undertaking. Burt (1955a) provides an introduction to the problems involved by taking the four main hypotheses about human ability, outlined in the previous section, and indicating the particular pattern of correlations which would be predicted by each hypothesis. Then we may ask which hypothesis most closely predicts the pattern actually observed.

Position (i) – that 'intelligence' may be analysed into a collection of unrelated abilities or faculties – would predict that all tests of a particular faculty would correlate highly together, but would show low or zero correlations with tests of other faculties. All tests of memory, for example, would correlate highly because all would be assessing the same distinctive capacity; but they would show little correlation with tests of perception or attention. Alternatively expressed, the tests would fall into distinct groups, each measuring its own 'group factor'.

Position (iv) – that 'intelligence' lacks all structure – would predict that all correlations would be zero or very low. Alternatively expressed, each test would measure its own, highly specific, factor, and would therefore show little or no connection with other tests (though if enough tests are involved some high correlations might occur by chance).

Burt argued that these two hypotheses could be ruled out. Each implies that there would be numerous low or zero correlations: position (i) among tests of different, unrelated, faculties; position (iv) among all tests, for all would be unrelated. But in practice, Burt observed, all investigators have found positive and significant correlations among all tests, whether or not they were supposed to involve different abilities. Spearman's matrix certainly illustrates this contention. On position (i) some at least of the coefficients should be zero, while on position (iv) all should be. But in fact all are positive. In practice, supporters of these two positions would find reasons for ignoring the apparent departure from their expectations, but we need not follow out these complications. Accepting Burt's argument, we are left to decide between the remaining two hypotheses.

Position (ii) – the hypothesis of a unitary general ability – predicts that all correlations would be positive. All tests must, at least to some extent, involve the same common ability, or 'general factor', and therefore all must show some relation. This hypothesis would, of course, rule out position (iv), which with its absence of all correlations is the antithesis of position (ii). It would also, if nothing else were involved, rule out position (i): there should be no evidence for the existence of groups of related tests, over and above what is due to the general factor.

At this point, Burt argued that prolonged research had shown that there always is evidence for some 'group factors'. In addition to relations which could be explained in terms of a general factor, there were always certain groups of tests which showed a special affinity and which contrasted with certain other groups. In other words, position (iii) is confirmed by the accumulation of evidence. Burt (1955a: 164) concluded: 'We are thus left with hypothesis (iii) as the only alternative consistent with the facts. And, accordingly, the unavoidable inference is that *both* a 'general factor' *and* a number of 'group factors' must be at work.'

However, not everyone would agree that all is such plain sailing as Burt's account may suggest. Inspection of Spearman's matrix shows that it is by no means immediately obvious whether hypothesis (ii) or hypothesis (iii) is more strongly supported, and many other similar tables have also lent themselves to varying interpretations. Factorial analysis attempts to provide agreed methods of analysing a table statistically, so that a valid interpretation can be made, and a decision reached among the various theories of intelligence. But unfortunately different theorists recommend different methods of analysis, and we are not surprised to discover that each recommends a technique which supports his own theory. As so often in psychology, the methods which were intended to settle the disputes themselves become a bone of contention.

To many psychologists, the arguments among the various schools of factor analysis will seem as pointless as the squabbles among the various derivatives of psychoanalysis, or the numerous versions of learning theory. It would be a bold man who would venture to disagree. But to those who believe that these statistical tables contain the key to the final analysis of human intelligence, their study may justify a lifetime's dedication. We shall briefly review the main historical landmarks in these arguments, in so far as they are relevant to the Burt affair.

Some of the earliest attempts to apply Galton's correlational methods to mental tests produced disappointing results. In America at the turn of the century, Sharp (1899) and others found such small correlations among the tests they used that it seemed there was little mental structure to be investigated. Position (iv) seemed to be substantiated. This view was strongly defended by the great American educational psychologist E. L. Thorndike, and has been perennially influential among behaviourists.

Spearman's appearance on the scene marked a reassertion of the significance of the biometric contribution from the British point of view. He believed that the low coefficients obtained were due mainly to imperfections in the methods of calculation employed; and, as we have seen, he urged the development of a 'Correlational Psychology' to exploit the 'brilliant work' being carried out by the Galton–Pearson school. However, the aspect of Spearman's early work which was most original, and which was destined to have greatest influence – either because it elicited support or provoked opposition – concerned the interpretation which Spearman proposed to place upon the coefficients once obtained.

Spearman claimed that a table of coefficients would always be found to display what he called 'hierarchical order'. When a number of tests are inter-correlated, the resulting coefficients will vary in magnitude. It follows that the tests may be arranged in the matrix in the order of magnitude of their average correlation, the test with the highest correlations being placed to the left, and the remainder declining progressively across the table. When this order followed a precise proportional pattern, Spearman described it as 'hierarchical'; and this was extremely important in his theorizing because it led directly to his fundamental claim to be able to demonstrate position (ii) – the hypothesis of a unitary general ability.

According to Spearman, the precise definition of hierarchical order, and the mathematical demonstration of its occurrence, required the calculation of 'tetrad difference equations'. This will be described in the appropriate place below. Here we may anticipate two important points. First, it is not always appreciated how long it took Spearman to perfect his mathematical technique. It was not until the twenties that he had brought it to the point where he could use it in practice; and until then he had to content himself with a variety of secondary methods (Banks 1983). Second, Spearman's methods always involved a piecemeal examination of the matrix: the 'tetrad equation' involved taking the correlations in groups of four (hence the name), which was a very lengthy process. This method contrasts strongly with those which take all the coefficients into account in a single process, like the techniques of Burt or Thurstone.

Once hierarchical order had been demonstrated, there was in Spearman's view only one way in which it could be explained. It required the hypothesis of a single general factor entering into all the tests, though more into some than others. Those tests which correlated highly with other tests would require a great deal of the general factor, or 'g' as Spearman termed it, and progressively less as the correlations declined. Inspection of the tests would then suggest what was the crucial ingredient requiring 'g', which Spearman identified as the capacity to grasp and apply relations. These were the bare bones of the theory which Spearman adumbrated in 1904, and elaborated and defended for forty years until his final paper of 1946 (Spearman 1946).

By the time that Spearman had perfected his method in the twenties, his influence was already beginning to wane. Whereas Spearman maintained that hierarchical order was regularly found, and that it admitted of only one interpretation, his critics were claiming with increasing assurance that the order was very frequently breached, and that even when found it could be explained in other ways. At least as early as 1917, Burt was exploring alternative possibilities. His method of analysing the matrix, in contrast to that of Spearman, took the table as a whole as the basis for its calculations; and claimed to find marked departures from the straightforward hierarchy, departures which were best accounted for by group factors in addition to a general factor (Burt 1917). Rather later, Thomson (1939) argued that hierarchical order itself was more plausibly explained as the outcome of the random sampling of large numbers of 'neural bonds'.

Very similar doubts and alternatives were also occurring to American critics. The most influential was undoubtedly Thurstone, whose 'multiple factor analysis', as mentioned above, reintroduced a sophisticated version of the faculty theory embodied in 'hypothesis (i)'. Thurstone's ideas parallel Burt's in two respects: first, in employing analysis of the table as a whole; and second, in finding evidence for 'group factors'. The crucial difference was that Thurstone preferred to exclude the general factor, whereas Burt preferred to retain it. American tradition had always been resistant to the notion of 'g', and welcomed Thurstone's solutions as an alternative to it.

We shall later have occasion to return to these different procedures and conclusions. Here we may note that Thurstone and other American writers did not, perhaps, always recognize how far their criticisms of Spearman had been anticipated by British writers. They were sometimes inclined to write as if, in superseding Spearman, they were superseding British work in the field in general, as Cronbach (1979) observes. This was naturally not to Burt's liking. He could with some plausibility see his own combination of general and group factors as rendering Spearman's and Thurstone's views no more than partial aspects of the whole.

Burt's interest in heredity

Galton was the first to offer detailed evidence about human heredity. His *Hereditary Genius* (1869) studied family trees and records of achievement and, noting the large differences among individuals, suggested that ability runs in families. Further, he suggested that 'individuality' arises from the single fertilized egg with which each organism begins. Galton's ideas are often criticized today as underestimating the importance of environment, but in 1869 the possible influence of heredity on intelligence was not generally appreciated. Even Darwin had taken for granted the Victorian view that a man could do anything he wanted if he worked hard enough, until he was converted by Galton's findings (Darlington 1962: 12). Galton's emphasis on heredity, at the time it appeared, may be seen as a much-needed corrective to a general neglect of its possible importance.

Galton's belief in the significance of the original fertilized cell also led him to appreciate the possible value of studies on twins in disentangling the relative importance of heredity and environment. He first proposed their study in a paper called 'The history of twins as a criterion of the relative powers of nature and nurture' (Galton 1875). It is interesting to note that Darwin had explained the remarkable similarity of twins by pointing to their living in the same womb, and then growing up together under the same conditions. Galton disputed this, and argued that twins must be of two kinds. Some had developed from two separate cells which happened to have been fertilized at the same time. These are now called fraternal or dizygotic (DZ) twins, and their genetic constitution is no more alike than that of ordinary brothers and sisters. But others had developed from a single fertilized cell. These are now called identical or monozygotic (MZ) twins, and possess identical, or nearly identical, genetic constitution. We also now know that twins – including both DZ and MZ – occur on average in about 2 per cent of the poulation; and that MZ twins constitute about 25 per cent of all twins – that is, about 0.5 per cent of the total population (see

Burt 1966a: 141). Galton suggested that two-egg (DZ) twins could be used to show the likely range of hereditary differences within a family; while one-egg (MZ) twins could be used to show environmental effects. Galton's paper, which was reprinted in *Inquiries into Human Faculty* (1883), contained many striking observations of twins and of their remarkable similarities, and stimulated further interest; but it lacked controlled and quantified data.

Like many others, including Darwin and Karl Pearson, Burt was from the beginning much impressed by Galton's data and conclusions. His first paper of 1909 included some observations which he believed supported the hereditary determination of ability. However imperfect Burt's evidence may seem to the modern critic, it impressed some of his contemporaries: 'the evidence as to heredity of intelligence is very striking,' declared Spearman in commenting on Burt's findings (letter from Spearman to Burt, 23 June 1909: 1). A paper contributed to the *Eugenics Review*, on 'The inheritance of mental characters' (Burt 1912), reviewed the position in general terms but did not report any fresh data.

Later, and especially during the period when he was working for the LCC, Burt collected much material on the mental and physical character-istics of schoolchildren in London and elsewhere. From the whole sample, he was able to extract data for particular kinship groups such as siblings, parents and children, cousins, and so on. He also claimed to have examined many twin pairs, both DZ and MZ. The results were reported in a succession of papers between 1943 and 1966. In general, the correlations varied with the degree of genetic similarity, echoing Galton's finding that the degree of similarity in achievement matched the degree of family affin-ity. Burt's claims, especially as regards twins, have figured prominently in the accusations made against him. Here a selection of his results are given to indicate the general tenor of his reported findings.

Table 1.2 gives the correlations reported by Burt for various kinship groups, using both group and individual tests of intelligence (extracted from Burt 1966a, Table I: 146). Inspection of the figures suggests that both heredity and environment have some effect. The high correlation for MZ twins reared together might be due either to their identical heredity or to their very similar environments; but the lower figures for MZ twins reared apart suggest that, though a difference of environment has some effect, heredity is exerting a powerful influence. Similar inferences may be made from a comparison of the remaining figures, the correlations for the last group – unrelated children reared together – suggesting that in the absence of genetic similarity, environment still exerts some pull. Burt himself (ibid.: 152) concluded that 'individual differences in "intelligence" . . . are influenced far more by genetic constitution . . . than by post-natal or environmental conditions'.

Burt reported many further correlations for various measures of

Table 1.2 Selected kinship correlations from Burt (1966a, Table 2: 146)

	Number of pairs	Group test	Individual test
MZ twins reared together	95	0.944	0.918
MZ twins reared apart	53	0.771	0.863
DZ twins reared together	127	0.552	0.527
Siblings reared together	264	0.545	0.498
Siblings reared apart	151	0.412	0.423
Unrelated children reared together	136	0.281	0.252

educational attainment, and for physical characteristics. The data which he claimed to have collected, together with his own high standing in the field, ensured that his research was widely regarded as exceptionally important.

Burt's involvement in public policy

Towards the end of his life, Burt found himself out of sympathy with some growing educational trends, especially the widespread scepticism about natural differences of ability with its accompanying hostility to selection. There was a tendency to see the traditional educational psychologist, with his intelligence tests and emphasis on heredity, as the accomplice if not the architect of a divisive class system, perpetuating unreal inequalities. Burt contributed to the 'Black Papers' (Cox and Dyson [eds] 1969a and b: 1970) on education which expressed opposition to these trends in the late sixties, and in consequence often found himself cast in the role of hidebound reactionary.

These debates raise difficult questions for psychology, and have direct relevance to the Burt affair. The psychologist's findings, and any advice he may offer on the basis of those findings, may well have implications for matters of current political and social concern, and may lend support to one side or the other. Facts and values are in danger of becoming mixed and muddled. The only certain way of avoiding such entanglements would perhaps be to refuse to participate in any applied problem, and those who do not take that drastic route are likely to need all the detachment and forebearance they can muster.

The critics were exaggerating the role which psychologists had played, as an examination of recent history shows. Between the wars the Board of Education, as it then was, instructed its consultative committees on a number of occasions to report on educational trends and problems in the state schools. There were three major reports – by Hadow in 1924, Spens in 1938, and Norwood in 1943 – which exerted considerable influence over the development of educational policy in the public sector, paving the way for the Education Act of 1944. Hearnshaw (1979), in his chapter on 'Developments in English education', provides a detailed account of the part played by educational psychologists in this process.

The Hadow Committee appointed a sub-committee to examine the use of tests in schools; and three psychologists, Ballard, Myers, and Spearman, were co-opted. Burt was consulted, and helped to draft the report, *Psychological Tests of Educable Capacity*, which appeared in 1924. The report accepted the need for selection, and encouraged local education authorities to adopt psychological tests for the purpose. In the same vein, the Spens Report of 1938 accepted that children should be allotted at 11+ to one of three kinds of school – grammar, modern, and technical which the Norwood Report of 1943 endorsed. Psychologists, including Burt, were certainly consulted in all this, and the majority seem to have favoured some selection. But it by no means follows that psychologists can be regarded as responsible for the system which emerged in 1945.

In the first place, as Hearnshaw (ibid.: 94) points out, the Hadow Report sounded a note of caution: 'any system of selection whatever, whether by means of psychological tests or by means of examinations, which determines at the age of eleven the educational future of children is and must be gravely unreliable'. But the advice went unheeded. Hearnshaw (ibid.) comments as follows: 'The report's warnings about selection at eleven, which if not contributed by Burt certainly accorded with his views, were ignored when the final decisions were taken.' As Hearnshaw (ibid.: 112) also observes, to a considerable extent such reports give voice and authority to changes which are already being introduced, as much as they stimulate new departures. He concludes that it would be unfair to hold the committees wholly responsible for developments derived from their recommendations; and adds, very pertinently, that

> It would be still more unfair to regard someone like Burt, who was not even a member of, but only a witness and adviser to, the Consultative Committee, as the architect of the selective system of schooling which emerged. Yet towards the end of his life he was cast in this role by many of his left-wing critics.

Yet another important limitation on the responsibility of psychologists in this matter is pointed out by Stephenson (1983), who has contributed an illuminating discussion of 'Cyril Burt and the special place examination'. Stephenson notes that a system of providing scholarships for the clever children of poor parents had been established for centuries, and has been called the 'cardinal principle' of English education. 'The Special Place Examination was meant to assess "native ability" . . . but that was decades before intelligence tests were heard of. . . . It should be clear that Burt had no influence whatever on this historical winnowing of bright children for the "directing class"' (Stephenson 1983: 49). He adds that Burt was not invited to present evidence to the Select Committee fashioning the 1944 Act.

Burt's own views on educational policy stemmed from his fundamental belief in the existence of large natural differences of ability, these differences being increased, not diminished, by education. For Burt, environment enhanced natural differences. These considerations are already prominent in Burt (1917), where primary attention is given to the task of selecting those who had proved educationally incompetent, so that they might receive special schooling. But Burt also noted, as a task for the future, that at the other end of the scale the bright children need special attention too. In proposing such classifications, Burt, and other educational psychologists of the day, would certainly not have seen themselves as trying to strengthen a divisive class system. A selective system for grammar and secondary education was already in operation. But entry depended primarily on ability to pay, and only a few could win scholarships. Moreover, many poor children received such a discouraging start in life that their chances of winning support were negligible. Burt's surveys convinced him that a great many 'working-class' children possessed the ability to profit by secondary education, but never received the chance. He himself had benefited from the scholarship system, and he wanted such opportunities to be far more widely and fairly spread (Burt 1943). Testing was a means of helping to ensure equality of opportunity, regardless of the origins or previous education of the child.

At the outset, Burt would have seen himself, and been seen by others, as an adherent of liberal views on education (see Hearnshaw 1979: 127); but while these views entailed a belief in selection, Burt also wanted to reform the existing selective system. Mistakes could easily be made at 11+, and better provision should be made for second thoughts at later stages, especially where special aptitudes were concerned. In so far as Burt's views implied selection, he was endorsing the 'cardinal principle' of English education; but in advocating the use of tests, he was trying to reform that system.

But the 1944 Act had not been in operation very long before more radical proposals for reform were heard. The principle of selection itself was increasingly attacked by left-wing critics as accepting and reinforcing class divisions. There was a tendency to regard all selection, whether with tests or without, as 'elitist'. Further, the testing movement was widely seen as being at the root of selection. This was historically inaccurate, as we have seen; nevertheless, psychology (or rather, the current establishment in psychology) could plausibly be seen as providing the chief intellectual justification, or excuse, for selection. The belief in large natural differences of ability could be regarded as supporting a stratified society, however modified from the existing one. As so often happens, those who had grown accustomed to thinking of themselves as in the van of progress, now found themselves relegated to the invidious position of reactionaries.

If selection itself was regarded as objectionable, the comprehensive school was the obvious solution, and its supporters became increasingly vocal in the years after the Second World War. Eventually the Robbins Report of 1966 gave official voice to the now widespread opposition to selection, while the Plowden Report of 1967 began to advocate 'positive discrimination' rather than 'equality of opportunity', rather as did the 'headstart' programme in America. These trends are important in understanding the origins of the Burt affair, and we shall return to them. Burt became involved in some of the controversies. He doubted the efficacy of the new comprehensive schools, retained a belief in the value of streaming, and believed that the bright children of the poorer classes would suffer most from the abolition of selection (Burt 1969a).

Those who defend Burt against the charge of political bias sometimes do so on the ground that, in so far as he held political views at all, they were progressive or liberal rather than reactionary; and they point to all he did, especially in his younger days, for the disadvantaged and underprivileged. No doubt this is true. But from the strictly scientific standpoint, there is no more virtue in the left than in the right. All that matters is that political views, whatever they may be, do not prejudice and distort supposedly factual conclusions. When the psychologist finds, as he often must, that his findings have some bearing on political controversies, he faces an extremely difficult and dangerous task.

It may be added that the assumption, so frequently encountered today, that a belief in the importance of heredity and eugenics necessarily entails right-wing views has not always been prevalent. Many of the eminent left-wing thinkers of the earlier part of the century were at the same time advocates of eugenic programmes, notably Graham Wallas, Haldane, Laski, Shaw, Wells, and the Webbs. It seems to have been the irrational excesses and cruelties of the Nazis which produced a left-wing revulsion against all forms of eugenics (Freeden 1979; Paul 1984). Hence the treatment of Burt as reactionary simply because of his hereditarian views is in some ways anachronistic, because it forgets that his views were moulded in a very different intellectual climate.

Assessing Burt's contribution

So long as Burt's integrity is in doubt, any attempt to assess his contribution is hazardous. It is impossible to tell how much, or how little, of his work will be trusted. But it is most important to notice that, even if Burt's honesty had never been questioned, his achievements would still be controversial. This is because so much of his work involved methods or assumptions which have yet to be scientifically established to general satisfaction. The reliability and validity of mental tests, the value of factorial analysis, and the influence of heredity may all be legitimately questioned; and frequently are. It is impossible to tell how far future research will confirm Burt's faith in these matters; and his scientific reputation must to a considerable extent stand or fall by the eventual answers to such questions. Only then will it be possible to say whether Burt, and others who worked in the psychometric field, contributed to a movement of great and lasting significance, or only helped to explore a blind alley.

Psychometricians are not alone in this respect. The most diverse opinions are still expressed about a number of psychological specialisms. The value of psychotherapy, for example, and with it the reputation of Freud, remains at least as controversial as does the measurement of intelligence. Where Burt is concerned, it is noticeable that the areas of his work where he has been accused of deception – especially the inheritance of intelligence, and the relative value of the different methods of factorial analysis – are also the areas which are in any case most controversial. This is a point of considerable significance. It can hardly be a coincidence. It raises the question whether this means that Burt was trying to obtain a dishonest advantage in relation to issues where he felt strongly, or whether his critics have persuaded themselves he was guilty because it is here that they are particularly anxious to discredit him.

However this may be, it is clear that the time has not yet come for any final assessment of Burt. But this necessary caution cannot alter the fact that, in his lifetime and for a great many of his contemporaries, Cyril Burt was a figure of outstanding achievement, who embodied many of the qualities they considered most essential to a psychologist, and who represented British psychology more fully than any other man of his day. Other psychologists might be better known, such as McDougall and Spearman. But they gave less time to British psychology than did Burt. McDougall emigrated to Duke University in 1920, when he was only forty-nine, and never returned. Spearman did not settle permanently in this country in an academic post until 1907, when he was already forty-four. Burt by contrast spent nearly the whole of his long life close to the centre of things in London; and in his old age none could rival his almost legendary associations with the great figures of the past, from Galton and Ward, through McDougall, Spearman, Pearson, Thorndike, Sherrington, and many others, to such later notables as Thurstone, Cattell, and Eysenck.

When Burt was knighted in 1946 he received, predictably, an immense flood of congratulations both from within the field of psychology and from beyond; and many other honours came his way, including election as an honorary Fellow of his old college, Jesus. The culmination came in 1971, just before his death, when the American Psychological Association granted him the Thorndike Award for distinguished services to educational psychology. During his lifetime Burt's reputation stood high and unblemished, and his death evoked all the sentiments of admiration which might have been expected. He was 'Britain's most eminent educational psychologist' (*Times Educational Supplement*, 15 October 1976); he gave 'a total impression of immense quality . . . of a born nobleman' (Jensen 1972: 117).

On 21 October 1971, a few days after his death, a memorial service was held at St Mary's Church, Primrose Hill. The church is only a stone's throw from the house at 9 Elsworthy Road, just north of Regent's Park, where Burt had spent the twenty-one years of his retirement. He had been a very private man, but the service was an occasion for a public recollection of all that he had achieved; and the feelings of his friends and colleagues were expressed in an eloquent and moving address given by Professor Leslie Hearnshaw (1972: 31–3) of Liverpool University.

> We are gathered here today . . . to commemorate the life and work of Professor Sir Cyril Burt, a man of rich humanity and outstanding gifts, whose achievements in the field of psychology will be remembered for many years to come . . . his place in the development of psychology in this country was of the first magnitude, and his reputation was worldwide. No one man has done more to shape the profession of psychology, as we know it today in this land. . . . His work can be regarded as the fulfilment of Sir Francis Galton's dream of a comprehensive psychology of talent and character, which could be employed in the service of mankind. . . . So long as his former students and colleagues are alive Cyril Burt will continue to live in their memories, and . . . as long as psychology remains a subject of scientific inquiry he will live in its halls of fame.

It will be observed that Galton's transformation of individual psychology into a reputable branch of natural science has now become a dream; and it is Burt who is credited with its fulfilment.

Burt's sister, Dr Marion Burt, thought highly of Hearnshaw's address, and knowing his reputation as an historian of British psychology, she invited him a few weeks later to undertake a full-length biography of her brother. Hearnshaw accepted the invitation. The contents were to be very different from anything which either of them envisaged.

Chapter two

Scandal

During his lifetime Burt's standpoint and conclusions were often criticized, especially where they concerned heredity and its influence on mental traits. His 1966 paper on twins, for example, was at once challenged. Stott (1966) argued that Burt's conceptual framework was not the only one which could be fitted to the data, and suggested that the observed differences could be ascribed to motivational rather than cognitive factors; Lewis (1966) considered that insufficient attention had been paid to the environment in which the twins had been raised, and doubted whether the conditions had been sufficiently different in the case of the twins reared apart to justify confident conclusions. But both critics accepted the data as genuine, and neither suggested that Burt had been careless or incompetent, still less that he had been dishonest. It was only his interpretations which they questioned. The points they raised might equally have been made about the twin research conducted by others. Indeed, Burt's kinship correlations were sufficiently similar to those reported earlier (for instance, Newman *et al.* 1937) for them to be generally accepted as genuine; and leading writers such as Jensen (for example, 1969, 1970) and Eysenck (for example, 1973b) treated Burt's work as wholly reliable.

But a foretaste of more damaging objections had already occurred in Shields's (1962) study of monozygotic twins. Shields mentioned Burt's early brief reference to twin data (Burt 1943), and noted that Burt had given little information about the twins reared apart. Burt undoubtedly wrote his 1966 paper in part to answer this comment, as he himself makes clear (Burt 1966a: 140). This line of criticism did not appear again until after Burt's death, when it began to take on a much more extensive character. However, this appears to have arisen independently of Shields's earlier remarks, for the posthumous critics do not refer to him in this connection.

The object of this chapter is to describe the mounting attacks on Burt's work which took place after his death. These reached a climax in the public accusation of dishonesty, which eventually came to be generally accepted. The aim at this stage is simply to trace the main events as they are generally understood to have occurred, and to avoid any controversial appraisal of these events.

Kamin, Jensen, and the Clarkes

Serious posthumous criticism began with two American psychologists, Professor Leon Kamin of Princeton and Professor Arthur Jensen of Harvard. Interestingly, their standpoints were contrasted, Kamin stressing environment, Jensen heredity. The trouble stemmed from an article by Jensen (1969) in the *Harvard Educational Review* entitled 'How much can we boost IQ and scholastic achievement?'. Liberal opinion in the United States at that time held out considerable hopes for the 'headstart' programme. It was supposed that many children were handicapped in their education by unfavourable environmental conditions, and that this might be redressed by giving them a 'headstart'. Jensen's article cast doubt on this view. It purported to show that the backwardness was primarily due to innate incapacity, not lack of opportunity, and hence that the environmentalist predictions were doomed to disappointment. Jensen relied heavily on Burt's twin data, and said nothing of any possible weaknesses in Burt's evidence.

It was after reading Jensen's article that Kamin, whose interests had so far been in animal behaviour, became involved. As early as April 1972 he gave a talk at Princeton criticizing the hereditarian evidence, and he repeated this at a number of American institutions over the next couple of years. He published a full account of his views in October 1974, in an influential book entitled *The Science and Politics of IQ*. This included several pages (pp. 55–71) highly critical of the evidence given by Burt, principally that concerning his separated identical twins. But Kamin's book was primarily a general onslaught on the hereditarian position, especially as it had been expounded and applied by American psychologists from the beginning of the century. A major conclusion was that the hereditarians had allowed their supposedly scientific conclusions to be biased by their political convictions.

However, a few months before Kamin's book appeared, Jensen had published a paper which also found fault with Burt. This paper, entitled 'Kinship correlations reported by Sir Cyril Burt' (Jensen 1974), made it clear that Jensen had drastically revised his opinions about Burt's work, and could now see many weaknesses. (There has been some argument about priorities here; see Appendix A). It was striking that, despite the strong contrast in their standpoint, the two authors made very similar criticisms and reached very similar conclusions. These are examined in detail below (Chapter 6). Here only the two most important common objections are listed.

First, perhaps the most damaging criticism, made by both Kamin and

Jensen, and very widely quoted, concerned certain of the correlation coefficients reported by Burt on different occasions. In order to appreciate this criticism, it is necessary to note how Burt published his data. Burt reported much of his data cumulatively; that is to say, when he had extra data to report in a particular category, he did not first describe it separately as additional evidence, and then combine it with the data previously given. He simply combined the new with the old to give a fresh total. Thus, to take the most frequently quoted example, in 1943 Burt described results for 15 pairs of separated identical (MZ) twins; in 1955, results for 21 pairs – which included the 15 already reported; and in 1966, results for 53 pairs – which included the 21 given in 1955. There was no reason why Burt should not do this; but there was, apparently, a serious difficulty concerning the coefficients which he reported on these successive occasions. Since the number of subjects differed from one occasion to the next, it was to be expected that the coefficients would differ too. Yet the coefficients given by Burt for a group test of intelligence remained remarkably constant: for 1943, 0.77; for 1955, 0.771; and for 1966, 0.771 again. An occasional identity could be accepted as a coincidence. But in Burt's twin papers as a whole there were, so it appeared, far too many such repetitions, despite changing numbers of subjects, for such a simple explanation to account for them all. Jensen counted more than twenty; Kamin rather fewer. But there certainly seemed to be far more than would be expected by chance, and an explanation was required.

Burt himself did not mention these repetitions, still less offer any explanation. Indeed, since he simply presented the new figures without recalling the old, it was not immediately obvious to the reader that there was anything to be explained. Unless someone actually compared the different reports, the repetitions could easily be overlooked. Kamin appears to have been the first to notice them (see Appendix A). But for both Kamin and Jensen there seemed no escape from the conclusion that the figures must be in error, and that in future no reliance could be placed upon them.

A second criticism which both writers made was what Jensen (1974: 24) called 'the quite casual description of tests and the exact procedures and methods of data analysis'. This echoes Shields's earlier observation that Burt had given too little detail, though neither of the critics seems to have picked up the point from Shields. This criticism covers a variety of instances. One which especially struck both authors was Burt's use of what he called 'final assessments'. Some of the correlations were based, not simply upon a test score, but upon a test score adjusted in the light of teachers' estimates, or upon some estimate (never very clearly specified) of an allowance that should be made for the effects of environment. Jensen objected that such procedures were not completely repeatable: they might be appropriate in clinical work, but not in psychometric research. There could be no assurance that the scores had not been unwittingly adjusted to accord with Burt's preconceptions. Kamin dealt with this feature more briefly than did Jensen: such procedures were unorthodox, and not to be relied upon (Kamin 1974: 61). Both men mentioned numerous other points where they were dissatisfied, elaborating and illustrating further alleged weaknesses.

Surveying the defects which each had independently listed, Jensen and Kamin reached parallel conclusions: 'the correlations are useless for hypothesis testing' declared Jensen (1974: 24); 'the numbers left behind by Professor Burt are simply not worthy of our current scientific attention' protested Kamin (1974: 71). It was notable that two men of such very different persuasions should reach such similar conclusions.

It was a further question why so able and eminent a writer as Burt should have left so many weaknesses in such important papers, and neither Jensen nor Kamin could offer a very confident explanation. Kamin, at least in one place, seems to suggest senility (Kamin 1974: 71): Burt would be eighty-three in 1966. Jensen, who knew Burt personally, and visited him in his last years, did not mention this; and his recollections of Burt rather imply that he was remarkably well-preserved in his old age (Jensen 1983: especially 15–17). So Jensen asked if perhaps Burt had simply lost interest in the empirical side of his work, regarding only the theoretical aspects as important (Jensen 1974: 24). One thing is clear: neither writer in these 1974 publications made any explicit and unambiguous accusation of dishonesty, nor of any other fraudulent or dishonest practice. Burt's competence might have been seriously dented, at least in certain respects, but his integrity remained intact.

Critical comments also appeared in that same year, 1974, in Britain. In the third edition of their *Mental Deficiency*, Clarke and Clarke (1974) expressed certain doubts about some of Burt's data. These doubts were much more briefly reported than those of either Jensen or Kamin, and seem to have arisen independently of the American comments. The Clarkes (ibid,: 168–71) mentioned 'puzzling features', 'surprisingly high intercorrelations', 'question begging', and results which 'appear suspiciously perfect'. Alan Clarke was Professor of Psychology at the University of Hull. He and his wife Ann, who also held an academic appointment at Hull, had been associated for many years in research on the development of cognitive capacities. A little later, Ann Clarke and another colleague at Hull, Michael McAskie, made several further critical references to Burt's work, also brief (Clarke and McAskie, 1976).

These British comments were so much shorter and less comprehensive than the American criticisms that they attracted much less attention. But they are significant because the Hull group was to play a central role in the next stage of the story, in which events took a much more dramatic turn. In fact, the Clarkes were to play a more crucial part in the Burt affair in the future than were either Jensen or Kamin.

Accusation

'The argument about Burt's data', remarked Kamin, '. . . might have tiptoed around the question of Burt's fraudulence were it not for Oliver Gillie' (Kamin 1981: 102). Kamin may well be right. As we have seen, by 1976 none of Burt's critics had yet made any explicit accusation of dishonesty or fraudulent practice; and, left to themselves, it seems likely that they would have shrunk from so damning a charge against so eminent a colleague. But Dr Oliver Gillie was not a psychologist. He had been trained in genetics at the University of Edinburgh in the fifties, and his interests in human biology had brought him eventually to the post of medical correspondent to the *Sunday Times*. It was through his initiative, more than any other single influence, that the explicit and public accusation was eventually made.

Gillie (1980) has given an account of how he came to be involved. In 1976, while reading Kamin's *Science and Politics of IQ*, he began to have doubts about the authenticity of Burt's work, and decided to investigate. He first tried to trace a Miss Margaret Howard and Miss Jane Conway, two people mentioned by Burt as having helped him in his kinship research. Their names appeared on papers published in the fifties in the *British Journal of Statistical Psychology*, while Burt himself was editor. So in August 1976 he telephoned the British Psychological Society for information about their current whereabouts. He describes what happened next as follows:

I was amazed to be told by Mr Harry Partridge, an official of the Society, that he thought Howard and Conway were pen-names used by Burt in the journal which he edited. Dr Ralph Hetherington, another of the Society's officials, confirmed that he had heard it said that the names were 'fictitious'. The Society had often been asked to locate Miss Howard and Miss Conway and had asked Burt several times how they might contact these ladies. Each time Burt had told them politely that they were abroad or unavailable.

When I put the telephone down after that first inquiry I paused for breath. In the context of what I already knew from Kamin this appeared to confirm the suspicions of fraud. Fudged statistics might make a newspaper story but non-existent people, invented in order to perpetrate a fraud, really catch the popular imagination. In newspaper terms this began to look like a big story.

(Gillie 1980: 9–10)

Gillie next contacted Professor Jack Tizard of London University's Institute of Education (the old Day Training Centre where Burt had worked in the twenties). Tizard too said that he had tried to trace the assistants, and having failed had become convinced they never existed. Gillie then conducted his own search of the records of London University, because the published papers gave University College as their institution. But again he drew a blank. He also questioned, he said, some eighteen people who had known Burt well, and who might have come across these supposed research assistants or have heard of them. Not one could recall either of them.

Gillie's next move was to prove decisive. Tizard had suggested that he should contact the Clarkes, who as we have seen had criticized Burt's work; and accordingly, his suspicions now thoroughly aroused, Gillie travelled to Hull in the summer of 1976 to discuss the matter with them. 'We spent a long time . . .', he writes, 'discussing Burt's work and how certain we could be that fraud was involved' (Gillie 1980: 10). The details of these discussions have not been recorded, but it is plain – although Gillie does not actually say this (see Chapter 11) – that the upshot was that the Clarkes, together with their colleague McAskie, agreed to support Gillie if he exposed Burt. After advertising in the Personal Columns of the *The Times* for information about Howard and Conway, once more without success, Gillie decided to go ahead.

The fateful article duly appeared on the front page of the *Sunday Times* on 24 October 1976. It was headlined 'Crucial data was faked by eminent psychologist', and began with the following words:

> The most sensational charge of scientific fraud this century is being levelled against the late Sir Cyril Burt. Leading scientists are convinced that Burt published false data and invented crucial facts to support his controversial theory that intelligence is largely inherited.
>
> (Gillie 1976b)

It will be seen that, in this article, Gillie implied that he was primarily concerned to report what 'leading scientists' were saying, and was not making the charges on his own authority. Later in the article he said that he had conducted a *Sunday Times* inquiry, but this 'followed up independent academic criticism' (ibid.). In the course of the article it became plain that the 'leading scientists' were the Clarkes and McAskie, and Gillie quoted a number of their comments derived, presumably, from the discussions in Hull. One of the most pointed remarks was attributed to McAskie who, with reference to a finding of Burt that the intelligence of children showed greater variance than that of adults, was reported as saying, 'It is impossible to see how Burt could have obtained these observations without deliberately fiddling the figures to produce the results he desired.' The Clarkes were quoted as saying that there was 'a probability of dishonesty', and also, in some later editions of the paper, as concluding that 'Scientifically, Burt's results were a fraud' (see Gillie 1980: 10).

The article listed four main charges. These were: (1) that Burt had often guessed the intelligence of parents and then treated these guesses as hard scientific data; (2) that two of Burt's alleged collaborators 'may never have existed'; (3) that Burt's identical coefficients across varying samples showed that he was adjusting his samples to fit his theories; and (4) that he had worked backwards to supply data to fit his favoured genetic theories.

Gillie did not elaborate these charges in any great detail, and although he mentioned both Kamin and Jensen he gave few references. He went straight on to indicate that the charges were especially serious in view of the practical significance attaching to Burt's work, both as supporting selective education, and as lending plausibility to some pronouncements about racial differences. Thus the implications of the deception went far beyond a purely scientific controversy. There was a deliberate manipulation of data to serve ideological ends.

The following day, 25 October, *The Times* published a similar article, by its education correspondent, Tim Devlin. This repeated several of the previous day's allegations, but now Tizard and not the Hull group was named as the supporting authority. Tizard was quoted as saying that Burt's work was 'completely discredited', and also as being sceptical of much of Burt's earlier work, especially his *Young Delinquent* (1925) and his *Backward Child* (1937a). Tizard had apparently asked Burt to let him see some of the material he had collected for these books, but had received evasive replies, so he said. Already no less than four academic psychologists had publicly expressed their conviction that Burt had been thoroughly dishonest.

Controversy

The situation now contained all the ingredients for a considerable explosion, and Gillie would hardly have been human if he had not surveyed with some satisfaction the uproar which his article provoked. To the scientific community no offence is more repugnant than the deliberate fabrication of evidence, and any instance of it is likely to attract wide attention. But in Burt's case there were at least two further factors which ensured that there would be an exceptional outcry. If Burt had been some young and impoverished research student, struggling to make a name for himself, such behaviour would have been intolerable, but at least it would have been understandable. But Burt had been among the most eminent psychologists in the country, and the alleged frauds belonged mainly to the latter part of his life, when he was already distinguished, and when his work was not unnaturally regarded as especially worthy of trust. It was unforgivable that such a man should repay the honours he had received from his country and his colleagues with such contemptible dishonesty.

But another, and even more important factor, concerned the nature of the alleged frauds. As Gillie (1976b) had been quick to point out, the question of the inheritance of intelligence bore directly upon one of the most controversial political and social issues of the day. The argument between selective and comprehensive education – between elitists and egalitarians – was crucially affected by convictions about the relative importance of heredity and environment in determining educational progress. When it was now alleged that much of Burt's evidence had been invented to defend what many saw as no more than a class prejudice, old passions were aroused with renewed bitterness. Accusations and counter-accusations were flung back and forth, some rejecting the charges as malicious slander, others extending the catalogue of Burt's delinquencies.

A relatively dispassionate review of the arguments, as so far available, was published by Wade as early as 26 November 1976. He concluded that it was not yet possible to decide among 'systematic fraud, mere carelessness, or something in between. . . . The facts so far available do not allow any of these explanations to be ruled out' (Wade 1976: 919). But the very uncertainty left room for a variety of opinions, and for several weeks *The Times* and other journals carried a succession of letters and articles, while Gillie acquired prestige in media circles as an investigative journalist.

Support for the accusations soon came from the Clarkes and McAskie. In a letter to *The Times* (13 November 1976), they endorsed Gillie's accusations, and declared that in their opinion Burt was 'either a fraudulent scientist or a fraud as a scientist'. (The distinction has never been clear to me.) This letter was something of a milestone on the road to Burt's condemnation, for it was the first signed public statement in which psychologists themselves accused Burt of dishonesty. It was followed shortly by Kamin (1976), who wrote from America to say that he was satisfied that the charges of fraud had some substantial basis, adding a little later that in his opinion Burt's earlier work was also suspect (Kamin 1977b). Tizard did not commit himself to print until the following May, when a review article endorsed the accusations (Tizard 1977); but since he had not objected to the use of his name by *The Times* in October 1976, it was already obvious that he too was convinced. Thus five psychologists of standing – the Clarkes, McAskie, Kamin, and Tizard – had endorsed the charges made in Gillie's article. Undoubtedly, their support made Gillie's position a strong one.

However, Burt was by no means without defenders. The accusations sparked off a lengthy correspondence in *The Times*, much of it directed primarily to the question of heredity, but much of it also concerned with Burt's behaviour. Among the numerous contributors, Eysenck played a prominent role. His first letter (*The Times*, 8 November 1976) attacked Gillie's evidence. His second (12 November 1976) declared that the evidence so far produced justified no charge stronger than carelessness, and accused Gillie of a political smear campaign and of character assassination. A letter to Burt's sister (16 November 1976) assured her that 'the future will uphold the honour and integrity of Sir Cyril without question'. A little later, in a letter to the *Bulletin of the British Psychological Society*, Eysenck (1977a: 22) wrote that the allegations were based on grounds 'so weak that they would never be judged even remotely adequate by an unprejudiced person. . . . It is an example of the worst kind of witch-hunting smear campaign which has come to my attention in the scientific field'. He added that he thought the British Psychological Society should publicly dissociate itself from it, and suggested that the society should set up a 'Committee of experts' to look into the whole question. A longer article in *Encounter* (Eysenck 1977b) gave a more detailed and considered defence.

Eysenck's stand was strongly supported by many other letters in *The Times*. They included one from Anita Gregory (2 November 1976), who pointed out that Burt's early tests had been designed with the particular aim of helping the backward child; one from Banks (6 November 1976), who affirmed her faith in Burt's integrity; another from Jensen (9 December 1976), who wrote that nothing more than carelessness was involved, a view which he repeated later when he added that the mistakes were odd ones for an experienced statistician to make if he were really intent upon forging his results (Jensen 1978); and one from Jonckheere (20 November 1976), who argued that a similar consideration applied to the allegation that Burt had invented his research assistants, and described Gillie's article as 'an example of innuendo unworthy of scientific journalism'. In the same vein, Cattell (1978: 18) later remarked that 'if deception had been his aim he would not have done the crude and obvious substitutions now being interpreted as deceptions'.

Perhaps the most effective of these early defenders was Cohen, an old student of Burt's who had been at University College before the war. Gillie had given particular prominence to the matter of the missing assistants. Why could they not be found? Jonckheere and Cattell might argue that their absence did not prove deception; but they offered no positive evidence for their existence. Now Cohen offered the first positive claim. He said (*The Times*, 10 November 1976) that he could recall a Miss Howard from before the war (see also Cohen 1977). Of course, she was not necessarily the Miss Howard apparently known to Burt, and even if she was there was no proof that she had helped him. Nevertheless, this was the first indication that perhaps the assistants, or at least one of them, might be genuine after all. It was odd that Gillie, in his enquiries among those who had known Burt, should have overlooked someone so closely connected as Cohen; and it is noticeable that in subsequent references to the missing assistants, Burt's critics concentrate on Conway and make less of Howard, if they mention her at all (for example, Clarke and Clarke 1977).

So in these first weeks Burt's fate hung in the balance. The 'detractors', as Cohen called them, had certainly not established Burt's dishonesty to everyone's satisfaction. On the other hand, the defenders had not managed to dispose of the case against him. Wade (1976) had suggested that a decision was not yet possible, and now Hearnshaw (1977) underlined that conclusion. His recent retirement had left him free to concentrate on the biography of Burt which he had embarked upon soon after Burt's death. Now he avoided aligning himself with either side. He wrote that the evidence so far presented was by no means conclusive, and that the proper course was 'to suspend judgement until all the evidence can be fully and fairly assessed' (ibid.: 23). He added that, as Burt's biographer, he possessed much of the relevant evidence in the shape of Burt's letters and diaries. He concluded (ibid.), 'I venture to suggest that until I have finished my job no one is in a position to pass a final judgement on Burt.'

Verdict

Hearnshaw's biography was published in July 1979. Much of the book conformed closely to the conventional academic study, tracing the intellectual influences which had moulded Burt's development, and the innumerable ways in which Burt had in turn shaped the psychology of his day. But this was probably not the feature of the book which many of Hearnshaw's readers found most absorbing. Hearnshaw's verdict concerning the accusations was the aspect most eagerly awaited.

When he had embarked upon his task, Hearnshaw had had no doubts about Burt's integrity. It was only gradually, as the evidence accumulated, that he became convinced of Burt's guilt (see Hearnshaw 1979: vii–ix). The later parts of the volume were increasingly concerned with the accusations, and Hearnshaw left the reader in no doubt about what conclusion he had reached. He did not by any means accept every charge which had been brought; indeed, as we shall see, he disagreed strongly with some of the views expressed by the Clarkes. But that Burt had been dishonest, repeatedly and wilfully, he did not doubt.

The charges had so far been concentrated in the area of Burt's kinship research, especially the missing assistants. On this problem, Hearnshaw thought it quite likely that the assistants were real enough, and had worked for Burt before the war. But he could find no evidence in Burt's diaries or other documents that they had been in touch with him after the war, or had collected any material for him then. So he reached the conclusion that Burt's twin data were, at least to some extent, fabricated. The increase in the reported number of identical twins reared apart, from 21 in 1955 to 53 in 1966, especially roused his suspicions. In this respect, therefore, Hearnshaw gave detailed corroboration to the most sensational of the accusations.

That Hearnshaw, a detached and balanced writer who had begun as an admirer of Burt, should thus endorse the major charge was striking enough. It was even more striking that Hearnshaw also added new and extensive misdemeanours. The first and most impressive concerned the early history of factor analysis. Hearnshaw said that, from the mid-forties onwards, Burt had undertaken a sustained campaign of falsification of that early history, designed to deprive his great predecessor, Spearman, of the credit for originating factor analysis, and to insinuate himself into Spearman's place. According to Hearnshaw, it was here that Burt's dishonesty was first displayed on a massive scale; and the circumstance that Hearnshaw was a reputable historian no doubt lent extra weight to his conclusions. As Burt's life unfolded, this was the first of the delinquencies which Hearnshaw described; and the addition of so much extra and previously unpublished material, coming before the kinship charges were examined, undoubtedly made a powerful impression upon the reader, and rendered those subsequent misdeeds only too plausible.

Another new charge brought by Hearnshaw involved fewer misdeeds, but was of greater practical significance. It concerned papers written by Burt at the end of his life on the question of changing standards of scholastic achievement in British schools. Burt (1969c) gave figures which purported to show that contemporary standards had declined, and Hearnshaw said that he could not possibly have collected some of the post-war data which he reported, and must have fabricated it.

After reviewing all this evidence, Hearnshaw (1979: 259) delivered a magisterial judgement:

> The verdict must be . . . that at any rate in three instances, beyond reasonable doubt, Burt was guilty of deception. He falsified the early history of factorial analysis; he produced spurious data on MZ twins; and he fabricated figures on declining levels of scholastic achievement.

So far Hearnshaw had given Burt's critics considerable cause for satisfaction. But there were other features of his analysis which did something to redress the balance, and might be expected to mollify Burt's defenders. The first concerned the timing of Burt's offences, and the second the reasons for his misbehaviour.

First, in Hearnshaw's view, Burt's misdeeds were essentially a feature of his later life. There were possibly some signs that Burt's character was deteriorating in the thirties, but Hearnshaw dated the first definite fabrications, concerning factorial history, to 1947 (ibid.: 171); the first indications of fraudulence over kinship data to shortly after 1955 (p. 252); and the deceptions about scholastic achievement to 1969 (p. 259), only two years before his death. Thus Burt's misbehaviour was said to be mainly a feature of his later life and retirement. As Hearnshaw (ibid.: 286) put it, 'Had Burt died at the age of 60 [that is, in 1943] his reputation would have been unblemished, and his standing as a psychologist generally acclaimed.'

A major implication of this dating is, of course, that for the greater part of Burt's life his behaviour was unexceptionable. It would follow that his colleagues had been quite justified, in those earlier years, in accepting him without question. It would follow, too, that his major promotions and honours had all been awarded before his behaviour deteriorated, and need not be questioned; nor need suspicion attach to his earlier work. So far, therefore, as Burt's life and work down to 1943 were concerned, the biographer could justifiably deliver the same favourable judgements that he would have given if Burt had never lapsed.

This conclusion on timing ran counter to the opinions expressed by some of Burt's other critics. The Clarkes have repeatedly said that in their view Burt had always been dishonest, and that the record of his misdeeds would be found to stretch back to the beginnings of his career, a conviction which they continued to express after the biography had appeared. In their opinion, Burt had always been a 'confidence-trickster' (Clarke and Clarke, 1980a and 1980b). Hearnshaw's view was, of course, more favourable to the reputation of psychologists in general, and made it much easier to excuse the long delay in uncovering the villain.

Second, when Hearnshaw had decided that Burt was guilty, he faced the further question of what had brought about the lapse. As Hearnshaw (1979: viii) expressed it: 'the problem became that of explaining how a man of Burt's eminence and exceptional gifts could have succumbed in this way.' This is indeed a puzzle, and we may note that it is deepened by Hearnshaw's conclusion that the lapse began when Burt was about sixty years of age. If Burt's dishonesty had begun very early in his life, his behaviour would always have been consistent and in character; and if his dishonesty had begun very late, it might have been ascribed to senility. But neither of these relatively simple interpretations could be applied to a deterioration which began a few years before his retirement. Something is required which will cause him to break the habits of a lifetime, and then, when he is at the height of his powers, risk all that he has achieved. Hearnshaw, in what is in many ways the most intriguing section of the biography, makes a sustained attempt to solve this problem, elaborating a full-length analysis of Burt's character and development from his earliest days. As he remarks (1979: 261), 'The psychologist must himself be psychologised.'

Hearnshaw's solution is that Burt suffered from a 'psychological disturbance' which undermined his character in later life; and he examines the circumstances which gave rise to the condition, the particular form which it took, and the way in which it finally produced Burt's delinquent behaviour. This explanation will be examined later, but it plays such a central part in Hearnshaw's thinking that its main features must be described here.

The conditions producing the 'disturbance' were, according to Hearnshaw, in part innate and in part environmental, and unfolded as follows. It seems likely that Burt suffered from an innate weakness of the type called 'psychosomatic', where certain bodily ills are associated with emotional tensions. This was exacerbated by certain features of Burt's childhood environment. Until young Cyril was nine years old, the family lived on the edge of one of London's poorest Victorian slums, Petty France, and he attended a school in which, so Hearnshaw supposes, he would be forced to adapt himself to the behaviour of the slum children – the *gamins* who roamed the back streets, living by every dodge and underhand trick. Then, when Cyril was nine, his father obtained a practice in the rural peace of middle-class society in Warwickshire. The transition would be a profound shock to the impressionable Cyril, and a certain 'dualism' began to acquire a permanent hold over his character. Fortunately, his intellectual gifts enabled the lad to embark upon a successful academic career, and to lead a stable and productive life throughout his youth and middle years. These were the years of achievement for which he would have been mainly remembered if his later delinquencies had never come to light.

Under favourable circumstances, Burt's latent instability might never have surfaced; but unfortunately, from about 1940 onwards, there occurred a series of major shocks and setbacks which gradually undermined his mental balance, always somewhat precarious. There were some half-dozen of these shocks. One of the first was the breakdown of his marriage, which showed signs of strain in the early forties and which finally collapsed at the time of his retirement. Then, in 1941, there came in rapid succession the onset of Ménière's disease (a disorder of the inner ear), and the loss of his accumulated research material in an air raid on University College. Following his retirement, he became embroiled in disturbing disagreements with his successor at University College, which resulted in a request that he keep clear of his old department. Subsequently, his high-handed behaviour as editor of the *British Journal of Statistical Psychology* resulted in his being forced ignominiously to resign. Finally, the ideas about the inheritance of intelligence and selective education, on which so much of his career had been based, were increasingly challenged and abandoned in his old age. It must have seemed to Burt – all this is Hearnshaw's view – that everything for which he had lived and worked was falling apart.

Burt's fragile balance could not withstand such a succession of hammer blows. A deterioration of his personality took place in which the less attractive features gradually gained the upper hand. Burt became increasingly impatient of any opposition, any challenge to his reputation and position. He resented the inevitable loss of influence which old age brought, and tried to hold on to it for far too long. He became suspicious, self-assertive, and aggressive. In short, all the signs pointed to an 'incipient paranoia', often hidden behind his old urbane good will, but ever ready to take over when he felt himself threatened.

It was from this 'personality disturbance', according to Hearnshaw, that Burt's dishonesty stemmed. By the well-known mechanism of regression, he reverted when challenged to the '*gamin*-culture' of his early childhood, and to the dishonest and underhand tricks which he had then acquired. In those days, he had been forced to cheat to survive, and now he turned back to those well-tried methods. 'In the end he chose to cheat rather than see his opponents triumph' (Hearnshaw 1979: 291). The paranoid personality was thus the natural soil which permitted Burt's malpractices to grow, whether expressed in the 'devious' behaviour which many of his colleagues noted while he was alive, or in the full-blown fraudulence which came to light only after his death.

By restricting Burt's misbehaviour to the later part of his life, Hearnshaw had seemingly limited the damage to Burt's reputation and achievements. By suggesting that mental instability was the primary cause, he had further reduced the blame to be ascribed. As he put it: 'there were mitigating circumstances in the psychological disturbances from which he suffered' (Hearnshaw 1979: 319). Thus, while Hearnshaw had sided with Burt's critics in finding him guilty, his further analysis took some of the sting out of the verdict. Undoubtedly Burt had done what he was accused of, and more. But at least the greater part of his life had been blameless; and when he did succumb, he was the victim of mental illness, as much to be pitied as blamed.

Hearnshaw claimed to have struck a balance between Burt's defenders and his detractors. Certainly, he had not sent either party away empty-handed. But we may ask whether in the long run he would not prove to have given far more to the detractors. It was much more significant that Hearnshaw had accepted those three major deceptions, than that he had limited them to the later part of Burt's life. Scientists are immensely dependent upon one another's honesty, and everyone knows how easy it would often be to fabricate results. In the nature of things Hearnshaw could never demonstrate that Burt's earlier years were blameless. There must always remain a suspicion that evidence for those years was missing only because the trail had long since faded. Nor could Hearnshaw prove that Burt's mental instability, assuming it to have been genuine, provided a valid excuse. It might have been a coincidental accompaniment of his fraudulence, rather than a causal influence. Even if it does exonerate Burt, that does not reinstate him as a character to be trusted; it only provides him with an excuse for being untrustworthy. The scientific community cannot compromise with dishonesty. If Hearnshaw's verdict was accepted, Burt was finished.

Endorsement

The biography tipped the balance. Until it was published, Burt's fate was undecided. A few month's later, the climate of opinion had hardened, and his guilt was widely accepted. References to the affair increasingly took it for granted that Burt might now be pilloried as a prime example of scientific fraud. Differences of opinion undoubtedly remained, especially about when the misbehaviour had begun, how extensive it had been, and how far 'psychological disturbance' could be held to excuse him. There was also a hard core of Burt's old friends and colleagues who steadfastly maintained his innocence. But opposition was swamped by the overwhelming tide of condemnation.

There were probably a number of reasons why the biography was so influential, and opinions may differ as to their relative importance. The author himself already enjoyed a reputation as a reliable and balanced historian, and since he had not been previously involved in any of the controversies, he was readily accepted as unbiased. This estimate was heightened by the circumstance that he had started as an unquestioning believer in Burt's integrity, and had only gradually and with reluctance abandoned this position as evidence accumulated. In addition, Hearnshaw enjoyed the advantage of being able to discuss Burt's misdeeds in the context of a wide knowledge of his life and character in general: as the official biographer, he was accepted as an authority on his subject. The book itself also possessed a number of attractive features. It was written in a clear and lively style; it contained much information about the growth of British psychology; and its analysis of Burt's personality was likely to appeal to the professional student of human nature. Chiefly, perhaps, it possessed the flavour of a high-brow detective story. For all these reasons, a reader was likely to be predisposed to give Hearnshaw's case a sympathetic hearing, long before he came to examine the detailed arguments employed.

The evidence which Hearnshaw presented was undoubtedly highly plausible. He began with the alleged historical falsifications. The very fact that these had not been published before, that there seemed to be an extraordinary number of instances of deceit, and that Hearnshaw as a historian might be presumed to possess a special knowledge and capacity in this field – all these considerations ensured that the first charge would make a powerful impact. Hearnshaw could hardly be mistaken about dishonesty on such a scale, conducted over so long a period; and so the reader approached the central question of Burt's alleged invention of twin data already strongly predisposed to find the charges proved. Here too Hearnshaw's case was impressive, for he was able to claim that Burt's letters and diaries, hitherto unavailable, failed to confirm that the supposed research assistants were in touch with him after his retirement. The third charge, of falsifying evidence about educational standards, was almost a foregone conclusion. All in all, the case which Hearnshaw had assembled must have seemed much stronger than most of those who believed in Burt's integrity could have believed possible.

A further characteristic of the biography which probably helped to secure its ready acceptance was simply that it reached a definite conclusion. Many psychologists were, naturally enough, distressed and annoyed that 'the Burt affair' had occurred at all, with the attendant bad publicity which psychology received. The last thing they wanted was a protracted wrangle which kept the wretched business in the public eye. If Hearnshaw had cautiously concluded that the evidence was too incomplete to permit a definite verdict, the controversy could easily have dragged on for many further weary months. A verdict of 'innocent' would also, perhaps, have been likely to produce the same effect: it would have provoked complaints of a 'cover-up', and renewed attempts by Burt's critics to establish their case. A verdict of 'guilty', on the other hand, probably offered the best hope of a quick settlement and a speedy oblivion; and Hearnshaw had sweetened the pill for Burt's defenders by limiting the damage. I do not wish to suggest that Hearnshaw had these considerations in mind when he reached his verdict; but only that his verdict satisfied a widespread feeling, and this was a factor in its rapid acceptance.

Once the book was launched, there were a number of further factors which helped to ensure a successful voyage. The first was the character of the notices which it received. It was very widely reviewed, and most reviewers concentrated on the question of Burt's guilt, ignoring the remainder of the biography. Almost without exception, they accepted Hearnshaw's verdict. The comments which appeared in the *British Journal of Psychology* may be taken as representative. Four different reviews appeared, all in the same issue, from psychologists of very different background and standpoint. Chown (1980: 171–2) summarized the main conclusions concerning Burt's guilt and the explanations offered. She concluded that Hearnshaw had shown 'scientific detachment in his assessments yet has written with compassion'. The Clarkes (1980b: 172–3) expressed their opinion that Burt's malpractices had begun early rather than late in life. Mackintosh (1980: 174–5) again found no reason to doubt Burt's guilt, but he was less satisfied with Hearnshaw's explanations and psychological analysis. Where Chown had thought this a 'believable portrait', Mackintosh was more impressed by the suggestion that the deceptions were an immediate response to what he, Burt, saw as 'ill-informed, politically motivated, sociological criticism'. Finally, O'Neill (1980: 175–6) accepted Hearnshaw's conclusions, and spoke of his 'balance and fairmindedness'. The biography was, he said, 'singularly free of errors of detail'. None of these reviewers entered any reservations about Burt's guilt, and such unanimity among persons chosen as worthy of the responsibility which they discharged could only tend to move general opinion powerfully towards acceptance of the guilty verdict.

A second factor was that three of Burt's most influential supporters changed their minds when the biography appeared. Jensen (1981) explicitly accepted Hearnshaw's appraisal, and later described his book as 'a masterpiece of psychological biography and history . . . thorough and scholarly investigation . . . eminently judicious and fair' (Jensen 1983: 14). Eysenck (1980b) admitted that Burt was guilty. Lastly Vernon, who had collaborated with Burt and was a prolific writer on psychometrics and factor analysis, wrote that Hearnshaw 'has a reputation as a psychological historian of the utmost integrity and objectivity', and said that the book 'stills all doubts that . . . Burt did commit fraud' (Vernon 1980: 325). When three such commanding figures changed sides, the ordinary mortal could only suppose that the battle was all but over.

A third factor was the publication of one or two further papers, which had come too late for Hearnshaw to mention them, and which claimed more evidence against Burt. The most notable was a statistical analysis of one of Burt's last papers by Dorfman (1978). This claimed that Burt had invented some of his figures to support a preconceived conclusion; and though the paper was at once challenged, Dorfman maintained his position. These matters are examined below (Chapter 8); here we simply note that every fresh piece of evidence seemed only to confirm Burt's condemnation. The tide was running strongly against him.

Perhaps the most important single endorsement came in February 1980, when the Council of the British Psychological Society made it know that, at a meeting held earlier on 20 October 1979, it had discussed the Burt affair in the light of Hearnshaw's biography. It now announced that, 'with the evidence of fraud before it', the Council had decided to take a number of steps. Only the first two need concern us here. They were:

1 that at the Annual Meeting at Aberdeen in March 1980 Professor Hearnshaw should be invited to give a paper assessing the impact of Burt's falsifications;

2 that a symposium should be organized in which Burt's deceptions should be seen in the wider context of scientific method in psychology, and that in this symposium, Dr Oliver Gillie should be invited to speak (see 'Monthly report', *Bull. Brit. Psychol. Soc.* 1980, 33: 71–2).

This announcement plainly implied that Council had agreed, apparently without dissent, that the biography established Burt's guilt beyond question, and that this might now be taken for granted.

The Council's action met some strong objections, notably from Professor Audley of University College, who considered it wrong to pronounce sentence on the basis of a single book, however eminent its author, and argued that a special inquiry ought to have been held if so severe a judgement was to be accepted (Audley 1980: 135). Halla Beloff, a member of Council, defended the decision, declaring that 'scientific probity' demanded that Burt's misdeeds be acknowledged (Beloff 1980a:

294). So far as most psychologists were concerned, who were not themselves immediately implicated in these events nor directly interested in Burt's fate, it must have seemed that most of those who persisted in defending Burt had been in some way connected with him, and that there was no reason to suppose that their elected representatives had any motive for condemning him, other than a desire to see justice done and to protect the good name of the society.

It is arguable that Council's conclusion, though quietly and tardily announced, was by no means the least influential of the various factors making for the acceptance of Burt's guilt. Council's endorsement expressed much more than mere passive acceptance of Hearnshaw's verdict. It implied that any further inquiry by the society, such as some had demanded, was unnecessary; that, in so far as British psychology could be said to have any 'official' view, this was it; and that accordingly any psychologist who continued to dispute it was at odds with the considered decision which his colleagues had taken through their duly elected representatives.

None of these reflections are intended to imply that the council ought to have held its own inquiry. It might well have refrained from adopting any position in the matter at all since Burt was now dead. It could have been treated like any other controversial matter: something to be settled, if at all, by the ordinary process of discussion. That would have been a prudent course to take. However this may be, one consequence of Council's action was undoubtedly to strengthen still further the general view that Burt was guilty, for those who knew little of the minutiae of the affair – the great majority – would naturally suppose that so responsible a body would only have taken such a decision if, after due consideration, they had found the evidence to be incontrovertible.

The weight of opinion which had now gathered against Burt was formidable. The original accusation in the *Sunday Times* had been supported by five 'leading scientists'; it had been largely corroborated and considerably extended by Hearnshaw; reviewers had almost without exception endorsed it; three of Burt's chief erstwhile supporters had capitulated; further findings had told the same story; and now finally had come the considered condemnation by the Council of the British Psychological Society. True, there were one or two loyal friends of Burt who still refused to give way; but this was to be expected, and none had produced any detailed refutation of the massive case which had accumulated. Burt was finished, officially.

From Primrose Hill to Aberdeen

The symposium proposed by Council duly took place at Aberdeen, and the proceedings, together with Hearnshaw's invited paper and one or two extra comments, were published later that year under the title 'A balance sheet on Burt' (Beloff [ed.] 1980b). This publication opened with a short introduction by the President, Professor Connolly. He accepted Burt's guilt: 'From the meticulous work of Professor Hearnshaw we now sadly accept that Sir Cyril was guilty of violating a fundamental canon of science' (ibid. i). He said that the society had been criticized both for dragging its feet and for accepting the verdict too readily. If attacked simultaneously for two opposite reasons, the council had probably done the right thing, he suggested. The contributors took a similar line. There was some disagreement about the extent of Burt's misdeeds, but nobody defended him. The symposium was not a debate about the validity of Hearnshaw's verdict. It was not intended to be. It was entitled 'The Burt Scandal'; and it was intended, in the words of Council's announcement of February 1980, to enable 'Burt's deceptions to be seen in the wider context of scientific method in psychology'. Thus the symposium, together with Beloff's collection of papers, was a public demonstration by the society that Burt's guilt had been accepted.

Hearnshaw's (1980) paper began by saying that nothing which had happened since the publication of his book had led him to make any substantial change in his views. Indeed, it was clear that he was somewhat relieved to find that he had encountered much less opposition than he had expected, especially from Burt's old colleagues at University College: 'From the pro-Burt faction there has been not a murmur of dissent. . . . My book has been received with a stunned silence' (Hearnshaw 1980: 1–2). He was in fact placed in a very strong position by the absence of any support for Burt. He could take it for granted that Burt's guilt had been established, and concentrate on indicating where he disagreed with those he called the 'anti-Burters'. This was his name for Kamin, the Clarkes, and Gillie. He suggested that they had performed a valuable service in exposing Burt's delinquencies, but had gone too far in the 'virulence and extent of their denigration of Burt' (ibid.). It was necessary, in the interests of accuracy, to counter these extreme views. 'Burt, after all, is not here to speak for himself', he reminded his audience, perhaps a shade super-fluously, 'and although I am not setting out to defend Burt, I am concerned that history be accurately and fully recorded' (ibid.). Thus the remarkable situation arose in which Hearnshaw, whose work had been decisive in establishing Burt's guilt, was the only person who spoke on his behalf. Hearnshaw's chief concern was to re-emphasize the conclusion of the biography, that, contrary to the 'anti-Burters', the delinquencies were primarily a feature of Burt's later life, and should not be allowed to obscure his earlier achievements. There was indeed an absence of rancour in Hearnshaw's discussion, an awareness of the tragic features of Burt's fall, and a willingness to see him as a mixture of good and evil, which combined to secure for Hearnshaw a sympathetic reception.

The symposium proper began with Gillie (1980). His title, 'Burt: the scandal and the cover-up', sufficiently indicates a rather more journalistic approach. Gillie's brief was to tell the story of how he had become involved, and this he proceeded to do with gusto. Gillie gradually took a more active part in the affair. Initially, in 1976, he presented himself primarily as the reporter, passing on what was said by the experts. But as Burt's guilt became accepted, he began to express his own views with greater confidence. Now he expressed scepticism about the various setbacks which, according to Hearnshaw, had precipitated Burt's decline. Rejecting these as mere excuses, he condemned Burt in uncompromising terms: 'Burt was the classic confidence-trickster – the white-collar criminal whose currency happened not to be cash but ego inflation' (Gillie 1980: 14). Next were inserted some brief comments by the Clarkes (1980: 17–19), which had not been given at the symposium. They summarized their own part in the business, and echoed Gillie's belief that Burt had probably always been a confidence-trickster.

There followed three papers by speakers who were less concerned with Burt's character or conduct than with the wider implications and consequences of the affair. Kline (1980: 20–3) discussed 'Burt's false results and modern psychometrics', arguing that Burt's findings had resembled the most recent data so closely that there had been no reason to suspect him. He then passed on to the nature of intelligence and the question of heritability. Blackman (1980: 24–31) spoke about 'Data and experimental psychology', and although he did not try to exonerate Burt, the general tenor of his remarks was that those without sin should cast the first stone – an observation not out of place at this stage. Farr (1980: 32–6), who had been the discussant at the symposium, then made 'Some observations on the nature of probity in science', which again did not attempt to comment directly on Burt's misdeeds. These three papers together introduced a refreshing detachment from personal abuse, and a constructive attempt to see the matter in a wider context. A note on heritability (Clarke, Ann, 1980: 37–8) closed the publication.

The star of the occasion was undoubtedly Hearnshaw. His knowledge of Burt's life and work was greatly superior to that of the other contributors, and this, together with his detached and fair-minded handling of the explosive issues, gave him an overwhelming authority. At the same time things were to a considerable extent made easy for him at Aberdeen. The 'anti-Burters' were most inadequately represented by a journalist, who could never carry the authority of a professional psychologist; while the two-page article, little more than a note, from the Clarkes was only added later. The 'pro-Burters' were not represented at all. The remaining contributors did not pretend to know very much about Burt or his misdeeds; they were concerned with the wider implications. Thus Hearnshaw's performance was not so much a victory as a walkover.

But if the final stage was plain sailing, we must not forget that it had been a long, hard road for Hearnshaw, from the 'Memorial Address' at Primrose Hill to the 'balance sheet' at Aberdeen; and he must have been heartily relieved that he could at last feel that the journey was safely completed. He had shouldered an enormous burden, and resisted as fairly as he could the pressures to side with one party or another. His handling of the contentious issues, and the conclusions he had reached, had gone far towards reconciling a bitter division of opinion, and towards resolving a threatening and damaging dispute. The message which he had delivered at Aberdeen had been dramatically different from that which he had presented at Primrose Hill. But both messages had been admirably adapted to the needs of the occasion; and after his address at Aberdeen he received what a senior member described as the longest ovation he had ever heard at an annual conference (Letter from J. R. Morrison, 3 April 1980).

For Burt – or rather, for Burt's reputation – the journey was less satisfactory. In October 1971, at the memorial service, his record had been unblemished and his achievements universally acclaimed; but thereafter the decline had been continuous. After some years of critical rumbling, there came the public accusations of 1976, supported by a number of 'leading scientists'; within three more years, Hearnshaw's biography, originally intended to record an honoured and honourable place in the history of British psychology, had furnished a detailed documentation of the major charges, and a massive elaboration of further misdemeanours; and all this had now been accepted, not least by the Council of the British Psychological Society. After Aberdeen, Burt was finished. His guilt had been publicly acknowledged by the society of which he had been one of the earliest members, one of the staunchest supporters, and for nearly half a century one of the brightest adornments.

Chapter three

Discoveries

On first reading Hearnshaw's biography, there seemed no reason to doubt that Burt had been thoroughly and repeatedly dishonest. It was especially striking that Hearnshaw had begun as a sympathetic admirer of Burt's work, and had been gradually forced to revise his opinions as the evidence accumulated. Moreover, he had not only confirmed and strengthened many of the charges originally brought by others; he had also, it appeared, discovered extensive additional misdemeanours in the historical field. Even if there proved to be occasional inaccuracies in this mass of evidence, the damning conclusion would surely hold: that Burt's goose was well and truly cooked.

If there was any fault in Hearnshaw's assessment, it seemed to me initially that it might lie, not in being too hard on Burt, but in being too lenient. This seemed especially likely with regard to Hearnshaw's two mitigating arguments: that Burt's misdeeds began only in the latter part of his life; and that he was 'psychologically disturbed'. Both propositions seemed too convenient to be readily believable.

The first argument enabled Hearnshaw to include, unaltered, much of the material he had already gathered for the earlier part of the biography, and to preserve almost unchanged the favourable judgements he had always made about the greater part of Burt's career. In addition, this belief largely exonerated psychologists from the charge that they had been culpably lax in failing to detect Burt's misdeeds sooner. All Burt's earlier promotions and honours could be justified, and the eventual failure to detect his misdeeds became comprehensible – for who could have predicted that such a paragon would fall from grace?

Second, the belief that Burt was psychologically disturbed seemed even more convenient. 'Mental illness' has become a highly popular plea among many accused persons, and its diagnosis is such an uncertain matter that there is often little difficulty in finding some supposed expert who will testify that he can detect it. If the belief that Burt's misdeeds began late in life helped to preserve much of his earlier reputation, the further belief that he became mentally ill tended to mitigate his eventual guilt. It also tended to reinforce the exoneration of psychologists in general. Burt's failure became a private and individual tragedy, which might equally have befallen a scientist in any field. It did not reflect upon his colleagues in general, by suggesting, for example, that such behaviour was in any way typical of psychologists as such, or that psychological standards were inferior to those of other disciplines, or that psychology might be more prone to such lapses than other sciences. Burt was just the rotten apple in the barrel.

It should not be supposed, of course, that explanations must be false just because they are convenient. The main point of mentioning these matters here is to stress that my initial impression was that Burt might well have been more guilty than Hearnshaw supposed. I was inclined to doubt the assertion that Burt was disturbed, and prepared to believe that his misbehaviour had begun much earlier than Hearnshaw allowed. In short, the more plausible position appeared to me to be that adopted by Burt's more extreme critics, the Clarkes and Kamin, that Burt had always been a 'confidence-trickster' and was perfectly sane; while Hearnshaw's pleas in mitigation seemed a little too opportune.

Looking back on this first reaction now, it seems to have been determined in part by the revulsion which Burt's alleged behaviour is likely to arouse in anyone who believes he was guilty. One may easily be so incensed by such dishonesty that anything which might be interpreted as an attempt to excuse it can arouse strong opposition.

Influenced by this initial impression, I thought it would be worthwhile to attempt to strengthen the evidence that Burt's dishonesty had begun early. For this purpose, *The Young Delinquent* (Burt 1925) seemed a good place to start. As one of Burt's best-known works, it had greatly enhanced his reputation in the earlier stages of his career. It had also been Tizard's complaint that Burt had failed to produce his research material on delinquency when requested (*The Times*, 25 October 1976). It might be possible to demonstrate fraudulence here.

An examination of this book quickly brought one, perhaps predictable, conclusion. This was that any attempt to demonstrate deception in a book published more than fifty years earlier, on the basis of internal evidence alone, verged on the foolish. It is of course possible that Burt invented much, even all, of the material he records; but this could be true of most similar works, and his failure to produce his material – many years later, after several moves, in his old age – is hardly decisive. However, Burt had also given a preliminary account of his findings in an earlier paper (Burt 1923a). I therefore compared his earlier and later reports, in order to determine whether he had touched up his original findings to improve his case. I could find nothing to support this. In fact, the material does not lend itself to such 'adjustment', for Burt was not trying to establish some favoured hypothesis; he was only presenting an initial survey of the field in order to isolate the main factors which required explanation. It may be that my inquiry was altogether too superficial, but it did impress upon me the enormous difficulty of demonstrating deception after so long a time.

It also brought another conclusion. This was that *The Young Delinquent* deserved its high reputation. It contained a mass of interesting data; it was refreshingly free from special pleading and preconceived conclusion; and it was tolerant and humane in its outlook. No doubt its methods and findings could now be criticized, but they seemed to be admirably adapted to the needs of the day and the resources available. Burt was also generous in his comments on the work of other criminologists, and aware of the incompleteness of his own contribution. His general conclusion was that both hereditary and environmental factors were important, and there was no obvious sign that he was blind to the importance of the latter.

The upshot of this first tentative inquiry was to suggest that it would be hard to demonstrate any further major delinquencies by Burt, particularly in the earlier part of his life. The failure to demonstrate earlier delinquencies did not, of course, demonstrate that Hearnshaw was right to reject the possibility. But it did suggest that there was little likelihood of proving him wrong.

The origin of this study

The assertion that Burt was suffering from 'incipient paranoia' seemed more open to criticism. But here my scepticism concerning Hearnshaw's conclusion was checked by one argument for Burt's mental instability which seemed particularly strong. This argument arose in the course of Hearnshaw's accusations of historical falsification, and since it was this point which proved to be the origin of this study, it will be worth considering more fully.

Hearnshaw's accusation of historical falsification occurs mainly in chapter nine of his biography, and is concentrated in section six. This begins with the following words:

> It is a strange story. Burt's account has convinced few; it is totally at variance with the evidence and replete with misrepresentations; it might be dismissed as an unimportant aberration of Burt's declining years were it not for the fact that it provides documentary evidence for the peculiarities of his personality, and, probably, for a pathological streak in his make-up.
>
> (Hearnshaw 1979: 169)

It certainly was very strange that Burt, who (according to Hearnshaw) embarked upon these falsifications in 1947 when he was only sixty-four years old and widely recognized as an authority upon the subject, should nevertheless have written an account 'totally at variance with the evidence' and which 'has convinced few'; and of which Hearnshaw later writes that 'Burt might have known it would be regarded with incredulity' (ibid.: 178). Hearnshaw can see only one way of explaining such mysterious behaviour: Burt must have been mentally ill. So Hearnshaw (ibid.: 179) concludes that Burt's 'apparently total blindness to the implausibility of his story suggests that a delusional system had taken over. . . . Could any well-balanced individual have supposed that he could get away with this?'

This argument seemed strong, for such strange behaviour surely suggested that Burt was unbalanced. There seemed no way of avoiding Hearnshaw's conclusion. However, I remained dissatisfied, until another thought occurred to me – influenced perhaps by the more favourable attitude to Burt induced by reading *The Young Delinquent*. The alleged historical falsification was indeed a strange story. But was it strange because Burt was suffering from delusions? Or was it strange because Hearnshaw was mistaken about the facts? Had Burt really produced an account which was, in Hearnshaw's words, 'totally at variance with the evidence'? It seemed most unlikely that Hearnshaw could be wrong, yet the accusations made against Burt were immensely damaging. Before one finally accepted them, some attempt ought to be made to check the alleged historical facts. Unlikely as it seemed, Hearnshaw might be wrong.

A check, it seemed, should not be too difficult. Much of Hearnshaw's evidence consisted of claims made by Burt in the forties and fifties, both about his own early papers and those of Spearman – claims which could not be confirmed, so Hearnshaw alleged, by a study of those papers. It would not, I supposed, be necessary to check every one of the many instances given by Hearnshaw. There was no question of having to repeat all Hearnshaw's research. It would be enough to check a sample; and if Hearnshaw's statements were confirmed, the remainder could be accepted on trust. Then it would be possible to say with assurance, whether the story was strange because Burt was behaving oddly, or – remote possibility – because Hearnshaw was mistaken.

The very first misrepresentation of which Burt was accused concerned Spearman's 1904 paper on 'General intelligence'. I happened to possess a reprint of this paper, so it was a convenient place to start. I was in no real doubt as to what the outcome would be: Hearnshaw's charges would be substantiated. He might possibly make one or two slips, but no responsible historian of Hearnshaw's standing was at all likely to prove repeatedly unreliable, especially in a matter of such importance.

'General intelligence' and 'Sensory discrimination'

The first example which Hearnshaw gives of Burt's alleged falsification of factorial history comes from a passage which Burt wrote in the Michotte

Festschrift of 1947. This is said to misinterpret the views expressed by Spearman (1904b) in his famous paper on 'General intelligence', and to mark the 'very tentative beginnings' of a 'new story' (Hearnshaw 1979: 171). According to Hearnshaw, Burt had until 1947 accepted that factor analysis originated with Spearman, but now he began to sing a different tune. Hearnshaw describes the misrepresentation as follows:

> Spearman's role was played down, and his conclusions misrepresented. Spearman did not, as Burt stated, propose 'the identification [of general intelligence] with general sensory discrimination'; he held merely that 'discrimination has unrivalled advantages for investigating and diagnosing the central function', and added that 'Discussion as to the psychical nature of this fundamental function has been reserved until a more complete acquaintance has been gained concerning its objective relations'. Burt was perfectly well aware of Spearman's position on this matter as he had added a footnote to page 165 of his 1909 article to clarify it. So he was unquestionably misrepresenting it in his Michotte paper.
>
> (Hearnshaw 1979: 171; the phrase in square brackets was added by Hearnshaw)

The first question to be settled here is whether Spearman did (as Burt said), or did not (as Hearnshaw claims), propose 'the identification [of general intelligence] with general sensory discrimination'. On examining Spearman's paper (1904b), I found the following three statements. They are taken from pages 269, 272, and 284 respectively. The emphasis is that of Spearman.

1 Thus we arrive at the remarkable result that *the common and essential element in the Intelligences wholly coincides with the common and essential element in the Sensory Functions.*

2 . . . we reach the profoundly important conclusion that *there really exists a something that we may provisionally term 'General Sensory Discrimination' and similarly a 'General Intelligence', and further that the functional correspondence between these two terms is not appreciably less than absolute.*

3 . . . there is also shown to exist a correspondence between what may provisionally be called 'General Discrimination' and 'General Intelligence' which works out with great approximation to *one or absoluteness.*

I found these statements both surprising and puzzling. Surprising, because the very first check of Hearnshaw's allegations seemed to lend such obvious and strong support to Burt; puzzling, because Spearman gives them great prominence in his paper, yet Hearnshaw seemed to have overlooked them entirely. But Spearman's statements require much more careful study before reliable conclusions are possible. The accusation occupies only a dozen lines. It requires many more to set out what Spearman and Burt actually held.

Certainly it seems that nowhere in his paper did Spearman ever use the word 'identification' to describe the relation between 'general intelligence' and 'sensory discrimination'. This might be regarded as the end of the matter: if Burt alleged that Spearman said this, and Spearman did not, does it not follow that Burt is misrepresenting him? But before we come to this conclusion, we should study exactly what Burt said in his Michotte paper, and what Spearman said in 1904 – and a great deal more besides.

Burt's actual words were as follows:

> He [Spearman] thus claimed to have secured objective evidence, first for the existence of general intelligence, and secondly for its identification with general sensory discrimination.
> (Burt 1947a: 55; the name in square brackets has been added by the present writer)

It will be seen that Burt does not purport to be quoting Spearman's actual words, nor does he state that Spearman actually used the word 'identification'. He is only purporting to state Spearman's conclusion in his, Burt's, own words. But Hearnshaw's report is ambiguous. The manner in which he describes what Burt said could easily give the impression that Burt was putting words – false words – into Spearman's mouth. This is because Hearnshaw places the words in quotation marks without making it clear whether the words are the words of Burt himself, or whether they are words which Burt alleges Spearman used. Since this phrase is followed at once by two further sentences in quotation marks ('discrimination has unrivalled . . .' and 'Discussion as to . . .') which do appear to be intended as direct quotations from Spearman, the reader might very well suppose that the phrase about 'identification' was also intended to be a direct quotation. And if it was, and if Spearman did not actually use the word, then to this extent at least Burt would have misrepresented him.

But since Burt was only purporting to describe Spearman's views in his, Burt's, own words, he cannot be accused of misrepresenting Spearman by misquoting him. He might still, of course, have misrepresented Spearman by ascribing to him views he did not hold; however, the relevant question is not 'Did Spearman use the word "identification"?' but 'Did Spearman write anything which might justify Burt in describing his views in this way?'

The three statements of Spearman, quoted above, certainly seem to lend considerable plausibility to Burt's claims. It may be that these quotations are not by themselves sufficient to demonstrate that Spearman did intend to assert the 'identification' of general intelligence and general sensory discrimination; but the least that can be said is that anyone might be forgiven for thinking that he did. At first sight, these quotations seem to make the point in forceful and unequivocal language, giving it great prominence as an important conclusion. The third extract, in particular, appears in Spearman's 'summary of principal conclusions' at the end of the paper. If Hearnshaw had only wanted to conclude that Burt had misunderstood Spearman, we might perhaps think it was odd that he had failed to draw our attention to these passages, which suggest so strongly that Burt had not misunderstood. But Hearnshaw is claiming that Burt misrepresented Spearman: that is, that Burt understood Spearman perfectly well, but deliberately presented what he knew was a distorted account of Spearman's conclusions. Accordingly, Hearnshaw's failure to mention these passages is puzzling. He omits what must be a major piece of evidence in Burt's favour. Can it be that Hearnshaw was unaware of these passages?

The two statements, mentioned above, which Hearnshaw ascribes to Spearman (namely, 'discrimination has unrivalled . . .' and 'Discussion as to . . .') do indeed appear in Spearman's paper, on pages 274 and 284 respectively. Thus these accurate quotations are taken from the same section of the paper as the three quotations we have given concerning Spearman's views on the relation of general intelligence and general sensory discrimination; indeed, one of these accurate quotations has been taken from the very same page. This circumstance can only serve to reinforce the question whether Hearnshaw can possibly have been unaware of these passages which seem to support Burt's interpretation so strongly. How was it possible to read the relevant pages with sufficient care to extract the sections which Hearnshaw quoted, and yet fail to notice the phrases which he did not quote?

The two quotations in question are mentioned by Hearnshaw as if they were to be contrasted with the notion of 'identification', and demonstrate Spearman's real views on the matter ('he held merely . . .'), as opposed to the views falsely ascribed to him by Burt. But Hearnshaw nowhere explains or justifies his implication. Had he tried to do so, he would surely have realized that the statement 'discrimination has unrivalled advantages for investigation and diagnosing the central function' in no way qualifies, contradicts, or reduces Spearman's emphasis on 'identification'. On the contrary, unless Spearman were intending to assert an identity, it is hard to understand why he should suppose that discrimination would have these advantages. Again, there is no indication that Spearman's caution about the psychical nature of the 'fundamental function' limits or contradicts an 'identification'. It is simply a reservation as to what its ultimate nature will prove to be. There seems no good reason, then, for taking these quotations as supporting Hearnshaw's accusation; rather the reverse.

We may conclude that, on the evidence we have so far examined, Spearman's own statements in 1904 seem to support Burt's formulation, and the statements quoted by Hearnshaw, so far from refuting it, also seem consistent with it.

If Hearnshaw is to persuade us that Burt was deliberately distorting Spearman's views, he must explain in what way the alleged distortion would discredit Spearman. Unless good reason can be shown why Spearman would be discredited, the supposed motive vanishes, and we have no reason for thinking that any distortion was deliberate. It is remarkable that Hearnshaw does not appear to realize what he has to do, and simply ignores this part of his task. Yet, once again, if he had looked into the matter, he would surely have come to realize that the view which Burt is ascribing to Spearman, so far from discrediting him or misrepresenting him, actually seems to be entailed by Spearman's own theories. This matter of the relation of 'General intelligence' (GI) and 'General sensory discrimination' (GSD) is so important for the understanding, both of the various views on intelligence in general, and for that of the Burt affair in particular, that it is essential to set out what is involved in some detail. Unless the rival theories are appreciated, it is impossible to assess fairly what Burt said.

Spearman's central belief, expressed in his own words, was that 'all branches of intellectual activity have in common one fundamental function, whereas the remaining or specific elements seem in every case to be wholly different' (Spearman 1904b: 284). Burt quotes these words of Spearman as providing the justification for his own summary of Spearman's conclusions: 'He thus claimed to have secured objective evidence, first for the existence of general intelligence, and secondly for its identification with general sensory discrimination' (Burt 1947a: 55). The reasoning behind this conclusion is as follows. When Spearman referred to 'all branches of intellectual activity' he was thinking of a very wide range of performances. Thus he writes that 'All examination in the different sensory, school, or other specific faculties may be considered as so many independently obtained estimates of the one great common Intellective Function' (Spearman 1904b: 272). All these 'independently obtained estimates' would be positively correlated, in Spearman's view, simply because they all had 'one fundamental function in common'. The degree of correlation would vary from case to case, and it need not be large. It would depend upon the extent to which the particular activity depended upon the 'one great common Intellective Function' (the 'general factor'), and the extent to which it involved 'the remaining or specific elements' (a 'specific factor').

The application of these general principles to the case in question is straightforward. If a number of different tests of sensory discrimination – for example, of visual acuity, of sound intensity, and so on – are administered, and if these tests correlate positively among one another, the correlation suggests that there is a capacity for 'general sensory discrimination' as contrasted with distinct capacities for 'specific sensory discrimination' in visual acuity, in sound intensity, and so on. In other words, these tests correlate in so far as they all have 'one fundamental function in common'. But, and this is the crucial point, for Spearman this common function is simply 'the one great common Intellective Function', it is the same 'general factor' which explains the positive correlation found among all the 'different sensory, school and other specific faculties'. To put it crudely: for Spearman, tests of sensory discrimination, in so far as they correlate, are measuring the same 'general intelligence' as any test of relations, logical powers, or whatever. Hence the conclusion quoted above: 'Thus we arrive at the remarkable result that the *common and essential element in the Intelligences wholly coincides with the common and essential element in the Sensory Functions*' (Spearman 1904b: 269).

Spearman's standpoint becomes clearer when compared with the remaining theories of intelligence summarized earlier. A 'multiple factor' theory, such as that of Thurstone, would also expect all tests of sensory discrimination to correlate positively, but the explanation would differ. In Thurstone's theory, the correlation would be ascribed to a 'special aptitude' for sensory discrimination, akin to a traditional faculty, which would bear no relation to any common intellective function – indeed, for this view there would be no common intellective function. For Thurstone, therefore, it would be mistaken to refer to an 'identification' of GI and GSD, because there would be no such thing as GI. In contrast to such a faculty theory, Spearman was justified in calling his own conclusion 'remarkable'.

For the view that there is no structure of intelligence at all – as proposed by Thomson, for instance – both Spearman and Thurstone would be mistaken. Correlations among different mental tests, if found at all, would merely reflect the chance sampling of highly specific functions, each independent of the rest. For this view, an 'identification' of GI and GSD would be erroneous because there is in reality nothing to correspond to either GI or GSD. In contrast, Spearman's result is again 'remarkable'.

The final possibility is that of Burt himself. Involving both a general factor and group factors, Burt's view is the most complex and hence the most easily misunderstood. Burt agrees with Spearman in accepting a general factor, but rejects his denial of group factors. Burt agrees with Thurstone in accepting group or multiple factors, but rejects his denial of a general factor. Burt would expect there to be a correlation among different tests of sensory discrimination. Here he would be in agreement with both

Spearman and Thurstone, and in disagreement with Thomson. But Burt's reason for expecting such a correlation would be more complex than that of either Spearman or Thurstone. Where Spearman and Thurstone would argue about whether such a correlation was due to a 'common intellective function' (general factor) or to a general discriminatory function unrelated to any common function (a multiple factor), Burt's view is that it is due to both. Burt supposes that the correlation can be resolved into two components, both the general and a group factor.

The use of the term 'identification' as a shorthand way of describing Spearman's view of the relation of GSD and GI is perhaps open to misunderstanding. But it seems a reasonably fair and accurate description if we bear the alternative possibilities in mind. Burt, of course, would wish to deny that GSD and GI should be 'identified'. But this was not because he wished to deny Spearman's 'common intellective function'; it was because he wished to include Thurstone's 'multiple factors'.

The upshot at this point is that both Spearman's own very positive statements in 1904, and his theoretical position, seem in accordance with Burt's statement that he 'identified' GSD and GI. In particular, there seems to be no reason whatever for supposing that Burt was trying to misrepresent Spearman. But there remains much further evidence to consider before a decision can fairly be reached.

An old story

According to Hearnshaw, Burt's 1947 statements about 'identification' were part of a 'new story' which he was then just beginning to invent with a view to discrediting Spearman, who had died in 1945 and was unable to defend himself. But was it a 'new story'? Plainly, such a statement can only be made with confidence by those who have studied Burt's earlier writings with sufficient care to assure themselves that Burt had not said this before, when Spearman was alive. If Hearnshaw is right, and Burt was in the later forties setting out to falsify past history and steal Spearman's credit, then it may very well be that it is in 1947 that the 'story' first appears. But if, as our examination has so far suggested, Burt was only reporting what he genuinely believed Spearman thought, and what indeed seems to be in accordance with Spearman's writings and theories, then Burt may well have said this often enough before. Indeed, since it seems to concern a central theoretical issue, it would be surprising if he had not. To find earlier instances would accordingly go far towards deciding between Hearnshaw's position and that of Burt.

In fact, there is no difficulty whatever in finding a number of earlier occasions, when Spearman was still alive, when Burt made very similar statements. In his major work, *The Factors of the Mind*, Burt (1940: 4, footnote 1) remarks that in 1904 Spearman 'identified' a 'common and essential element underlying all the intelligences' with 'general sensory discrimination'. Spearman can hardly have failed to read this work, and notice this ascription; but there is no record that he complained.

Actually, Burt had been saying this for years – nearly forty years. As a young man, Burt attended the British Association meeting at Sheffield in 1910, and there gave an account of the experiments he had described in the *British Journal of Psychology* in 1909. The report of the meeting contains a brief paper by Burt which includes the following significant statement:

> Views attributing to sensory discrimination, whether general or specific, an intimate functional correspondence with general intelligence were not confirmed.
>
> (Burt 1911a: 804)

This statement does not, it is true, either use the word 'identification' or name Spearman as the person whose views were not confirmed. But if there is any real doubt about it, Burt does both things in another publication of the same year which appeared in *Child Study*. This paper also described Burt's 1909 experiments, and in it Burt criticizes Spearman by name for interpreting correlations between general intelligence and general sensory discrimination as 'a manifestation of a fundamental identity between General Intelligence and Sensory Discrimination' (Burt 1911b: 40). This paper was based upon an address given to the Manchester Child Study Society on 22 October 1909. We do not, of course, know whether the address itself contained the phrase quoted; but if it did, this would actually pre-date the appearance of Burt's 1909 paper itself, which was published in December 1909. However this may be, we seem justified in concluding that not only was this not a 'new story', it was a very old story indeed, going back to the time of Burt's very earliest publications.

Perhaps, then, Burt was already trying to misrepresent Spearman before the First World War? If so, he was not alone. Burt was only one of a number of psychologists who were in those days criticizing Spearman along these lines. Thorndike, the great American learning theorist and educational psychologist, became interested in the mathematical approach to intelligence at the beginning of the century, and followed Spearman's work closely. Moreover, it is clear that as soon as Spearman published his 1904 papers Thorndike was puzzled and concerned by Spearman's discussion of the relation between sensory capacity and general intelligence. A letter from Thorndike to Spearman, dated 17 October 1904, expressed his dissatisfaction with Spearman's interpretation of correlations between the two functions (see Appendix B). Then in 1909 he published a paper in the *American Journal of Psychology* entitled 'The relation of accuracy of sensory discrimination to general intelligence' which referred to Spearman's conclusion, given in our third extract above, and reported a special investigation he had conducted to test it. His conclusion was: 'The measurements obtained in the present investigation do not in the least support this hypothesis' (Thorndike, Lay and Dean 1909: 367).

Meanwhile, in Britain, William Brown, in his influential *Essentials of Mental Measurement* of 1911, mentioned Spearman's conclusion given in our first extract above, and referred approvingly to Thorndike's paper and conclusions (Brown 1911: 86–90). Brown added (page 120) that 'In all results hitherto quoted in support of the ultimate identity of general intelligence and general sensory discrimination, the correlations contributed by the latter are so small compared with their probable errors that nothing definite can be inferred from them.' Here, then, we have another instance of a psychologist who finds the word 'identity' suitable for describing Spearman's view of the relation between GSD and GI. The upshot is not merely that Burt himself had told this 'story' long before 1947, but that other psychologists of impeccable credentials had long ago criticized Spearman for holding this view. If Burt could have known, in 1947, that he would one day be pilloried for inventing a new story to discredit Spearman, he would surely have been astonished.

A further point emerges. Thorndike's 1909 paper appeared towards the beginning of the year. Burt's 1909 paper was not published until December. Thus it was Thorndike, not Burt, who first publicly criticized Spearman for holding this view. Moreover, Burt's paper refers to Thorndike's (Burt 1909: 165), so Burt would be aware that the criticism had already been expressed by Thorndike. Actually, the idea of a possible relation between GI and GSD may well be of considerable antiquity, for Burt subsequently mentions an observation of Galton, that acute sensory discrimination is characteristic of persons of high intelligence, adding that 'It was this observation that led Spearman later on to put forward his well-known hypothesis that general intelligence and general sensory discrimination are identical, and that intelligence can best be measured by tests of sensory discrimination' (Burt 1961a: 14).

Footnotes, obscurities, and misrepresentations

But Burt is not out of the wood yet, for we have not yet asked what Burt said on this issue in his 1909 paper itself. This is especially important because the nub of Hearnshaw's case is that, in his 1909 article, Burt knew that Spearman had not intended to identify GI and GSD, because Burt had added a footnote to make this plain.

> Burt was perfectly well aware of Spearman's position on this matter as he had added a footnote to page 165 of this 1909 article to clarify it. So he was unquestionably misrepresenting it in his Michotte paper.
>
> (Hearnshaw 1979: 171)

Hearnshaw does not tell his readers what the footnote said, nor in what context it appeared. These points require examination.

In his 1909 article, Burt (1909: 159) summarized Spearman's 1904 conclusion by quoting three key extracts from Spearman (1904b: 273, 272, and 272 respectively) as follows:

1 Whenever branches of intellectual activity are at all dis-similar then their correlations with one another appear wholly due to their being all variously saturated with some fundamental common Function (or group of Functions). . . .

2 All examination in the different sensory, school, or other specific faculties may be considered as so many independently obtained estimates of the one great common Intellective Function.

3 [Hence] there exists a something we may provisionally term 'General Sensory Discrimination', and similarly a 'General Intelligence' and . . . the functional correspondence between these two is not appreciably less than absolute.

On the same page, Burt appends a footnote to the final word – 'absolute' – in the above summary. This footnote concludes with the words: 'See however Dr Spearman's comment quoted below, p. 165, note 1.' The note referred to is the footnote on page 165 which Hearnshaw mentions. It is appended to a passage in the text, which reads as follows:

It is clear, however, from our extension of the tests into regions representing a stage of mental development higher than sense-perception, that the absolute identification of General Intelligence and General Sensory Discrimination (if it has ever been suggested by any but its opponents) cannot be maintained.

(Burt 1909: 165)

The footnote is attached to the word 'opponents', and reads as follows:

With reference to my criticism of the passage cited above (p. 159) formulating his view of the relation of General Sensory Discrimination and General Intelligence, Dr Spearman has written to me: 'This conclusion of mine was very badly worded. I did not mean (as others have naturally taken it) that general intelligence was based on sensory discrimination; if anything, the reverse. I take both the sensory discrimination and the manifestations leading a teacher to impute general intelligence to be based on some deeper fundamental cause, as sketched in the *Zeitschrift für Psychologie*, vol. XLI, p. 110, para. 5.'

61

A number of points need to be made:

First, although Hearnshaw's statement that Burt 'added a footnote' is literally correct, it is misleading. Hearnshaw's readers would naturally suppose that the footnote was written by Burt – that it was Burt who was clarifying the position. Now we see that it was Spearman. What had happened was that Burt had written to Spearman requesting his comments on a draft of the paper (Burt to Spearman, 19 May 1909). In a lengthy reply, Spearman made numerous suggestions and observations, many of which Burt incorporated in his paper, including the passage just quoted, which ended with the sentence 'I should be glad if you could mention this in a footnote or elsewhere' (Spearman to Burt, 23 June 1909, p. 4, note 31). It is clear, then, that Spearman's 'clarification' would not have appeared if Spearman had not asked Burt to publish it. It is also clear that, whatever Burt may have thought about it, he had little option but to publish it, when asked to do so by such a senior figure.

Second, Hearnshaw's account is also misleading in that it gives the impression that Burt agreed with whatever clarification was made: 'he had added a footnote . . . to clarify it'. But no expression of opinion from Burt appears in this footnote. He merely reports, without comment, what Spearman had asked him to report. Indeed, the words with which Burt prefaces Spearman's comments – 'my criticism of the passage . . . formulating his view of the relation' – suggest that Burt still adheres to the criticism which he expresses in the text (on page 165: 'the absolute identification . . . cannot be maintained') of the passage he had cited from Spearman (on page 159).

Third, it will be seen that in 1909, in his first published paper, Burt is to be found criticizing the 'identification' of GSD and GI, just as we have seen he does subsequently in 1911, in 1940, and in 1947.

Fourth, Spearman's note says that his conclusion had been badly worded, and that he had been misunderstood. But he does not then deny that he had intended to identify GSD and GI. Indeed, he does not mention 'identification' at all. The issue he is concerned about is that he has been misunderstood as meaning that GI was based on GSD, whereas he thinks both are based upon 'some deeper fundamental cause'. This formulation suggests that some critics supposed him to have been *distinguishing* between GI and GSD – for how else could one be based upon the other? If they had supposed that he *identified* them, as Burt supposed that he did, they could not have thought he was basing one on the other. On the other hand, the belief that Spearman is concerned to defend – that both were based upon 'some deeper fundamental cause' – seems to be quite consistent with their identification.

All this seems to suggest that the footnote does not indicate that either Burt or Spearman is rejecting the identification of GI and GSD. There is, however, a difficulty in this interpretation. If Spearman was not concerned to protest against the belief that he intended to identify GI and GSD, why does Burt attach the note to his criticism of Spearman for 'the absolute identification' of GI and GSD? And why should Burt immediately qualify that criticism by adding 'if it has ever been suggested by any but its opponents'? Does not this qualification express some doubt whether Spearman had really intended an 'identification'? Does it not follow, then, that Hearnshaw is after all correct in implying that in 1909 Burt recognized that Spearman did not hold this view, even though the recognition appears in the text and not in the footnote?

I think this is a defensible view, yet it raises its own difficulties. If Spearman objected to Burt's formulation – of an 'identification' – why did he not say so, and ask Burt to withdraw it? And if Burt thought that this misrepresented Spearman, why did he not withdraw it? And why did Burt continue to use this formulation in subsequent publications? And why did Brown also use this formulation? And why did not Spearman object to these later repetitions?

At this distance of time, and in the absence of the parties concerned, it is hardly possible to settle the matter conclusively. But the weight of evidence seems to me to be strongly in favour of the view that Burt believed that Spearman intended an 'identification' and that Spearman himself was not opposed to this formulation. A possible explanation for the difficulty just mentioned may be as follows. It may be the word 'absolute' which is causing the trouble. The note on page 159 (Burt 1909) is attached to the word 'absolute' in Spearman's conclusions; and the qualification on page 165 is attached to the phrase 'the absolute identification'. This is the only occasion I have found where Burt refers to 'the absolute identification' instead of simply to 'the identification'. Perhaps, then, it is the word 'absolute' which had been responsible for the misunderstanding Spearman complained of, and that this had implications which Spearman now regretted. Burt therefore suggests that it is 'the absolute identification' which had only been suggested by its opponents.

It may be that Thorndike's letter to Spearman, mentioned above (see Appendix B), throws some light on this point. It there appears that Thorndike and others had at first understood Spearman to mean that the correlation between GI and GSD ought to be complete (that is, 1.00 or 'absolute'), whereas Spearman in fact supposed that the tests involved would be influenced by numerous specific factors which must reduce the coefficients.

The upshot of this involved inquiry would therefore seem to be that the discussion in Burt (1909) is by no means straightforward, and one is hardly entitled to express dogmatic conclusions. In particular, it is flimsy evidence on which to assert that Burt knew he was misrepresenting Spearman in 1947, especially since Hearnshaw has provided no detailed foundation whatever for such a conclusion.

Finally, there are two things we must not forget: (1) that Burt's reference to 'identification' in 1947 was far from being a 'new story', so that if he was misrepresenting Spearman then, he was also misrepresenting him in 1940, and also in 1911 and in 1909, as were Spearman's other critics of those early years; and (2) that Hearnshaw has never explained how he supposes that 'identification' would discredit Spearman, an explanation which is especially necessary since 'identification' is so plainly in accord, not only with what Spearman himself said in 1904, but also with his theory of the general factor.

Consequences

The upshot of this first attempt to verify Hearnshaw's allegations is to suggest rather strongly that, in this particular instance, he seems to be an unreliable guide. In this case at least, there seem no very adequate grounds for supposing that in 1947 Burt was just beginning to invent a new story with intent to discredit Spearman, then recently deceased. On the contrary, there is ample evidence that Burt and others had criticized Spearman for identifying GI and GSD many years previously, long before Spearman died. Moreover, three considerations strongly suggested that Spearman had 'identified' these functions: (1) his repeated statements in 1904; (2) the implications of his theory of the general factor; and (3) the fact that Spearman did not withdraw or deny this ascription.

It must be added that the evidence upon which Hearnshaw based this particular accusation seems to have been slender. Hearnshaw does not appear, in this case, to have studied what either Spearman or Burt wrote at all closely. Nor does he seem to be familiar with other relevant writers of the period, such as Thorndike and Brown.

This outcome was extremely surprising to me. I had imagined that, after a brief routine check, I should have confirmed the general accuracy and reliability of Hearnshaw's statements. Instead, after a long and often difficult search, I seemed in this instance to have discovered the very opposite. Yet no sweeping conclusions should be drawn from this episode alone. One swallow does not make a summer. There are at least two possible explanations which might account for the outcome, without seriously damaging Hearnshaw's case. The first is that I had myself misinterpreted or misunderstood what was involved. The second is that I had by chance hit upon one of the very few instances in which Hearnshaw happened to have been mistaken, and that further inquiry would soon show that he was for the most part entirely correct.

Plainly it was necessary to study further instances before any safe conclusions could be drawn; and it seemed to me that much the most likely outcome was a general vindication of Hearnshaw's position. But the result of this first attempt to check Hearnshaw's case was undoubtedly a strong encouragement to continue. The matter could not be left as it was. It must be settled, one way or the other.

As I gradually extended my examination of the numerous examples of historical falsification alleged by Hearnshaw, there seemed to be far more to be said for Burt's standpoint and claims than Hearnshaw allowed. In almost every instance, Hearnshaw seemed to give an inaccurate account. At first I was astonished. How could Hearnshaw be so mistaken? Surely, I must somehow be mistaken myself?

Such reflections prompted an exceptionally careful examination of the evidence. This inevitably proved a long and often tedious task. As the first instance has shown, it may require many pages to unravel the truth behind an accusation which needs only a few lines to express. But once embarked upon the task, it became increasingly difficult to imagine abandoning it.

It was the historical aspect of the case against Burt which interested me most, and for a long time I continued to explore this as opportunity offered. It was only gradually, as I became increasingly confident that my scepticism was well founded, that I began to realize that this would have considerable repercussions for the remainder of Hearnshaw's account.

First, my original belief that Hearnshaw had been too lenient to Burt was finding little support. Rather, it seemed that he might have been too severe. If the charge of historical falsification was mistaken, one of Hearnshaw's three major accusations collapsed. Moreover, the beginning of Burt's major misdeeds would have to be postponed a full ten years from 1947, when the Michotte *Festschrift* appeared, to 1957, when Hearnshaw thought that Burt first began to invent twin data. It would follow that Hearnshaw's theory that Burt's fall was precipitated by setbacks first encountered in the forties became much less plausible. If Burt's major deceptions began in 1957, he would already be seventy-four years old when he embarked upon them. No doubt this was a possibility, but it would favour the simple theory of senility rather than anything so complicated as the explanation proposed by Hearnshaw.

Second, if Burt's historical statements were well founded, one of Hearnshaw's prime reasons for supposing that Burt was mentally unbalanced had been undermined. Burt was not after all telling a tall story which he might have known would be rejected. He was a rational man defending his own point of view. My original scepticism about Hearnshaw's appeal to mental illness now seemed to be reinforced.

Third, if Hearnshaw's case was so unreliable in the historical area, where his reputation principally lay, what reliance could be placed upon his evidence concerning the remaining charges, where he could claim no particular expertise? His second and third charges would have to be regarded with caution until they too had been exhaustively examined.

By the beginning of 1983 I had largely completed my investigation of the historical aspect, and as I was now convinced that Hearnshaw was indeed mistaken, I began to prepare a paper for publication. However, it proved extremely difficult to compress the mass of information into the required space, and I soon abandoned the attempt and settled down to prepare a book. In August 1983, when I was already fairly launched on the task, events took another entirely unexpected turn.

Dr Charlotte Banks

The discovery that many of Hearnshaw's historical allegations could not be confirmed was a first surprise. A second discovery occurred in the summer of 1983, when my attention was drawn to a special issue of the *Journal of the Association of Educational Psychologists* (JAEP), which had been published earlier that year to mark the centenary of Burt's birth (Mcloughlin 1983). This was devoted to the observations and reminiscences of a number of Burt's former colleagues and acquaintances; and contained a number of contributions which stoutly defended his reputation. The journal could not be accused of bias. It included papers by psychologists who now accepted Burt's guilt, such as Jensen and Eysenck, as well as by those who still believed in his innocence, such as Banks and Cohen. All contained much valuable detail about Cyril Burt; but Banks's paper, entitled 'Selected reminiscences', struck me immediately as particularly significant.

Down to 1983, a number of Burt's former colleagues and pupils had expressed their continued faith in his probity, sometimes in the most forceful terms. But such confidence, however sincere it might be, could have little impact in face of the mass of evidence presented in the biography. This must be particularly true for the great majority of psychologists who, like the present writer, had never known Burt. In the long run, then, the charges could only be effectively challenged, if they could be challenged at all, by a thorough critical examination of the case which had been built up against Burt, especially as it had been confirmed and extended by Hearnshaw. The significance of Banks's contribution, so it seemed to me, was that she was the first of Burt's defenders to appreciate what was required and to set about providing it. Here for the first time was a detailed examination of some of the main charges, and a sustained exposition of evidence to be presented on Burt's behalf.

Banks (1983) examines the first two of the three major charges listed by Hearnshaw: the historical falsifications, and the twin frauds. Her paper does not deal with the third charge, concerning educational standards. The historical section impressed me most initially because I could see at once, from my own recent study of the relevant literature, how accurate and reliable Banks's critique was. Many of the main points which I had slowly and painfully unearthed were already well known to her, as well as other considerations which had escaped my notice. (The question which I had first examined, of the identification of GI and GSD, was not, however, mentioned.) Working quite independently, we had both reached very similar conclusions for very similar reasons. Any lingering doubts I still retained concerning the inaccuracy of Hearnshaw's work in this field were swept aside by Banks's detailed exposition of conclusions which I had independently reached.

Dr Charlotte Banks is uniquely well placed to contribute to 'the Burt affair' by virtue of her long and close association with him. Born in 1915, she enrolled in the intermediate course at University College in 1938, when Burt was well established as head of the Department of Psychology. She moved with the department to Aberystwyth in 1939 and, after graduating, became a research student with Burt, during which time she carried out many calculations for Burt's wartime memoranda. Her Ph.D. thesis, presented in 1945, was entitled 'Factor analysis applied to current psychological problems, with special reference to data from HM Forces'. She subsequently worked on a number of problems in which Burt was interested, and their first joint paper, 'A factor analysis of body measurements for adult British males', appeared in 1947 (Burt and Banks 1947). Banks was a lecturer in psychology at University College until 1965, when she moved to the Home Office to concentrate on prison research. She retired in 1975.

Banks was probably in closer touch with Burt after his retirement in 1950 than was any other psychologist. Burt had many occasional visitors during this period, but, as Hearnshaw (1979: 209) observes, Banks was probably the only regular caller: 'weeks would sometimes go by with no other callers than Charlotte Banks'. So she is probably the only academic who can give a first-hand account of the last fifteen years of Burt's life, which are so crucial for the charges against him. In 1965 she was joint editor with Broadhurst of a *Festschrift* written by Burt's old colleagues and pupils, *Stephanos: Studies in Psychology presented to Cyril Burt* (Banks and Broadhurst 1965); and after Burt's death she prepared the posthumous *Gifted Child* for publication (Burt 1975).

From all these circumstances, it is clear that Banks is better placed than any other psychologist to give an informed account of the last thirty years of Burt's life – that is, from the beginning of the war until his death in 1971. Her long and continuous acquaintance with Burt, combined with her expert knowledge both of factor analysis and of Burt's general contribution to psychology, make her views on the problems of Burt's later life of special interest. It was unfortunate that her paper appeared in a relatively restricted specialist journal, and so escaped the wide attention which it deserved. Shortly after reading Banks's paper, I got in touch with her and explained my own position. Since then, she has generously commented upon the historical chapters of this book (especially Chapters 3, 4, and 5), and my thinking has greatly benefited from her critical remarks.

Hearnshaw (1984a) replied briefly to Banks's (1983) arguments. Although he pointed out, with justice, that there were a number of matters she had not dealt with, he failed to reply to, or even to mention, any of the positive criticisms which it contained. He concluded: 'I find nothing in Banks's contribution which forces me to amend in the slightest detail what I wrote in Chapter IX of my biography' (Hearnshaw 1984a: 6). Since Hearnshaw makes no attempt to indicate what Banks's criticisms were, still less to explain why he considers them mistaken, his blank rejection of them is unjustified.

It seems even more unjustified in the light of a further finding. Among the many things I learned from Banks's paper was that Cronbach, a leading American writer on differential psychology, had already expressed the opinion that Hearnshaw's historical allegations were unreliable. In a review of the biography, Cronbach (1979: 1392) wrote as follows:

> Spearman's theory of a unified ability was superseded by multiple factor analysis which Burt pioneered. Thurstone's important book, *Multiple Factor Analysis* . . . underplayed Burt's influence and ignored his priority, which stimulated Burt to tell the story in his own way. The defence can read many of Burt's supposed falsifications as consistent with the printed record of 1909 and after, making Hearnshaw's reading seem tendentious and defusing the charge.

That was exactly what I was finding myself. It was also becoming clear that my discoveries, like so many discoveries, had already been made by others. But that does not make them less worthwhile; only more reliable.

Conclusion

The origins of this research have been described in order to make it clear that it was as a consequence of routine historical study, rather than through any special interest in the Burt affair, that the writer became involved. I had no pre-formed opinion about the likelihood or otherwise of Burt involving himself in deception. But by late 1983 it was clear to me that the historical accusations were poorly established, and accordingly that the whole case against Burt ought to be investigated. What the outcome would be, I still did not know.

The next five chapters examine the three main charges which have been brought against Burt. They will be considered in the chronological order in which Burt is said to have embarked upon them: first, the historical falsifications (Chapters 4 and 5); next, the kinship frauds (Chapters 6 and 7); and finally, the allegations concerning scholastic standards, and parent–child intelligence quotients (Chapter 8). The conclusions are summarized at the end of Chapter 8.

Chapter four

Burt's historical claims: the early papers

The assessment of Burt's historical claims is an extremely complex undertaking. Ideally, it requires a clear grasp of the evolution of statistical methods from Galton onwards, and an accurate appraisal of Burt's contribution in relation to the whole factorial movement. This would include at least the major figures: Pearson and the biometric school, Spearman, Brown and Thomson, Stephenson, Thurstone, and many others. Such a study calls for both factorial expertise and historical interest – two qualities rarely found together. Under these circumstances, the need for caution becomes obvious, and the opinions expressed here are tentative.

There are additional complications. Burt published his historical claims in numerous and scattered sources, though a good many of his comments appear in his own statistical journal. Often his remarks are incidental to other issues, and may appear in lengthy footnotes rather than in the text. Comments also appear in other journals, in books, in book reviews, and in correspondence. Many of these are post-war, but there are also important observations in earlier publications. Burt never drew all these remarks together into a single comprehensive statement, so it is hard to be sure that one has given a fair and complete account of his views. Further, in order to check the accuracy of the claims it is necessary to study numerous early papers by Burt and others, which are not always easy to obtain. For all these reasons, dogmatism is more than usually out of place.

The conventional view has been that factor analysis began with Spearman. Hearnshaw begins his own account by expressing the conventional view categorically and without qualification. 'It is universally agreed by every leading factorist,' he writes (1979: 155), 'except Burt in the final phase of his factorial work, that factor analysis had its origins in Spearman's 1904 article.' Hearnshaw calls this the 'orthodox view' (p. 169).

Those who accept this view often, then, see factorial history as comprising two main phases. The first, dominated by Spearman's theory of the general factor, lasts into the thirties, when it is replaced by the second phase, the rise of Thurstone's multiple factor theory. This is the picture presented, for example, in Oléron's (1957) lucid survey. It was also the view of Thurstone himself, in his *Multiple Factor Analysis* of 1947. This treated other British factorial writers as secondary to Spearman, so that in disposing (as Thurstone thought) of Spearman's general factor, they too might now be ignored. Burt could not be expected to welcome this treatment, and Hearnshaw (1979: 173) may well be right when he suggests that Burt was influenced by the publication of Thurstone's book.

> Burt . . . was provoked, as his review [Burt 1947d] of the book makes clear, by Thurstone's disregard of British work other than that of Spearman. Burt felt that the methods being advocated by Thurstone had in fact been anticipated by British workers, and that Thurstone was not giving them credit for this. He himself had anticipated Thurstone's 'centroid' method, and the 'principal axes' method praised by Thurstone was identical with the procedure described by Pearson in *Biometrika* in 1901.

It should be noted that Burt's disagreement with Thurstone's treatment did not prevent him from expressing appreciation in other respects, and a second review (Burt 1947c: 71) described the book as 'a most valuable addition to the literature of factorial-analysis.' Cronbach (1979) also considered that Burt was reacting against Thurstone's neglect; but whereas Cronbach believed that Burt's claims had substance, Hearnshaw supposes that Burt was inventing a 'new story'.

Whether Burt was right or wrong in his claims, and whether he was over-stating his case or not, his position and achievements entitle him to a fair hearing. In asserting his own independent contribution, Burt made two main claims, as follows.

First, that over a long period, from his earliest papers, he had been presenting his own position with regard to intelligence, distinct from that of Spearman. Accordingly we find Burt stressing (a) that he had from the beginning recognized the importance of group factors, in addition to the general factor; and (b) that he had always employed his own factorial technique. In both these respects, Burt was claiming that he had anticipated Thurstone's major ideas, long before Thurstone had even entered the field; and thereby had also anticipated Thurstone's main criticisms of Spearman.

Second, that his own distinctive views were in fact derived from Galton and Pearson: the combination of general and group factors being derived from Galton, and the statistical technique from Pearson.

In my opinion, the central aim of Burt's historical observations was to portray his own position as a continuation of the original English standpoint, stemming from Galton and Pearson. This was, of course, a tradition which pre-dated not only Thurstone, but Spearman too. From this point of view, both Spearman and Thurstone appeared as partial theorists, the one concentrating exclusively upon the general factor and the other equally exclusively upon group or multiple factors. Neither of them could be expected to greet Burt's position with enthusiasm, for he was placing both of them in a less important position than they allotted to themselves. The question to be asked here is whether Burt's historical formulation was a deliberate falsification, designed, as Hearnshaw maintains, to feed Burt's self-importance, or whether it was put forward in good faith as a sincere attempt to depict the actual course of historical events.

Hearnshaw's account

According to Hearnshaw (1979: 154ff.), Burt's factorial work falls into three phases, the historical falsifications belonging to the third. However, all three phases must be considered, since Hearnshaw's argument depends upon drawing a contrast between the first and the final phases.

The first phase began while Burt was a student at Oxford in the early years of the century, and continued until his appointment at University College in 1932. In Hearnshaw's account, factor analysis was only a secondary interest of Burt during these years, and he took his ideas and methods on the subject from Spearman. Thus he states that 'Burt's first acquaintance with factorial techniques arose through his contacts with Spearman while still an Oxford student' (p. 154); that 'Burt's first venture into factor analysis was wholly derivative from Spearman's work' (p. 159); and that 'These early ventures were not worked up in any detail' (p. 155). Hearnshaw summarizes his view of this first phase in the statement that 'Factor analysis remained secondary to Burt's essentially practical interests, and Burt's recognition of Spearman's leadership was virtually complete' (p. 155).

The second phase lasted from Burt's appointment at University College in 1932 until Spearman's death in 1945. Now factor analysis 'moved increasingly to the centre of the stage' (p. 155). Burt elaborated his views much more fully, and they diverged in several respects from Spearman. The period culminated with the publication of *Factors of the Mind* in 1940. However, Burt 'still publicly acknowledged Spearman's priority and pre-eminence in the field' (p. 155); and also 'accepted the orthodox view, that factor analysis originated with Spearman's 1904 article' (p. 169).

The final phase 'lasted from 1947, when he launched the statistical journal with Godfrey Thomson, until the early 1960s' (p. 155). Now Burt 'largely rewrote the early history of the subject' (ibid.). At this stage Burt was 'mainly concerned in de-throning Spearman as the founder of factor analysis, and asserting his own claim to priority as the first user of factorial method in psychology' (ibid.). According to Burt's 'new story', factor analysis had originated with Pearson in 1901, and Burt's own work 'was derived from this source and not from Spearman at all' (p. 179). Thus so far from Spearman having been the originator and first user of factor analysis in 1904, as everyone including Burt himself had hitherto supposed (we are still following Hearnshaw's account), the originator had been Pearson in 1901, and the first user in psychology had been Burt in 1909.

Burt had waited until Spearman was dead before setting out to steal his credit and to propagate this 'new story'. Then the story gradually became more elaborate and extravagant: 'After Spearman's death the campaign of belittlement became increasingly unrestrained, obsessive and extravagant' (1979: 130; and see p. 176). Burt is alleged to have bolstered his malign tale with a series of detailed falsifications of what he himself had written in his early papers, of misrepresentations of Spearman's views and early papers, and by false claims of what he himself had derived from Pearson. Burt must have known that all this was false because he had for so many years believed something so very different.

It is to be noted that Hearnshaw does not treat Burt's claims as a reasonable possibility, proposed by an honest but mistaken man, which we find to be unsound after careful inquiry. Nor does he treat it as the plausible invention of a clever rogue. He treats it as the implausible claim of an unbalanced mind. Hearnshaw describes it, as we have seen, as a 'strange story', whose implausibility suggests that Burt has become psychologically disturbed, and that 'a delusional system has taken over' (p. 179). Yet there are certain prominent features of Burt's account which ill accord with this interpretation. Is it really so strange to suggest that one's work is part of a long-standing tradition? And is it really a sign of overweening self-importance to trace one's main ideas to others? It seems that Hearnshaw's account of the three phases through which Burt's factorial work passed is inaccurate and misleading. In particular, he exaggerates both the extent of which Burt derived all his ideas from Spearman in the early days, and the 'campaign of belittlement' after Spearman's death, deriving from the false contrast an argument which bears little relation to reality.

It does not follow that everything Burt said about the origins of factorial analysis is to be taken as gospel. No prudent historian would accept without careful inquiry an account of events furnished by one of the chief actors therein. The motives for distorting the record, for exaggerating his own part and diminishing the contribution of rivals, are powerful. But even if inaccuracies or exaggerations are detected in Burt's account, it does not follow that Burt is necessarily to be convicted of dishonesty. It may be that any such inaccuracies demonstrate nothing more culpable than that rather too favourable view of oneself and one's achievements which a person may quite honestly hold. Each of us would surely admit such inclinations.

The problem is compounded by the circumstance that some of the issues at stake are controversial, and some of the evidence is incomplete, so that 'what really happened' is genuinely a matter of opinion – as in many historical debates.

Burt's historical account, as we noted, contains two distinct strands: (a) that concerning the content of his early papers, and his assertion that these contained the beginnings of his own distinctive contributions – the group factors and the simple summation method; and (b) that concerning the origins of these ideas, and in particular the contribution of Pearson. These two elements are both equally involved in Burt's historical accounts, and they are closely related: there would be little point in Burt making claims in relation to Pearson if he had not put forward his distinctive ideas at an early stage. But there are two important differences between these two aspects: (1) the first aspect is relatively easy to check by looking back to Burt's papers, whereas the second aspect depends upon negative evidence, and (2) the first aspect was not at all a new story – Burt had been telling it for years, whereas the second aspect does seem to have been new in the late forties. Hearnshaw fails to note this distinction. He treats both aspects alike as part of a 'new story' which is completely false.

The remainder of the present chapter is concerned with the first strand – the content of Burt's early papers. The following chapter deals with the second strand – the origin of Burt's ideas.

'The distribution and relations of educational abilities' (1917)

One half of Burt's historical claim consists, as we have seen, in asserting that from his earliest papers he had been expressing his own distinctive views on intelligence, and had not simply echoed Spearman; and in particular that he had from the beginning supported (a) the conception of group factors in addition to a general factor, and (b) his own 'simple summation' technique of analysis. The papers in question are principally those published between 1909, the date of his first paper, 'Experimental tests of general intelligence', and 1917, the date of his monograph on 'The distribution and relations of educational abilities'. In examining these papers, we shall begin with the 1917 article, and work backwards to 1909. This is because the contents of the 1917 paper are both clear and generally agreed, and it becomes easier to understand the earlier papers in the light of what Burt undoubtedly said and did in 1917. Banks (1983: 23–7) covers the same ground in chronological order, and should be consulted throughout.

It has been widely accepted – not least by Hearnshaw – that Burt's 1917 monograph does indeed advocate the two features of Burt's historical claim which we have just listed. Thus Vernon (1950: 15) described it as a landmark since it provided clear evidence (which Spearman continued to ignore) of verbal, numerical and practical group factors in school subjects, in addition to the general factor. Also he arrived at the fundamental formula for the *Simple Summation* technique of analysis, later rediscovered by Thurstone and named the *Centroid* method.

Hearnshaw (1979: 161) himself echoes this opinion when he writes that the monograph was 'a landmark. It more clearly demonstrated the presence of group factors than any previous analysis had done, and it introduced a number of procedural innovations which anticipated the "centroid" method developed by Thurstone in the 1930s.'

In making his statement, Hearnshaw is also making an admission of the first importance, though he does not seem to realize it. For the 1917 monograph is as relevant to Burt's 'new story' as are any other of the early papers to which Hearnshaw refers. If it be agreed that, at least as early as 1917, Burt's claims for his early work are in these two respects correct, then it becomes absurd to assert that Burt's 'new story' is 'entirely contrary to the evidence'. It demonstrates that, as early as 1917, Burt was indeed expressing the views he claimed. This gives Burt's account a plausibility which Hearnshaw cannot deny. It cannot be nothing but the sheer falsification and delusion which Hearnshaw suggests. Moreover, these two points constitute Burt's main contribution to factor analysis, even if in 1917 still in embryo, so it must be incorrect to say, as Hearnshaw does, that 'The key advances occurred when Burt moved to University College' (p. 162).

Burt's 1917 paper is described by Hearnshaw (p. 160) as 'the most elaborate and significant of his early ventures'. Indeed, this work goes far towards refuting Hearnshaw's earlier and contrasting remark that 'These early ventures were not worked up in any detail' (p. 155). Such comments contribute to an impression that Burt was later trying to make altogether too much of his early work, and such an impression is unfair.

Burt (1917) consists of three memoranda prepared for the London County Council. Most of the relevant material is to be found in the third section, entitled 'On the relations between ability in different subjects in the school curriculum' (pp. 45–79). It described a study of 120 school-children, aged between ten and twelve. They were of varied ability, though 'differing but little in . . . zeal, attendance and social status, taught by the same teacher and for about the same period of time' (p. 46). Burt himself drew up, and applied personally, some thirteen special tests in the various school subjects. All the children were tested at least twice in each subject on different days. A standard scale of marking was devised to secure an approximately normal distribution of marks, and comparable standard deviations in the various tests. Each test was then correlated with every other, and the coefficients presented in a conventional matrix (see Burt 1917: 52, Table XVIII). These observed coefficients are given in our

Table 4.1 (Correlations between school subjects, (A) Observed coefficients).

It should be noted that the table contains the actually observed coefficients; they have not been adjusted by Spearman's well-known 'correction for attenuation' – a small example of Burt's independence from Spearman. The tests have been arranged in order of their average correlation. The table also gives, in the diagonal in brackets, the 'self-correlation' or correlation between the first and second application of the test. These indicate how far the test tends to give the same answer on successive applications, and are usually called 'reliability coefficients'. Here they range from 0.85 for Arithmetic (rules) to 0.54 for Drawing, which suggests a satisfactory consistency; and the great majority of the coefficients (68 out of 78) are more than three times their probable error.

One of the most obvious facts about this table, as of most such tables, is that all the coefficients are positive. Here they vary from 0.08, between Arithmetic (rules) and Reading (comprehension), to 0.76, between Arithmetic (rules) and Arithmetic (problems). As Burt (1917: 51) remarks, 'ability in any one subject tends on the whole to be accompanied, to a greater or less degree, by ability in nearly every other subject'.

Reflection on this finding leads to the most important single question in the field. Thus Burt notes that the existence of a correlation between two tests is more naturally explained by supposing that the same ability is common to both – in other words, by supposing that the correlation provides evidence of a common factor. But in this table there are numerous such correlations. Burt (1917: 53) therefore asks: 'But is the common factor one and the same in each case? Or have we to recognise a multiplicity of common factors, each limited to small groups of school subjects?' This is the great central problem concerning the structure of ability: is it the outcome of a single common factor, as Spearman supposed, or of a number of group factors, as Thurstone later preferred?

The most important part of the memorandum concerns the procedure which Burt adopts for answering this central question, together with the answer which he gives. The procedure involves two steps. The first step is to ask what the correlation among the tests would in theory have been *if they had been due to one and the same common factor*. This gives a second table of 'theoretical coefficients' (see our Table 4.2) which have been 'so calculated that all the correlations are due to one factor and one only, common to all subjects, but shared by each in different degrees' (ibid.: 53). The next step is to compare the observed with the theoretical coefficients, in order to determine whether any differences justify a departure from the hypothesis of a single common or general factor; and, if so, what this departure should be. Burt's statistical procedures will next be examined in greater detail.

(Burt describes his statistical procedures briefly in a note to page 53,

Table 4.1 Correlations between school subjects

(A) Observed coefficients

Data: special tests; 120 children, aged 10- to 12-years; 2 schools; 3 classes, standards V and VI (reliability coefficients in brackets)

	Composition	Science	Arithmetic (problems)	Geography	History
Composition	(.76)	.71	.65	.70	.71
Science	.71	(.70)	.63	.65	.67
Arithmetic (problems)	.65	.63	(.81)	.51	.60
Geography	.70	.65	.51	(.72)	.71
History	.71	.67	.60	.71	(.78)
Reading (comprehension)	.58	.51	.49	.51	.57
Dictation	.47	.32	.40	.45	.41
Writing (speed)	.50	.38	.22	.39	.32
Reading (speed)	.49	.31	.34	.38	.35
Handwork	.30	.49	.38	.40	.31
Arithmetic (rules)	.27	.37	.76	.25	.27
Drawing	.38	.19	.21	.30	.28
Writing (quality)	.30	.26	.29	.22	.17
Average	.50	.46	.46	.46	.45
Hypothetical general factor	.85	.76	.76	.75	.74
General educational ability (.79)	.71	.55	.67	.58	.60
General intelligence (.74)	.63	.56	.52	.35	.39

Source: (From Burt 1917: Table XVIII).

Reading (compre-hension)	Dictation	Writing (speed)	Reading (speed)	Hand-work	Arith-metic (rules)	Drawing	Writing (quality)
.58	.47	.50	.49	.30	.27	.38	.30
.51	.32	.38	.31	.49	.37	.19	.26
.49	.40	.22	.34	.38	.76	.21	.29
.51	.45	.39	.38	.40	.25	.30	.22
.57	.41	.32	.35	.31	.27	.28	.17
(.68)	.52	.21	.56	.10	.08	.15	.14
.52	(.82)	.25	.38	.09	.31	.12	.18
.21	.25	(.80)	.35	.28	.32	.36	.30
.56	.38	.35	(.79)	.19	.16	.15	.22
.10	.09	.28	.19	(.61)	.33	.50	.46
.08	.31	.32	.16	.32	(.85)	.09	.18
.15	.12	.36	.15	.50	.09	(.54)	.57
.14	.18	.30	.22	.46	.18	.57	(.72)
.37	.33	.32	.32	.32	.28	.27	.27
.59	.52	.52	.52	.51	.45	.43	.43
.64	.62	.43	.46	.37	.29	.24	.40
.51	.28	.48	.37	.50	.09	.17	.06

Table 4.2 Correlations between school subjects

(B) Theoretical values

To illustrate the nature of a 'hierarchy' constructed on the assumption of a sole and single factor, shared by all subjects in different degrees. Data: 'Hypothetical general factor' coefficients of Table XVIII

	Compo-sition	Science	Arith-metic (prob-lems)	Geo-graphy	History
Composition	(.72)	.65	.65	.64	.63
Science	.65	(.58)	.58	.57	.56
Arithmetic (problems)	.65	.58	(.58)	.57	.56
Geography	.64	.57	.57	(.56)	.55
History	.63	.56	.56	.55	(.55)
Reading (comprehension)	.50	.45	.45	.44	.44
Dictation	.44	.39	.39	.39	.38
Writing (speed)	.44	.39	.39	.39	.38
Reading (speed)	.44	.39	.39	.39	.38
Handwork	.43	.38	.38	.38	.37
Arithmetic (rules)	.38	.34	.34	.34	.33
Drawing	.36	.33	.33	.32	.32
Writing (quality)	.36	.33	.33	.32	.32

Source: (From Burt 1917: Table XIX).

Reading (compre-hension)	Dictation	Writing (speed)	Reading (speed)	Hand-work	Arith-metic (rules)	Drawing	Writing (quality)
.50	.44	.44	.44	.43	.38	.36	.36
.45	.39	.39	.39	.38	.34	.33	.33
.45	.39	.39	.39	.38	.34	.33	.33
.44	.39	.39	.39	.38	.34	.32	.32
.44	.38	.38	.38	.37	.33	.32	.32
(.35)	.31	.31	.31	.30	.26	.25	.25
.31	(.27)	.27	.27	.26	.23	.22	.22
.31	.27	(.27)	.27	.26	.23	.22	.22
.31	.27	.27	(.27)	.26	.23	.22	.22
.30	.26	.26	.26	(.26)	.23	.22	.22
.26	.23	.23	.23	.23	(.20)	.19	.19
.25	.22	.22	.22	.22	.19	(.18)	.18
.25	.22	.22	.22	.22	.19	.18	(.18)

which is reproduced in Appendix C. It gives three main formulae, (iii) being derived from (ii), and (ii) from (i). In making the calculations, these formulae are used in reverse order. I may add that I have not assumed that Burt's 1917 calculations are accurate. I have re-calculated a sufficient proportion to satisfy myself both that his calculations are accurate, and that my account of his procedures is correct.)

Burt first calculates the correlation of each test with what he calls the 'Hypothetical general factor' (the h.g.f. coefficients). The formula is as follows:

$$h.g.f. = \frac{a_1}{\sqrt{A}} \ldots \text{(Burt's formula (iii))}$$

where a = total (or average) of the entire row of observed correlations for any test, 1;

and   A = total (or average) of correlations in entire table.

The second step is to obtain the 'theoretical coefficients' by the following formula:

$$r_{12} = r_{13}.r_{23} \ldots \text{(Burt's formula (ii))}$$

where r_{13}, r_{23} = h.g.f coefficients, 1 and 2 indicating any two tests, and 3 the h.g.f.

These theoretical coefficients are given in Table 4.2, and may now be compared with the observed coefficients.

The theoretical values possess the characteristic of 'hierarchical order', as Spearman called it, in that they diminish gradually and regularly from the top-left corner to the bottom-right. This is a predictable characteristic of such theoretical coefficients. Burt describes hierarchical order as 'a rough and useful criterion of the presence of a single general factor' (p. 53), and notes that the observed values do 'to some extent, conform to this criterion' (p. 55). But Burt then goes on to observe that there are certain cases where the observed values are far too high, for instance, Arithmetic (rules) with Arithmetic (problems), and Drawing with Handwriting, and also with Writing (quality). Burt comments, however, that these exceptions occur precisely where we might anticipate that special factors would operate, over and above the universal factor common to all subjects, to produce an enhanced correlation between specific subjects, as general mathematical ability or general manual dexterity. Burt (ibid.: 55) continues by saying that

These apparent exceptions, therefore, are not inconsistent with the general rule. Since, then, the chief deviations from the hierarchical arrangement occur precisely where, on other grounds, we should expect them to occur, we may accordingly conclude that *performances in all the subjects tested appear to be determined in varying degrees by a single common factor* [Burt's italics].

(Note that Burt's conclusion here is based, not upon statistical considerations alone, but upon these in conjunction with what might reasonably be expected on the basis of logic and ordinary experience.)

As to the nature of this single common factor, Burt obtained, for each child, estimates of its 'general educational ability' and of its 'general intelligence', made by its teachers independently of the test results. Table 4.1 (bottom two rows) gives the correlation of each test with these two estimates. Burt concluded that we may identify the hypothetical general factor more closely with general educational ability than with general intelligence, since the coefficients are more alike.

The exceptions to the general rule, however, suggest that there may also be certain special abilities affecting performance in school subjects, apart from the general educational ability. Otherwise expressed: if the influence of the hypothetical general factor could be excluded, what special correlations would still remain? Burt tackles this question with a straightforward application of what he calls (ibid.: 53, note 1) the usual formula for 'multiple correlation', namely:

$$r_{12.3} = \frac{r_{12} - r_{13}.r_{23}}{(1 - r_{13}^2)^{\frac{1}{2}} (1 - r_{23}^2)^{\frac{1}{2}}} \ldots \text{(Burt's formula (i))}$$

(In this formula, $r_{12.3}$ is the required specific correlation between Tests 1 and 2 when the influence of 3, the h.g.f., is eliminated; r_{12} is the original observed coefficient, and $r_{13}.r_{23}$ the theoretical coefficient. In brief, the specific coefficients are the difference between the observed and the theoretical coefficients, divided by the denominator in the formula above. Banks (1983: 25) indicates that Burt was working from Yule's *Introduction to the Theory of Statistics* (1912). Yule had in fact read Burt's memoranda in typescript – see Burt 1917: 3, note 1.)

These special or specific correlations are given in Table 4.3, Specific coefficients (Burt's Table XX, p. 57). The coefficients are fewer and smaller; only 25 out of the total 78 are significant, 16 being positive and 9 negative. The positive correlations fall into four groups, and Burt (p. 64) now draws his general conclusion:

School achievements are due to mental qualities of two kinds: first, a

Table 4.3 Correlations between school subjects

(C) Specific correlations

Data: coefficients in Table XVIII

	Compo-sition	History	Geo-graphy	Science	Arith-metic (prob-lems)	Arith-metic (rules)
Composition	–	.23	.18	.18	.00	−.23
History	.23	–	.37	.25	.09	−.10
Geography	.18	.37	–	.19	−.14	−.14
Science	.18	.25	.19	–	.12	.05
Arithmetic (problems)	.00	.09	−.14	.12	–	.74
Arithmetic (rules)	−.23	−.10	−.14	.05	.74	–
Handwork	−.28	−.10	.03	.19	.00	.12
Writing (quality)	−.13	−.25	−.17	−.12	−.07	−.01
Drawing	.04	−.07	.03	−.24	−.20	−.12
Writing (speed)	.13	−.10	.00	−.02	−.31	.12
Reading (speed)	.10	.05	.02	−.15	−.09	−.09
Dictation	.06	.05	.11	−.13	.02	.11
Reading (comprehension)	.19	.26	.13	.11	.08	−.25

Source: (From Burt 1917: Table XX).

Hand-work	Writing (quality)	Drawing	Writing (speed)	Reading (speed)	Dictation	Reading (compre-hension)
−.28	−.13	.04	.13	.10	.06	.19
−.10	−.25	−.07	−.10	.05	.05	.26
.03	−.17	.03	.00	.02	.11	.13
.19	−.12	−.24	−.02	−.15	−.13	.11
.00	−.07	−.20	−.31	−.09	.02	.08
.12	−.01	−.12	.12	−.09	.11	−.25
−	.31	.36	.03	−.09	−.23	−.28
.31	−	.48	.10	.00	−.05	−.15
.36	.48	−	.18	−.09	−.13	−.14
.03	.10	.18	−	.11	−.03	−.14
−.09	.00	−.09	.11	−	.15	.36
−.23	−.05	−.13	−.03	.15	−	.30
−.28	−.15	−.14	−.14	.36	.30	−

general ability entering into all school work; secondly, special aptitudes for particular subjects.

Since the positive correlations fell into four main groups, Burt concluded that the special aptitudes comprised at least the following corresponding types: Arithmetical, Manual, Linguistic, and Compositional. But Burt also noted that the demarcation between these special aptitudes was not sharp. They could be arranged in a circular chain, such that each is correlated with its neighbour, and the last with the first. This he called 'cyclic overlap'. It is illustrated by a circular diagram, and he subsequently (Burt 1948b: 187) said that 'the method of construction was suggested by the circular diagrams sometimes used by Karl Pearson to exhibit the correlations between two or more variables' (giving a reference to Pearson's *Grammar of Science*, 1899: 436, Fig. 31).

(Since Burt uses the term 'specific' to describe these special aptitudes, it might be supposed that he is in fact here simply echoing Spearman's doctrine of the 'two factors' – general and specific. However, Spearman and Burt were using the word 'specific' in different senses. For Spearman, a specific factor was one which was measured by one test, and one only, of all those included in the matrix. It therefore referred to a very narrow ability, and was to be contrasted with a group factor, which was a broader ability running through several, but not all, the tests. Burt, however, is thinking precisely of such group factors, which will produce such a correlation among a number of tests. This is the sense in which Galton referred to special aptitudes. Burt discusses the ambiguity of the word 'specific', and makes this point very clearly, in *Factors of the Mind* (1940: 141, note 1). So Vernon and others are undoubtedly correct in seeing Burt's 1917 conclusion as an early assertion of the reality of group factors.)

We seem entirely justified, then, in following Vernon, and indeed Hearnshaw himself, and accepting that Burt (1917) put forward these two propositions, at least in a preliminary form. If this be accepted, we have already gone far towards establishing that, so far as one half of Burt's historical account is concerned, it was accurate at least so far back as 1917. To this we may add that Burt did not first begin to make this claim about his early work in 1947. It will be found stated very clearly in both Burt (1940: 140, note 1) and in Burt (1924: 19).

But if Burt was expressing these views in 1917, it becomes at least a reasonable possibility that this was not in fact the first occasion when he expressed them, and that we may find adumbrations in still earlier papers. It might, after all, have taken Burt some time to work out and develop his ideas, and that process might well have begun before 1917. In fact, Burt (1917) itself contains two strong hints that this was not the first time that he had broached these ideas, but that he had referred to them previously.

1 *Group factors*. Burt's conclusion, quoted above, that mental qualities

are of two kinds, has the following note attached: 'For a further discussion of this distinction I may perhaps refer to my address to the Manchester Child Study Society (1909), reprinted in Child Study, Vol. IV., Nos. 2 and 3, esp. pp. 94–95.' (See Burt 1917: 64; and 1940: 140.) In other words, in 1917 Burt considered that he had already been thinking along similar lines in 1909, some eight years previously.

2 *Statistical procedures*. The second hint comes in a footnote attached to 'cyclic overlap'. Noting that this raises difficulties for the demonstration of a general factor, Burt adds: 'I drew attention to these difficulties, when first noting the existence of cyclic overlap in an attempt to establish a general factor underlying the primary emotions (*Brit. Ass. Reports*, Manchester, 1915, sub-section I)' (see Burt 1917: 60, footnote). It was 'simple summation' which led Burt to mention 'cyclic overlap' in 1917. If he was also talking about cyclic overlap in 1915, this suggests that then too he may have been using the same statistical method.

Our conclusion is that it is not unreasonable to expect to find Burt mentioning these two points earlier, not merely on general grounds, but also because of his own statements in 1917.

'General and specific factors underlying the primary emotions' (1915)

If Hearnshaw finds nothing to complain of in the accounts which Burt later gave of the content of his 1917 paper, he finds a great deal to criticize in Burt's subsequent accounts of his 1915 paper. It is odd that there should be such a contrast concerning papers separated by only two years; so odd that we need not be surprised to find that Hearnshaw is mistaken.

Burt (1966b: 37–8) described his 1915 research in the following words:

> In a research carried out partly in collaboration with R. C. Moore, in which both impressionistic assessments and objective tests were used, we applied the modified Pearsonian procedure ('simple summation') to determine 'the general and specific factors underlying the primary emotions'. We found a large general factor of 'emotionality', and two significant bipolar factors distinguishing first what we called 'sthenic' from 'asthenic' emotions . . . and secondly 'euphoric' and 'dysphoric' emotions.
>
> (Burt 1915; Reymert 1950 and refs)

Hearnshaw (1979: 160), after quoting this passage, describes it as

> both inaccurate and misleading. Burt did not use objective tests, only estimates of emotional tendencies; he did not employ modified Pearsonian procedure (simple summation) until the data were re-worked many

years later; and he did not at the time derive two significant bipolar factors. Burt read back into this investigation far more than it originally contained, and since the pronoun 'we' clearly implies that these procedures and findings related to the period when he and Moore were working together in Liverpool his later account must be regarded as a fabrication.

It is true, as Hearnshaw (1979: 159) remarks, that this research was 'very briefly reported' in 1915; but it is also true, as Banks (1983: 26) observes, that papers given at the annual meetings of the British Association have to be reported in summary form. It is also by no means correct to add, as Hearnshaw does, 'no details being given of the methodology employed or of the mathematical working' (p. 160). Brief as the report is, it contrives to pack a good deal of information both about methodology and about statistical analysis.

As regard methods, it is incorrect to state that 'Burt did not use objective tests, only estimates of emotional tendencies'. Burt specifically refers to a 'Method of Indirect Estimate' in which 'selected items of behaviour are systematically recorded in a way comparable for all members of the group observed' (Burt 1915: 694). Moreover, in another account, to which Hearnshaw does not refer, Burt (1967c: 216) writes that 'The methods employed – tests, observations, behavioural reports, etc. – are fully described elsewhere'; and then gives a cryptic reference to 'J. Exp. Pedag., p. 355ff. and refs'. This can only be the second part of Burt and Moore (1912), namely 'The Mental Differences between the Sexes' in J. Exp. Pedag., vol. 1 (5): 355–88. In this paper, on pages 379–84, the reader will indeed find a much fuller description, from which it is clear that Burt and Moore then used 'objective tests', as Banks (1983: 27) has already pointed out. Burt and Moore (1912: 382) state that they have found pneumographs and sphygmographs unsatisfactory, but that they did employ 'measuring and recording upon double revolving drums the rate and rhythm of utterance by means of a lip-key and a 1/5-second chronograph'. Their account also mentions some of the earliest experiments in this country with the psychogalvanic reflex. If Hearnshaw had recalled his own earlier reference (1979: 28) to these experiments by Burt and Moore, he would perhaps have been less ready to accuse Burt of fabrication.

As regards statistical analysis, Burt gives no formulae in the 1915 report; but he gives enough information for us to see what he did, especially if we bear in mind the procedures he was to use in 1917. Burt first provides a table of observed correlations, based upon 172 children, each given 11 emotional assessments. This table includes the average coefficients for each test, and the h.g.f. coefficients, so that it is very similar to Burt's Table XVIII of 'observed coefficients' in 1917. I have checked a sample of these figures on the assumption that Burt was most likely using his 1917 formulae, and the assumption seems to be justified since they come out correctly.

Burt does not, however, next give a table of theoretical coefficients as in 1917, but proceeds direct to the calculation of specific factors. He states that 'By means of "partial correlation" the influence of the h.g.f. may be eliminated, and the partial or specific intercorrelations calculated' (Burt 1915: 696). Once again, I have repeated a sample of these calculations on the assumption that Burt was using the same formulae as in 1917, and again I have obtained the coefficients which Burt gives. This evidence points to the same conclusion which has been reached by Banks (1983: 26):

> Reading the 1915 summary and the 1917 account and recalculating a few of Burt's figures suggests very strongly that the same method was used in each analysis. . . . Hearnshaw . . . appears to accept Burt's own claims [for the 1917 paper], namely, substituting summation for weighted summation and testing residuals for significance. It follows, for there is no doubt at all that the two analyses are similar, that what holds for the latter also holds for the earlier one.

Burt also states that his second table of partial or residual correlations 'suggests that the specific tendencies may form a circular series, each member being most closely related to its immediate neighbour, less closely related to remoter members, and antagonistically related to members half-way round the circle' (1915: 696). These are again depicted with the diagram of 'cyclic overlap' (see Banks 1983: 26). In this, Anger-Subjection (-0.49) and Anger-Tenderness (-0.31) are the highest negative correlations. Banks also mentions that Burt (1939b) indicates that the original paper contained five tables of observed correlations and ten of residuals, which 'suggests that Burt may have indeed extracted two bipolar factors from the five original correlation tables' (Banks 1983: 26–7).

Finally, Burt's concluding paragraph in 1915 seems to show very clearly – if we bear in mind that Burt was in those days using 'specific' in Galton's sense of a special aptitude, or what would now be called a group factor – that he was then already advocating a combination of a general and group factors, in contradistinction both to an exclusively general, and to an exclusively group, factor theory:

> The theory of a general factor is commonly associated with the view that specific factors are negligible and that the general factor is simple. The problem arises as to whether the above specific correlations invalidate the hypothesis of a general factor, and, in particular, whether the peculiar relations between the specific factors may not themselves produce the appearance of a general factor. Independent evidence, however, appears to confirm the existence of both general and specific

factors underlying emotional reactions and to indicate that both are highly complex.

(Burt 1915: 696)

Although Burt does not say who he has in mind in this passage, I think there can be no doubt that he is referring to the views of Spearman on the one hand and Brown on the other, and indicating that his own view combines their positive aspects. These identifications would be far more obvious to his audience in those days, among whom these views were currently debated.

In summary, there can be little doubt that Burt's later accounts of his 1915 research were substantially correct, and in particular that he was then thinking in terms of a combination of general and group factors, and that he was using simple summation in his statistical analysis. There may well be some excuse for misunderstanding the 1915 paper, either on account of its brevity or because of the terminology used, but there are no good grounds for accusing Burt of fabrication. (Several of Burt's later publications contain references to his early work on the emotions, among the more important of which are Burt 1938, 1939b, 1945, 1948b, 1949d, 1950a, 1966b, and 1967c.)

'The experimental study of general intelligence' (1911b)

Published in the journal *Child Study*, this paper is a much abbreviated and somewhat popularized version of Burt's 1909 paper on general intelligence. It demonstrates Burt's extraordinary flair for expressing complex ideas in simple and vivid language, even at this early stage in his career. It is also of considerable interest in throwing further light on his early views on 'general' and 'group' factors, though it does not add to our knowledge of his statistical procedures.

Hearnshaw (1979: 172–3) states that, in reviewing Thurstone's *Multiple Factor Analysis*, Burt (1947d) 'went on to claim that what was called a "three-factor hypothesis" was put forward in his 1911 paper in *Child Study*, though in actual fact there is no reference in the article to any factor other than the general factor, and nothing at all to suggest the presence of any group factor'.

Strictly speaking, there is no reference in the article even to a 'general' factor, because Burt did not employ the term 'factor' at all. But it would be pedantic to maintain that the paper has therefore no relevance to the problem of factors. Where later writers speak of 'factors', Burt in 1911 used words such as 'capacity', 'function', and 'ability'. So when Burt, in 1911, refers to 'general', 'common', or 'all-pervading' capacities or functions, he is referring to what is later called a 'general factor'. It follows that Hearnshaw is entirely correct when he implies that Burt refers in this article to the 'general factor': he does, though without using the phrase. By the same token, we should recognize that there are plenty of references in the paper to 'group factors', though they appear in the guise of 'special abilities', 'specialized forms of intelligence', and 'specific capacity'. Here, as elsewhere in these early papers, Burt is following Galton's usage and employing 'specific' to refer to 'special aptitudes', and is not following Spearman's usage. These papers are only to be understood if we appreciate the changes which have taken place in terminology.

In 1917, it will be recalled, Burt refers his readers to pages 94–5 of Burt (1911b) for a further discussion of the distinction between general ability and special aptitudes. In truth, the whole of this section (pages 92–101) deserves to be read, though here we have space for only a few short extracts.

> We have thus to distinguish . . . between capacities applicable in one direction only, and capacities applicable in several directions, or even in all. [He then quotes Carlyle on heroes: 'I have no notion of a great man who couldn't be all sorts of men – Poet, Prophet, Priest, King, or what you will.'] . . . We have, therefore, to avoid confusing two kinds of capacity: on the one hand, general capacity, like that of Julius Caesar . . . – capacity which would have been successful no matter what tasks were imposed upon its owner by the circumstances of his life . . . [On the other hand] specific capacity, like that of Rembrandt . . . – capacity which was applicable specifically to painting . . . but to no other purpose . . . . Surely it may be urged, intelligence is more multiplex and specialized than any other faculty.

(It is of interest that when Burt (1967a) discussed the problem many years later he again used this same reference to Carlyle, thus showing that his ideas remained fundamentally the same.)

Burt's *Child Study* paper was published in two parts, the first part appearing on pages 33–45 of volume IV, 1911, and the second part on pages 92–101 of the same volume. In the first part, Burt discusses in some detail the hypotheses involved in his study. He suggests that, in the early stages of research, the investigator is best advised to begin with that of 'general intelligence' as being the simplest hypothesis. This should prove relatively easy to check, Burt continued, and 'The investigations made upon the simpler assumptions will themselves test its legitimacy, and show whether the simpler hypothesis has to be replaced by a more complex. . . . [On the other hand] to start with the assumption of special abilities and specialized forms of intelligence . . . [would be] a task indefinitely more arduous' (Burt 1911b: 34).

From these remarks it seems clear that, at this stage (namely, 1909–11), Burt's primary aim was to check the hypothesis of a general intelligence –

that is, the central tenet of Spearman's system. Accordingly we find that, at the conclusion of the paper, when Burt is giving a summary of the factual outcome of his 1909 experiments, he refers only to his confirmation of 'general intelligence' and makes no mention of specialized abilities or 'group factors'. It does not follow, however, that Burt's attitude was, at this early stage, identical with that of Spearman, either with regard to the 'general factor' or with regard to 'group factors'. He seems to have differed from Spearman on two counts.

First, for Spearman, the general factor was an alternative to group factors, and he believed that, in establishing the existence of a general factor, he was excluding the possibility of group factors. For Burt, on the other hand, establishing a general factor was a preliminary to investigating group factors, and was compatible with their existence.

Second, Burt's references to 'specialized abilities' indicate that he is far more interested in this possibility, and far more sympathetic towards establishing it, than Spearman ever was. Burt's conclusion to his references to Carlyle's distinction seems to show clearly that Burt expected that group factors would one day be established: 'Surely, it may be urged, intelligence is more multiplex and specialized than any other faculty we have' (Burt 1911b: 95).

It seems that many years later, in 1947, Burt was more than a little irritated by what he saw as a tendency on Thurstone's part to elbow his way to the front, ignoring the part which Burt and other British writers had played in this field long before Thurstone himself had appeared on the scene. I do not think that Burt had in 1911 put forward the 'three-factor' theory in the kind of emphatic and formal style that would make the matter immediately obvious. Yet a careful reading shows clearly enough that even at that early stage Burt thought that the 'simpler hypothesis' would one day be replaced by the 'more complex'. The worst that can be said against him is that he exaggerated a good case: but it was a good case, and it is unjust to accuse him of deception.

Why were these points not clear to Hearnshaw? Part of the answer might lie in the brevity of Burt's discussion. But possibly Hearnshaw also encountered some difficulty in locating the full reference. As mentioned above, Burt (1911b) appeared in two parts, namely, on pages 33–45 and 92–101 of *Child Study*, volume IV. The reference is given correctly in the list of Burt's publications on page 321 of Hearnshaw (1979). But in the text, when Hearnshaw is discussing the paper, he twice gives incorrect page numbers: on page 159 he gives 'pp. 92–100'; while on page 172 he gives 'pp. 77–100'. On neither occasion does he mention the first part, pages 33–45; while page 77 is an advertisement for Benger's Food for Backward and Ailing Children.

A further oddity lies in the peculiar contrasts and contradictions which one encounters between a number of the statements Hearnshaw makes in his account of Burt's supposed 'new story', and some of the references earlier in the bibliography to the same papers. We have just noted Hearnshaw's explicit denial that Burt used objective tests in 1912, whereas he had himself earlier specifically mentioned such tests. Additional such contradictions will be noted below. Hearnshaw's right hand sometimes does not seem to know what his left hand is doing.

'Experimental tests of general intelligence' (1909) – A: statistical methods

Burt's first published paper provides evidence about both his statistical methods and his views on the structure of intelligence in these early years. Whatever conclusions are reached about the origins of this paper, it is likely to remain an important document in the history of psychometrics.

Hearnshaw's description is as follows:

> Thirteen tests were intercorrelated, and the results analysed using the tetrad equation, which was derived from Spearman's work. The theoretical values calculated from the tetrads were compared with the observed coefficients, and the agreement between theoretical and observed values was found to be so close that it was roughly equal to the probable error. 'A neater agreement between observation and theory could scarcely be desired' (p. 163). . . . There is no evidence in Burt's 1909 article, as he subsequently claimed, that he proceeded to subtract the theoretical figures from the observed correlations and to factor analyse the residuals, thus inaugurating multiple factor analysis. . . .
> (Hearnshaw 1979: 158–9; the sentence in quotation marks refers to
> p. 163 of Burt's 1909 paper.)

This passage is a curious mixture of truth and error. Burt presented his statistical findings in two tables, headed 'Hierarchy of coefficients' (see Burt 1909, Tables V and VI: 161 and 162). The first table gives the results for an elementary school, and the second for a preparatory school. (Table V only is reproduced here; see our Table 4.4. It is to be noted that in all such tables the coefficients in the upper right half should be identical with the corresponding coefficients in the lower left half. Careful study of Burt's table reveals numerous discrepancies between the two halves – presumably a consequence of careless copying at some stage in the production of the table. I have not noticed any similar errors in Burt's second table.) These two tables contain large and elaborate matrices, much larger and more elaborate than any which Spearman had published at that date, together with further statistics.

For each of the thirteen tests, Burt gives first the observed correlations and second the theoretical correlations. Thus, whereas in 1917 he gave the observed and theoretical coefficients separately, in 1909 he gives them

Table 4.4 Hierarchy of Coefficients (amalgamated series)

(A) Elementary school

		Dotting apparatus	Alphabet	Sorting	Imputed intelligence	Dealing	Spot pattern	Tapping	Mirror	Sound	Lines	Touch	Memory	Weight
Dotting apparatus	Observed coefficient	–	77	67	60	69	57	57	50	52	48	38	20	16
	Theoretical value	–	80	73	72	72	67	63	49	45	33	28	27	05
	Deviation	–	03	06	12	03	10	06	01	07	15	10	07	11
	P.e. of coefficient	–	05	07	08	06	08	08	09	09	09	11	12	12
Alphabet	Observed coefficient	77	–	74	61	66	59	54	29	52	16	62	31	07
	Theoretical value	80	–	69	69	69	65	60	46	43	32	26	25	05
	Deviation	03	–	05	08	03	06	06	17	09	16	36	06	02
	P.e. of coefficient	05	–	06	08	07	08	09	11	09	12	07	10	12
Sorting	Observed coefficient	67	74	–	52	72	45	61	34	52	14	22	19	23
	Theoretical value	73	69	–	62	61	59	54	42	39	28	24	23	04
	Deviation	06	05	–	10	11	14	13	08	13	14	02	04	19
	P.e. of coefficient	07	06	–	09	06	10	08	11	09	12	11	10	19
Imputed intelligence	Observed coefficient	60	61	52	–	44	76	47	67	40	29	13	57	–13
	Theoretical value	72	69	62	–	69	58	53	41	39	28	23	23	04
	Deviation	12	08	10	–	16	18	06	26	01	01	10	34	17
	P.e. of coefficient	08	08	09	–	10	05	10	07	10	08	12	08	12
Dealing	Observed coefficient	69	66	72	44	–	76	47	67	40	29	13	57	–13
	Theoretical value	72	69	61	60	–	58	53	41	39	28	23	23	04
	Deviation	03	02	11	16	–	07	12	01	05	19	00	04	03
	P.e. of coefficient	06	07	06	09	–	10	07	11	12	10	11	12	12
Spot pattern	Observed coefficient	57	59	45	76	51	–	41	41	47	25	03	26	11
	Theoretical value	67	65	59	58	58	–	48	37	35	35	26	21	04
	Deviation	10	06	14	16	07	–	07	04	12	01	18	05	07
	P.e. of coefficient	08	08	09	05	09	–	10	10	10	11	12	11	12

		1	2	3	4	5	6	7	8	9	10	11	12	13
Tapping	Observed coefficient	57	53	61	47	65	41	—	41	47	08	26	-05	22
	Theoretical value	63	60	54	53	53	48	—	36	34	25	20	20	04
	Deviation	06	06	07	08	12	07	—	05	13	18	06	25	18
	P.e. of coefficient	08	09	08	10	08	10	—	10	10	12	11	12	12
Mirror	Observed coefficient	50	29	34	67	40	45	45	—	34	16	08	05	-05
	Theoretical value	49	46	42	41	41	37	36	—	25	19	15	15	03
	Deviation	01	17	08	26	01	04	05	—	09	03	07	10	08
	P.e. of coefficient	09	11	11	17	10	10	10	—	10	12	12	12	12
Sound	Observed coefficient	52	52	52	40	34	47	47	34	—	-07	-01	01	-13
	Theoretical value	45	43	39	39	39	35	34	25	—	17	14	14	02
	Deviation	07	09	13	01	05	12	13	09	—	24	15	13	15
	P.e. of coefficient	09	09	09	10	17	10	10	12	—	12	13	12	12
Lines	Observed coefficient	48	16	14	29	47	25	08	16	-07	—	26	06	19
	Theoretical value	33	32	28	28	28	26	26	25	17	—	10	10	02
	Deviation	15	16	14	01	19	01	17	03	24	—	16	04	17
	P.e. of coefficient	09	12	12	08	10	11	12	12	12	—	11	12	12
Touch	Observed coefficient	38	62	22	13	23	03	26	08	-01	26	—	16	29
	Theoretical value	28	26	24	23	23	21	20	15	14	10	—	08	01
	Deviation	10	36	02	10	00	18	06	07	15	16	—	08	28
	P.e. of coefficient	11	07	12	12	12	12	11	12	12	11	—	12	11
Memory	Observed coefficient	20	31	19	57	19	26	-05	05	01	06	16	—	05
	Theoretical value	27	25	23	23	23	21	20	15	12	10	18	—	01
	Deviation	07	06	04	34	04	05	25	10	13	04	08	—	04
	P.e. of coefficient	12	10	11	10	12	11	12	12	12	12	12	—	12
Weight	Observed coefficient	16	07	23	-13	01	11	22	-05	-13	19	29	05	—
	Theoretical value	05	05	04	04	04	04	04	04	03	03	01	01	—
	Deviation	11	02	19	17	03	07	18	08	15	17	28	04	—
	P.e. of coefficient	12	12	12	12	12	12	11	12	12	12	11	12	—

Average deviation = .100 Average p.e. = .101

Source: (From Burt 1909: Table V).

together, in the same table. As in 1917, the observed correlations have not been adjusted using Spearman's 'correction for attenuation'; as in 1917 also, the theoretical coefficients are calculated in order to indicate what the coefficients would have been if due to a single general factor (that is, in order to furnish a 'hierarchy' for comparison). The formula which Burt used to obtain the theoretical calculations, and its origin, needs to be examined with care.

Burt had sent a preliminary version of his paper to Spearman asking for 'any criticisms or suggestions' (Letter from Burt to Spearman, 19 May 1909). Unfortunately, no copy of this preliminary version has survived, so we do not know exactly what it contained. Hence there is some doubt how much of the final version was unadulterated Burt, and how much was added or altered on Spearman's advice. However, it is clear that that original included a hierarchy of theoretical correlations, because Burt mentioned in his letter that he was 'diffident' about this; and Spearman, in his reply, remarked that the 'theoretical values for the hierarchy may be got by various formulae' (Letter from Spearman to Burt, 23 June 1909). The 'simple formula', as he called it, which Spearman suggested in his letter, and which Burt then used in his final version, was as follows:

Let r(s,t) denote the required theoretical value, satisfying the condition

$$\frac{r(A,P)}{r(B,P)} = \frac{r(A,Q)}{r(B,Q)}$$

and at the same time agreeing as well as possible with the correlations actually observed.
Then

$$r(s,t) = m_s \cdot m_t,$$

where

$$m_s = \frac{a_s}{\sqrt{2\Sigma - a_s}} \cdot \sqrt{\frac{n-2}{n-1-\frac{n \cdot a_s}{2\Sigma}}}$$

a_s = the sum of all the correlations with the performance s,

Σ = the sum of all the different correlations altogether,

n = the number of performances,

and m_t has a value analogous to m_s.

Burt (1909: 163, footnote) repeated this formula, prefacing it with this remark: 'The following simple formula has been supplied for this purpose by Dr Spearman (to whom I am here particularly indebted for several improvements on my own demonstration of a hierarchy).'

Spearman begins by remarking that the required theoretical coefficient will satisfy the condition

$$\frac{r(A,P)}{r(B,P)} = \frac{r(A,Q)}{r(B,Q)}$$

This ratio is known as the 'proportionality criterion', and this is its earliest publication. It is a way of saying that the required theoretical coefficients will form a hierarchy – that is, will display a regular proportional decline, as exemplified in a selection of four coefficients related as the ratio indicates. As Spearman said, 'I now find [it] the most brief and precise manner of expressing the law of the hierarchy' (Spearman to Burt, 23 June 1909: 4). It plays an important part in factorial history.

Spearman then gives the formula for obtaining the theoretical coefficients, $r(s,t) = m_s.m_t$. Although it may not be immediately evident, this formula is closely similar to that which Burt uses in 1917. In 1917, the formula is

$$r_{12} = r_{13}. r_{23}, \text{ where } r_{13} = \frac{a_1}{\sqrt{A}} \text{ and } r_{23} = \frac{a_2}{\sqrt{A}}$$

where a = the sum of all the correlations with a particular test, and A = the sum of all the correlations. This is a simplified version of the first part of the 1909 formula

$$m_s = \frac{a_s}{\sqrt{2\Sigma - a_s.}}$$

The second part of the 1909 formula is a correction for the number of performances, or tests, and is omitted in 1917. A further difference is that in 1917 Burt fills the diagonals, but not in 1909. However, down to this point Burt's procedure in 1909 is closely similar to what it was to be in 1917.

The next step on both occasions is to compare the observed and theoretical coefficients. But here there is a marked difference. In 1917, it will be recalled, Burt used partial correlation. In 1909, however, he simply subtracts the theoretical from the observed, without regard to sign, so that his method is here much simpler. This is the third item of information given for each test, and is labelled 'Deviation'. It is the amount by which the observed coefficients deviate from the coefficients to be expected if all the correlations were caused by a single general factor, and nothing else. The fourth item given is the probable error of the observed coefficients. Burt also gives the average deviations (that is, the mean difference between observed and theoretical coefficients), which are 0.100 and 0.165 respectively; and the average probable errors which are 0.101 and 0.162 respectively.

Returning now to Hearnshaw's description of Burt's 1909 paper, it will be seen that he is correct when he says that 'The theoretical values . . . were compared with the observed coefficients.' This is what Burt is doing when he gives the 'deviation'. Hearnshaw is also correct when he states that this was roughly equal to the probable error. But it is incomprehensible that Hearnshaw should then go on to say that 'There is no evidence in Burt's 1909 article . . . that he proceeded to subtract the theoretical figures from the observed correlations'; for this, again, is exactly what Burt is doing when he gives the 'deviation'. The two operations are one and the same. Hearnshaw appears not to have realized that 'comparing' and 'subtracting' and finding the 'deviation' are simply different ways of describing the same thing. It follows that if Hearnshaw is correct to say that Burt compared the theoretical and observed coefficients – as Burt plainly did – then Hearnshaw is also incorrect to deny that Burt subtracted them – as Burt equally plainly did. As Banks (1983: 23–4) has written: 'Burt did subtract his theoretical figures from the observed; they are on pages 161 and 162 of the 1909 article for all to see.'

Hearnshaw's tenuous grasp of Burt's procedure – and indeed of Spearman's procedure, too – is shown even more clearly when he says that the results were 'analysed using the tetrad equation'. He appears to have confused what Spearman (1927: 73) termed the 'tetrad equation' with the 'proportionality criterion', which is what Spearman sent to Burt in 1909. The tetrad equation is derived from the proportionality criterion by a simple transformation:

$$\text{if } \frac{r(A,P)}{r(B,P)} = \frac{r(A,Q)}{r(B,Q)} \ldots \text{ (the proportionality criterion)}$$

then $r(A,P) \times r(B,Q) - r(B,P) \times r(A,Q) = 0$ . . . (the tetrad equation)

Spearman indicated to Burt in 1909 that the theoretical coefficients should meet the proportionality criterion; but in the form presented there was nothing that could be done with it except to demonstrate that the various 'tetrads' of theoretical coefficients met this criterion. This would merely illustrate that they conformed to 'the law of the hierarchy'. So Burt could not have 'analysed his results' in 1909 using this formula. Spearman did not intend that he should. Spearman was merely offering the formal definition of a hierarchy which the theoretical coefficients were designed to exemplify. It could not be applied to the observed coefficients, except to demonstrate the way in which they departed from ratios shown by the theoretical coefficients. Burt was interested in the difference between the theoretical and observed coefficients, but, as we have just seen, he studied this by subtracting the one from the other, not by applying the proportionality criterion to the observed coefficients, which Spearman said nothing about. Spearman gave the criterion as a preliminary to giving the formula Burt was to use to calculate the theoretical coefficients.

The proportionality criterion does, however, point to an alternative way of comparing the theoretically expected coefficients with those actually observed. If it is transformed into the tetrad equation, then, if the theoretical coefficients are entered into the formula, the result must always be zero. If now the observed coefficients met this criterion perfectly – that is, if there was a perfect hierarchy – the result again would always be zero. But we cannot expect perfect results; there must always be chance errors to distort the outcome. The question becomes, what distribution of tetrad differences is to be expected by chance, and how great must the deviation be to indicate that the observed coefficients depart from it? This was the route which Spearman ultimately adopted. But in 1909 he had not yet got so far. The tetrad equation could only be used when some method of testing for error had been devised. This proved difficult to find: as Spearman (1927: 79) said 'To discover this . . . has been the greatest trouble in the whole development of the doctrine.' It was not until 1924 that this was achieved by Spearman and Holzinger (1924; see also Spearman 1927: 79, and Appendix: ii–iii and x; Banks 1983: 24). Thus the tetrad equation was not actually in use, even by Spearman, until the twenties; and to suggest that Burt used it in 1909 is an anachronism. Spearman, so far as I can find, nowhere indicates who in fact first derived the tetrad equation from the proportionality criterion, or when. According to Burt (1949b: 172, note 2), it was first suggested by W. F. Sheppard at a British Association discussion on factors in 1920.

Until Spearman had worked out a method of calculating the probable error, he used other techniques. In 1912, for example, he was using the method of 'intercolumnar correlation', in which the similarity between the successive columns of coefficients was calculated. Even when the tetrad difference method was perfected in the twenties, it was enormously laborious. Thousands of tetrad differences would have to be calculated, even for a modest matrix (Banks 1983: 24). As Stephenson (1983: 46) remarks, 'We used the ponderous tetrad-difference methodology in Spearman's laboratory, while Burt was busy elsewhere with factor analysis as we know it now.'

So did Burt use 'simple summation' in 1909? It seems one can certainly see the beginnings of the method in Burt's comparison of observed and theoretical coefficients. Burt later claimed that 'the first attempt at fitting a theoretical matrix to a set of observed correlations was, I think, that shown in Tables V and VI of my paper of 1909' (Burt 1940: 295). This seems justified, as Banks (1983: 24) maintains. But Burt went on to claim that 'the residual correlations were obtained in a way which has since become fairly general' (ibid.); and this too has been endorsed by Banks (ibid.) when she states that 'he did test the residuals for significance'. This further claim is perhaps open to question. As we have noted, in 1909 Burt simply subtracted the theoretical from the observed coefficients, to obtain the 'deviations' (but see also Burt (1940: 447, note)). He certainly seems to have been trying to do something in which Spearman was not interested.

There can be little doubt, then, that the beginnings of 'simple summation' are to be found in the 1909 paper. It may be added that, since Burt expressed this claim very clearly in his major work of 1940 (page 295), scholars had by his death had over thirty years in which to challenge it. Nobody, including Spearman, did so in all that time. It is a lamentable state of affairs that Burt should first be challenged, forty years later, by a writer who appears to misunderstand the elements of the problem; and that this challenge should then be generally accepted by psychologists without anyone attempting to examine it adequately, with the sole exception of Banks.

'Experimental tests of general intelligence' (1909) – B: group factors

Hearnshaw is once more emphatic in his rejection of Burt's claims. 'Burt's claim to have enlarged Spearman's two-factor theory into a three-factor theory as early as 1909 is not supported by the published reports of his work' (1979: 159). 'There was no question at this stage of any "three-factor" theory. The emphasis was entirely on the confirmation of Spearman's hypothesis of a general factor' (p. 176). We have seen that in 1909, in his talk to the Manchester Child Study Society, Burt was already envisaging the possibility of enlarging Spearman's theory by including what are now called 'group' factors; and Burt himself (1940: 140) said that this was his first suggestion. How far does the 1909 paper confirm this conclusion?

Anyone who goes to Burt's first paper expecting to find Burt confronting Spearman with a proposal to modify his views by adding 'group' factors will be disappointed. On the other hand, he will certainly find Burt placing considerable emphasis upon his support for Spearman's 'general intelligence'. But in my opinion, the emphasis is by no means entirely upon this confirmation. Hearnshaw (1979: 158–9), it will be recalled, described Burt's 'confirmation' in the following words: 'the agreement between theoretical and observed values was found to be so close that it was roughly equal to the probable error. A neater agreement between observation and theory could scarcely be desired' (p. 163).

Spearman, of course, would regard this agreement between theoretical and observed values as confirming the 'general factor'; and also – and more importantly in the present context – as simultaneously excluding 'group factors'. The sentence which Hearnshaw quotes from Burt (1909: 163) – 'A neater agreement . . .' – appears therefore to indicate Burt's full endorsement of Spearman's position. Indeed, there appears to be further evidence that Burt was here simply echoing Spearman's views. In his letter to Burt of 23 June 1909, Spearman, noting the probable errors, wrote that 'a prettier agreement between observations and theory is not often seen' (p.4). It is plain that Burt's sentence is a paraphrase of Spearman's statement to him.

But unfortunately for this whole argument Hearnshaw has misquoted Burt. Burt did not write, 'A neater agreement . . . could scarcely be desired.' He wrote, 'So far, then, a neater agreement . . . could scarcely be desired' (Burt 1909: 163). Hearnshaw has omitted the first three words. No doubt these three words are capable of more than one interpretation, but to me they suggest that Burt is saying, 'Yes, so far so good; but do not make up your mind until we have finished looking at the evidence'. These three omitted words appear to me to indicate an essential qualification – that all the evidence was not yet in. So Burt's paraphrase of Spearman's statement to him might be read as carrying a special emphasis for Spearman: 'I know this is what you think, but just wait and see.'

If Hearnshaw had included those three preliminary words in his quotation, the effect of unqualified support for Spearman which he wanted to convey would have been destroyed. It is an accepted convention in quotation that omitted words are indicated by appropriate stops, whenever the omission might be significant, so that the reader is warned that the quotation is incomplete. Hearnshaw has not observed this convention.

However, in his very next sentence Hearnshaw writes: 'Nevertheless Burt did note that "the tendency for subordinate groups of allied tests to correlate together is discernible, but small" (p. 164)'. This quotation is a clear indication that in his 1909 paper Burt did report some evidence for 'group factors'. It refutes Hearnshaw's assertion that the emphasis in 1909 was *entirely* upon the confirmation of the 'general factor'. Moreover, this seems to me to be the reason why Burt qualified his confirmation of Spearman by adding 'So far, then'. This evidence for 'group factors' is the qualification Burt had in mind. Hearnshaw, on the other hand, makes it appear that this phrase about subordinate groups was an unimportant afterthought on Burt's part.

That Burt did recognize group factors as early as 1909 has in fact been widely recognized. Vernon (1950: 15) writes that 'As early as 1909 Burt had obtained suggestive evidence of a sensory discrimination group factor beyond g.' Butcher (1968: 47) states that in his first paper 'Burt foresaw to some extent that intermediate [that is, group] factors would be needed to provide a full account of the structure of abilities.' Most striking of all, perhaps, Hearnshaw (1979: 54) himself, when describing the 1909 paper on an earlier page, wrote as follows:

the outcome was to confirm Spearman's main conclusion of a universal general factor, though Burt also noted discernible, if small, group factors. From this support for a general factor Burt never deviated, though he was soon to accord more weight to group factors than Spearman was ever prepared to do, or than he himself had done in this first piece of work.

With this judgement, I would entirely agree; but once again, Hearnshaw's right hand does not seem to know what his left hand is doing.

One may certainly agree that Burt's support for 'group factors' in his first paper is neither very clear nor very confident. Indeed, Burt himself (1949b: 172) only claims that his 1909 research gave 'some slight evidence' of a special factor for sensory discrimination. But there are at least three further pointers to his views. Burt's criticism of Spearman for identifying general intelligence with general sensory discrimination is the first. In effect, Burt is advocating a 'group factor' for sensory discrimination, whereas Spearman sees no need for anything more than his 'general factor'. The second point is connected with this. Early in his paper, Burt indicates that one of his reasons for undertaking his experiments is to extend the range of mental activities tested: 'to determine whether higher mental functions would not show a yet closer connection with "General Intelligence"' (Burt 1909: 95). Previous tests, he suggests, have been too much restricted to the sensory functions, and have given poor correlations with intelligence. The use of tests dealing with the 'higher mental processes' of reasoning and problem solving should give better results. Here again it is a great pity we do not possess the first draft of the paper, which Burt sent to Spearman before he had heard the latter's comments. It could be that it gave greater emphasis to 'group factors' and that this was toned down in the final paper in deference to Spearman's views. Third, again early in his paper, Burt writes as follows: 'Whether Intelligence consists of a single elementary faculty; whether it is the complex resultant of a number of faculties . . .; or whether there is really no such thing . . . these are controversies still awaiting the evidence of experiment' (Burt 1909: 96–7). This surely makes it plain that Burt was not simply accepting Spearman's belief in 'a single elementary faculty' but regarded the question of the nature of intelligence as open.

Conclusion

It has been widely accepted that Burt (1917) provides clear evidence of support both for group factors and for the method of simple summation. This makes it plausible that Burt had been thinking along these lines in earlier years, and examination of his writings from 1909 onwards demonstrates that this was indeed so. Burt's 1917 contribution did not spring out of the blue. His whole sequence of inquiries from 1909 to 1917 form a related series in which we can see these two points gradually emerging and strengthening. Burt also supported Spearman's notion of a 'general intelligence'; and Hearnshaw is correct in stressing this. But even in Burt (1909) there is evidence that for Burt the notion of 'general intelligence' did not exclude Galton's conception of 'special aptitudes'. When we also take into account Burt's Manchester address of October 1909 (Burt 1911b), we can only conclude that there are so far no grounds for accusing Burt of historical falsification.

If Burt was beginning to publish his point of view in 1909, it would not be unreasonable to suppose that he had already begun to think and work along these lines even earlier. So Burt may well be right when he claims, with reference to 'simple summation', that 'This method was first used by Burt and his research students in early studies from 1907 onwards' (Burt 1968: 68). It is impossible now to confirm this claim; and the term 'research students' for those who helped him is questionable. But 1907 is a not unreasonable date for the beginnings of Burt's distinctive contribution. There seem to be no good grounds for accusing him of lying here.

Hearnshaw describes Burt's early papers in disparaging tones. 'He employed factor analysis on a small scale in his early investigation into intelligence. . . . These early ventures were not worked up in any detail' (1979: 155). 'Factor analysis during this phase of Burt's career had been an adjunct to his main practical tasks, and neither psychologically nor mathematically had his conclusions and his methods been worked out in any detail' (p. 162).

If Burt's early papers are compared with subsequent factorial studies, no doubt they will prove to be slighter and less elaborate works. But if they are compared with those of his contemporaries, which provide the most appropriate yardstick, I think such dismissive judgements are out of place. Burt packs a remarkable amount of information into his papers, and his economical style demands careful reading. Perhaps the most relevant comparison to draw is with Spearman's early work. By 1917 Spearman had produced a great deal of theoretical speculation, methodological advice, and critical assessment of the work of others. But so far as evidence collected by himself was concerned, he had supported his conclusions with only the slender empirical data given in 1904. The reader may compare Spearman's matrix of 1904 (our Table 1.1) with Burt's matrix of 1909 (our Table 4.4). Again Spearman and Hart (1912) support the general factor theory, not with fresh evidence, but by re-analysing data furnished by others. Burt, whatever the inadequacies of his work, had collected much more data, and had also expressed his conclusions more cautiously. Cronbach's (1979: 1393) observations seem justified when he writes that Hearnshaw 'mocks Burt's 1909 paper, which I find sophisticated and painstaking, a precocious work for a science still in knee pants'.

In my opinion, there is no substitute for collecting data oneself. It corresponds in empirical work to the need in historical enquiry to read the original sources. Nor should Burt's factorial work be characterized as 'an adjunct to his main practical tasks'. Burt had embarked upon his studies in intelligence as part of Galton's anthropological survey for the British Association, and it is a mistake to regard his scientific interests as secondary to his practical aims. Burt's early contributions stand comparison well with those of his contemporaries in this pioneering field. His claims concerning their contents are reasonable.

Chapter five

Burt's historical claims: Spearman and Pearson

Having confirmed Burt's claims concerning the content of his early papers, we must turn to the second question: that of the origin of his ideas and methods. This resolves itself mainly into an examination of Burt's relations to his two famous senior colleagues, Charles Spearman (1863–1945), who was twenty years older than Burt, and Karl Pearson (1857–1936), who was twenty-six years older. But the enquiry is of more than personal interest, since it is concerned with the origins of factorial analysis itself.

It is far harder to determine exactly what Burt owed to these two men than it is to discover the content of his early papers. The evidence is less complete and definite, and sometimes Burt's own word is all we have to go on. The fact that we have so far found him to be a reliable guide in historical matters naturally makes us more ready to trust him further. There are, however, considerable grounds for caution. There is an important difference between the two strands in Burt's claims. His statements about his early adherence to group factors and to simple summation had been put forward over many years. They are not made for the first time in the forties, and cannot be part of a 'new story', as Hearnshaw supposes. On the other hand, his claims concerning the influence of Pearson do seem to be of later date, possibly no earlier than 1936. Here, therefore, Hearnshaw's theory of the pathological 'new story' acquires greater plausibility.

Burt's claims about the origins of his ideas are widely scattered, but three sources seem to be especially important. These include two papers which appeared in his own journal in 1949 – 'Alternative methods of factor analysis and their relation to Pearson's method of "principal axes"' (Burt 1949a), and 'The two-factor theory' (Burt 1949b); and his autobiographical study written three years later (Burt 1952a). Throughout this examination, it is essential to study what Burt himself actually claimed, and to distinguish this from the exaggerated or inaccurate versions which have too often been fathered upon him.

Spearman as the founder of Factor Analysis

Undoubtedly Spearman has usually been regarded as the originator of factor analysis. Thus Flugel (1933: 311) wrote that Spearman 'founded one of the most important modern schools – the "Factor School"'; while Butcher (1968: 44) remarks that he is 'generally recognised as both the inventor and first user of factor-analytic methods'. Burt challenged this accepted view. The first question which arises is whether he was right or wrong. If he was right, the question of dishonesty does not arise; if he was wrong, we have to ask whether he was simply mistaken, or whether he was lying.

Hearnshaw deals with the first question with remarkable dispatch. He begins his case against Burt with the following sentence:

> It is universally agreed by every leading factorist, except Burt in the final phase of his factorial work, that factor analysis had its origins in Spearman's 1904 article.

> (1979: 155)

He calls this 'the orthodox view' (p. 169), and proceeds to regard it as beyond dispute. Thus if he can show that Burt originally believed that this view was correct, he has secured a conviction. But this is altogether too hasty.

First, the only support which Hearnshaw offers for his assertion that it is 'universally agreed by every leading factorist' is a quotation from Guilford's *Psychometric Methods* (1936: 459) which runs: 'No single event in the history of mental testing has proved to be of such momentous importance as Spearman's proposal of his famous two-factor theory in 1904.' But Guilford does not say that factor analysis had its origins in 1904; only that Spearman's two-factor theory did. There is not the slightest reason to suppose that Burt would have wanted to deny that this paper marked the origin of the two-factor theory. The question is whether it was the origin of factor analysis. Hearnshaw has only managed to provide one unsatisfactory example, and that from a book written forty years earlier, before the whole question was raised. It does not demonstrate universal agreement today by every leading factorist.

Second, *Modern Factor Analysis*, by Harman (1967: 3), shows that there is not in fact universal agreement. He writes:

> The birth of factor analysis is generally ascribed to Charles Spearman. His monumental work goes back to 1904 ... Of course, his 1904 investigation was only the beginning of his work in developing the Two-Factor theory, and his early work is not explicitly in terms of 'factors'. Perhaps a more crucial article, certainly in so far as the statistical aspects

are concerned, is the 1901 paper by Karl Pearson [reference to *Phil. Mag.*, 1901, II: 559–72] in which he sets forth 'the method of principal axes'. Nevertheless, Spearman, who devoted the remaining forty years of his life to the development of factor analysis, is regarded as the father of the subject.

Third, the most important objection to Hearnshaw's position is, however, his equation of 'orthodox' with 'correct'. Having established to his own satisfaction what 'every leading factorist' thinks, he takes it for granted that such an authoritative view must be accepted by everybody, and that it requires little further defence or explication. In other words, he supposes that 'universally agreed' may be equated with 'established beyond question'. But to reject Burt out of hand, simply on the grounds that he challenged accepted views, is absurd. On this principle, the 'orthodox view' could never be debated, let alone rejected. Burt was one of the few in this field who was interested in the history of factorial enquiry, and who wrote at all extensively about it. His achievements surely entitle him to a hearing, not to automatic rejection because what he says is unusual.

However unorthodox Burt's view may be, there is nothing particularly odd about his suggestion that factor analysis originated before 1904. The origins of the other major psychological schools, which also began around the turn of the century, provide an illuminating comparison. There is usually some outstanding figure who is recognized as founding the movement: as Watson for behaviourism, Freud for psychoanalysis, and Wertheimer for Gestalt theory. Commonly, also, some one paper or publication is picked out as marking the great event: Watson's lecture of 1912, and Wertheimer's paper on perceptual motion of the same date, for example, or Freud and Breuer's *Studies on Hysteria* of 1895. These are convenient ways of pinpointing influential men and decisive events. But none of these movements sprang fully grown out of thin air. In every case there had been a lengthy period of preparation, in which many of the crucial ideas and methods had been mooted, and sometimes carried a long way.

Behaviourism provides a good example. The objective standpoint had been brewing for a long while before Watson. Among its antecedents were the whole materialist trend of the nineteenth century, with its declaration that only physico-chemical explanations were acceptable; the arguments about whether psychology as a science of mental life had any place in such a system; the work of Thorndike and the objective study of animal behaviour, including the Russian reflexologists and much more. Similarly, Freud was preceded by Charcot and Janet, and Wertheimer by von Ehrenfels and others. Schultz (1975) provides an instructive survey of such 'antecedent influences'. He does not include factorial work, but what is true elsewhere might very well be true here. Moreover, if there were important antecedents, a likely place to find them would be in the Galton–Pearson biometric movement.

Boring (1950: 194) described a frequent occurrence by saying that 'When the central ideas are all born, some promoter takes them in hand, organizes them, insists upon them, and in short "founds" a school.' Schultz takes up this idea and suggests a distinction between the 'founder' and the 'originator' of a school. The 'originator' comes first and hits upon the key ideas or methods; then the 'founder' develops and exploits them. Thus Fechner, in the nineteenth century, originated some of psychology's major experimental methods, while Wundt founded the first laboratory and organized and advertised the movement. Perhaps we should do well to think of these as primarily distinct functions, which may sometimes be combined in a single individual. There also seems to be a tendency for whoever does the 'founding' to be credited with the major contribution, and perhaps to be allotted more originality than is really his due. It is much easier, especially in teaching, to talk of one man as beginning it all, and one work where he did it, than to fill out the full complexity. But this becomes misleading if we forget that a leading figure, and a leading work, are being singled out to represent many people, producing numerous works, over an extended period.

There can be little doubt that Spearman deserves the major credit as 'founder', in the above sense, of the factorial movement. Thus it is entirely appropriate that Flugel (1933: 311) should describe how Spearman became head of a small and new department at University College in 1907, how he gradually built this up over the years as a centre for factorial research, 'and in his twenty-four years' work in London he founded one of the most important modern schools'. There are no grounds for supposing that Burt wished to deny to Spearman the credit for this achievement. At the same time, Spearman also showed great originality in his formulation of the two-factor theory; so we ought not to think of him as a mere 'founder'. But this is not incompatible with certain other people exercising an antecedent originality in certain respects, and thereby playing an important part. Indeed it would be odd if, in sharp contrast to other schools, there were not prior events and discoveries and theories which, at least in part, paved the way for Spearman's work or for other developments in factorial analysis.

Flugel (1933: 132) himself makes the general nature of the relevant background clear: 'Galton is the true father of the mental "test" and of all that later sprang from it – of the practical application of testing . . . of statistical analysis and the discovery of "factors" by the correlation method.' Spearman, of course, was very well aware of the general significance of Galton and his follower Pearson. His first paper (1904a: 96) expresses regret that 'psychologists never seem to have become acquainted with the brilliant work being carried out by the Galton–Pearson school'.

His second paper championed the need for a 'Correlation Psychology', as he called it (Spearman 1904b). Many psychologists certainly responded to these pleas, both in Britain and America. Brown (1911) acknowledges Pearson in particular, as does Kelley (1923: vi), who wrote, 'my greatest inspiration has been that master analyst, Karl Pearson'.

All these are no more than general acknowledgements of indebtedness. They contain nothing as yet to suggest that factorial analysis itself owed any direct debt to the biometric school. But these considerations do suggest that it is not unreasonable to look for some antecedents, and that Pearson is a not unplausible person to be involved. At this point we must look more closely at the claims which Burt made, and at the account of those claims which Hearnshaw provides.

Burt's claims – and Hearnshaw's account of them

Burt's central claim about the origins of factor analysis is contained in the following extract:

> From a mathematical standpoint the methods of factor analysis in vogue at the present time resemble in their general approach, not so much the somewhat specialized technique which Spearman proposed on the basis of his own somewhat specialized hypotheses, but rather the older procedures first outlined by Edgeworth and Karl Pearson for reducing correlated variables to uncorrelated components . . . The principle eventually adopted (in my 1909 investigation) was suggested by Pearson's procedure for fitting theoretical values to contingency tables in cases of manifold association.
>
> (Burt 1949b: 177; quoted by Hearnshaw 1979: 175)

When Burt wrote this passage, Spearman's two-factor theory and his tetrad equation had been largely abandoned. They had been supplanted by multiple analysis, whether in the form of Thurstone's centroid method or Burt's simple summation. Burt's claim was that the mathematical ancestry of multiple analysis is to be found, not in Spearman, but in the biometric school; and that his own work provided a link between the 'older procedures' of Edgeworth and Pearson and 'the methods in vogue at the present time'.

There is no suggestion here that Spearman was not the first to propose the 'two-factor theory'; nor that Spearman had derived his methods from Pearson; nor that Spearman was not the founder of the 'factor school'. If Spearman's approach had never been abandoned, and if in consequence 'factor analysis' had continued to mean his approach, then of course the origins of factor analysis would have rested with Spearman in 1904. But in 1949 'factor analysis' meant first and foremost 'multiple analysis', and this had a different pedigree. A new and broader history of factorial analysis was needed now that the historical background of the new methods was to be included.

From Thurstone's standpoint such a revision was not necessary. Thurstone appears to have believed that multiple analysis began with his own contributions, and that only Spearman's work had previously been significant. Burt, by contrast, contended that Thurstone was ignoring relevant earlier work; that the origin of multiple analysis – and therefore factor analysis *as now understood* – rested with Pearson; and that his own paper of 1909 represented the first use of *these* methods in psychology. We have already seen that Burt's claim to have been using these methods from 1917 is generally conceded, and also that his claim to have been using them from the beginning is sound. The question now concerns the origin of his ideas.

Hearnshaw is adamant that Burt's first work on intelligence, and his first uses of factor analysis, were derived entirely from Spearman and owe nothing whatever to Pearson. Thus he writes that 'Spearman was certainly the starting-point of Burt's own work on intelligence' (p. 170); 'Burt's first venture into factor analysis was wholly derivative from Spearman's work' (p. 159); 'A perusal of Burt's article [of 1909] makes it perfectly clear that Pearson had no influence on it whatever' (p. 174). Further, he maintains that Burt fully recognized Spearman's priority and leadership right down to at least 1940. It will be seen that Hearnshaw leaves no room for the possibility that Burt derived something from both men: everything is derived from Spearman; nothing from Pearson. But after Spearman's death in 1945, according to Hearnshaw, everything changes. Now Burt claims the exact opposite. It was, Hearnshaw writes,

> Burt's contention from 1947 onwards that Pearson founded factor analysis in his 1901 articles, that his (Burt's) work was derived from this source and not from Spearman at all, and hence that he (Burt) was the first factorist in psychology. We can say at once that these claims by Burt about his early work were completely false.
>
> (p.179)

Burt must have know that this story was false, because he had for so many years believed something so different. Yet now his story became gradually more elaborate: 'After Spearman's death the campaign of belittlement became increasingly unrestrained, obsessive and extravagant' (p. 130; and see p. 176). Burt falsifies history in the interest of self-aggrandisement (p. 180).

Hearnshaw would have been correct if he had said that Burt was initially diffident about expressing his own views on factor analysis, and placed considerable reliance on Spearman's advice; and that as he grew older and more experienced he displayed increasing independence, and showed an increasing boldness in asserting his own standpoint. In so far as such a trend occurred, it is nothing remarkable. It is no more than might be expected of the relations between two men who were separated by some twenty years in age, and where the elder occupied for most of the time the senior academic position. Nor would it be surprising if Burt sometimes chafed under Spearman's long predominance, and if, when he eventually succeeded Spearman, he wished to make his own mark in the world. The history of psychology is full of such relationships, taking different courses on different occasions. The relation between Burt and Spearman recalls that between Jung and Freud, or that between Lashley and Watson. But there are also considerable differences. Burt was never so closely associated with Spearman as Lashley was with Watson, and as Jung was with Freud.

Hearnshaw would have been correct, in my view, if he had simply noted that Burt as he grew older became less deferential to Spearman. There is nothing remarkable in such a change of emphasis in the relationship between senior and junior colleagues. But Hearnshaw has, in my opinion, painted the contrast too starkly, greatly exaggerating both the extent to which Burt was originally dependent on Spearman, and the nature and strength of his more independent behaviour in maturity. The accusation of dishonesty depends upon this exaggeration, because it is only if the contrast is extreme that Burt can be described as misrepresenting his own earlier contribution, and denying his debt to Spearman. It is only in this way that Hearnshaw's charge acquires plausibility. But we have already seen that Burt's account of his early work is substantially correct. It remains to ask whether the remainder of Burt's story is also trustworthy.

Burt's debt to Spearman

Hearnshaw repeatedly emphasizes Burt's dependence upon Spearman in his early days: 'Burt's recognition of Spearman's leadership was virtually complete' (p. 155); 'Burt's first venture into factor analysis was wholly derivative from Spearman's work' (p. 159); 'Spearman was certainly the starting-point of Burt's own work on intelligence' (p. 170). All these sweeping statements are open to question. We may begin by recalling Spearman's position at that time.

The stereotype of a 'school' with its 'leader' may mislead us into assuming that all those in Britain who were interested in psychometric work followed meekly in Spearman's footsteps. This was never true. In the early years there was considerable opposition to some of his statistical proposals, notably from Pearson (1904; see Banks 1983; 30), whose ideas were pointedly preferred by William Brown in his influential *Essentials of Mental Testing* (first edn, 1911). Godfrey Thomson at Edinburgh always took an independent line, and his *Factorial Analysis of Human Ability* (1939) entirely rejected the general factor. By the twenties Spearman had certainly built up a strong following at University College, but even here some of his most distinguished students, such as William Stephenson, were notable for their independence. Some writers, influenced perhaps by Burt's London connections and by his long-continued support for the general factor, have supposed that the intellectual association between the two men must have been very close. Thus Oléron (1957: 72) describes Burt as Spearman's pupil. But this seems to be a slip, for Burt was never a student, either undergraduate or postgraduate, at University College; nor did he hold an appointment there while Spearman was in charge. Indeed, with the exception of Spearman's comments on Burt's first paper, there does not seem to have been much collaboration between the two men, either in research or publication, though there were personal contacts. Burt cannot be described as a member of Spearman's 'school'.

In contrast to all such notions, Burt was a pupil of McDougall at Oxford, and it was McDougall who encouraged his early interest in intelligence and secured his co-operation in Galton's survey. It is odd that in his chapter on 'Influences shaping Burt's psychology', Hearnshaw (1979, chap. 2) gives pride of place to McDougall and Galton; and he makes only one mention of Spearman (p. 16), a reference which contains no suggestion that Spearman exerted any influence over Burt at all. These early chapters were apparently written before Hearnshaw suspected Burt's honesty, and provide a further instance of his inconsistencies. Certainly most of the material for Burt's first paper was collected while he was at Oxford, and it was written mainly in his first year at Liverpool (1908–9).

It does not follow that Spearman had little or no influence over Burt in those years. But our aim should be to estimate the nature and degree of that influence, rather than to force an unrealistic choice between 'wholly derivative' and 'wholly uninfluenced'. Burt must certainly have read Spearman's two 1904 papers, and it is obvious from his own first paper that these were a great stimulus to him, whether positively, as in his lifelong belief in 'general intelligence', or negatively, as in his desire to develop more effective tests of 'higher mental processes'. There may also have been a more direct personal influence while Burt was still at Oxford. Thus according to Burt (1952a: 60): 'On McDougall's lawn at Boar's Hill Spearman and I used to meet and submit tentative ideas to him for criticism and suggestion.' However, it appears that this must have been during Burt's last year at Oxford (1907–8), because, according to Mrs Spearman, she and her husband were in Germany until 1907: 'We went to Germany in December 1902, and were there until July 1907, mostly in Leipzig. . . . I think my husband came to England, possibly during the Easter term, 1907, for an interview, otherwise we were all that time in Germany' (Mrs Spearman to D. F. Vincent, 2 December 1951). Mrs

Spearman's testimony seems to indicate that Burt must have been well launched upon his work on intelligence before Spearman had any opportunity of exerting a direct personal influence.

In support of his own interpretation, Hearnshaw quotes the acknowledgements in Burt (1909). But his quotation is selective, and gives the impression that Burt was making a much more exclusive acknowledgement to Spearman than was in fact the case. The quotation is repeated here with the parts which Hearnshaw omitted included in italics, so that the reader may see that the complete passage makes a markedly different impression from that given by Hearnshaw's selective quotation.

The investigation reported in the following pages was commenced with a view to testing in practice the mathematical methods of Dr Spearman, *and to verifying the experimental results both of Dr Spearman and of Professor Meumann. . . . Throughout almost the whole period of the experimental part of the work I enjoyed the invaluable co-operation of Mr J. C. Flugel . . . while* the mathematical part of the work is especially indebted to the generous advice and assistance of Dr Spearman. *The whole research however, owes its origin to the suggestion of Mr W. McDougall and its completion to his constant encouragement and advice . . . .* Dr Spearman and Mr McDougall have been kind enough to read through my pages in manuscript, and to allow me to make use of their criticisms and embody their suggestions
(Burt 1909: 95–6; compare Hearnshaw 1979: 170)

At first sight, perhaps, the omitted phrases do not make a great difference. But the omission of 'the whole research owes its origin to the suggestion of Mr W. McDougall' enables Hearnshaw to state that 'Spearman was certainly the starting-point of Burt's own work on intelligence' (1979: 170). It is through the accumulation of minor inaccuracies that a misleading impression is created.

Spearman's main opportunity to influence Burt came in the spring of 1909, when Burt sent him a draft of his projected first paper, and asked for his criticisms and suggestions (Burt to Spearman, 19 May 1909; an annotated edition of the 1909 correspondence between the two men has been compiled by Lovie 1985). Apparently Burt did this at the instigation of McDougall, or of Ward who was then the editor of the *British Journal of Psychology*. Neither of these two knew much statistics, and were consequently nervous about Burt's forays into this terrain. Spearman replied to Burt's request in great detail (Spearman to Burt, 23 June 1909). Burt was certainly strongly influenced by Spearman's suggestions, and a careful comparison of Spearman's commentary with Burt's paper reveals many striking similarities. However, as Banks (1983: 24) points out, no copy of Burt's first draft to Spearman has survived, and this makes it hard to estimate the exact degree of Spearman's influence. It is clear that it was considerable, especially in statistical matters, but there are a number of considerations which taken together strongly suggest that Hearnshaw goes much too far when he suggests that Burt's first venture into factor analysis was 'entirely derivative from Spearman's work'.

Much of the evidence has already been reviewed in the previous chapter. Burt's strong support for the general factor certainly lends colour to this suggestion; yet even here his attitude to it was fundamentally different from that of Spearman. Burt regarded this as a necessary preliminary to the investigation of group factors; Spearman as eliminating any need for group factors. In 1909 Burt was already finding some tentative evidence for group factors, and was already taking the first steps towards the method of simple summation. We have also seen that Burt did not use the 'proportionality criterion' – nor its derivative, the 'tetrad equation' – to analyse his observed coefficients; this criterion was nothing more than a mathematical way of expressing the 'law of the hierarchy', as Spearman called it, to which the theoretical coefficients must conform. Many years later, however, in 1937, there was a correspondence between Spearman and Burt about this proportionality criterion, and who had first expressed it. Hearnshaw makes much of this, implying that Burt had made a claim to which he was not entitled; that he was forced by Spearman to withdraw it; and that the whole incident is an early example of Burt's growing proclivity to making false claims. These assertions require critical examination.

Hearnshaw describes the 1937 exchange as follows:

The correspondence which took place in 1937 resulted from a claim made by Burt in the *British Journal of Educational Psychology* of that year that the 'proportionality criterion' which he had used in 1909, though derived from an article of Spearman and Kruger, was in fact first employed by Burt himself. The equation (later known as the tetrad equation) was in fact supplied by Spearman in a letter dated 23 June 1909. After the claim in Burt's 1937 article Spearman wrote, 'I am a little concerned with the priority of this enunciation of the "proportionality criterion". I am afraid throughout all these years I have been rather claiming this priority for myself, on the strength of my letter to you being dated 23rd June, 1909, whereas your article in the *British Journal of Psychology* was only published in December 1909'. In answer to this letter of Spearman Burt completely withdrew his claim. 'There can hardly be any real doubt,' he wrote, 'The whole idea of a hierarchy is your own; and since the essence of a hierarchy is its proportionality, surely you have a prior claim here.'

(Hearnshaw 1979: 170)

Hearnshaw does not quote the claim which Burt is said to have made in

1937, and the reader is therefore unable to judge, without consulting the reference, how far Hearnshaw's remarks are justified. The passage in question repays study. It appears in a footnote on page 185 of Burt (1937b), and is as follows:

> The proportionality criterion was first given in my article on 'Experimental Tests of Intelligence', *Brit. Journ. Psych.*, III, 1909, p. 159. As I there indicated, however, it is immediately deducible from equation (f) as given by Spearman and Kruger in *Zeitschr. F. Psych.*, XLIV, p. 85.

It can now be seen that Hearnshaw's statements are misleading. Note first that Burt does not claim, as Hearnshaw alleges, that the criterion was 'first employed by Burt himself'. He says it was 'first given' in his article. Nor does Spearman complain that Burt has claimed to have been the first to use it. He says that he is concerned with 'the priority of this enunciation', that is, with who had first stated it, pointing out that he had been the first, in his letter of 23 June 1909.

But even if Burt had claimed to be the first to use it, Spearman had no possible cause for complaint, because he had sent it to him. Moreover, Hearnshaw himself has told us that Burt used it in 1909; and, if he did, this must have been the first time it had ever been employed, because it was 'first enunciated' by Spearman on 23 June 1909. According to Hearnshaw's own account, therefore, Burt must have been the first to employ it; and it is absurd for him now to treat this as a false claim. The absurdity is heightened by the circumstance that Burt does not claim this; nor does Spearman object to it. It is raised to an even greater pitch by the further fact that, as we have seen, Burt could not have used it for the analysis of his observed coefficients, even if he had so desired.

Spearman makes it very clear that he is concerned about who first expressed the criterion, and his concern presumably arose because of Burt's remark that it was 'first given' in his 1909 article. If by 'first given' is meant 'first made generally available', or 'first published', then Burt is justified. He was the first to publish it. But Spearman was the first to state it, in his prior letter. The real question therefore appears to be this: when Burt said 'first given', was he trying to claim that he, not Spearman, had priority in the formulation of the criterion, as Spearman seems to have suspected?

My own interpretation of Burt's 1937 footnote is that Spearman is reading altogether too much into it. The mere fact that Burt put it all in a footnote seems to me to indicate that he regarded it as a minor matter. The phrase 'first given' seems to me to mean nothing more than 'first published'. And the immediate indication that it was deducible from Spearman and Kruger's earlier article seems to me to mean, not that Burt is claiming authorship, but that he is disclaiming it. Burt seems to me to be saying to the reader: 'It was first published in my article of 1909, but the real credit is due to the reference given.'

It is Spearman's behaviour in this matter which seems to require explanation, rather than Burt's. The correspondence of 1937 needs to be judged in the light of what had happened before this, which Hearnshaw does not mention. In 1912, Spearman does not seem to have been in the least concerned to ensure that his priority in formulating the criterion was recognized. He actually refers to it as 'Burt's equation' (Spearman and Hart 1912: 65). His first concern comes in 1919. In that year Garnett referred to it as 'Burt's equation'; and Spearman wrote to him and objected to this. Garnett pointed out, reasonably enough, that it was Spearman's own phrase, but agreed that it was misleading (see Banks 1983: 23–5). Against this background, Burt's 1937 footnote seems innocent enough. We can only speculate about why Spearman should have blown hot and cold about it. Perhaps he was at first so secure in his superiority over Burt that he did not worry about priority; but later he became nervous about Burt's growing reputation and independent approach, and anxious to preserve every advantage he could. The proportionality criterion was important to Spearman, as foreshadowing the tetrad equation; it was far less significant for Burt, who used a different method of analysis.

A final argument used by Hearnshaw concerns the acknowledgements in Burt's *Factors of the Mind* (1940). He quotes Burt's statement that Spearman's 'brilliant work has after all inspired, directly or indirectly, the numerous alternative methods put forward to supplement or supersede it'; and also that 'Spearman's pre-eminence is acknowledged by every factorist' (Burt 1940: 269 and x). These seem to me to be conventional compliments rather than considered historical judgements. As Hearnshaw himself says, 'When he wrote *The Factors of the Mind* Burt was not greatly concerned with historical background' (1979: 169). Burt's remarks recall the couplet describing the mutual flattery of two noted historians:

Ladling butter from alternate tubs,
Stubbs butters Freeman, Freeman butters Stubbs.

Burt's debt to Pearson

If one-half of Hearnshaw's argument is that Burt's early ventures into factor analysis owed everything to Spearman, the second half is that they owed nothing to Pearson. According to Hearnshaw (1979: 172), Burt traces the origins of factor analysis to two papers by Karl Pearson which appeared in 1901: 'On the systematic fitting of curves to observations and measurements' (Pearson 1901a, in *Biometrika*, I: 265–303); and 'On lines and planes of closest fit to systems of points in space' (Pearson 1901b, in *Philosophical Magazine*, II: 559–72). This is the essence of Burt's fictitious 'new story' which is influenced by two events: Spearman's death (1945) which removes the man who could have given him the lie; and Thurstone's work on *Multiple Factor Analysis* (1947) which ignores his contributions. Hearnshaw (1979: 171ff.) maintains that Burt only begins to express indebtedness to Pearson in the Michotte *Festschrift* of 1947, and only begins to involve the *Biometrika* paper in October 1947 (Burt 1947b), and the *Philosophical Magazine* article in 1948 (Burt 1948a). Hearnshaw maintains that there is no reference in any of the earlier writings of either Burt or any other factorist to either of these papers. Burt's repeated claims that his early work was derived from Pearson can therefore be regarded as fictitious. The claims gradually became more extreme until eventually they became so absurd that he must have been losing his mental balance.

But Hearnshaw's account of Burt's claims is inaccurate in essential respects. So far as Pearson (1901a) is concerned, Hearnshaw appears to have completley misunderstood Burt's references. First, he seems to have misread Burt (1947b). This was Burt's inaugural article for the new statistical journal – 'A comparison of factor analysis and analysis of variance'. Hearnshaw (1979: 172) states that it is in this paper, on page 21, that Burt first refers to the *Biometrika* article of Pearson (1901a). But Burt's reference is not to Pearson (1901a). The reference (see Burt 1947b: 21, and footnote 2) is attached to a passage which reads as follows:

> The idea of reducing a number of correlated variables to an equal number of uncorrelated variables, by choosing the 'principal axes of the correlation ellipsoid' to represent the new 'dimensions', appears to have been first put forward by Karl Pearson.

The footnote reads simply '*Biometrika I,* 1901, p. 209.' Burt's reference cannot be to Pearson (1901a), because the page numbers of that paper are

Table 5.1 Macdonell's matrix of 1901

(as abbreviated from five figures to three figures by Spearman (1927: 141); decimals omitted)

	1	2	3	4	5	6	7
1 Head length	–	402	394	301	305	339	340
2 Head breadth	402	–	618	150	135	206	183
3 Face breadth	394	618	–	321	289	353	345
4 Left mid-finger	301	150	321	–	846	759	661
5 Left cubit	305	135	289	846	–	797	800
6 Left foot	339	206	363	759	797	–	736
7 Height	340	183	345	661	800	736	–

265–303. The page actually referred to, page 209, is part of a paper by Macdonell (1901) entitled 'On criminal anthropometry and the identification of criminals'. This contained, on page 202, a matrix of correlation coefficients among seven physical variables (see Table 5.1). The correlations were based on measurements of 3,000 male 'non-habitual' criminals furnished by the Central Metric Office at New Scotland Yard. The relevant passage which Burt has in mind is on page 209, which begins, 'Professor Pearson has pointed out to me that the ideal index characters would be given if we calculated the seven directions of uncorrelated variables, that is, the principal axes of the correlation ellipsoid.'

Hearnshaw (ibid.: 173) also states that Burt refers to Pearson (1901a) again in his review of Thurstone (Burt 1947d). But here too he is mistaken. Burt's review (1947d: 165, note 1) once more gives the reference 'Biometrika I (1901) p. 209'. Burt's cryptic references have confused Hearnshaw; but they are not untypical of Burt's generation. Spearman's references in his *Abilities of Man* are highly abbreviated by today's standards: Spearman's (1927: 141) own reference to this paper by Macdonell (whose name he spells in his text as McDonnell) was simply '*Biometrika*, 1901, i'.

Spearman's reference, like Burt's, is perfectly adequate for anyone who wants to look up the paper, because there is only one paper by Macdonell in the first volume of *Biometrika*. Nothing is gained by giving the wrong reference in superfluous detail.

I have not in fact been able to find any reference to Pearson (1901a) anywhere in either of these two places where Hearnshaw states that Burt first introduced it, nor indeed in any of Burt's writing on the origins of factor analysis. However, too much weight should not be placed on this negative observation, as a failure to find a reference in the vast and scattered corpus of Burt's writings means very little. But Hearnshaw has not established that this paper has any place in Burt's accounts, and therefore his emphasis on Burt's failure to mention the paper earlier is irrelevant. All that Hearnshaw has established is that he literally does not know what Burt is talking about.

Hearnshaw's errors here are especially significant, because they also show that he is unaware of the account which Burt himself gave of the origin of his ideas. Burt (1952a) states that he originally derived his own ideas, not from Pearson's two papers mentioned by Hearnshaw, but from Macdonell's paper and from a talk given in Oxford by Pearson. Macdonell (1901) is the paper on which Burt places most emphasis in his account both of the origins of factor analysis, and of his own ideas. It is the paper which Burt (1952a: 60) in his autobiographical study claims to have read, and been influenced by, in his early days. In a letter to Vincent, dated 15 October 1951, Burt mentions 'the part played by Pearson and his immediate disciples in working out suitable formulae for what we now call factor analysis', and instances the 'closest fit' paper in the *Philosophical*

Magazine, and 'a paper published under his supervision in the first volume of *Biometrika*' by Macdonell.

It is also the paper to which Burt gives pride of place in the origins of factor analysis. In his major statement on 'Alternative methods of factor analysis and their relation to Pearson's method of "principal axes"', Burt (1949a: 103) writes that the matrix furnished by Macdonell was the first such table to appear: and he adds (ibid., note 2) that 'this was the first table which it was suggested might be analysed into a series of uncorrelated components or "factors"; it marks as it were, the birth of factor analysis as a biometric method'.

This, like so many of Burt's footnotes, recalls a remark of Wrigley, in a letter to Vincent of 23 September 1958, that Burt's footnotes contain a remarkable wealth of information, and that 'Burt's Collected Footnotes' would make an invaluable volume. Wrigley himself contributed a re-factorization of Macdonell's matrix (Wrigley and Neuhaus 1952); and he says, in the same letter, that the passage from Pearson in Macdonell (1901: 209) is that which he, Wrigley, read as indicating that Pearson had grasped the essential idea of the principal axes method.

Hearnshaw seems to be correct in stating that there is no relevant reference in any of Burt's earlier writings to the two 1901 papers of Pearson; but this by no means shows that Burt was uninfluenced by Pearson when he wrote his early papers from 1909 onwards. Burt's main claim was that he was influenced, not by Pearson's papers, but by Macdonell's paper and by the lecture which Pearson gave in Oxford at McDougall's invitation (Burt 1952a and 1952b). So it is not necessary for Burt's defenders to maintain that he was in those days familiar with any of Pearson's early papers; and indeed Banks (1983: 27) believes that it was only when Burt returned to London after the war that he had the time and the opportunity of looking into the early literature. If Hearnshaw's account is studied with care, it will be found that he nowhere provides any quotation from Burt's post-war papers in which Burt does claim that his early work was based on Pearson's 1901 papers, though Hearnshaw repeatedly talks as if he did. Burt (1948a: 101) says that his 1909 paper looked for the factor which gave the closest fit to all the observed coefficients, and adds, 'To obtain such a factor as this we have to adopt the principles previously adopted by Pearson for calculating what he termed the "lines of closest fit".' Hearnshaw comments that 'This claim wholly ignores the fact that Burt's 1909 work was entirely derived from Spearman' (1979: 174). Quite apart from the fact that Burt's 1909 work was far from being wholly derived from Spearman, Burt has not here claimed that in 1909 he took his principles from Pearson's papers, only that they had previously been adopted by Pearson. Hearnshaw, however, argues that Burt claimed his early work was based on Pearson's principles, though (a) his early writings did not refer to Pearson and his early papers, and

117

(b) his early writings did not contain the principles and methods he claimed.

So far as (b) is concerned we have seen that they do contain the anticipation of the multiple factor methods. But if this was so, where did these ideas come from? Burt might have evolved them entirely independently, but in that case why did he not claim priority for himself, instead of ascribing them to Pearson? If Burt was really so concerned with self-aggrandisement, as Hearnshaw alleges, this is what he might have been expected to do. Yet he ascribes priority to Pearson. This surely suggests that he genuinely thought that Pearson deserved the credit. Indeed, one may imagine that if Burt had claimed originality for himself, instead of ascribing it to Pearson, he might have been accused by his critics of trying to steal what was due to Pearson.

So far as (a) is concerned, it is remarkable that Hearnshaw ignores Burt's main account of how he originally became acquainted with Pearson's ideas. The most detailed source is the autobiographical study of 1952. While he was at Oxford, McDougall suggested to Burt that he should undertake the standardization of psychological tests for the anthropometric survey which the British Association was planning at Galton's instigation. Burt (1952a: 60) continues:

> I had already purchased the first volume of *Biometrika*, a new periodical just founded by Galton. This number contained a fascinating article on 'Anthropometry and the identification of criminals.' Here Pearson suggested calculating from a table of correlations for bodily measurements (collected at Scotland Yard according to the Bertillon system) metrical assessments for a hypothetical set of 'index-characters', or 'factors' as they would now be called, from which the observable traits could more readily be predicted. It seemed to me that this kind of analysis might also be tried for psychological measurements. As it happened, about this date Pearson himself came at McDougall's invitation to address a college society on the subject of 'correlations and lines of closest fit,' and I was invited to attend. In this way I first met Karl Pearson.

The *Biometrika* article is, of course, that by Macdonell (1901). It may be true, as Hearnshaw says (1979: 159), that Burt would not have been able in those days to grasp Pearson's mathematics; but why should he not have been able, from this paper and Pearson's talk, to understand the logic of Pearson's methods, as Banks (1983: 27) suggests? This is plausible since Pearson presumably adapted his talk to his audience, and offered a non-technical explanation. Burt does not give a precise date for this talk, but Hearnshaw (p. 12) seems to accept it, and it was almost certainly before he met Spearman in his last year at Oxford. It is also not without significance that in this autobiographical study Burt does not claim that it was in those early years that he became familiar with Pearson's 'closest fit' paper. Yet surely this is just what he would have claimed if he had been attempting to secure acceptance of a false story.

Burt (1952a: 61–2) continues his account by recalling a talk he gave to a society in Jesus College entitled, so he says, 'The calculation of index-characters for intellectual differences'.

> Here I outlined a method of factorizing correlations (modified from Pearson's) which I subsequently used in my 1909 and 1917 articles. . . . My own contribution lay chiefly in the idea of fitting the tables of inter-correlations with a set of hypothetical correlations deduced from the 'highest common factor', and then testing the residuals for 'specific abilities'. This method was in effect a simplified substitute for Pearson's method of principal axes.

It is very possible, then, contrary to what might be expected, that Burt met Pearson and was influenced by him, some time before he met or was influenced by Spearman. It must also be remembered that Pearson was a far more prestigious figure in those days in the university and statistical world than was Spearman. Spearman did not obtain his first academic post until 1907, and was not in those days the leader of a factorial school of world-wide reputation. Pearson, on the other hand, had been an academic figure of distinction for many years already, and was leader of the biometric movement. It was far more natural for a budding statistical psychologist to turn to Pearson for guidance than to Spearman. Burt (1952b: xi) writes as follows:

> Galton had suggested that the efficiency of the tests should first be checked by the correlation techniques which he and Karl Pearson had worked out; and accordingly McDougall invited Pearson to Oxford to give a brief exposition of his new methods of statistical analysis. McDougall . . . strongly encouraged his earlier pupils, Brown, Burt and H. B. English, in their attempts to use or develop Pearson's procedures for the study of mental processes.

We have no independent confirmation of this, but it is plausible, and there seems to be no positive reason for doubting it. Hearnshaw (1979: 23) himself – in one of his early chapters written before he suspected Burt – gives the background:

> Pearson and his school had provided psychologists with many of the

basic tools they were to use in their rapidly expanding science. Burt was one of the first to grasp the importance of these developments in statistics . . . and from his Oxford days onwards he worked intensively to acquire not only a knowledge of statistics, but an understanding of their mathematical foundations.

Hearnshaw himself also, in his chapters on Burt's early life and the influences which impinged upon him, states (p. 12) that it was in Burt's final year (namely, October 1907 to June 1908) that Burt had his first contacts with Spearman. All in all, there is nothing preposterous in the suggestion that in those days Burt was influenced by Pearson, and more by Pearson than by Spearman. There is no positive evidence that this was so, other than Burt's own accounts, but we ought to have definite grounds for scepticism before we accuse Burt of dishonesty here.

A question arises why we have to wait until the late forties before Burt raises the matter of Pearson's influence. Hearnshaw's answer, of course, is that he was waiting for Spearman's death, lest his 'new story' be exposed. But this assumes that Burt was romancing. There are many possible reasons, consistent with the truth of Burt's story.

First, Burt seems in fact not to have studied Pearson's early papers until after the Second World War. He probably would not have understood them when he was preparing his first paper, as Hearnshaw and Banks agree. He had simply got the idea for something like simple summation from Pearson's talk, and developed that himself.

Second, Burt says (Letter from Burt to Spearman, 6 November 1937) that his paper was read by Pearson, who 'strongly criticised all the mathematical methods'. This would make Burt cautious about acknowledgements to Pearson, which might be taken to imply that his methods could claim Pearson's authority.

Third, an important consideration must surely have been the notorious quarrel between Spearman and Pearson. This originated in 1904, as mentioned above, when Spearman, in his very first paper, ventured to criticize certain aspects of Pearson's work (Spearman 1904a: 96–9). Banks (1983: 30–1) describes the origin and development of this rift. Burt would certainly be aware of this. In a letter of 10 October 1909, Spearman asked Burt to include in his paper a note of clarification. He added: 'I hope you do not mind putting in the note. It is the sort of thing that a man like Pearson might try to get hold of.' For Spearman to write in such disparaging terms of a colleague to someone as junior as Burt indicates the strength of his feeling. The persistence of the quarrel was extraordinary. In his *Abilities of Man* (1927), Spearman gives an account of the origins of correlation without once mentioning Pearson – a considerable achievement. The significance of this in the present context is that whoever gave too much credit to Pearson could expect short shrift from Spearman, who was rapidly becoming one of the most powerful figures in the small world of British psychology. If Burt had any ambitions he would be unwise to express too much indebtedness to Pearson.

Fourth, after Spearman's death, Burt expresses more openly the idea that Pearson's contribution had been undervalued, as in a letter to Vincent (Burt to Vincent, 15 October 1951), and in his review of *Human Ability* (Burt, 1950b: 193): 'Now that the long and heated controversy between these two protagonists has become a thing of the past, it is to be hoped that Pearson's profound and original suggestions will once more be fully recognised. . . . Factor analysis as a statistical method owes far more to Pearson's papers of 1901 than to any later contributions of Spearman.' It is easy to imagine Spearman's fury if anyone had suggested that Pearson had originated factor analysis, or indeed had anything to do with it. Burt was wise to avoid any such clash. So Burt might have delayed bringing up the matter until after Spearman's death; but not because he feared Spearman's arguments, but because he did not wish to provoke an unseemly quarrel, and because, perhaps, he simply did not wish to hurt Spearman's feelings.

Fifth, it may well only have been as the development of factor analysis unfolded that Burt began to appreciate the full significance of Pearson's influence over him. He could not possibly know in 1909 that multiple analysis would one day sweep away Spearman's cumbrous methods; and that his own technique would thereby acquire a much more significant position in the development of factor analysis than he had previously envisaged. So to a very considerable extent, this aspect of Burt's new story could indeed be new; but this does not show that it is a false tale which Burt is inventing. It may be in part a genuine discovery of historical connections and antecedents which he was only now making.

It could well be that Burt, in delving into these mathematical connections, and searching his own recollections for relevant incidents, sometimes improves upon what actually happened, to make the connections clearer or more definite, and so to tidy up his story – rather as in Bartlett's processes of rationalization and conventionalization. As in any record depending upon human memory, we must take it with a pinch of salt. But this does not make Burt a deliberate liar. The main outlines of his story are highly plausible. It is wide of the mark to describe it as so preposterous that he might have known it would be rejected.

Finally, we may emphasize that it is particularly striking that Hearnshaw attacks Burt's views about the influence of Pearson without mentioning what Burt himself said (see Burt 1949c, 1952a, 1952b) about how that influence had originated: namely, through Macdonell's paper and through the talk given by Pearson at Oxford. Indeed, there does not appear to be any reference whatever in Hearnshaw's biography to Macdonell's paper, though this plays so central a part in Burt's own account of the origins of factor analysis.

Burt's motives

An allegation that Burt falsified history, if it is to carry conviction, must include a plausible motive. Hearnshaw supposes that the motive was to enhance his own reputation, and calls it 'self-aggrandisement'. But this motive is at once too plausible and not plausible enough.

It is *too plausible* in the sense that it is extremely likely that Burt would have some such motive; but extremely likely because everyone might be expected to possess it, and not because there was anything special about Burt. Few people could honestly say that they were driven by nothing but a pure desire for truth; there is almost always some admixture of personal pride, of self-assertive involvement. But it is a motive of which we judge very differently in others and in ourselves. In myself, I call it a proper self-respect. When others display it, I rather easily see them as self-important and over-ambitious. So Hearnshaw is on very safe ground in suggesting that Burt possessed this motive – whatever name we care to give it. Of course Burt did, for everyone has it. But Hearnshaw, by calling it 'self-aggrandisement' and suggesting that it led Burt to dishonesties, also suggests that this is a motive which is rare, which is discreditable, and to which you and I are strangers.

There is also a special difficulty about this motive. This is that ambition and a concern for his reputation would be at least as important motives if Burt were telling the truth as if he were lying. If Burt sincerely thought that he was making a justified claim, his pride would make him even more concerned to establish his story than if he were lying. For in this case he would believe he deserved it; and his sense of justice would be offended by the denial of what he saw as his rightful due. But in this case we should call it by more respectable names: ambition, self-assertion, and so on. The name we give to the motive is coloured by our moral appraisal of the behaviour involved. We are already halfway to accepting Burt's guilt if we call his motive 'self-aggrandisement'.

The proposed motive is also *not plausible enough*. It is odd that Burt's self-aggrandisement should take the form of claiming that factor analysis originated with someone else, in this case Karl Pearson. Hearnshaw forgets to explain why, if he was ambitious, he should propose someone else as the originator, and allot himself the humbler role of first user. Why, if self-aggrandisement were his motive, and especially if he was suffering from incipient paranoia, did he not claim that factor analysis originated with himself? Why drag Pearson into it at all when the story, if false, might only serve to arouse suspicion without doing much credit to himself. It is unlikely that anyone else would have developed Pearson's claims if Burt had not done so. But however this may be, at least it is a relatively modest form of self-aggrandisement which ascribes first place to another, and second place to oneself.

There are other considerations too. Burt is supposed to have embarked upon his falsifications around 1947. It would have been hard to find a point in Burt's career when he had less reason to indulge in grandiose claims. He was then at the top of the tree, recently knighted, the senior professor of psychology in the country. Why should he risk everything by embarking upon a story which was, in Hearnshaw's view, completely implausible? It is the supposed implausibility of the 'new story' which makes Hearnshaw say that Burt was mentally unbalanced. But it is Hearnshaw who has invented the story, and who then has to make Burt unbalanced to account for it.

The accusation of wanting to destroy Spearman's reputation is also wholly unrealistic. In 1909 Burt had been one of the very few to support the idea of the general factor and to provide evidence for it. Most of the prominent writers such as Thorndike and Brown were in those days attacking the idea. And Burt remained throughout his life a staunch defender of this central tenet of Spearman's system. After Spearman's death in 1945 Burt continued to defend it, when it was threatened by Thurstone's multiple approach. Burt rescued the general factor from the wreck of two-factor theory. It is grossly unfair to Burt to accuse him of lying to undermine Spearman's position when he had throughout been the most dependable supporter of his central idea. Of course, Burt also advocated group factors; and in this respect he was bound to criticize Spearman; but the criticisms should not be so exclusively stressed that a biased picture is presented. Hearnshaw's hackneyed anthropological theme of killing the father–king does not meet the case.

None of this means that self-assertion, pride, and ambition were not important for Burt – especially if he believed his claims were justified. But in recognizing this motive, we ought to describe it carefully and examine its nature. It may well be that Burt felt, from the mid-thirties onwards, that Thurstone and his supporters were giving British factorists other than Spearman too little credit, and in particular that his own contribution was undervalued. But this was as much an ambition for British psychology as for Burt himself.

Burt's story consists essentially in setting out the long tradition of British psychometric and statistical work from Galton onwards. There was more to this tradition than the contribution of Spearman, important as that contribution had been. Thurstone was forgetting the biometric school and everything which had made Spearman's work possible. Spearman was as much to be blamed for this as anybody, because in his anxiety to secure his own position he had so often ignored Pearson.

Burt is presenting himself as a link in this long chain of events. He regarded this tradition as the central contribution of modern British psychology. Of course, such an interpretation is easily exaggerated because it reflects favourably upon his own contribution; and others will consider other aspects of British psychology to be far more important. But at least we should understand what Burt's story was: it was something much bigger and of much greater potential significance than any personal self-aggrandisement could possibly be. It is strange that Hearnshaw – an historian of British psychology – should have shown himself so blind to the essential meaning of Burt's historical account.

Hearnshaw's account of Burt's motives is also coloured by his belief that Burt was 'psychologically disturbed'. This affects both his account of Burt's claims, and their effect on others. According to Hearnshaw, Burt's claims were 'entirely at variance with the evidence' and 'convinced few'. He might have known they would be rejected. Yet he continues to put forward these highly implausible claims. Hearnshaw can see only one way of explaining such puzzling behaviour: Burt must have been mentally unstable. 'His apparently total blindness to the implausibility of his story suggests that a delusional system had taken over. . . . Could any well-balanced individual have supposed he could get away with this?' (1979: 179). Thus Burt's motives have to take on a pathological flavour. The evidence for Burt's madness is examined later: here we have removed any immediate need for such speculation because the story is not 'entirely contrary to the evidence'.

In order to appreciate fully the character of Hearnshaw's explanation of Burt's supposed behaviour, it may be compared with another explanation which can be imagined, again on the supposition that Burt was dishonest. It might have been alleged that Burt was a sane and plausible rogue, who used his great knowledge of factor analysis in an attempt to impose a most ingenious deception. This interpretation might have said that Burt cleverly included much which was patently true in order to obscure the numerous deceptions. Hence many of Burt's colleagues were taken in, and only painstaking historical research has revealed his dishonesty. This story would surely have been far more appropriate for a man of Burt's calibre, who was never seriously supposed during his lifetime to be suffering from mental illness. On some such view Burt's behaviour would have been well calculated to achieve the desired end, and would have been rational enough. It would also explain why Burt's colleagues were deceived for so long.

Why, then, does not Hearnshaw adopt this far more plausible position? If he had tried to do so, he would have found it far more difficult to persuade the reader that Burt was lying. For this would have made the story plausible; and, if plausible, Burt might have believed it himself. Worse still, the reader might have started to believe it too. So it is crucial in Hearnshaw's story that Burt's account should be 'entirely contrary to the evidence'. Only in this way can he also convince us that Burt was being deliberately dishonest. Moreover, if he had adopted the position that Burt's story was plausible, he would have had to provide a far more knowledgeable and detailed refutation of it. He would not have been able to dismiss it as unbalanced.

This leads to a final difficulty for Hearnshaw's account. He himself asks: 'Why were these falsifications and misrepresentations not exposed by his colleagues at the time of their perpetration?' (1979: 180). This is indeed an awkward question – for Hearnshaw. He earlier said that 'after Spearman's death the campaign of belittlement became increasingly unrestrained, obsessive and extravagant' (p. 130); and also that there were 'numerous articles' between 1950 and 1968 in which 'the same story was repeated and elaborated' with the claims getting 'more and more extravagant' (p. 176). Hearnshaw can only suggest that Burt's articles were probably little read and that 'Those who spotted the oddity of Burt's views either dismissed it as an unimportant quirk, or, in deference to Burt's eminence and reputation, either said nothing, or merely expressed surprise' (p. 180). Hearnshaw provides no evidence for any of this, nor does he explain how it was possible for a man of Burt's eminence to carry on such a campaign for so long and apparently attract so little attention. It must have been very galling for Burt, to expend so much time and effort in trying to boost his ego, only to be so universally ignored.

But in contradiction to all this, it seems to me that Burt invariably expressed his historical views in a modest and polite way, and that there are no good grounds for talking about a 'campaign of belittlement' against Spearman. In fact, a number of those who noticed Burt's views expressed at least some agreement. Butcher (1968: 16) wrote: 'Spearman, developing the technique of factor analysis first suggested by Karl Pearson, produced extensive statistical evidence for the predominance of general ability.' Eysenck (1952: 45) wrote: 'Factor Analysis . . . is indeed a logical and historical outgrowth of the work of Galton and Karl Pearson on correlation analysis. (It is not always realised that we owe the original formulation of factor analysis to Pearson and not, as is often believed, to Spearman.)' We have already noted Harman's remarks. Hearnshaw neglects such instances of the acceptance of Burt's views, and alleges instead that Thomson was 'uneasy' (1979: 180). However, he gives no authority, and we shall see later (Chapter 12) that it is probably untrue. The only instance I have myself found of a psychologist criticizing Burt's historical accounts in any detail is in Oléron (1957), and Hearnshaw does not mention this. Oléron, incidentally, makes no suggestion of dishonesty.

So Burt's views seem to have attracted modest attention, some favourable, some unfavourable. But the simple and obvious explanation of why his 'campaign' attracted little attention is that there was no such campaign. Burt's views were put forward quietly, and unsensationally. He regarded the evolution of factorial ideas as an interesting and significant aspect of psychological history. The notion of a mounting campaign against Spearman is a fiction of Hearnshaw's imagination. Burt was a sane man pursuing a rational purpose.

Concerning the content of Pearson's papers

There is also another feature of Hearnshaw's case against Burt which, though Hearnshaw only mentions it towards the end of his argument, is of great importance and throws much light on that argument. In setting out his case, Hearnshaw repeatedly emphasizes that Burt's account was wholly false: 'Burt's account . . . is totally at variance with the evidence' (p. 169); he 'never seemed to have appreciated the complete contradiction between his new story and the evidence' (p. 178). Burt is not allowed to include even a modicum of truth in his story – though it would have been far more plausible to suppose that Burt cleverly mixed truth and falsehood. Now the prime feature of the 'new story' is, of course, the assertion that factor analysis originated with Pearson, not Spearman. We should expect, therefore, that Hearnshaw would maintain that this aspect above all is false; and indeed, as we have seen, he opens his case with the dogmatic assertion that Spearman was the originator. After all this, the reader is unprepared for the recognition, which Hearnshaw eventually makes, that Pearson's early articles were not irrelevant to the problems of factor analysis.

Towards the end of the argument (p. 179), Hearnshaw asks whether there was any element of truth in Burt's story so far as Pearson's role was concerned – a question he might rather have asked at the beginning. He then refers to Lawley and Maxwell's *Factor Analysis as a Statistical Method* (1963) on the relation of Pearson's method of principal components to factor analysis, and comments as follows:

> According to Lawley and Maxwell . . . the techniques though different are related. It would of course, have been perfectly legitimate for Burt to have pointed out this relationship, and the relevance of Pearson's 1901 articles to the problems that factorists had been concerned with . . . . What Burt was not entitled to do was claim that, as a matter of historical fact, Pearson's articles were the decisive influence in the early days of factor work, and the main inspiration of his own first endeavours. This claim is entirely contrary to the evidence and involved a falsification of history.
>
> (Hearnshaw 1979: 179–80)

Nothing in Hearnshaw's previous account had prepared the reader for this admission that there was a 'relationship' between Pearson's method and factor analysis, whatever the precise nature of that relationship might be. If this had been mentioned at the beginning, instead of at the end, the reader would have received a very different impression. Down to this point, the reader has been given to understand that there was no truth whatever in Burt's story; indeed, that it was so preposterous that he must have been mentally unbalanced to suppose anyone would believe it. But if there was a 'relationship', we at once want to know what that relationship was, and whether perhaps Burt had some justification for his point of view after all. A man is much more likely to make claims if he believes that they are well founded, than if he thinks they are false. So if there was a 'relationship', Burt may have believed that his claims were justified, even if others disagree.

We have already seen that there is nothing implausible in the suggestion that there were significant antecedents to factor analysis, nor that they are to be sought in the work of the biometric school. If it is now admitted that there was a 'relationship', Burt's claims immediately acquire a greater plausibility. They still might not be acceptable. But they cease to be so wholly absurd and without foundation. As if sensing that he is on dangerous ground in admitting the relationship, Hearnshaw at once contrasts this with what Burt is supposed to claim. Burt is supposed to claim that Pearson's articles were 'the decisive influence in the early days' and his own 'main inspiration'. But Hearnshaw does not support these alleged extreme claims with any quotation from Burt's writings, nor have I been able to find such statements. What he should have done at this point, if he was to establish his argument, was to compare Burt's article 'Alternative methods of factor analysis and their relation to Pearson's method of "principal axes"' (1949a) with Pearson's article 'On lines and planes of closest fit to systems of points in space' (1901b), and explain why Burt was falsifying history. Why did he not do this?

Further, it is generally admitted that Burt had by 1917 clearly formulated both the conception of 'group factors' and of 'simple summation'. Was it, then, a coincidence that Burt should develop these ideas only a few years after Pearson had mentioned the method of 'principal axes'? If Burt had not been stimulated to think along these lines by Galton and Pearson, were they then original to himself? And if they were, why did he give the credit to others? It seems that Hearnshaw has not thought through the full implications of the views he is expounding. What, after all, does the hypothesis of deliberate deception require? That Burt, knowing that Pearson's early papers had no relevance to the origins of factor analysis, nevertheless set out to persuade expert statisticians that they had? And all this simply as an indirect way of demoting Spearman, and pushing his own claim as 'first user' of factor analysis in psychology – though so obscurely that, despite the increasing extravagance of his claims, few noticed?

It is a great deal simpler, as well as much more plausible, to suppose that things were much as Burt said they were – especially since his historical writing is in general so accurate. This is not to claim that Burt is invariably unbiased in his history. Perfection is not to be found in such studies, which must always be open to numerous shades of interpretation. Least of all is it to be expected or demanded where a man is describing events in which he himself played an important part. It may be that Burt overstated the contribution of Pearson; it may be that Hearnshaw overstates the contribution of Spearman. Such disagreements are legitimate and understandable. But accusations of dishonesty are best avoided unless the evidence is both solid and overwhelming.

There is a final consideration. Hearnshaw does not claim that he has himself read Pearson's papers and formed his own opinion about any possible relation with Burt's ideas. He simply accepts the vaguely formulated remarks of Lawley and Maxwell. Nor have I read Pearson's paper (1901b) myself. The reason is simple: the mathematics is entirely beyond me. But this emboldens me to ask a question. How many psychologists have read it, and understood it sufficiently to give an informed opinion as to its relation to multiple analysis, and to the charge that Burt falsified history? How absurd it is that Burt, in his lifetime an acknowledged authority on factorial analysis, should now be accused of fraudulence by psychologists who have yet to demonstrate that they understand the crucial papers.

Conclusion

We may now summarize our conclusions concerning Burt's historical claims. Burt's account of the content of his early papers appears to be substantially accurate. It has been generally recognized that in 1917 he reported evidence for 'group factors', obtained with the method of 'simple summation'; and, as Banks (1983) has argued and we have confirmed, these features may be traced back to his first paper of 1909. Burt may sometimes give the impression that these ideas were stated more clearly and forcefully than was in fact the case, but it is evident that they were in Burt's mind from the beginning. Moreover, Burt repeatedly made these claims long before he embarked upon any 'new story' in the late forties.

As regards the origins of his ideas, Burt undoubtedly owed a great deal to Spearman, especially in his first paper, and especially with regard to his lifelong adherence to the 'general factor'. But any suggestion that his work was entirely derivative from Spearman, even in those early days, is incorrect. Spearman was always reluctant to recognize the role of 'group factors', and never employed 'simple summation', so that from the beginning Burt was making his own contribution.

Burt's debt, if any, to Pearson is far harder to establish. Here we are almost entirely dependent upon Burt's own recollections of events, and upon a difficult assessment of the relation, if any, between 'simple summation' and 'principal components'. It seems unlikely that Burt became familiar with Pearson's 1901 papers until the forties, but he does not claim that he did. He claims that he was influenced by a remark of Pearson in Macdonell's paper of 1901, and by a talk which Pearson gave to

McDougall's students at Oxford in the early years of the century. From these sources, he derived certain simplified ideas which eventually proved to be an anticipation of Thurstone's multiple analysis.

Many different views may be held concerning the origins of factor analysis, and Burt's interpretation like others is open to debate. But Burt's views were expressed far too reasonably and coherently to be rejected out of hand as 'totally at variance with the evidence', or as entirely moulded by self-interest. The attempt to confirm Hearnshaw's account has failed; not occasionally and incidentally, but repeatedly and crucially. If Burt's story had really been wholly false, then it would indeed have been strange. But the impression of strangeness which Hearnshaw detects arises, not because the account which Burt actually gave is riddled with error, still less because of a pathological streak in Burt's character. It is because Hearnshaw has misunderstood Burt's account.

There is one further important implication of these findings. The errors in Hearnshaw's account are so frequent and widespread that they are highly likely to be discovered by anyone who sets out to check, wherever they begin their enquiry. It was not a lucky chance which led the present writer to find errors as soon as he began to look; they are everywhere. It follows that few if any of those who have publicly accepted Hearnshaw's conclusion, whether in reviews and articles, or in other public statements and decisions, can have made any real attempt to verify his case.

In Hearnshaw's biography of Burt, the alleged historical falsifications play a crucial role. These are the first important instances of dishonesty which the reader encounters, and they are likely to make a powerful impression. The catalogue of deceit seems far too extensive and detailed to be refuted. Moreover, these charges had not previously appeared in print, and it inevitably made a strong impression upon the reader that, in addition to the accusations already made public this further extensive list should have been discovered. The reader is now fully prepared to find Burt guilty of the major deceptions.

It is important, however, to avoid making the same error in reverse. Just because we have found grounds for scepticism about the historical allegations, it does not follow that we can assume that all the remaining charges will also prove false. Every charge has to be examined without presupposition, and decided on the basis of the relevant evidence.

Initially I had supposed that Burt was likely to be more guilty than Hearnshaw allowed; but so far the evidence has moved in the opposite direction. First, the attempt to extend the dishonesty to an earlier period failed; and now one of Hearnshaw's three major charges has collapsed. The earliest time for the onset of Burt's dishonesties now becomes 1955, so that they are postponed to the final fifteen years of Burt's life. To these matters we must now turn.

Chapter six

Burt's kinship studies:
the invariant correlations

Although the allegations against Burt have been many and varied, they have from the beginning centred on his kinship studies. It was here that Shields, in 1962, noted the slender information about the separated twins given by Burt in 1943; here that Kamin and Jensen, soon after Burt's death, pointed to puzzling numerical inconsistencies; here too that Gillie, unable to trace Howard and Conway in 1976, voiced the first public accusation of dishonesty; and here finally that the Clarkes and Hearnshaw based their major arguments. The historical falsifications were in comparison an obscure and academic issue, with no very obvious implications for matters of current importance. But the invention of false data, by non-existent research assistants, on a subject of heated contemporary controversy, was – if it had occurred – a clear-cut and scandalous misdemeanour which everyone could readily appreciate. As a journalist, Gillie knew a good story when he heard it.

This chapter is concerned with the first phase of these criticisms, before Gillie appeared on the scene. At this stage, the critics are principally concerned with the many cases where correlation coefficients are invariant though numbers of subjects alter. Carelessness or incompetence, occasioned perhaps by old age, are mooted as possible explanations; while Jensen suggested that Burt might have lacked interest in the empirical side of his work, Kamin hinted at more serious faults, but nobody was yet prepared to venture an explicit accusation of deliberate fraud. After Gillie's article, however, fraud was openly proposed, so that our discussion must include this possibility. The later criticisms, after Gillie's accusation, centre on the missing assistants and are examined in the next chapter.

There are two preliminary points concerning Burt's kinship studies which it is essential to keep in mind. The first is the very early date at which Burt began to collect his material. He lived to a great age, outliving most of his contemporaries – and composing many of their obituaries. When he died in 1971, it was nearly sixty years since his appointment as educational psychologist to the LCC in 1913, when he first began to make his school surveys. In those early days the conditions under which research had to be conducted were very different from anything that people nowadays experience. In particular, the necessary tests and statistical techniques had to a large extent to be developed as the research progressed, and the assistance, both personal and financial, which today is taken for granted, was simply not available. Burt was a pioneer, subject to all the constraints and limitations of his kind. His critics today sometimes fail to appreciate that, in studying his early work, they are stepping back into a different world. The second point to be remembered is the considerable time that elapsed between the collection of the greater part of the material and its publication. Most of the material, as we shall see, was almost certainly collected before the Second World War, but it was not until 1955 that Burt began to publish with any degree of completeness. These two general characteristics must be considered in detail before we try to proceed further.

Preliminary points

(a) The origin of the kinship data

Although the quality of some of Burt's early work has been criticized, nobody could reasonably doubt that, during the period of his appointment with the LCC, Burt conducted many surveys in London schools. The work was carried out for the LCC, and much of it was published by them. Thus Burt's well-known 'Distribution and relations of educational abilities' (1917) consisted of three reports presented by Burt to the council, and it was published by the council. Burt's brief was clearly stated by Sir Robert Blair, the Chief Education Officer, in his preface to the volume: 'Arising out of his immediate duties in connection with special (M.D.) schools and following on some previous inquiries, the results of which have already been published by the council, Mr Burt has pursued his investigations into the distribution of educational ability among the whole of the children in the special (M.D.) schools and in the ordinary elementary schools within a representative borough' (see Burt 1917: vii). Burt himself acknowledged his indebtedness 'to numerous head and assistant teachers, who have so readily helped me by compiling lists, schedules and estimates, or have arranged for me to carry out experiments and tests upon the children in their charge' (ibid.: 3, footnote). Burt's tests and methods were subsequently described in detail in *Mental and Scholastic Tests* (1921; 4th edn, 1962), and in a *Handbook of Tests for Use in Schools* (1923b; 2nd edn, 1948).

Nobody has ever seriously proposed that Burt managed to bamboozle all these people all this time, and did not actually collect a great deal of the material which he described. The point may seem so obvious as not to be worth mentioning, but it has extremely important consequences, which become evident when we consider the character of the material and the uses to which it could be put. Burt gives the immediate purpose of the survey as threefold: '(1) to discover both the actual and the most suitable lines of demarcation between children in the ordinary schools and children admitted to special schools for the mentally defective; (2) to obtain some estimate of the number of backward children in the ordinary schools; and finally, (3) to verify the hypothesis of a "general educational ability" underlying work in all school subjects' (ibid.: 1). However, once the material had been collected, it could be put to many other uses, such as the identification of the exceptionally bright child, the investigation of the delinquent child, and so on. Various samples of children with distinctive characteristics could in this way be extracted from the data for more detailed study. Thus Burt's survey had presented him with material of great potential value.

Among these possibilities, the one of most immediate concern is kinship data. The material must have contained individuals related in various ways to other children in the sample. Many would be unrelated; but there would be numerous instances of different degrees of family relationship – siblings, cousins, and so on – and of course twins, both DZ and MZ. Obviously the numbers falling into these different categories would vary greatly, corresponding roughly to their incidence in the population at large. MZ twins raised apart would be among the least frequent. Nevertheless, it is virtually certain that, among the large numbers studied, there would be some representatives of all the twin types. It follows that there is no plausibility in the suggestion that Burt did not collect any data on twins at all. Twin data could only have been missing from Burt's records if they had been deliberately eliminated.

One of the things that the material would enable Burt to do, therefore, was to compare the correlations between the IQs of the children in these different groups; and accordingly it is not surprising that, in his paper 'Ability and income' (1943: 91), we find him writing as follows:

> In London, during a survey with the Binet tests covering 3,510 children, we found 68 twins of whom 19 appeared to be 'identical' (monozygotic). During subsequent years an additional 121 cases have been added to the data. The correlations between the IQs are as follows: non-identical twins (156 cases), .54 . . . twins of like sex and 'identical' in type so far as could be judged (62 cases), .86 . . . (in the few cases – 15 in number – where the 'identical' twins had been reared separately the correlation was .77).

There do not appear to be any references to kinship correlations in Burt 1917, 1921, or 1923b, so presumably at this early stage he had not yet begun a specific study of this aspect of his data. The earliest reference to

Burt's own kinship data which I can confirm has been pointed out to me by Banks in *The Backward Child*, where Burt (1937a: 446, note 2) gives a correlation between parent and child (153 pairs) of 0.46, and a correlation between siblings (326 pairs) of 0.53; though where children had been brought up away from their parents a 'distinctly smaller correlation' was found: 0.28 to 0.34. The same volume provides evidence that his kinship data also contained twin material: after discussing handedness in twins, he adds that 'in a separate inquiry upon the mental characteristics of twins, I found, in a group of eighty-four, four instances where both twins were left-handed' (ibid.: 297). However, he gives no further details.

Burt (1943) appears to contain the only reference to Burt's own kinship data between Burt 1937a and Burt 1955a, but thereafter references become very frequent. In mentioning the origin of the twin data, Burt invariably traces it mainly to his years with the LCC and to the years before the Second World War (for example, Burt 1943: 91; Burt 1966a: 138–40); and in the last year of his life, in a letter to Eysenck dated 27 July 1971, he again said that 'Most of our own studies of separated twins were accumulated bit by bit between 1913 and 1939' (quoted by Hearnshaw 1979: 239).

From these considerations, a number of consequences follow which are crucial to a proper understanding of some of the puzzling characteristics of Burt's material.

First, Burt's kinship data did not necessarily originate from a study specifically undertaken with a view to investigating the relationship between heredity and environment in determining intelligence. Such problems proved to be one of many for which the 'London survey' provided suitable material, or at least a suitable starting-point.

Second, the term 'kinship data' is somewhat ambiguous. In one sense it may refer to the original individual record sheets, with their test marks and assessments, of Burt's sample of eleven-year-old London schoolchildren. In another sense it may refer to the various kinship categories extracted from the pool, and perhaps to the various stages of analysis thereafter (see Banks 1983: 22).

Third, while the 'London survey' would provide Burt with a rich pool of data for initial work on various samples of children, it would not necessarily provide him with all the data he needed. The representation of different groups of subjects would be likely to be very uneven. Thus there were more than enough siblings reared together (853 in Burt 1955a), but too few MZ twins, especially of the rare group reared apart (only 15 in Burt 1943). Thus it would often be desirable to collect additional data to supplement the original survey; and we can readily understand Burt's remark in 1943, quoted above, that an additional 121 twins had been collected 'during subsequent years' (that is, during the twenties and thirties).

Fourth, in order to gather all this material, Burt needed help. But research funds were far harder to obtain in those days, and trained assistants even harder. Burt was forced to rely upon help from teachers, school medical officers, and care committee workers, and to train them himself. Burt several times mentions assistants by name. Burt (1955a: 167) states that Miss Conway had collected 'further data' for the 1943 paper, and had also been responsible then for the final calculations; and her name appears jointly with that of Burt over the table of correlations on page 168. Later in the same paper Burt (1955a: 172, note) mentions four further assistants: Miss Pelling, Mr Seymour, Miss Richardson, and Miss Howard. Burt (1966a: 141, note) mentions five assistants to whom he had been specially indebted over the years: Miss Pelling, Miss Molteno, Mr Lewis, Miss Howard, and Miss Conway. We return to this controversial matter in the next chapter.

Fifth, it would often be necessary to go outside the London schools to obtain the additional material needed. Two instances are especially important: (1) the class of 'unrelated children reared together' were best found in foster homes and orphanages, and special surveys were initiated to obtain these; (2) in the case of twins, whether MZ or DZ, both members of a twin pair would not necessarily have been included in the initial trawl. A missing member, especially if reared apart, might well attend a different school, perhaps in a different part of the country. Here the additional material would have to be obtained by an individual search and assessment. As Burt said: 'If, as was often the case, a certain amount of travel was involved to examine the separated twin, then the job was usually delegated to Miss Conway or Miss Howard' (Letter to Jencks, quoted by Hearnshaw 1979: 240). Whether or not Conway and Howard were real people, the task which they were here allotted seems to have been real enough.

Sixth, although much of this extra twin material seems to have been collected before the war, some may have been added during the war. It seems unlikely that all of this could have been ready for the 1943 paper; but what could not be included then was available in 1955 when the numbers rise, specifically of MZ apart to 21. But even in 1955 Burt was apparently not satisfied with the numbers obtained, for we find him appealing to be notified of further cases (Burt 1955a: 167, note 3).

Seventh, just as it would be difficult for Burt to ensure the requisite numbers of subjects in the various categories, so it would also be realistic to expect some difficulty in ensuring that every subject received the full quota of assessments. From Burt (1955a) we learn that there were in fact some eleven assessments, including educational and physical as well as intellectual tests. The exigencies of time, space, and material could well result in some tests being omitted for some subjects. Over the twenty-odd years that material was collected, and the hundreds of children and numerous assistants who were involved, it would not be unreasonable to expect that, at the end of the day, some tests for some subjects would be incomplete. The physical tests, in particular, might be expected to have rather smaller samples, for a number of reasons: (1) since physical measurements are more accurate than mental, fewer data would be needed to secure reliable results; (2) the physical measurements might sometimes be harder to obtain (measuring weight, for instance, requires scales, not necessarily always conveniently to hand); (3) in a psychological enquiry, more interest attaches to the mental measurements, and especially to the intelligence scores, so Burt would be keen to collect more of these. These are important points when one comes to consider the reports of his data which Burt eventually produced.

All these limitations may be summarized in the reminder that Burt was a pioneer. He was the first to devise and standardize mental tests on any scale in the United Kingdom, and to use these to tackle important questions, both theoretical and practical. In order to collect information from schools and other institutions, he had to gain the co-operation of teachers and school medical officers, and he had to ensure that he did not move too far from sound practical judgement. The methods he employed, like those of any pioneer, were sometimes rough and ready; but Burt was the first to draw attention to this, and moreover himself did a great deal to improve them (Banks 1983: 31–2).

(b) The publication of the kinship data

Burt's twin references are not all of equal importance. They differ greatly in their purpose and in the amount of detail they give. Many of them do nothing more than repeat information already given, and comment in passing upon its application to whatever topic he happened to be discussing. For our purposes, the important papers are those which purport to give fresh kinship correlations, whether we believe these to be genuine or not. There are precisely four such papers: Burt (1943), Burt (1955a), Conway (1958), and Burt (1966a). The remaining papers may occasionally be useful in containing a correction to figures previously given, but otherwise they throw little fresh light on Burt's kinship data.

But even the four papers which contain new information vary greatly in the attention they give to the kinship data, and in the detail they provide. A brief survey will bring this home to the reader. Burt (1943), as he himself said (Burt 1966a: 140), 'was concerned primarily with the "influence of innate ability and parental income on entrance to the universities", and the mention of twins was merely incidental'. From our point of view, the paper is significant mainly because it provided the first preliminary account of the twin data which was available at that time, rather than because it gave (or could possibly have been intended to give) anything like a comprehensive report of completed research. There is no table of results, and only some twenty lines are devoted to twins. As we have seen, Burt indicated that 68 twins had been found in the initial London survey, of whom 19 were MZ; and that 121 were added later, making presumably 189 in all, of whom 62 were MZ, and 15 of these reared apart.

The first comprehensive table of kinship correlations appeared in Burt (1955a: 168). Once again, however, reporting kinship material was not the sole, or even the primary, purpose of this paper. Entitled 'The evidence for the concept of intelligence', it was a twenty-page review of ideas about and definitions of intelligence, and of the various ways of obtaining relevant evidence. This was the kind of survey which Burt was particularly adept at handling. It received wide notice, and no brief summary could do it justice. In the second half of the paper, Burt discussed multifactorial inheritance and the relative importance of heredity and environment, and it was in this connection that he published his table. Although there was still no comprehensive account of the research, it became possible to appreciate the outlines of what Burt claimed to have obtained.

Eleven different tests or assessments were mentioned, as follows:

for intelligence –
  a group test; an individual test; a 'final assessment';

for educational achievement –
  reading and spelling; arithmetic; general attainments;

for physical characteristics –
  height; weight; head-length; head-breadth; eye colour.

Burt's table (see Table 6.1 page 137) credits his data to 'Burt and Conway'. It shows the various categories or types of subjects who had taken these tests, but it gave no information about numbers of subjects. This was given in the text, which indicated how many subjects there had been in the various categories; but it is important to note that Burt specifically excluded the last three physical measurements (for head length and breadth, and eye colour) from these numbers. They were, he said, based upon 'much smaller numbers' in each batch (Burt 1955a: 167). As we have just observed, smaller numbers among the physical tests are not surprising.

Burt 1955a, though much more informative than Burt 1943, still falls far short of furnishing a comprehensive description, and numerous important details such as the age of the twins at separation, the length of separation, and the exact nature of any environmental differences, are not specified.

(Burt (1958) is the printed version of the Bingham Memorial Lecture, which was entitled 'The inheritance of mental ability' and was delivered on 21 May 1957 at University College. It is notable as saying, with reference to MZ twins reared apart, that 'We have now collected over thirty such cases'

Table 6.1 Kinship correlations

[IMPORTANT QUALIFICATIONS. Burt's table gave no information about the number of pairs on which his correlations were based. The numbers given below are taken from his text; but some uncertainty must remain for at least two reasons: (1) Some correlations may have been calculated from a sub-set of the total number in the group (see below, p. 153); (2) The last three physical measurements were based upon 'much smaller numbers' (Burt 1955a: 167.]

	MZ twins reared together	MZ twins reared apart	DZ twins reared together	Siblings reared together	Siblings reared apart	Unrelated reared together
Number of pairs	83	21	172	853	131	287
Intelligence						
Group	944	771	542	515	441	281
Individual	921	843	526	491	463	252
Final ass.	925	876	551	538	517	269
Educational						
General	898	681	831	814	526	535
Reading etc.	944	647	915	853	490	548
Arithmetic	862	723	748	769	563	476
Physical						
Height	957	951	472	503	536	069
Weight	932	897	586	568	427	243
Head length	963	959	495	481	536	116
Head breadth	978	962	541	507	472	082
Eye colour	1.000	1.000	516	553	504	104

Source: From Burt 1955a: 168, Table I.

(Burt 1958: 7). But the table of correlations contained no new information: as Burt later informed Jensen, it 'was transplanted whole from his 1955 article' (Jensen 1974: 8, footnote). Clearly, for whatever reason, the coefficients for the MZ twins had not yet been re-calculated to take account of the extra number claimed.)

Conway (1958) is entitled 'The inheritance of intelligence and its social implications'. It is only towards the end of the paper that the subject of kinship correlations arises, and then only a couple of pages are devoted to it, one of which is a table of correlations (Table II, p. 187) (see Table 6.2, page 138). The main interest is that new correlations are now provided for all MZ twins, whether raised together or apart (except for the figures for eye colour, which of course remain at 1.0). All the coefficients for the remaining categories, however, remain the same as in 1955. This naturally suggests that new cases have been added to the earlier data on MZ twins, but not to the data on the remaining groups. Once again, the numbers of subjects are not given in the table but in the text, where it is stated that there are now 42 pairs of separated MZ twins. No figure is given for the number of MZ twins reared together, though presumably they must have increased as well, since these correlations have altered too. It seems reasonable to assume that, in the case of the remaining, non-MZ, groups, the correlations remain the same because these figures had simply been copied from Burt (1955a), just as in Burt (1958) – the sample sizes remaining the same. Once again, the data are credited to 'Burt and Conway'.

Table 6.2   Kinship correlations

[IMPORTANT QUALIFICATIONS. As in 1955, the number of pairs was not given in the Table, and only the figure for MZ twins reared apart was given in the text. The correlations for the non-MZ group are assumed to be reproduced from Burt 1955a, so these are bracketed.]

	MZ twins reared together	MZ twins reared apart	DZ twins reared together	Siblings reared together	Siblings reared apart	Unrelated reared together
Number of pairs	?	42	(172)	(853)	(131)	(287)
Intelligence						
Group	936	778	542	515	441	281
Individual	919	846	526	491	463	252
Final ass.	928	881	551	538	517	269
Educational						
General	894	629	831	814	526	535
Reading etc.	943	645	915	853	490	548
Arithmetic	870	726	748	769	563	476
Physical						
Height	956	942	472	503	536	069
Weight	929	884	586	568	427	243
Head length	961	958	495	481	536	116
Head breadth	977	960	541	507	472	082
Eye colour	1.000	1.000	516	553	504	104

Source: From Conway 1958: 187, Table II.

After this, there is an interval until Burt (1966a), which is the last paper to report any new data. This paper is something of a new departure. In the three papers considered so far (Burt 1943; Burt 1955a; and Conway 1958), it has never been the sole or even the main aim of the paper to describe the kinship research. The accounts given have always been incomplete, and seem to have been introduced primarily to illustrate or support some aspect of the main theme, rather than for their own sake. In this respect, Burt (1966a) marks a radical change. It differs from the previous papers, and from all subsequent references, in that its primary aim is the presentation of the kinship research, and especially the twin data. This concentration is reflected in its title – 'The genetic determination of differences in intelligence: a study of monozygotic twins reared together and apart'. Perhaps it indicates the importance which Burt attached to this paper that it was published in the *British Journal of Psychology*, where it would be assured of a wide audience, rather than in the more specialist journals in which the previous papers had appeared.

Whatever limitations it may have, Burt (1966a) contains much fuller information than had been given previously (see Table 6.3, page 140). Just as in 1955, correlations are given for the six groups of subjects, and for the eleven assessments (Burt 1966a: 146). But now for the first time, the numbers of subjects in the various groups are given at the top of the table. In the following list, the 1966 numbers are compared with the 1955 numbers, and it will be seen that in every category there is some alteration, half increasing and half decreasing.

	1955	1966	Change
MZ together	83	95	+12
MZ apart	21	53	+32
DZ together	172	127	−45
Siblings together	853	264	−589
Siblings apart	131	151	+20
Foster children	287	136	−151

In a note attached to Table 2, Burt specifically excludes the last three physical measures (head length and breadth, and eye colour), as he had in 1955. These measures 'were based on samples of 100 only' so far as the last four groups of subjects were concerned. Once again, we find smaller samples among the physical tests. In 1966 the correlations are credited to 'Burt *et al.*'.

From this brief account of how the data were collected, and how they were published, it becomes clear that both phases of the research were spread out over many years – far longer than would ever be envisaged or tolerated today. When the final account was eventually published in 1966, some at least of the data on which it was based were almost certainly derived from the original London survey dating from the First World War, fifty years earlier; and much from the period between the wars.

Table 6.3 Kinship correlations

	MZ twins reared together	MZ twins reared apart	DZ twins reared together	Siblings reared together	Siblings reared apart	Unrelated reared together
Number of pairs*	95	53	127	264	151	136
Intelligence						
Group	944	771	552	545	412	281
Individual	918	863	527	498	423	252
Final ass.	925	874	453	531	438	267
Educational						
General	983	623	831	803	526	537
Reading etc.	951	597	919	842	490	545
Arithmetic	862	705	748	754	563	478
Physical						
Height	962	943	472	501	536	−069
Weight	929	884	586	568	427	243
Head length	961	958	495	481	506	110
Head breadth	977	960	541	510	492	082
Eye colour	1.000	1.000	516	554	524	104

* Figures for boys and girls have been calculated separately and then averaged. In columns 3, 4, 5 and 6 the correlations for head length, head breadth, and eye colour were based on samples of 100 only.

[These correlations are credited to 'Burt *et al.*'.]

Source: From Burt 1966a: 146, Table 2.

With these preliminary points in mind, we may consider the criticisms of Kamin and Jensen. These are very similar, and fall into two broad categories: criticisms of the numerical data reported, and especially the invariant correlations; and criticisms of Burt's procedures, including the information given – or not given – about his subjects, his tests, and so on.

The problem of invariant correlations

Kamin appears to have been the first to raise the problem of invariant correlations. According to Jensen (1974: 12, footnote), it was Kamin who, at a colloquium in Pennsylvania on 19 September 1972, pointed to the appearance of an identical correlation for MZ twins reared apart, despite changing sample size. Burt (1943) gave a coefficient of 0.77 for a sample of 15; Burt (1955a) a figure of 0.771 for a sample of 21; and Burt (1966a) 0.771 again for a sample of 53. Kamin (1974) gave several further instances, and Jensen (1974) added still more.

To some extent, of course, such invariances could be coincidental. The literature contains some remarkable instances of unlikely events, and it is curious that in this matter of MZ twins reared apart Shields (1962) also reports a figure of 0.77, as Jensen observes (1974: 13–14). Jensen also points to two further good reasons why Burt's correlations (r) might be expected to be fairly similar on successive occasions, despite changing sample size (N):

(1) the rs are not a random sample of all possible rs, but a sample of rs where the poulation (or 'true') value ρ is probably very close to 0.77, and in this range of high correlations the sampling error is much smaller than for low values of ρ, and (2) the Ns going from 1943 to 1955 and 1966 are cumulative, so that the added cases are much less likely to result in variations in the newly computed rs than if the rs were based on completely independent samples drawn from the same population.

(Jensen 1974: 12)

Table 6.4 Burt's invariant correlations

[These are the correlations given in Burt (1966a) which had already appeared, apparently with a different number of subjects, in Conway (1958) and/or Burt (1955a). Starred correlations are invariant from Burt (1955a) only. The figures have been corrected for minor slips and errors.]

	MZ twins reared together	MZ twins reared apart	DZ twins reared together	Siblings reared together	Siblings reared apart	Unrelated reared together
Number of pairs						
Burt (1955a)	83	21	172	853	131	287
Conway (1958)	?	42	(172)	(853)	(131)	(287)
Burt (1966a)	95	53	127	264	151	136
Intelligence						
Group		771*				281
Individual						252
Final ass.	925*					
Educational						
General			831		526	
Reading etc.					490	
Arithmetic	862*		748		563	
Physical						
Height			472		536	−069
Weight	929	884	586	568	427	243
Head length	961	958	495	481		
Head breadth	977	960	541			082
Eye colour	–	–	516			104
Total	5	4	7	2	5	6

Even so, in the instances drawn up by Kamin and Jensen there seem to be far too many invariant rs, despite changing Ns, for these explanations to be accepted as adequately accounting for everything. Jensen himself (ibid.: 24) concluded that 'error there must surely be', and Kamin thought likewise.

Before we consider possible explanations, it will be advisable to find out as much as possible about the anomalies themselves. How many are there? When do they first appear? How are they distributed among the various categories of subject and test? This is a tedious task, but it throws an unexpected light on the problem.

Locating the anomalies

The first task is to determine where, among Burt's numerous references to kinship correlations, the anomalies are to be found. It is necessary, of course, to distinguish the relevant cases, in which sample size changes, from the numerous irrelevant cases, in which Burt is merely restating correlations reported earlier in which there is no question of any change in N. Thus to distinguish the relevant from the irrelevant invariances depends, obviously enough, upon distinguishing those instances where N changes from those where it does not. This is not, however, in practice so straightforward as it sounds, because it is by no means always clear whether or not sample size has changed; and consequently it is sometimes doubtful whether a given correlation is a genuine instance of the kind in question. We shall have to return to this problem of numbers. Here we may emphasize that, whenever there is a doubt whether or not N did change, we shall assume that it did. In other words, we shall maximize the anomalies. This is in order to avoid any suspicion that we are attempting to minimize them, with a view to exonerating Burt.

Kamin (1974) lists some thirteen invariances, which he gives in two tables. The first table (Table 2, p. 58) compares siblings reared apart, and also DZ twins reared together, taken from Burt (1955a) and (1966a). The second table (Table 3, p. 59) compares MZ twins reared apart, and also MZ twins reared together, from Burt (1955a) and (1958), Conway (1958), and Burt (1966a). Kamin does not explain why he made this particular selection. If he thought it included every plausible possibility, he seems to have been wrong, for Jensen found several more. Perhaps he simply thought that thirteen was enough for his purpose, namely, to show that Burt's results were thoroughly unreliable; and assumed that if there were more anomalies to be found they could only strengthen his case. If this was his supposition, it prevented him from obtaining an adequate appreciation of the problem as a whole.

Jensen (1974) made a more extensive search, and he reported some twenty invariances. He claimed, indeed, to have based his conclusions on 'all of the various kinship correlations reported throughout Burt's writings' (p. 2). But thorough as Jensen was, some references escaped him. He included Burt (1943), (1955a), (1958), (1966a), (1971), and (1972), and also Burt and Howard (1956) and (1957); but he omitted Burt (1937a), (1967a), (1967b), and (1969); he also omitted Conway (1958) – which perhaps he regarded as outside the Burt corpus; and Burt (1975) – which of course would not have been available to him at that time.

It might be supposed that we shall now attempt a still more extensive survey than that provided by Jensen, but this would be inadvisable. This is partly because Burt published so prolifically and widely that material is easily overlooked, so it would be unwise to claim complete coverage. But a much more important reason is that complete coverage of all Burt's references to twin correlations is not necessary. A great many of Burt's references purport to do nothing more than repeat what he had reported before, numbers of subjects and all; and therefore contain nothing new. This is especially true of all references after Burt (1966a). Thus Burt (1971) and (1972), which Jensen includes, simply repeat Burt (1966a) and therefore add nothing to the picture. (These references may be important for other reasons, such as including the occasional correction to figures given earlier.) In short, what is required is not a complete coverage of all the correlations ever reported, but a complete coverage of all the relevant, anomalous correlations.

We criticized Kamin for making too brief a selection, and now we have criticized Jensen for covering too much. How, it might be asked, can we be sure that we have included all the anomalies? We need a presentation of invariant correlations of which we can say that it includes everything which is relevant and nothing which is irrelevant; which avoids both an arbitrary and limited selection, on the one hand, and confusing the picture with much that is irrelevant, on the other. A way to secure the desired presentation is not far to seek, and the reader may already have anticipated it.

An anomalous correlation – one which is invariant despite changing sample size – can only occur in a paper which reports changing sample size. If Burt does not report a change in N, the phenomenon of the invariant coefficient, in the relevant sense, cannot occur. If a change in N is reported, it is not of course inevitable that identical coefficients will appear; and there are numerous instances in Burt's data where sample size varies and correlations alter too. But it is only where sample size varies that the offending invariances could possibly occur. Thus we can exclude all those papers in which the numbers are the same as those reported earlier. Queries can only arise in regard to papers which report an alteration in sample size.

This reduces the papers to be included to those which report fresh material – and these can be none other than the four in this category listed above: namely, Burt (1943), Burt (1955a; see Table 6.1), Conway (1958; see Table 6.2) and Burt (1966a; see Table 6.3). These papers contain all the correlations which either Kamin or Jensen included, and some which neither included, giving a total of nearly thirty anomalous coefficients. Finally, it may be stressed again that the object of this analysis is not to minimize the number of instances requiring explanation, but to maximize it, thereby ensuring that the survey is as complete as possible.

Minor slips and errors

Before we list the relevant instances, it is necessary to note that Burt's reports, like many reports, contained several unintended slips and errors, several of which Burt later corrected, either in published papers or in correspondence. These errors, where relevant, have not been corrected in the tables taken directly from Burt's papers (that is, Tables 6.1–6.3), but they have been corrected in our final table of invariant correlations (Table 6.4; and in Table 6.5 – hence Tables 6.4 and 6.5 are marked 'Corrected for minor slips and errors'). It has sometimes been suggested that Burt's papers contained more of such errors than are usually found; but I have seen no good evidence for this.

Only the first item in the following list is directly relevant to the problem of the anomalies. This item is important, because it includes one of those given by Kamin. Consequently, that was not a genuine instance of an invariance. The remaining items are included for the sake of completeness, and readers uninterested in such details may omit them.

(1) One of Kamin's examples (1974: 38) of an invariant correlation concerns the figure for MZ twins reared together (group test of intelligence). This is given as 0.944 in Burt (1955a) and again in Burt (1966a), despite the increase in numbers from 83 to 95. However, according to Jensen (1974: 8), Burt told him (apparently in 1968) that the figure of 0.944 given in 1955 was a typographical error, the correct figure being 0.904. The correlation appears as 0.904 in Burt and Howard (1956: 124), but then reverts to 0.944 in Burt (1958). According to Jensen (ibid.), Burt also told him that the recurrence of the error in 1958 was because in that paper he had 'simply reproduced' the original table from 1955, and so 'unwittingly transferred' the error. Jensen then assumes that the figure of 0.944 in 1966 is correct, and is a genuinely new calculation, the number of MZ twins having changed. In my opinion the balance of evidence here favours Jensen.

(2) The correlation of 0.453 given by Burt (1966a) for DZ twins (final assessment for intelligence) was later corrected by Burt to 0.534 (see Jensen 1974: 18, footnote c; also Skanes 1978: 201). It appears as 0.534 in Burt (1975, Table 7).

(3) The figure of 33, which Burt (1966a, Table 4: 150) gives as the

number of investigations of siblings reared apart made by other research workers, was said by Burt himself to be a misprint for 3 when the original figure was queried by Jensen (see Jensen 1974: 20; Skanes 1978: 201). This mistaken 33 was also used by Kamin to discredit Burt (ibid.).

(4) The correlation of 0.983 given by Burt (1966a) for MZ twins reared together (for general educational attainments) is improbably high; moreover, in the text Burt refers to correlations of 0.83 and 0.80 as being 'nearly as high as those for identical twins reared together' (1966a: 147). If 0.983 were a misprint for 0.893, it would fit much better, and it does in fact appear as 0.89 in Burt (1967a: 274). The corresponding figure in Burt (1955a) is 0.898; and in Conway (1958) is 0.894. It therefore appears extremely likely that the 1966 figure was a misprint, corrected by Burt in 1967, and that it should have been 0.893.

(5) Jensen (1974: 10) also states that there were 'peculiar inconsistencies and, at points, sheer inaccuracies' in Burt's tabulation of correlations from Newman *et al.* (1937), which were quoted for comparison in 1955, 1958, and 1966. Jensen concluded that 'The reason for the seemingly unsystematic inconsistencies . . . can now only be a matter for idle speculation' (ibid.: 12).

Returning to the problem of locating the anomalous correlations, it is necessary next to compare the relevant papers. The comparisons to be made are as follows:

1 *Comparing Burt (1943) and Burt (1955a)*. There are two candidates, both involving the group test of intelligence. The first is the much-discussed correlation for MZ twins reared apart, given as 0.77 in 1943 and as 0.771 in 1955, though the number of subjects apparently increases from 15 to 21. The second is the correlation for DZ twins, given as 0.54 in 1943 and as 0.542 in 1955, though N appears to increase from 157 to 172. However, neither case can be reliably established as one of repetition. The figure of 0.77 in 1943 might have been reduced to two figures from anything between 0.766 and 0.774; and that of 0.54 from anything between 0.536 and 0.544. Moreover, in both cases a large proportion of subjects are common to both years, since the reports are cumulative, rendering the coefficients likely to be similar in any case. These two cases cannot be reliably established as instances of invariance where N changes.

2 *Comparing Burt (1955a) and Conway (1958)*. So far as the DZ twins, siblings, and unrelated children are concerned, all the correlations in Conway (1958) are identical with Burt (1955a) (see Tables 6.2 and 6.1); but, as mentioned above, these figures were in all probability copied directly from the earlier paper, and there is no suggestion that the numbers of subjects had changed. Hence these are not anomalous. As for the MZ twins, Burt only mentions that the number of MZ twins reared apart increased, but all the correlations alter so there are no anomalous cases here either. The only exception concerns the correlations for eye colour,

which remain at 1.0; but since this could hardly be otherwise, it is not a relevant instance. Thus down to and including Conway (1958) there are no reliable instances of anomalous invariant correlations.

It is with the publication of Burt (1966a), the major twin paper, that the anomalies appear; and all are to be found when this paper is compared with Conway (1958) and Burt (1955a). In the final analysis, then, it is only necessary to compare Burt (1966a) (Table 6.3) with these two preceding papers (Tables 6.1 and 6.2).

3 *Comparing Burt (1966a) with Conway (1958).* Table 6.4 ('Burt's invariant correlations') lists every correlation reported by Burt in 1966 which had already been given in 1958, though apparently with a different number of subjects. (The table has been 'corrected for minor slips and errors'.)

4 *Comparing Burt (1966a) with Burt (1955a).* Table 6.4 also includes the comparison with Burt (1955a). Here we have only to compare the correlations for MZ twins. This is because all the remaining figures in Conway (1958) were simply copied from Burt (1955a), as we have seen, so these have already been included. There are only three extra correlations to be included, two from MZ twins reared together, and one from MZ twins reared apart. These are starred in Table 6.4.

No fewer than 29 coefficients are repeated out of a possible total of 64. Thus some 45 per cent of the correlations are anomalous. However, as we have mentioned, the exact total is somewhat indeterminate, because the number of subjects involved is by no means always clear. Inspection of the table indicates that the distribution of anomalies among the three types of assessment is as follows:

Intelligence:	4 out of 24, or 16.1 per cent
Educational:	6 out of 24, or 25 per cent
Physical:	19 out of 36, or 52.8 per cent

Thus the anomalies appear least frequently in the intelligence tests, and increase towards the physical tests. On the other hand, the distribution appears to be random with regard to category of subject (Table 6.4, bottom row), there being no obvious tendency for any one category to be over-represented.

These observations lead to a striking conclusion. The invariant correlations are not to be found concentrated in the crucial area of tests of intelligence, nor in relation to MZ twins, as might have been expected if Burt was primarily concerned to fabricate false evidence about the inheritance of intelligence in twins. Rather, they appear predominantly among the physical measurements, and are scattered across every category of subject.

This conclusion would be strengthened if we accepted a further possibility. Banks reports a recollection concerning the much-discussed coefficient of 0.771 for the group test of intelligence for MZ twins reared apart. She (Banks 1983: 22; also p. 33) recalls that 'one day . . . he [Burt] showed me two correlations, identical and 0.7 something, although obviously based on different numbers of subjects. He seemed most astonished, but I was not attending very closely and did not enquire into it.' Burt's reaction is perhaps consistent with the possibility that he was surprised by a coincidence. However, this suggestion is not essential to the argument which follows.

Interpretations of the invariant correlations

Kamin's account

Kamin's account is neither complete nor accurate. He begins by referring to Burt's correlations for *intelligence*, and describes these as 'astonishingly stable, seeming scarcely to fluctuate as the sample size was changed' (Kamin 1974: 57). He then presents two tables which purport to illustrate his assertion. The first (ibid., Table 2: 58) compares the correlations reported in 1955 and 1966 for 'Siblings reared apart' and 'DZ twins reared together', giving the figures for intelligence, school attainment, and height and weight. There are no invariances at all here for the measures of intelligence (see our Table 6.4), nor are these correlations markedly stable. But in the remaining, non-intelligence, assessments nine out of ten correlations remain constant. Kamin's second table (ibid., Table 3, p. 59) compares the correlations reported in Burt (1955a), (1958), and (1966a), and also Conway (1958), for 'MZ twins reared apart' and 'MZ twins reared together', giving the figures for the group test of intelligence only. These are the two coefficients of 0.944 and 0.771. We have just seen that Burt himself corrected the 0.944 in Burt (1955a) to 0.904, and that the 0.771 may be a genuine coincidence. As evidence for the stability of Burt's intelligence correlations, Kamin's data are remarkably inadequate. He has managed to produce only two instances, and those doubtful. The figures he has selected, if they suggest anything, suggest that the repetitions are concentrated – as we have shown – among the educational and physical assessments. Kamin seems to be so eager to demonstrate flaws in Burt's intelligence data that he is unable to see the plain meaning of his own selection of figures.

But even if Kamin had satisfactorily established that Burt's intelligence coefficients were 'astonishingly stable', it would still be necessary for him to explain what he supposes this stability would demonstrate. This is the crucial problem. It is not hard to show that there are a large number of invariant correlations, at least among the educational and physical measures; and certainly these cannot all be ascribed to chance. But if not to chance, to what?

Kamin wants his readers to suppose that Burt deliberately introduced these anomalous figures into his work in order to give it a spurious stability and consistency; and that he, Kamin, can see through the imposture. Thus he adopts a tone of sarcastic disbelief, talking of the 'remarkable stability' (p. 59) of the correlations, and the 'marvellous consistency' which 'taxes credibility' (p. 71). He speaks scathingly of a 'benign Providence' smiling upon Burt's labours so that 'in 1966, his three-decimal-place correlations were back to where they had been at the beginning' (p. 59). Some readers, perhaps, would be carried along by Kamin's emotional rhetoric; but the logic of his argument is elusive. It is not at all clear what he, Kamin, actually believes, and what he is only pretending to believe.

Does he, for example, think that Burt supposed that his case would be strengthened if the correlations remained stable, however the number of subjects altered, and therefore deliberately repeated them knowing they were false? If this is what Kamin believes, one may say with confidence that it has little to recommend it. Nobody with the slightest statistical sophistication could imagine that such consistency was anything other than highly suspicious. Burt would have been utterly incapable of entertaining such a belief. Moreover, Burt did not draw attention to the consistency. Nobody noticed it until Kamin came along and pointed it out; and then, of course, everyone realized at once that something must be wrong. It is absurd for Kamin to suppose that Burt was statistically so ill-informed that he would believe the invariance would strengthen his case; and for Kamin simultaneously to assume that he has only to point it out and everyone else will at once see that it is a transparent falsehood.

Does Kamin, then, think that Burt, though not taken in himself, believed that his colleagues were so ill-informed that they would be taken in? It is just conceivable that Burt might have supposed that a few of his colleagues might be so ignorant; but by no stretch of the imagination could he have supposed that all would be deceived. To Burt, the error in question would be so elementary, so foolish, that he cannot have imagined that, if noticed, it would impose itself for a moment. And of course it did not. Kamin has only to draw attention to the anomaly for it to be generally recognized. Otherwise expressed, Kamin seems to believe that Burt is quite capable of believing that the deception will succeed, while he, Kamin, can confidently assume that he has only to point it out for everyone else to see through it.

Kamin is trying to pretend that Burt had something to gain by including these invariant correlations, when of course Burt had absolutely nothing to gain, would have know that he had nothing to gain, and could not have imagined that his colleagues would for one moment have been deceived. Certainly these invariances show that there is an error somewhere; but we cannot credibly suppose that Burt has deliberately introduced them because he thinks he has something to gain. On the contrary, it would have been in Burt's strongest interest to conceal them, because they immediately suggest something is wrong. There seems no good reason, then, to suppose that Burt deliberately introduced the anomalies because he thought he had something to gain thereby.

This conclusion is strengthened by the analysis we have just completed, for it has shown that the repetitions appear predominantly among the physical measures, and not among those of intelligence. In other words, they become less and less frequent as we approach the area, namely intelligence, where Burt is supposed to have had some interest in deception.

Jensen's account

In Jensen's account (1974: 24) it is also accepted that the invariances 'unduly strain the laws of chance and can only mean error, at least in some of the cases'. But Jensen did not suggest deception on Burt's part. He simply noted that the various mistakes in Burt's empirical data stood in 'strange and marked contrast' to his theoretical writings, which were 'elegantly and meticulously composed' (ibid.: 25). The reader is left to suppose that Burt, at least in later life, was simply not very interested in the empirical side, and 'regarded the actual data as merely an incidental backdrop' (ibid.).

But this explanation, too, is implausible. Throughout his life Burt had shown a marked positive interest in collecting empirical data: his career is punctuated by the appearance of massive publications testifying to this interest; and he had always insisted upon the most meticulous accuracy from his students (Cohen 1983: 70). It would be out of character for Burt to cast aside in his old age the habits of a lifetime; and there is plenty of evidence to suggest that he never lost this interest. Indeed, it is precisely because he retained it that he was setting out his kinship findings in 1966. It would be odd indeed if this paper provided evidence for his lack of interest in empirical data. There is also the circumstance that, on several occasions, Burt took care to correct even quite minor misprints and errors.

Cohen's interpretation

Cohen's interpretation (1983) concedes that it was unwise of Burt to use identical correlations when sample sizes had altered; but Cohen, like Jensen, denies that this constitutes evidence of fraud. If Burt had wanted to commit a fraud, Cohen argues, he would have fabricated different coefficients; and the identical coefficients were quoted merely because the statistical differences, in the particular context, 'did not really matter one

149

way or the other' (Cohen 1983: 72). In other words, Cohen believes that Burt did indeed possess extra material in these cases, and could therefore have calculated fresh coefficients if he had wished; but did not do so because it 'did not really matter'. I do not think this entirely exonerates Burt. It seems to imply that he knew his coefficients were inaccurate, but was too lazy to re-calculate them. It suggests a generally cavalier attitude to empirical data which is unacceptable. The explanation might be correct, but as a defence it is inadequate. In my opinion, however, it is an implausible explanation because the care which Burt takes to correct minor errors strongly suggests that he was concerned with strict accuracy.

Banks's discussion

Banks's discussion (1983: 32–6) employs different kinds of explanation on different occasions. In contrast to Kamin and Jensen, she believes that rather more of the invariants, particularly those for the physical correlations, may be 'genuine' – that is, identical correlations may have turned up from different sample sizes. Perhaps there are more such instances than has usually been supposed, but the observable pattern of physical correlations does not fit this hypothesis very well. For MZ twins, none of the physical correlations remain invariant between 1955 and 1958, but then between 1958 and 1966 all except the correlations for height remain constant. This is most naturally interpreted as indicating that the Ns changed between 1955 and 1958, and the correlations changed with them. But then the Ns remained constant between 1958 and 1966, and so the correlations remained constant too. But if these invariants were 'genuine', one would have expected a much more varied distribution.

In other instances, Banks suggests that Burt repeated old figures because he did not possess any new data, and therefore could not calculate fresh coefficients. Thus where Cohen says that Burt possessed the extra material but did not use it to calculate fresh coefficients, Banks suggests that he did not in fact possess the extra material, so could not calculate fresh coefficients. Banks (ibid.: 36) strongly denies, however, that this constitutes evidence of fraud, because Burt could not have imagined that anyone would be deceived: 'I do not think it would have occurred to him that anyone would think that he could possibly believe that such a large number of coefficients could be really invariant. Equally, had he wanted to fake them, nothing could have been easier.'

This last suggestion (that Burt repeats old figures where he did not possess new data) seems to me to be very plausible, for a number of reasons. First, because if Burt had possessed the extra data there would be no good reason for him not to give fresh coefficients. Second, because there are numerous other instances where Burt makes it plain that he is repeating old figures because he has no fresh data, and this explanation would simply extend the amount of data to be covered in this way. Third, because the invariant coefficients predominate among the physical and educational measures, and these are precisely the measures which are likely to have been dropped when extra material was being collected. Burt would consider he already possessed enough of these, so that attention could be concentrated on collecting more intelligence data. However, if this seems a plausible explanation, there are a number of aspects which require further discussion.

Clarifying the problem

In discussion of this matter, it sometimes seems that assumptions are being made which have not been fully articulated. Consequently, if one mentions the assumption, one is often uncertain what the response will be. To some, it may seem that the problem has been clarified. But others may say that the assumption is obvious – so obvious that there is no need to raise it. At the risk of offending the latter, the problem may be further examined.

The 'problem of the anomalous correlations' is usually posed in the form 'why are so many correlations invariant when the numbers of subjects have changed?' Only a relatively few can be due to statistical chance, or human error. We do not know how many such identities there are likely to be in Burt's data, but there must remain very many which cannot be accounted for in either of these ways. But there is only one way in which so many identical correlations can possibly be explained. They must have been copied from the earlier reports. What has to be explained is why the later correlations are so often identical to those given before. Most cannot be explained by statistical considerations or human error. *That* is what makes them anomalous. *That* is what makes them a problem. But they can only have been copied from the previous reports, otherwise so many identical figures could never have reappeared. The chances of the same figures recurring by chance are so remote that they must have been copied. They cannot have originated in any other way.

It follows that Burt has not been recalculating these coefficients from fresh data – and strangely obtaining identical results. There has been no fresh calculation at all. They are simply the old figures which were calculated previously on the original sample. Burt is not really reporting correlations which have remained the same, even though the sample changed. He is reporting again what he had reported before. In short, strictly speaking there are no 'anomalous' correlations; there are only correlations which appear to be anomalous. Genuine anomalous correlations – except in the rare instances where statistical oddity or human error are at work – are a sheer impossibility. There cannot be such things.

But if Burt must be copying the correlations from old tables, this still leaves many questions. First, is he repeating old figures because he has no fresh data to work on, as Banks suggested; or did he possess fresh data, but did not trouble to re-calculate, as Cohen thought? Banks's suggestion seems more plausible for the reasons given. But does this explanation exonerate Burt? In his defence it might be said that, if he had no fresh data, there is absolutely no reason why he should not repeat the previous coefficients. It is a perfectly sensible and harmless thing to do: if they were valid the first time, they will be valid the second. But there is one important matter which the argument fails to explain: namely, why Burt did not say what he was doing. Why did he not indicate clearly the correct numbers upon which the coefficients were based? Why did he leave it to be supposed that the numbers had altered, if in these cases they had not altered? After all, it would have saved a great deal of trouble if he had mentioned it.

So it is Burt's failure to give the correct numbers that has to be explained. Instead of asking, 'Why did the coefficients remain the same when the numbers changed?', we should be asking 'Why has Burt given the impression that the numbers changed, when in these cases they did not change?' Was Burt trying to conceal something? Was it deliberate or inadvertent? Until we have satisfactory answers to these questions, Burt is not out of the wood.

There are, of course, many other instances where Burt repeats old figures without any difficulties arising. Usually it is obvious enough what he is doing. In Burt (1958), for example, there was really no need to say, because the whole table was identical, and no new subjects were mentioned. So it had obviously been copied. But in the 'anomalous' cases, in Burt (1966a), it is only part of the table which has invariant coefficients, and the numbers at the top of the table suggest that sample sizes have changed (sometimes up and sometimes down). So here, if Burt is just copying from earlier data, it is far less obvious.

This same explanation must be correct for all or most of the remaining anomalies, because there is no other way in which the re-appearance of the old figures could possibly be explained. Moreover, we have seen that the anomalies predominate among the physical measures, which is exactly where there was good reason to expect that there would be a likelihood that fewer data would be added. So why did not Burt indicate clearly what he was doing?

The problem of numbers

Throughout Burt's kinship papers the reporting of the numbers of subjects is unsatisfactory in one way or another. Among the more important instances are the following.

First, already in 1943, the numbers given for the various groups of twins are inconsistent, as both Hearnshaw (1979: 230, footnote 15) and Banks

(1983: 35) have observed. Burt (1943: 91) first says that there were 68 twins in the original survey, and that 121 were added later, which gives a total of 189. He also says that 19 of the 68 twins in the original survey were identical, and that the total number of identical twins was 62. But shortly afterwards Burt refers to 156 non-identical and 62 identical twins, which gives a total of 218 – inconsistent with the first total.

Banks (ibid.) suggests that the figure of 156 non-identical twins is an error, which arose through a confusion between numbers of twin pairs, and numbers of individual twins. Most of the numbers refer to twin pairs, but the figure of 156 may refer to the number of individual non-identical twins. So there would have been 78 twin pairs in this instance. This would be an easy mistake for Burt to make if he was given the figures by an assistant. Banks suggests that an advantage of this analysis is that the total number of non-identical twins which it yields, namely 127, is the same as the eventual number given by Burt (1966a), by which stage he had probably discovered the mistake. The number given in 1955 – namely, 172 – is then interpreted as a mistake arising from the reversal of adjacent figures. The ramifications of this suggestion are too complex to be followed further here.

Second, moving on to 1955, we again find grounds for uncertainty about the exact numbers involved. Burt (1955a: 167, footnote 3) states: 'The figures for head-length, head-breadth, and eye colour are based on much smaller numbers in every batch.' But there is no indication of the precise number, nor of how much the number varied from batch to batch. A possible explanation here would be that the last three physical measures would be relatively unimportant, and also somewhat difficult to collect. It would not be surprising if they were sometimes missed out, and if there was considerable variability from one batch to another.

A further source of uncertainty in 1955 is pointed out by Jensen, in relation to the number of 'unrelated children reared together'. He writes:

> This N is rather ambiguously reported: 'she [Miss Conway] also secured data for 287 foster children' (Burt, 1955, p. 167). Is this then the N for the correlation between 'unrelated children reared together' given in Table I, p. 168? Or are 'unrelated children reared together' only a subset of the total number of foster children?
>
> (Jensen 1974: 22)

When we recall that the N of 172 for DZ twins is also uncertain, we find that, of the total 66 correlations reported in 1955, the numbers on which they were based is uncertain in no less than 34 instances.

Third, Conway (1958) adds a further uncertainty. No N is given for MZ twins reared together, even though the correlations have altered. We can only suppose that it must lie somewhere between the 83 of 1955 and the 95 of 1966.

Fourth, Burt (1966a) certainly seems to offer greater precision. We are now told that the last three physical measures – for DZ twins, siblings, and unrelated children – are each based on 100 subjects. The number of subjects is also for the first time given in the table, so that it is easier to see what Burt is claiming. But even if we are now prepared to accept all the numbers as correct, this does not clear up all the uncertainties. In order to determine which are the anomalous correlations, we have to know not only how many subjects there were in the sample in 1966, but also how many there were in the earlier years. However accurate the figures may be in 1966, the earlier numbers remain as uncertain as before. It is because these earlier numbers are so often uncertain that we said at the outset that the total number of repeated correlations is itself problematic. Our study of the numbers explains at least to some extent why this is so. But it does not make the total any less problematic.

Perhaps, however, we are a little further forward. The question to which we sought an answer was: 'Why did Burt not say that he was repeating old figures where he had no fresh data?' We have seen that it is only in 1966 that repeated correlations make their appearance. It is when we compare the 1966 figures with those given earlier, in 1958 and 1955, that we notice the anomalies. If we do not make those comparisons, we are not aware that there is anything to explain. So it was several years after the 1966 paper was published before anyone made the comparison and raised the problem. So it comes to this: why did not Burt, when writing his 1966 paper, point out that, if the reader compared the current figures with the old, he would find anomalies – some correlations remaining unchanged though the numbers had apparently altered?

I think the answer to this is probably that Burt did not think about it. Burt would be concentrating on the figures for intelligence. The repeated coefficients predominate in the physical and educational measures. Even if he had reflected on the number of those correlations that were repeated, he would have thought it would be obvious to the reader that he did not need any more, so had not collected any more. Moreover, deception would be so far from his mind with regard to these measures, that he would not begin to appreciate what a suspicious mind might think.

To provide a full explanation, he would have had to go back to the earlier papers, and provide further information about the numbers which had been involved then. Since Burt can no longer be questioned, it seems unlikely that we shall now ever know exactly what had happened. Burt might not have been able to say himself. It may be that, in those earlier papers, he was relying chiefly upon the reports and calculations sent to him by Conway; and that some errors or misunderstandings had crept in. It may have been only in 1966, when all the data had been recovered, that Burt was able to check through them for himself, finding some inaccuracies and obscurities in the process. But he would only concern himself with giving an accurate account of the figures as he now possessed them. It would not occur to him that anyone would think it necessary to go back to Burt (1955a) and Conway (1958) and explain any difficulties. In any case, the anomalies would be found principally in the physical measures, which were the least important for his arguments.

How was it, then, that the matter eventually came to light? The most important coefficients were those for the tests of intelligence in MZ twins, especially those reared apart. In this case, therefore, it was not unnatural that someone would remember what the figure had been on earlier occasions, including the figure of 0.77 for the group test. And so the possibility arose that the repetition of the 0.77 would be noticed, together with the odd circumstance that, although the number of subjects had changed, the correlation had remained the same. This figure does indeed appear to have been one of the first which Kamin noticed, and it led him to look for other instances of the same thing. If it had not been for that repeated 0.77, it is likely that nobody would ever have raised the matter of the anomalous coefficients at all. It is ironic, then, that what probably sparked off the whole enquiry was an instance in which a genuine coincidence may well have been involved.

From all this, it follows that 'the problem of the invariant correlations' is something of a red herring. So many invariances can only arise from a deliberate repetition of previous material, and since they predominate among the educational and physical measures, this is perfectly understandable. If Burt had given fuller and more precise information about the numbers involved in each category on every occasion, the repetitions would never have been puzzling. If it occurred to him to do this at all, he may well have thought it would be a quite unnecessary complication. We can now never know what he thought about it, if he thought about it at all, but there is no good reason to imagine some guilty secret.

The new correlations

The realization that the invariant correlations are concentrated among the educational and physical tests leads us to realize also that certain other features of Burt's data are unexpectedly significant. Concentration upon the invariant coefficients has distracted attention from what is actually much more important: those which are new. It might seem that there can be nothing very interesting about new coefficients: the numbers of subjects have changed, so obviously we should expect the coefficients to change as well. But the interest of the new correlations lies in this very fact.

The distribution of the new coefficients is, of course, complementary to that of the invariant coefficients. It follows that, since the invariant coefficients were concentrated in the area of the physical measurements, the new coefficients are concentrated in the area of the tests of intelligence.

There are in fact two sets of new correlations to be considered. There are those which appear in Conway (1958) and those which appear in Burt (1966a).

In Conway (1958), it will be recalled, we are only told that the number of MZ twins reared apart has altered, from 21 to 42. Since the corresponding correlations also change, there are no anomalous correlations here when the figures are compared with Burt (1955a). Hence in Conway (1958) all the correlations listed for MZ twins in Table 6.2 are new.

In Burt (1966a), on the other hand, numerous anomalous coefficients appear. The new coefficients are inevitably complementary to the repeated correlations. They are given in Table 6.5 (below), which shows the new correlations predominating in the tests of intelligence and diminishing in frequency as we move to the physical assessments. Once again, this tendency would be enhanced if the group test for intelligence (MZ apart) was a genuine coincidence.

Table 6.5 Burt's new correlations

[These are the correlations given for the first time in Burt (1966a). They have been 'corrected for minor slips and errors'.]

	MZ twins reared together	MZ twins reared apart	DZ twins reared together	Siblings reared together	Siblings reared apart	Unrelated reared together
Intelligence						
Group	944		552	545	412	
Individual	918	863	527	498	423	
Final ass.		874	543	531	438	267
Educational						
General	893	623		803		537
Reading etc.	951	597	919	842		545
Arithmetic		705		754		478
Physical						
Height	962	943		501		
Weight						
Head length					506	110
Head breadth				510	492	
Eye colour				554	524	

The significance of these findings is as follows. Burt's critics have all along argued that the appearance of an anomalous, invariant coefficient shows that there is something wrong somewhere. We have accepted this argument; and we have suggested that what is wrong is simply that Burt has failed to give a complete and accurate account of the numbers. But by the same logic we must also now argue that the appearance of a new coefficient suggests that the data are genuine. There is nothing anomalous about the appearance of a new correlation when the sample size has changed. It is just what we should expect if the data are genuine. So, using the same logic as the critics, there are no grounds for supposing that in these cases the data are other than they purport to be. Let us pursue this argument in detail.

Conway (1958) states that the number of MZ twins reared apart is now 42, double the number reported in 1955. Hearnshaw (1979: 231) describes this as 'incredible', and regards it as the start of Burt's fraudulent invention of twin data; and Burt's critics have in general treated it as highly suspicious. In the next chapter we shall consider the question where the increased number came from. Here we are simply concerned with the correlations. In this instance every one of the eleven coefficients given in 1958 differs from those given in 1955: they are all new. To regard these as fraudulent would be directly contrary to the line of argument pursued in the matter of the invariant coefficients. There, every identity is treated as a sign that Burt is up to no good. But if repeated coefficients are to be regarded as an indication that Burt is inventing results, new coefficients ought to be seen as evidence that his claims are genuine. In this case, then, we have no grounds for rejecting the natural assumption, namely, that the coefficients change because there are genuine new data. The only alternative is to suppose that there were no new data, and that new figures were being invented in order to mislead the reader. If we take this course, we are simply assuming that Burt must be guilty, whether correlations are anomalous or not.

It is also true that Conway (1958) failed to give the number of MZ twins reared together, though here again all the coefficients have changed. Some may find this suspicious. Yet if the data were fraudulent, and if Burt had gone to the trouble of inventing the new coefficients – and also of inventing the increased number of twins reared apart – it is surely incredible that he should have failed to invent this last piece of required evidence. A guilty man would never have made such an error.

Burt (1966a) again claims to add fresh data, but here we get both new and repeated coefficients. Table 6.5 indicates that the new appear predominantly in regard to intelligence, where at least four of the six coefficients for MZ twins are new. On the other hand, most of the physical figures are repeated. This association is just what we should expect in view of the way in which the data were collected. The physical measurements were both less important and more reliable. Consequently, when adding further data they were the most likely to be omitted, and hence Burt was most likely to repeat a previous correlation. On the other hand, the intelligence data were much the most important, and therefore most likely to be included when fresh data were collected, giving rise to new coefficients.

Thus the unexpected and remarkable outcome of this investigation of the invariant correlations is to direct our attention eventually upon those correlations which are not invariant, but which have changed, and hence to suggest strongly that in these cases, which are precisely those where Burt's critics have been most concerned to show that his data are fraudulent, they are most likely to be genuine.

A number of writers (such as Rimland and Munsinger 1977; Rowe and Plomin 1978; Kline 1980) have argued, with supporting evidence, that Burt's reported kinship data differed so little from the findings of other studies that there was no reason to doubt that they were genuine. Further calculations which are also consistent with their authenticity may be made from the present data. If Burt was in 1966 producing fake data to support the hereditarian position, then it is reasonable to suppose that his 1966 data will show distinct trends in comparison with his 1955 data, the last occasion when, according to Hearnshaw, he was still using genuine data. In particular, two predictions might be made, namely (1) that the coefficients for MZ twins reared apart would show an increase in relation to the MZ twins reared together, thus *reducing* the difference between the two groups and thereby enhancing the effect of heredity; and (2) that the coefficients for MZ twins reared apart would also show an increase in relation to both DZ twins and siblings reared together, thus *increasing* the difference between the MZ twins and the remainder and thereby again enhancing the effect of heredity. (In the case of invariant correlations there could of course be no such trends, so these could not have been introduced in the

Table 6.6 Trends between 1955 and 1966

	MZ twins reared together	MZ twins reared apart	DZ twins reared together	Siblings reared together
Intelligence				
Group	UP	SAME	UP	UP
Individual	DOWN	UP	UP	UP
Final ass.	SAME	DOWN	DOWN	DOWN
Educational				
General	DOWN	DOWN	SAME	UP
Reading etc.	UP	DOWN	UP	UP
Arithmetic	SAME	DOWN	SAME	DOWN
Physical				
Height	UP	DOWN	SAME	DOWN
Weight	DOWN	DOWN	SAME	SAME
Head length	DOWN	DOWN	SAME	SAME
Head breadth	DOWN	DOWN	SAME	UP

interests of this particular form of deception.) Table 6.6 summarizes the actual changes, and it will be seen that, if anything, they are in the direction opposite to the predictions, the coefficients for MZ twins reared apart actually showing a general tendency to diminish. Thus the changes rather suggest a strengthening of the environmental influence, a strange effect for a scheming hereditarian to produce.

Burt's reporting

From Shields (1962) onwards, critics have repeatedly claimed that Burt's accounts of various aspects of his kinship material are seriously defective. Kamin has often been the most virulent, while Jensen and others have usually been less censorious. The main criticisms have centred on the subjects, the tests, and what Burt called his 'final assessments'. In reaching an opinion, it is important to remember that it was only in 'The genetic determination of differences of intelligence' (Burt 1966a) that Burt was primarily concerned to describe his kinship material, and observations which may apply to his other and more incidental references do not necessarily apply to this paper.

The subjects

Both Kamin and Jensen note that Burt gives too little information about his subjects, especially the twins. There are indeed a number of points on which fuller information would have been most desirable. Burt indicates that the MZ twins had all been separated before the age of six months; and he mentions that three cases had been dropped because their separation came later. But nothing is said about the length of separation or age at testing. Probably many would be examined at eleven years old, since this was the regular age for Burt's surveys; but Burt also says that some children, having been tested originally by a local teacher or school doctor, have 'all since been re-tested by Miss Conway' (Burt 1966a: 141, footnote), and in such cases there was presumably a considerable gap between first and second testing. Neither does Burt give the sex distribution of the MZ twins, nor provide detailed histories. He states that the two brightest were sons of an Oxford don who had died just before they were born, and he adds that 'their story is told in full by Conway, 1958, p. 186' (ibid.: 144), but that paper says little more, and certainly does not tell their story 'in full'. Such material would have occupied considerable space, but more detailed case-histories would have been of great interest and would certainly have added verisimilitude to Burt's account. Burt also gives far too little information about environmental differences. He provides a table of the occupational categories of the parents and foster parents of separated MZ twins (ibid.: 143), and also gives data comparing the effects of differences in cultural conditions and material conditions on test results and school attainments (p. 149); but the precise basis of these classifications is too often elusive.

The tests

Kamin (1974) makes numerous strong objections: 'The reports contain virtually no information about the methods employed in testing I.Q.' (p. 57). There is 'no way of knowing what test(s) he used, how well they were standardised, or how test scores might have been combined' (p. 63). Many of Kamin's points seem to be soundly based; but it is far from clear how far he is intending his criticisms to suggest incompetence or bias in Burt, and how far dishonesty.

Burt is by no means as incompetent as Kamin makes out. 'Virtually no information' is going too far. Burt (1966a) does mention the three sources (on page 140) and these are not so mysterious as Kamin would have us think. Jensen's treatment is rather more balanced. He notes that Burt 'never gave very detailed descriptions of the specific psychological tests he used in any given study' (1974: 2), but points out the very simple reason for the omission, namely that as Burt said, 'The tests employed have been fully described elsewhere (Burt, 1921, 1933)' (Burt 1966a: 140). Burt might with some justice have supposed that his readers would take it on trust or look it up. However, there is a possibility that there were in fact changes in the tests or the modes of administration over the years, so there is a problem of comparability here. That Burt often gave less information than was desirable, or less precise information, is a fair criticism; and some of this behaviour might have been motivated, at least in part, by a desire to present his material in a good light. But Kamin exaggerates when he suggests that 'virtually nothing is said of when or to whom tests were administered, or of what tests were employed' (ibid.: 55). Jensen concludes that the group and individual tests of intelligence, and the scholastic achievement tests, are 'quite straightforward' (1974: 2).

Burt's 'final assessments'

Burt was far from believing that the result of an intelligence test was to be accepted automatically, whatever the conditions in which it had been obtained. Noting the variety of special circumstances, such as health or emotional upset, which might disturb the score on a given occasion, Burt advised asking the teacher whether the result seemed satisfactory, and where the teacher thought not, he proposed that 'the child must be re-examined individually, preferably with tests of a non-verbal type' (Burt and Howard 1956: 121–2). Burt also thought it desirable and possible to look beyond such temporary conditions to more permanent influences in the child's surroundings: 'The interview, the use of non-verbal tests, and the information available about the child's home circumstances usually make it practicable to allow for the influence of an exceptionally favourable or unfavourable cultural environment' (ibid.; see also Burt and Howard, 1957; Burt 1958 and 1966a). Finally, Burt claimed that 'when test-results have been systematically checked and adjusted by these means, the reliability of the final assessments, and their correlation with the pupils' subsequent achievements, prove to be far higher than those of a single intelligence test, whether group or individual' (Burt and Howard 1956: 122).

Commenting upon Burt's procedure here, Jensen observes that 'in actual practice his approach to psychological testing and assessment was more that of the clinician than of the psychometric researcher' (Jensen 1974: 3). He adds that Burt's methods seem exactly right for decisions affecting individuals; but he expressed some concern whether there was not a subjective element which was not completely explicit and which made these procedures of doubtful value in scientific research, or at least which meant that they could not be wholeheartedly recommended. Kamin makes the same point in more forceful language: there was 'no adequate description of what rules were followed' in this 'unorthodox procedure' (1974: 60).

It should not be forgotten that Burt gave the correlations for the group and individual tests, as well as his 'final assessment', so the reader could always see what difference Burt's 'unorthodox procedure' was making. There would have been more cause for complaint if Burt had suppressed the test result. The truth of the matter is surely that we do not possess any 'orthodox procedure' which may be 'wholeheartedly recommended' in all circumstances as providing a scientific measurement of intelligence. Over-reliance on psychometric scales has been increasingly criticized. Heim (1954), for instance, spoke of the 'appraisal' of intelligence rather than of its 'measurement', and emphasized the importance of individual judgement. Although – or perhaps because – Burt had done so much to pioneer the various scales, he was very aware of the innumerable factors which could in practice impede their accuracy. Where Burt is, in my opinion, open to criticism is in the statistical expression of his 'final assessment'. Undoubtedly this must often contain a very considerable measure of personal judgement, yet Burt still formulated the outcome in a correlation given to three decimal places, thus implicitly claiming an unjustified degree of accuracy.

Conclusions

The invariant correlations do not provide evidence of deliberate manipulation of data on Burt's part. As many have pointed out, Burt of all people would have known that nothing could have been more suspicious; anyone wanting to deceive would have invented different, not identical, correlations. Moreover, Burt never drew attention to this 'marvellous consistency'. Most significantly, the repetitions appear most frequently in relation to the physical measures, and least frequently in relation to the intelligence scores, so they have the minimum implication for the inheritance of intelligence. The less reason Burt could have for distorting his data, the more the anomalies tend to appear.

Where the invariant correlations appear, Burt must be copying the figures directly from the earlier reports. There is no other way in which so many identities could occur. Two questions arise: (1) why did he do this? (2) why did he not say what he was doing? The most obvious answer to (1) is simply that he repeated the old figures because he had not got any extra data to report – an explanation which is underlined by the circumstance that the repetitions are most frequent among the physical and educational tests which, as we have seen, are precisely those where Burt would be less concerned to collect extra data, or have some difficulty in obtaining it. The answer to (2) is perhaps not quite so clear. But Burt could have no motive for concealing what he was doing: it was a perfectly innocent and sensible procedure. Probably he simply did not realize that any difficulty would ever arise. As we have seen, there were numerous occasions where he did repeat old figures, and where it was obvious enough what he was doing. It probably never occurred to him that it would not be equally obvious everywhere.

Both Kamin and Jensen passed severe verdicts on Burt's kinship data. 'The correlations are useless for hypothesis testing,' wrote Jensen (1974: 24). 'The numbers left behind by Professor Burt are simply not worthy of our scientific attention,' declared Kamin (1974: 71). They may be right, but it is not hard to find reasons for at least some of the deficiencies. The way it was collected over so long a period, by so many different people, inevitably meant that there would be great difficulty in ensuring that everything was complete and consistent. Burt's clinical approach to testing would also be responsible for some aspects which others might find unacceptable.

A further factor, which perhaps has not been given as much weight as it should, is Burt's age. He was over eighty years old when he wrote his main twin paper of 1966. It is not at all surprising if errors creep in which a younger man would avoid. Perhaps Burt's critics will find it salutary to reflect on the numerous errors in their own work.

However, when the many strong and justified criticisms have been made, the most striking outcome of this inquiry is to provide fresh grounds for supposing that Burt's most important data were in fact genuine, whatever deficiencies there may be in his mode of presentation. The new coefficients show a marked tendency to predominate among the tests of intelligence. This strongly suggests that the additional data were genuine.

This conclusion is not to be construed as implying that we can after all rely upon Burt's data. There remain too many obscurities and uncertainties for confidence to be placed in them. But we have so far found no good grounds for accusing him of deliberate fabrication.

Chapter seven

Burt's kinship studies: the missing assistants

With the appearance of Gillie's *Sunday Times* article in October 1976, the criticism of Burt took a dramatic new turn. Hitherto, the emphasis had been placed upon deficiencies in Burt's reports, and anomalies in his data; and explicit accusations of deception are hard to find. Thereafter, the fraudulent invention of data becomes the principal charge.

It is important to notice that the chief arguments which have been advanced for Burt's fraudulence are negative. They have been based primarily upon the absence of evidence that his data were genuine. The most convincing case for their authenticity would come either from the survival of the original records, or from the testimony of research assistants that they had been involved at the relevant times and in the relevant places. But neither of these confirmations has yet materialized. Their absence does not by itself establish Burt's guilt beyond reasonable doubt, because there might well be good reasons for the absence. So the argument between Burt's critics and his defenders hinges upon why these two kinds of evidence are missing.

The absence of the original records has in fact proved to be the less important of these two kinds of evidence. This is because there have been a number of occasions on which such records could easily have been destroyed. The first such occasion was during the air raids of 1941; other occasions arose in the frequent wartime moves that Burt was forced to make; and if any material survived so long, it might well have been destroyed after his death, along with many other of his papers. As regards the records, then, it is not particularly surprising if none have survived, and the arguments here have been more concerned with when they were destroyed – and whether there were any to be destroyed.

The brunt of the argument has therefore fallen on the question of the missing assistants. It has so far proved impossible to demonstrate conclusively that either Howard or Conway ever existed, still less that they helped Burt to collect his data; and reasons for their absence have been harder to find than in the case of the records. So it is the failure to trace them which has been the most important single factor in triggering and sustaining the accusation of fraud. It was this which originally convinced Gillie that he had a good case, and was one of the four main charges which he published in 1976. It was this too which the Clarkes (1977, 1980) advanced as their main argument, and this which Hearnshaw (1979: 239) places at the centre of his own discussion.

An important feature of these later criticisms is that there is not a single 'case for the prosecution', but two different versions. The critics have been divided over the question of when Burt's delinquencies began. A more extreme position, adopted by the Clarkes and some others, argues that Burt was a 'confidence-trickster' all his life. The Clarkes believe that in all probability Burt never collected any data on twins at all, either before, during, or after the Second World War; and that Howard and Conway were figments of his imagination. Burt's claims were a dishonest pretence from start to finish. A more moderate position is adopted by Hearnshaw. He supposes that Burt's delinquencies began only in the 1940s. Hearnshaw accordingly believes that Burt did genuinely collect twin data before the war, probably helped by Howard and Conway. After the war, however, when he wanted it to be thought that he was still actively gathering fresh material, he began to play tricks with his data, and to pretend that Howard and Conway were still helping him. Thus for Hearnshaw, Burt's deception consisted in pretending to continue with a mode of research which had once been real enough, but was real no longer; whereas for the Clarkes, the research was fraudulent from the start.

These two versions are in fairly close agreement concerning the post-war deceptions. Their dispute mainly concerns the genuineness of Burt's pre-war research. We shall begin by considering the evidence for pre-war deceptions.

Did Burt ever collect kinship data?

It is only in comparatively brief publications that the Clarkes have expressed their view that Burt never collected kinship data (Clarke and Clarke 1980a, 1980b), and they do not try to substantiate their conclusion in any detail. They assert that there is 'no evidence that Burt gathered data for himself' (Clarke and Clarke 1980a: 18); but they do not ask how far it is reasonable, after so long an interval, to regard the absence of evidence as significant. The most convincing demonstration today would be the recovery of the original records, but since so many of Burt's papers were destroyed after his death, this is not to be expected. It seems that it is no longer possible to prove that Burt did ever collect kinship data; but there are not in fact any very strong grounds for supposing that he did not, and there are a number of considerations which in combination make it extremely likely that he did.

The only independent support for the Clarkes' total scepticism is to be found in a paper by Sutherland and Sharp (1980), which studied certain aspects of Burt's career before 1940. The conclusion which they reach is, however, comparatively mild: 'The evidence presented here suggests that there are aspects of Burt's work before that date which, if not suspect, are puzzling' (Sutherland and Sharp 1980: 202). This is hardly a damning verdict: it is a considerable step from work which is puzzling to work which is suspect, and a considerable further step to work which is demonstrably dishonest.

After this moderate conclusion, it is not surprising that the evidence given by Sutherland and Sharp is inconclusive. They express surprise at what they describe as a lack of positive confirmation from the pre-war period that Burt collected twin material; and especially at the absence of specific references to Burt's data in the papers of Hogben (Herrman and Hogben 1933) and Cattell (Cattell and Molteno 1940). They are clearly unaware of the evidence already mentioned in Burt (1937a). They also make much of the fact that nobody has ever been able to find any material in LCC records or reports, where Burt (1943: 89) said that some of it had appeared. But such negative evidence can never be conclusive, and the failure to trace the LCC records, in particular, is of doubtful significance. The assumption that such records might have been expected to survive today is not well founded. As Sutherland and Sharp themselves state: 'Our survey of local authority archives 1919–1940 has dramatized the appalling randomness of such survivals' (Sutherland and Sharp 1980: 199). It also seems that Burt's 1943 reference, in which he said that much of the data was 'buried' in typed theses and LCC records, was intended to indicate that it would be hard to find there, not that it was accessible. All in all, this evidence does little to support the Clarkes' position.

Hearnshaw, on the other hand, is able to support his standpoint in a number of ways. Soon after his LCC appointment in 1913, Burt informed Dr Kimmins, the Chief Inspector, of his interest in twins, and asked permission to collect data (Hearnshaw 1979: 39). This does not, of course, prove that any data were collected, but it points that way. Hearnshaw (1979: 229) also states that both Hogben and Cattell were assisted by Burt in obtaining twin material in the 1930s, and there is some support for this in their papers. Hogben certainly acknowledges Burt's help, though only in general terms, and with no specific mention of twins (Herrman and Hogben 1933: 128). Cattell is rather more definite. His study employed some 53 DZ and 31 MZ twin pairs, and he thanks Burt for 'assistance in getting material' (Cattell and Molteno 1940: 46). Presumably this must refer to twins, and therefore strongly suggests that Burt had access to, and was interested in, twin data at that time, as indeed Burt (1937a) indicates. Hearnshaw also supports his case by mentioning that Luria was familiar with Burt's investigations on twins when he began his own work in the 1930s (Hearnshaw 1980: 3). Luria does not go into details, but simply says that 'at the time we undertook this work in the early 1930s, we were familiar with the work of K. J. Holzinger, Cyril Burt, and others' (Luria 1979: 81).

Positive testimony is also furnished by a distinguished geneticist, Dr J. A. Fraser Roberts, FRS, of Guy's Hospital. In a letter to *The Times* (25 November 1976) he wrote as follows:

> From the middle of the 1930s to the middle of the 1950s I was closely concerned with genetic studies on intelligence as measured by Binet IQ and other reliably established tests. . . . Much of our work overlapped with that of Sir Cyril Burt, with whom I was closely associated. I had many long personal meetings with him, during which we went through his data and ours. I found him thoroughly accurate and reliable and our results were in close accord. I should like to condemn most strongly the idea that he cooked his data.

In addition, Hearnshaw (1979: 229, footnote) states that Fraser Roberts informed him that he spent a whole day going through Burt's figures, probably about 1955. There is no specific mention of kinship data here, but it would be odd if it were not involved. It is hard to believe that Burt could have bamboozled Fraser Roberts over so long a period, and his testimony accordingly goes far towards establishing that Burt possessed some genuine material.

But the strongest reason for believing that before the war Burt possessed kinship data, including twin data, lies in a further consideration, which seems to have been overlooked by both Hearnshaw and the Clarkes. Burt always stated that the twins had come to light initially, not as a result of a special search for them, but as a by-product of his general surveys of schoolchildren. Nobody has ever questioned that Burt did in fact, in the course of his work for the LCC, test large numbers of children; and that these results formed the basis of the successive edition of his *Mental and Scholastic Tests*. The proportion of twins, MZ and DZ combined, to be expected in the general population is commonly given as of the order of 2 per cent. Since Burt's initial London survey contained 3,510 children, it should have included approximately 70 twins. Burt (1943) in fact reported that he had found 68 twins (1.94 per cent) in this group. Too much emphasis should not be placed upon the precise figure, if only because we do not know how often both members of a twin pair would be likely to be included in a school survey. The important point is that there must have been some twins, and that the likely number is of the order reported.

Further calculations can also be made. About one-quarter of all twins born are likely to be MZ. This follows (see Burt 1966a: 141) from the empirical observation that generally about 38 per cent of twins are of unlike sex. These must all be DZ. A further 38 per cent must be DZ twins of like sex, since twins of like and unlike sex are equally likely among the DZ population. The likely total for DZ twins is therefore 76 per cent, leaving 24 per cent for the MZ twins, all of whom will be of like sex. It follows that, among the 68 twins reported in the initial survey, around 17 could be expected to be MZ: Burt (1943) reported 19. Burt might, of course, have been inventing appropriate numbers; but since we have sound reasons for supposing that such numbers must have been present, he could have no pressing reason to invent them. The onus of proof is on those who think Burt was romancing.

These considerations strongly support Hearnshaw's conclusion that 'There is no doubt that with the assistance of teachers, medical officers and social workers Burt was able to build up, during the time he was at the LCC, a body of material on twins' (1979: 229). The contrary view of the Clarkes, by contrast, is inadequately supported. The significance of this conclusion must not, however, be exaggerated. In particular, it does not demonstrate that Burt's behaviour was in all respects above board before 1940.

Did Howard and Conway ever exist?

Gillie (1976b) was the first who publicly expressed doubts about whether Howard and Conway ever existed. But several others had already expressed reservations privately. Gillie's doubts were sparked off in the summer of 1976 by Harry Partridge, an official of the British Psychological Society, who told him that he thought Howard and Conway were pennames used by Burt in the journal which he edited; Hetherington confirmed that he had heard that the names were fictitious; and Tizard told him he was convinced they had never existed (Gillie 1980: 9–10). Gillie then conducted his own search, concentrating on the post-war period because this was when they were supposed to have published, and when therefore they were most likely to be known (see Gillie 1977: 257). He could find nobody who claimed to have known them, and nothing in the records of London University, so he too joined the ranks of the sceptics. This is still his position: 'there is no documentary evidence for the existence of Howard or Conway' (Gillie 1980: 12).

The Clarkes soon took up Gillie's theme, though with one modification. Cohen had claimed (*The Times*, 10 November 1976) that he could recollect a Miss Howard at University College before the war; and after this the sceptics concentrated on Conway. So the Clarkes, offering what they called a 'minimum documentation', urged that an important matter requiring elucidation was 'the status, qualifications, whereabouts in the 1950s and role of Miss Conway' (Clarke and Clarke 1977: 83). They placed especial emphasis on the difficulty of finding any evidence that Conway had actually been working with, or even in contact with, Burt during the post-

war period when the sample of separated MZ twins had increased so
markedly. If she had really been doing such important work in the 1950s,
they argued, someone would surely have encountered her and be able to
confirm her reality.

Hearnshaw (1979: 239–45) agrees that there is no trace of the two ladies
in the fifties and sixties, but thinks it likely that they had been genuine
enough before the war, and had helped Burt then. He gives a number of
reasons for this conclusion, in addition to Cohen's recollection, just
mentioned. W. H. Hammond, a research student at Aberystwyth who was
himself a twin, recalled Miss Howard.

> I had my intelligence assessed by Miss Howard, who I know was doing
> research in this field under Burt, together with another woman whose
> name I knew began with 'C', but my recollection of the full name
> escaped me until the present prompting of seeing it in print.
> (Letter of 30 November 1976; see Hearnshaw 1979: 243)

Burt's first published reference to Conway also comes from this period,
when he states that she had been responsible for testing foster children
(Burt 1943: 91, footnote). Hearnshaw (ibid.) comments that there 'seems
no good reason why, at that time, Burt should merely have invented her'.
Since neither woman appears to have been registered at London
University, Hearnshaw thinks it possible that they were 'care committee'
workers doing voluntary social work in connection with London elementary schools. Burt described them as 'the council's social workers' in a
letter to Dr Nichols on 17 March 1964; and he also mentioned the help of
'care-committee workers' in a letter to Eysenck on 27 July 1971. 'So the
most probable conclusion', writes Hearnshaw (1979: 244), 'is that Howard
and Conway were care-committee workers, who assisted Burt in his educational work in the 1920s and 1930s.' This would explain, of course, why
Gillie could find no trace of either woman in London University records.

Further support for the reality of Miss Howard has appeared subsequently. *The Journal of the Association of Educational Psychologists*
(Spring 1983: 40–1) has published a photograph of the Psychological
Society at University College in 1937. Burt is seated in the centre, and
standing immediately behind him is a dark-haired, bespectacled woman
who appears to be about thirty-five years old. Stephenson, who is also in
the picture, is confident that this is Miss Howard; and he adds a report that
she was also identified as Miss Howard by Mrs Raper, the wife of the
laboratory technician at University College at that time (Stephenson 1983:
52). However, Cohen says that she is definitely not the Miss Howard that
he knew (ibid.: 53). There is still no certain documentary evidence for the
existence of either, but Rawles (1977: 354) reports that a Miss M. A.
Howard was a member of the British Psychological Society in 1924, and

asks whether this could have been the notorious Margaret Howard. MacRae (1978) has also reported meeting a Miss Howard in 1949 or 1950, when she delivered to him proofs of a journal article written by Burt.

We seem justified in concluding that Burt did almost certainly collect kinship material, including twin data, down to the 1940s; and also, with rather less certainty, that he was assisted at that time by two care-committee workers, Howard and Conway. So Burt's claims to have possessed such data before the war are in accordance with a good deal of direct and indirect evidence – probably as much as could reasonably be expected to survive after so long a lapse of time. The more important question becomes what happened later on.

The post-war events

According to 'the prosecution'

If the Clarkes and Hearnshaw are sharply opposed in their interpretation of Burt's pre-war conduct, they are united in believing that there is a great deal to condemn in his post-war behaviour. Hearnshaw has set out the case for the prosecution in much greater detail than have the Clarkes, and his argument is as follows.

Hearnshaw believes that Burt collected little or no material after his retirement in 1950: 'it is probable that all his data, such as it was, had been collected prior to his retirement in 1950, most of it, indeed, prior to the Second World War' (1979: 239). Unfortunately, most of this material was destroyed, Hearnshaw believes, in the blitz in 1941, which was a terrible blow to Burt. He had, however, been able to abstract some of the crucial findings before this happened, and this enabled him to make his references to twin material in the 1943 paper on 'Ability and income'. Between the end of the war and his retirement, Burt was able to recruit some additional cases, and it is these which, in Hearnshaw's view, account for 'the small increases in the sample sizes of the various twin groups, and the slight changes in correlations between 1943 and 1955' (1979: 252). It follows that down to, and including, Burt (1955a) there is little scope for supposing that Burt invented very much, so Hearnshaw concludes that 'Burt can be presumed up to this point in time to have been working with authentic data' (ibid.).

Burt's deceptions in this field began, according to Hearnshaw, shortly after 1955 and were concentrated in the area of the MZ twin data, especially the crucial group who had been reared apart. We now encounter two major instances of fraudulent claims. The first concerned Conway (1958), which Hearnshaw regarded as being, at this stage, a front for Burt himself. Here the number of twins rises from the 21 reported in 1955 to no fewer than 42 – 'an incredible doubling of the number of this rather rare group in the space of three years!' exclaims Hearnshaw (1979: 231). The second offence concerns the further increase to 53 pairs of separated MZ twins in Burt (1966a), the largest number ever claimed by a single investigator. The two instances together produce what he called Burt's 'published claims to have collected no fewer than thirty-two pairs of separated MZ twins between 1955 and 1964 (when his 1966 article was sent for publication)' (1979: 240).

Hearnshaw devotes considerable space to explaining just why Burt could not have collected these thirty-two extra pairs of separated twins. In 1955 he was already seventy-two years old, rising to eighty-one by 1964. It is impossible to believe that an old gentleman in indifferent health could by himself have collected so many of this 'rather rare group', especially in view of the travelling and testing that would be involved. But there is also no evidence that either Howard or Conway was available to help during this period. Hearnshaw was unable to find any trace of them, even in Burt's diaries and correspondence: 'he was never visited either by Miss Howard, or by Miss Conway, or by any other assistant actively working for him. Nor is there any trace among his carefully filed correspondence of any communication from any of these supposed assistants' (1979: 240). Additionally, there is no record of anyone else ever meeting either woman during this period; no evidence of Burt ever applying for, or being granted, research funds to support what must have been a considerable under-taking; and no evidence that Burt was ever able to meet the requests for data which he eventually received. Accordingly, Hearnshaw (1979: 239) reached this conclusion: 'we can say with complete certainty that neither Burt nor any of his alleged assistants carried out any field work after 1955.'

Where, then, did the extra data come from which Burt reported after 1955? To Hearnshaw (1979: 252) the answer was only too plain:

It can only have come from three possible sources. It could have involved the reconstruction of data that had been destroyed; it could have been borrowed from other resources; and it could have been simply invented.

Hearnshaw thinks that the first possibility, reconstruction, is the most likely; but any of the three alternatives would, of course, involve inadmissible doctoring of evidence.

Burt has been accused of many lesser falsifications in connection with his kinship studies, but the nub of the prosecution case is that he claimed to have collected 32 extra pairs of separated MZ twins between 1955 and 1966, when in fact neither he nor any of his assistants did anything of the kind. This is essentially the prime accusation which Gillie and the Clarkes had been making since 1976, and Hearnshaw's contribution here is chiefly to elaborate and substantiate their basic suspicion.

According to 'the defence'

The most obvious fact about the case for the defence is that its most essential witness, Burt himself, can never be called, and we can never know how he would have replied to the accusations. The next best thing is to consult those who were most closely associated with him. We can no more assume that they will be unbiased than we can assume that the critics will be, but in elementary fairness to Burt judgement must wait upon a consideration of what is to be said in his favour.

Many of Burt's former associates have expressed their dissatisfaction with the accusations, and they have frequently attacked particular points. But only in Banks (1983) is there a detailed examination of many of the main arguments which have been advanced, and a sustained exposition of many of the chief points to be made in Burt's favour. Banks had not only worked closely with Burt in research and publication, she was also throughout his retirement a frequent visitor to Elsworthy Road. In this way, she became well acquainted with those who worked for him there: with his secretary, Miss Bruce, and his housekeeper, Miss Archer. Banks is thus unique in being well acquainted with both the professional and the domestic side of Burt's life.

The central accusation of Burt's critics – and this is common to Gillie, the Clarkes, and Hearnshaw – is that he claimed to have collected, with the help of Howard and Conway, some 32 separated twins between 1955 and 1966; and that he can have done no such thing. Hearnshaw believes that Burt did collect 21 separated MZ twins before 1950, whereas Gillie and the Clarkes doubt whether he ever collected any; but they all agree that he collected none after 1950. Accordingly, all concentrate their efforts upon showing that he could not have collected those extra twins. In so doing they take it for granted that the defence must respond by trying to show that Burt did collect all those extra MZ twins in the fifties and sixties, that Howard and Conway did help him to do this, and that they did at that time assist him in the preparation of the relevant papers.

But this is not the position adopted by Banks (1983). She accepts that Burt had collected most of his twins before his retirement – though possibly adding a few more later – and does not attempt to establish that Burt or his assistants collected an extra 32 separated twins between 1955 and 1966. In this respect, therefore, she is at one with the prosecution: it is attacking a position which is not defended. But Burt did, of course report an increasing number of separated MZ twins after the war: 21 in 1955; 42 in 1958; 53 in 1966. Where, then, did these additional data come from? Hearnshaw, it will be recalled, could see only three possibilities, all involving some trickery on Burt's part. But there is another possibility, so easily overlooked, as Banks (1983: 22) recounts:

Often, in the 1950s, when going to tea in the flat on a Saturday, I would see the study door open on my way upstairs to the kitchen, knock and interrupt a heated conversation about some papers that Burt needed and Miss Bruce could not find. One day she caught me as I left the study, seized my arm, pulled me into the drawing room next door and said in a hushed whisper, 'You won't tell anyone, not even Miss Archer, will you, Dr Banks, that we can't find Miss (Conway's) stuff on twins?' I said I would not and forgot about it. Some weeks later she met me on the stairs, beaming all over in her rather nervous, exaggerated way, and said, 'Isn't it lovely, Dr Banks; we have found Miss (Conway's) data on twins.'

Banks adds, by way of explanation, that

> I have put Miss Conway's name in parentheses because, although I am sure I recognize it – this took quite a time – and heard it several times in this context, whether or not I should have *recalled* it, I do not know.
>
> (Ibid.; Banks's emphasis)

So Banks believes that Burt possessed, before his retirement in 1950, not only the 21 twins reported in 1955, but a considerably larger number, much of it collected by Conway. But most of this was mislaid during Burt's wartime moves or thereafter, and only recovered in 1957, to be published in 1958. The further data added in 1966 then came either from a further recovery, or from extra cases which had been forwarded to him in response to his appeals for information, or from both sources. Burt merely added the extra data as they came to hand.

Banks's position is much closer to that of Hearnshaw than might have been expected. Both believe that Burt, aided by Howard and Conway, did indeed collect kinship data, including twin data, down to 1950. Both believe that much was lost during the forties – Hearnshaw permanently during the blitz; Banks temporarily during the moves. Both believe that little (Banks) or none (Hearnshaw) was collected after his retirement, when Burt lost contact with the women. The major divergence concerns whether the extra twin data published after 1955 were found or fabricated. These are the bare bones of the rival positions, and we shall next examine the pros and cons.

The collection and loss of the data

The collection of the data

The view of both Hearnshaw and Banks that Burt had collected most of his kinship data, including especially much of those on separated twins, by the Second World War is confirmed by Burt himself, who wrote in a letter to

173

Eysenck in 1971 that 'Most of our own studies of separated twins were accumulated bit by bit between 1913 and 1939' (Hearnshaw 1979: 239). Burt could hardly have done all this without assistance; but in those days research funds were hard to come by, and Burt had to rely mainly upon the unpaid help of those who had ready access to schoolchildren, such as teachers, medical officers, and social workers. Burt mentions especially Miss Pelling, who seems to have been one of the earliest but died young (she is mentioned in Burt 1917: 3, footnote), Miss Molteno (Cattell's co-author in his study of twins), Mr Lewis (about whom little seems to be known), and of course Howard and Conway (see Burt 1966a: 141).

Burt's opportunities for collecting data were probably somewhat curtailed when he moved from the London Day Training Centre to University College in 1933, and they would be still further interrupted by the outbreak of war in 1939. But it is very possible that not all the work had been completed by 1939. As we noted earlier, it is unlikely that both members of a twin pair would always have been tested in the initial surveys, and the unexamined member would have to be located and visited. It is not, then, surprising to find Burt writing that 'If, as was often the case, a certain amount of travel was required to examine the separated twin, then the job was usually delegated to Miss Conway or Miss Howard' (letter to Jencks, 1971). Burt also indicates (1966a: 141) that where a child had originally been tested by a teacher or medical officer, they were later re-tested by Howard or Conway. It is not improbable that some of this work remained to be done during the war years, and this would explain their appearance in Wales at that time.

Banks (1983: 35) suggests that, after the initial London surveys, and at the time when further data were being contemplated, the argument would run rather like this: 'We have enough DZ pairs, all reared together; it will now be better to concentrate on the MZ, especially the rare ones reared apart. These are far more important than the non-identical twins reared apart, about whom more is known and who behave very like ordinary siblings.' Burt certainly seems to have remained interested in collecting further cases of twins after his basic data had been collected, for he is still to be found appealing for more instances in 1955. So it seems unlikely that the twins mentioned in Burt (1943) were by any means all those who were coming along. They were simply those who had been tested so far, and Burt was expecting Howard and Conway to bring him the fruits of their further labours. Hearnshaw (1979: 252) recognizes this possibility when he writes that 'After his return to London, just prior to the ending of the war, it is probable that Burt . . . was able to recruit some additional cases.' There might then be two additional sources for extra MZ twins after the 1943 report: those still being tested from the initial surveys, and those later encountered on a more individual basis. How many there might be in either category we have no means of estimating. It should be added that, whereas most writers speak of the rarity of separated MZ twins, and the great difficulty of finding them, Burt's remarks about getting access to confidential records suggest that he did not think things were quite so hard (Burt 1966: 141).

Hearnshaw (1979: 239) is remarkably confident that Burt could have added nothing whatever after his retirement:

> Burt certainly added no data himself after leaving University College, and there is no evidence of any contact or communication with any assistants . . . we can say with complete certainty that neither Burt nor any of his alleged assistants carried out any field work after 1955.

Hearnshaw appeals to the lack of evidence for contact with assistants or for the possession of research funds. But such negative evidence again hardly justifies such dogmatic assurance.

The case for the defence, as already mentioned, does not in fact rest upon the contention that Burt collected any great quantity of data after 1950, either by himself or with assistance. It therefore has no need to suppose that Burt did possess research funds, and it is happy to accept the absence of assistants because, as already mentioned, Burt himself had indicated that they were not available after 1950. But we certainly cannot rule out all possibility that a small number of cases of separated twins were drawn to his attention after his retirement. In several of his papers, Burt appealed for information on further cases, and he would not necessarily seek formal permission from the education authorities for a brief testing session, possibly conducted in the child's home. Burt's retirement lasted some twenty years. He was fairly active during much of that time. There does indeed seem to be little or no positive evidence that he collected extra cases during this time; but this does not justify a dogmatic certainty that he did not. Hence if Burt claims a few more cases, we are not entitled to convict him of dishonesty forthwith.

This may be the source of the three extra cases which Burt, apparently, mentioned to Dr Sandra Scarr of Yale in a letter dated 22 May 1971. Jensen (1983: 19) is suspicious because Burt failed to mention this to him when he saw Burt less than two months later. But it must be remembered that Burt was then in his eighty-ninth year, and perhaps not eager to prolong the meeting. His reticence at least suggests that he was not, in this instance, concerned to demonstrate that he was still at work – an improbable motive in someone of that age.

Whether or not Burt collected more cases after 1950, Hearnshaw, like Banks, believes that some cases were probably tested during the war years or immediately afterwards. These could not be reported in 1943, and might have remained in the possession of Howard or Conway from some time before they were passed on to Burt. Conway, it will be recalled, was responsible for the calculations, so it may well have been she who had the data. This group may be especially significant in relation to the question whether Burt lost any material, and if so how.

The loss of the data

When Burt's department was evacuated to Aberystwyth at the outbreak of war, a good deal of material was perforce left behind at University College. Much of it was stored in the basement there, where it was hoped it would be safe; but the building was heavily damaged in April 1941, and Burt among others lost much valuable data. The question has been raised whether Burt's losses included kinship material, and especially twin data.

Hearnshaw believes that Burt lost all his original records of twins at this time, though not before he had been able to abstract some of the salient data, which then formed the genuine basis for his papers of 1943 and 1955. The Clarkes, however, cannot agree that Burt lost any such data because they deny that he had any to lose. They support their position by referring to a letter which Burt wrote to the college authorities in 1941, just before the evacuation, in which he requested storage space for some of his papers. Burt wrote that he possessed

> a very large number of documents [which] include many files of case-histories of defective, neurotic and delinquent children, rather large collections of children's drawings, compositions, etc., systematically gathered while I still had access to London schools. It would be both expensive and unnecessary to transport all this for storage to Aberystwyth, and, on the other hand, it would be a great pity to destroy the material.

> (See Hearnshaw 1979: 248–9.)

The Clarkes (1980a, 1980b) argue that what they call 'this catalogue' would surely have included the twin data if any such had existed, for this would have been the most important item; and also that Burt would surely not have referred to the possible loss of such data as 'a pity', when a far stronger word would have been appropriate. Accordingly they take the letter to be a strong indication that Burt had no twin data to leave behind.

Hearnshaw (1980: 3) comments that to call Burt's description a 'catalogue' – that is, a complete enumeration – is 'stretching language beyond its limits'. He contends that Burt was only listing some of the bulkier items, and the use of the phrase 'etc.' shows only that the list was incomplete. One may agree with Hearnshaw that Burt's letter does not exclude the possibility that twin records were left at University College, and were therefore destroyed; but this gives no positive evidence that they were there. On the other hand, if twin records were not included, this does not demonstrate that Burt possessed no such data. There is a third possibility, overlooked by both Hearnshaw and the Clarkes: namely, that Burt did not leave his twin records behind in London, but took them with him to Wales.

Burt's letter does not compel any very definite conclusion. Burt certainly took many documents with him to Wales: books, lecture notes, and so on. It would have been natural to take also any research materials which were either especially valuable or which were related to work he was currently doing. On both grounds the twin data would rate highly: their value is obvious, and Burt may already have been turning his thoughts to the topic of his 1943 paper on 'Ability and income'. It has also to be remembered that Howard and Conway may still have been collecting data on MZ twins in 1941 and subsequently, or have been in possession of such material, and Burt would probably receive such extra data after the blitz in 1941. Since the evidence is so inconclusive, this must be regarded as a real possibility; and in fact there is further evidence to render it plausible.

Hearnshaw's account contains a number of inconsistencies. Sometimes he asserts quite definitely that Burt lost all his research materials in the 1941 raid: 'It is extremely unlikely that his papers would have been dispersed in separate places, and so the presumption is that everything went [to University College]' (1979: 250); 'for practical purposes, there seems no doubt that the large store of data collected by Burt between 1913 and 1939 must be written off as a casualty of the war' (ibid.: 252). But at other times Hearnshaw talks as if not everything went to University College, and not everything therefore was destroyed: 'some papers were transported from the flat in Eton Road to Aberystwyth. It seems to have been a haphazard selection, and it is impossible to determine precisely what went to Wales' (ibid.: 250). Moreover, Hearnshaw writes as if Burt had authentic material with him at Aberystwyth when he was writing his 1943 paper, and, as the Clarkes (1980b) are quick to point out, this is incompatible with his insistence that everything was lost in 1941.

Useful evidence is also furnished by two letters written by Grete Archer, Burt's housekeeper, which are quoted by Hearnshaw but which do not seem to bear out his assumption that everything was destroyed. The first letter, written to Marion Burt on 31 August 1975, includes the following:

> I remember Prof telling me when someone asked about them that he really did not know what had happened to the test sheets from all the schools after he had extracted the twins from them. It was just before the college evacuated to Aberystwyth. As you know the packing was left to Joyce [Mrs Burt], Erna [domestic] and Miss Bruce [secretary]. And Miss Bruce mentioned that they had not enough boxes, and so put a lot

into sacks, which were thrown into a damp and dirty coal cellar on arrival at Aberystwyth.

(See Hearnshaw 1979: 251.)

The second letter, written to Hearnshaw on 16 February 1978, includes the following:

As far as I remember from remarks made either by himself or his secretary, Miss Bruce, neither of them really knew what went where, and whether some boxes were, or were not, left behind in Eton Road. Several times in my presence Sir Cyril asked Miss Bruce whether certain papers or correspondence were stored at University College, or sent to Aberystwyth, and she was never sure of it. Often she explained to me afterwards that at the time it was all a great muddle. The packing was done by different people in a hurry while she was occupied with Prof's correspondence. Everybody was upset and agitated, and nobody made a note of what went where. I also remember Sir Cyril asking Miss Keir and Charlotte [Banks] whether and where his boxes at college may be, but neither knew anything definite. The suggestions were, either still somewhere around, or thrown out when Professor Russell took over or when the whole department moved into new premises. . . . Whilst at Aberystwyth and then again at University College, Sir Cyril told me he was too busy with lectures, his students and college affairs to miss packed up material. It was only after his retirement, when he revised some of his books, and wanted to work on his accumulated material, that he realised that a lot of it had got lost somewhere, and started to ask for it. I think I told you once in which state I found material from Aberystwyth in one of the attic rooms, when I joined the household in 1950, and tried to sort it out and preserve and file somehow the still readable and usable remains of it. Sir Cyril was always very glad afterwards to find something 'useful' upstairs.

(See Hearnshaw 1979: 251)

These two letters by no means seem to confirm Hearnshaw's conclusion that, for practical purposes, everything was lost in 1941. They surely suggest that a good deal may have survived. They suggest (1) that Burt had extracted twin data from the test sheets just before the move to Wales; (2) that some material may have been sent to Aberystwyth, or left at Eton Road; (3) that material from Aberystwyth was stored in the attic (at Elsworthy Road) after the return; and (4) that Burt did not miss it until after he had retired, when he was always glad to find something 'useful' (that is, there was useful material to be found in the attic, and it was sometimes so found). These points can only be regarded as lending considerable plausibility to Banks's recollections about the finding of lost material, to which we may now return.

Archer's letter of 16 February 1978, indicating that after his retirement Burt realized that a lot of material had been lost, and started to ask for it, is consistent with Banks's recollections. There had certainly been plenty of opportunity of losing things, either during the wartime moves to Wales and back, or during the move to Elsworthy Road, or when Burt left University College – not to mention as a result of air raids. In addition, Miss Bruce, whatever her other merits, was not one to maintain a methodical filing system: Banks (1983: 22) recalls that 'There was an enormous amount of paperwork dating back a very long time, pretty higgledy-piggledy, and occupying much space in the attics in London. This filing muddle was a great drawback.'

Banks's recollections of the recovery of lost material have already been quoted. She had in fact given a rather fuller account in a letter to Jensen, dated 17 November 1978. Since this was written before the appearance of Hearnshaw's biography, it cannot be said that her story was concocted to counter his arguments. Some extracts follow:

I have quite clear memories about this and am quite sure in my own mind what happened. Some data of Howard's and Conway's was lost and could not be found on and after Burt's return to London after the war. This explains a lot. I didn't remember anything for a month or so, but then suddenly recollected that in the fifties Burt asked Miss Bruce, his secretary for 40 years, where Miss So-and-so's data on twins was. He asked her in front of me on purpose, I think. One day, when I went for tea, she lay in wait for me on the stairs, before I got up to the kitchen, clutched my hand (this was very characteristic behaviour) and took me into the drawing room and shut the door. She said 'You won't tell anyone, will you Dr Banks, about Miss So-and-so's data being lost? Not even Miss Archer, I feel so ashamed. I'm sure I haven't seen it, but the Professor is getting very cross', or words to that effect. I said I wouldn't tell anyone and put it out of my mind. Burt went on asking her about it, and then one day I was coming up the stairs as Miss Bruce was coming out of the study, and she leaned over the bannisters and said 'Isn't it lovely, Dr Banks, we have found Miss So-and-so's data?' She was wreathed in smiles and seemed very relieved. I didn't connect these rather insignificant memories at first with loss of twin data, but suddenly the penny dropped, some months after all the criticism had begun. I told Hearnshaw about it, and Professor David, and later Grete Archer.

This explains a great deal. All I can remember is that afterwards Burt was doing a great deal of calculating and it was to do with twins.

In order to understand this situation one needs to know something about Miss Bruce. . . . She was a marvellous shorthand typist, but had

had a bad breakdown, psychotic I would think. She was very accurate, but couldn't file for toffee, and was very sensitive to criticism. To give you one example, in the war, when Burt's elderly housekeeper had 'flu, someone important was coming to tea, so Miss Bruce said she would do tea. I went for a walk with Burt . . . and when we got back to the house Miss Bruce had burnt about 20 pieces of toast and gone to bed, terribly upset at having let the Professor down . . . and I think Miss Bruce stayed in her room for several days in tears, probably. No-one was allowed into her room in London, even to clean it. It was usually done while she was away. . . .

Burt often told me how much he owed her, and how accurate her work was; also how much he appreciated her loyalty. She died of cancer in 1958. [Hearnshaw also gives 1958 as the year of Bruce's death; but Banks, since writing the letter, has studied Burt's diaries and corrected the date to 1959.] I think she must have typed the draft of the Conway paper (1958). She could not, I am sure, [have] been persuaded to type any statement about data being lost. She would have taken this as a public criticism of herself broadcast for all the world to see, even if her name wasn't mentioned. . . . I am sure he would have promised her not to say the material had been lost. And, knowing him, he would not have published any statement after her death.

(Letter from Banks to Jensen, 17 November 1978)

These recollections certainly provide possible answers (whether we can accept them or not) to some urgent questions, especially where the extra material reported in Conway (1958) came from, and why Burt did not mention its origin. Furthermore, our examination of the correlation coefficients has stressed that, in Conway (1958), all the figures for MZ twins are new, which strongly suggests that they are genuine.

But of course this still does not account for the further eleven separated MZ twins reported in 1966; and why Burt was equally uncommunicative about their origin. Were these a further find somewhere in the attics? Or perhaps some extras derived from Burt's appeals for more cases? Or perhaps from a mixture of such sources? Or were these a figment of his imagination? There does not appear to be any very positive evidence that would allow us to decide among these possibilities, except, once again, in the arguments derived from our examination of the new coefficients. The extra eleven MZ twins may be regarded as suspicious; but one cannot convict Burt of fabrication on a suspicion, especially since he cannot defend himself.

Burt's eventual total of fifty-three separated MZ twins is the largest ever collected by a single investigator, and is certainly impressive. But it is by no means beyond the bounds of possibility. By 1966, exactly fifty-three years had elapsed since Burt had first expressed an interest in collecting twin data, back in 1913, and an average of one pair per year is not excessive. Shields reported the respectable total of thirty-seven separated pairs, collected over a shorter period, and nobody has questioned his probity.

Burt's claims

We have so far stressed that the 'defence', like the 'prosecution', believes that the greater part – though probably not all – of Burt's twin data was collected before 1950. But the 'prosecution' also asserts that Burt claimed to have collected many pairs after 1950; and it is this, of course, which leads to their charge of deception. Burt's critics have concentrated their attacks against what Hearnshaw (1979: 240) calls 'His published claims to have collected no fewer than thirty-two pairs of separated MZ twins between 1955 and 1964 (when his 1966 paper was sent for publication).' It is just as important for the critic to establish that Burt made these claims, as it is for the critic to establish that he could not have collected the data during those years. Yet far more attention has been given to the latter than to the former task. But did Burt publish such claims? And did he claim that Howard or Conway had helped him to collect the extra thirty-two pairs between 1955 and 1964?

Such claims might be either explicit or implicit. By an explicit claim I mean one in which the claim is clearly and expressly made in writing. By an implicit claim I mean one which is implied – for example, by the use of the names 'Howard' and 'Conway', without actually stating what it was that they did. Explicit claims will be considered first.

Explicit claims

The most obvious place for Burt to publish his claims would be in those papers where increased numbers are reported; namely, Burt (1955a), Conway (1958), and Burt (1966a).

Burt (1955a: 167) credits Conway with collecting 'further data' and undertaking 'final computations' for the 1943 paper; and also with having been able 'to increase the number of cases, particularly for the small but crucial groups of monozygotic twins reared together or apart'. But there is no possible way in which a paper published in 1955 can be regarded as making claims about what was collected between 1955 and 1964; and it is plain that Burt is talking about 'further data' collected since his original London survey.

Conway (1958: 186) states that 'Since the last review of our own cases was published' [reference to Burt 1955a] 'our collection has been still further enlarged. . . . The number of cases of this type – all identical twins reared apart from early infancy – now amounts to 42.' Obviously this phrase could be taken to mean that the data had been collected since 1955, as the Clarkes (1977:83) take it. But it is also a somewhat indirect way of talking. Conway does not, for instance, say that since the last review 'a further 21 cases have been collected, making a total of 42'. The phrasing is consistent with the possibility that Burt, in accordance with his promise to Miss Bruce, is concealing that they had been lost. It should be noted that this paper contains only a short reference to twin data, that the extra data play a minor role, and that all the MZ twin correlations differ from those given in 1955.

Burt (1966a: 140), after mentioning several previous papers from Burt (1943) to Conway (1958), continues:

Meanwhile, largely as a result of these various discussions, further cases of separated twins have been brought to our notice, and more information has been obtained for the earlier cases from the follow-up inquiries. The main purpose of the present paper therefore will be to bring together the evidence now available both from our studies and from more recent investigators.

In a footnote on the following page, Burt lists his helpers, including Howard and Conway, but there is no suggestion that any have been recently involved in gathering data. There is no specific claim that either Howard or Conway had collected data recently, and there is a definite suggestion, in the last line of the above quotation, that other investigations have been more recent than his own. In addition, there is a definite indication that some of his report will concern extra information about old cases. Nowhere does one find a claim that thirty-two pairs have been collected since 1955. If Burt is trying to claim recent research he is remarkably reticent about it.

Opinions may legitimately differ about the precise implication of Burt's published claims. In my opinion, the only plausible instance of a claim to have collected extra cases since 1955 comes in Conway (1958), in the passage quoted. The place where one would have supposed a clear claim was most likely to appear is Burt (1966a), yet this seems if anything to be stressing the antiquity, not the recency, of Burt's data. Hearnshaw passes over this remarkable silence without seeming to notice it. The Clarkes (1977: 83) give a curiously obscure reference: 'In 1966, Burt (p. 141) reports that he had now studied 53 pairs of separated MZ twins, and Miss Conway's 1958 paper is referred to (p. 140, where a detailed statement of the elaborate and unusual testing procedure is given, and in an important footnote p. 141).'

Hearnshaw (1979: 239–40) also refers to Burt's letter to Eysenck of 27 July 1971 in which he told Eysenck that 'Most of our own studies of separated twins were accumulated bit by bit between 1913 and 1939.' This is, of course, in flat contradiction to the repeated assertion that Burt published claims to extra MZ twins between 1955 and 1966. There would seem to be no good reason why Burt, who is supposed to have been trying to build up the impression of recent research, should so readily throw it all away and admit the truth to Eysenck. Rather it appears that Burt was simply not aware of any contradiction. Hearnshaw makes no attempt to explain why Burt should behave so oddly. He simply treats it as an instance of Burt's alleged 'inconsistency', asserting that 'the accounts given in his published papers were quite different' (1979: 240). He then offers three supporting items.

The first is the statement in Burt (1955a) that Miss Conway had collected further data. But this, as we have seen, is irrelevant to the point at issue, and is perfectly consistent with Burt's statement that most of the twin data were collected earlier; indeed, this is what the paper is indicating.

Second, Hearnshaw sees an inconsistency between a statement in Conway (1959) that many cases were ascertained through personal contact, and a letter to Jencks saying that all the assessments were done in the course of routine work. The truth seems to be that both sources were used, for Conway (1958: 186) writes that 'our earlier cases were encountered during the routine inspections . . . among our later cases most were discovered through personal contacts'. So this seems a very minor slip. Furthermore, Conway (1959: 11) states that the children were 'tested by Burt and myself in 1950'.

Third, in a letter to Humphries in 1968 Burt stated that since his Bingham lecture 'we have added considerably to the number of our separated MZ twins'. Hearnshaw (1979: 240) describes this as 'a direct contradiction of what he later wrote to Eysenck'. But is it any real contradiction to say (to Eysenck) that 'most of our own studies of separated twins were accumulated . . . between 1913 and 1939' and (to Humphries) that 'we have added considerably to the number'.

It is to be noted that the last two items are not only unconvincing; they also depend upon statements made in private letters. Hearnshaw has actually produced no clear evidence that Burt made the 'published claims' which he alleges. Burt does not seem to have been at all eager to make the claims that his critics ascribe to him.

Implicit claims

There can be no denying that Burt used the names of Howard and Conway either alone or in conjunction with his own, and that the number of subjects increased from 1955 onwards. We shall first ask whether there are good grounds for supposing that Burt intended to make an implicit claim of the kind ascribed to him by Hearnshaw, perhaps cleverly calculating that if challenged he could say that he had never intended the claim. Plainly, the use of these names implies that the owners thereof helped in some way. Archer recalls what Burt had told her:

He had trained them both in testing children and adults, and so they were able to assist him in collecting most of the data when he was still working for the London County Council and later at University College. Professor Burt told me that he had promised to acknowledge their great help later on, when he was retired and had more time to collate the data for the papers he intended to write and publish. He thought it only fair to mention and include both as coworkers in his articles

(Archer 1983: 53)

In so far as Howard or Conway do appear as 'coworkers', that is, where they are named as co-authors with Burt, the position is straightforward enough. Multiple authorship is a common practice, and often entails a senior author directing the work of junior colleagues or research assistants. The senior author is generally regarded as bearing the prime responsibility for the conduct of the whole enterprise, including the writing of any papers, their dispatch for publication, and the management of any correspondence which may ensue. He would also, almost certainly, bear the brunt of any resulting criticism, and be expected to defend the work in public. The nature and extent of the work done by the junior members may vary greatly from one case to another. They might assist in data collection, in statistical analysis, in writing particular sections, and so on. There is no reason whatever to assume that the junior members will be around when the paper is actually written. They might have moved to another job, in another university, possibly in another continent. They need not have read the paper before it is published, and perhaps not even afterwards. They might indeed be dead, as in the case of Eysenck and his research assistant Thelma Coulter, who died in a car crash before Eysenck, perfectly properly, wrote a research paper on their joint work (see Gibson 1981: 222).

The commonest abuse is for the senior author to give too little credit to his helpers. There would seem, therefore, to be no serious objection to the appearance of papers in which Howard or Conway are named as co-authors with Burt, though they might not have seen the papers before or even after they were published, and might indeed have emigrated or died years before. Burt may properly be regarded as giving them no more than their due – assuming that they really did help him – and he might indeed have been justly criticized if he had not used this accepted way of acknowledging their help.

It is a different matter, however, when a paper appears with the name of Conway alone, as in Conway (1958). It is clear enough in the paper that the writer has been working with Burt. The table of twin correlations in Conway (1958) is headed 'Burt and Conway', just like that in Burt (1955a). But there is no indication in these papers that Burt has been in any way involved in the writing, or bears any responsibility for what is said. On the contrary, the plain implication is that a certain J. Conway takes full responsibility. Yet we have every reason to suppose that, however much she may have done at some time in the past to collect and analyse the data, to draw the conclusions, and even perhaps to have written quite lengthy sections of the paper, nevertheless, it is most improbable that she saw the paper before it was published, and may never have known of its existence. It is most important to note, however, that, so far as the alleged fraudulent kinship data are concerned, Conway (1959) gives no data at all, while Conway (1958) makes it perfectly clear that the data given are the joint responsibility of Conway and Burt. Why, then, did Burt place her name alone upon the title page, especially when it would have been so easy to add his own name to place everything beyond serious objection?

This matter needs to be considered in relation to another, closely related, practice which Burt adopted. He frequently wrote letters, comments, and even occasional book reviews, and published them in his *Journal* under various pseudonyms. This behaviour has been interpreted in diametrically opposite ways. Hearnshaw sees it as 'a convenient device whereby Burt could express his views, and call attention to his own achievements . . . without his too obviously monopolising its space' (1979: 245). He sees it, in other words as an expression of Burt's self-aggrandisement. Banks (1983: 38) sees it in precisely the opposite light:

> Being shy and modest, he felt most embarrassed, when editing the statistical journal, at publishing so much himself. . . . The so called fake letters, some of which could well have been his, would have been simply an attempt to get replies and stimulate interest in the journal . . . surely there is nothing wrong in using a nom-de-plume in a good cause, successful or not.

Burt himself does not seem to have regarded the practice as reprehensible. He continued so long and on such a scale, and sometimes with such transparent pseudonyms, that he can hardly have been concerned about discovery; and in fact their true author was widely guessed well before his death. When Gillie tried to trace Howard and Conway he was told they were probably pseudonyms. Indeed, in a letter of 16 June 1970 to Mrs Heywood, Burt discussed and defended the use of pseudonyms in general. 'After all,' he wrote, 'no one thinks the worse of Daniel, Job or Ecclesiastes because they were not written by their ostensible authors: even pseudo-Dyonysus should not be decried as "a fraud by a monk of the middle ages" as a twentieth-century ecclesiastic declares. It was, as you say, quite a permissible device in those oriental cultures.' This is hard to assess. Was he just eccentric, as Cattell (1978) suggests? He certainly seems to have been oblivious to the suspicions which some of his colleagues were likely to entertain.

Returning now to the papers where Conway is given as the sole author: Burt's general use of pseudonyms must greatly strengthen the suspicion that Howard and Conway too were fictitious. Hearnshaw sees Burt's use of the names of both Howard and Conway as an extension of his general use of pseudonyms. They were 'members of a large family of characters invented to save his face and boost his ego' (1979: 244–5). Hearnshaw has no difficulty in divining an unworthy motive in Burt's behaviour – indeed, several unworthy motives. But the following passage shows on what slender evidence he is prepared to base conclusions: 'Firstly, they were a sop to Burt's feeling of isolation. Burt always fancied himself as the focus of an active school of researchers. One of his favourite phrases was "I and my co-workers." The truth was rather different.' (ibid.). Hearnshaw offers no evidence for any of these aspersions. It is not hard to suggest unworthy motives for the behaviour of others and thereby discredit them. Of course, if Burt felt as Hearnshaw alleges, his behaviour would become comprehensible. But his behaviour becomes comprehensible if we postulate a whole range of other motives. Why, for instance, should he not want to recognise Conway's help?

Hearnshaw (ibid.) continues:

> Finally, and most important of all, Howard and Conway enabled Burt to maintain the fiction that he was still actively engaged in research . . . he was fond of accusing his opponents of basing their criticisms 'not on any fresh evidence or new researches of their own, but chiefly on armchair arguments from general principles'. [Reference to Burt, 1966a, p. 139.] 'My co-workers and I', on the other hand, were engaged in on-going research. It was a powerful argument with which to belabour the environmentalists.

An incautious reader, who has not yet learned the advisability of checking Hearnshaw's references, would naturally conclude that in 1966 Burt contrasted the armchair arguments of the environmentalists with his own 'fresh evidence' and 'on-going research'. And it was, says Hearnshaw (ibid.), 'this pretence of on-going research which the evidence of the diaries reveals as a complete fabrication'. But the evidence seems incapable of bearing this interpretation. Burt makes the criticism of the environmentalists which is given in the quotation. But he is not in fact comparing their 'armchair arguments' with any 'fresh evidence' or 'new researches' produced by himself, or indeed by anybody else. He is not comparing their 'armchair arguments' with any *fresh* evidence whatever. He is comparing the arguments of the environmentalists with the whole long line of genetic evidence which had been brought forward from Galton onwards. He is objecting that, when the environmentalists criticize this long tradition they base their arguments 'not on any fresh evidence or new researches of their own, but chiefly on armchair arguments.'

Burt does not follow this by making any pointed comparison with his own 'on-going' research' or 'fresh evidence'. He does indeed go on to mention his own researches. But the phrase 'my coworkers and I' does not appear for another forty-two lines, and it is then followed by a reference to his first London survey in 1921. I have read and re-read these pages in Burt (1966a), and I can find no ground whatever for supposing that Burt has any intention of drawing the contrast which Hearnshaw alleges. Indeed, this first section of Burt's paper ends by stating that its main purpose is 'to bring together the evidence now available both from our own studies and those of more recent investigators' (Burt 1966a: 140). This phrasing seems rather calculated to indicate that Burt's studies are not among the most recent; indeed, the whole of this section (pages 137–40) seems to me to be far more concerned to stress how long ago Burt had started to collect material, than how recently he had been collecting it. If Burt had presented so distorted an account of the views of one of his opponents, as Hearnshaw has here presented of the views of Burt, then Burt would probably have been accused by his critics of deliberately twisting the evidence. Hearnshaw would rightly resent any suggestion that his own distortions were deliberate.

Burt's motives

The question whether Burt made the alleged claims becomes a discussion of what his motives were in publishing his kinship data. Burt's critics ascribe unworthy motives to him, and interpret his behaviour accordingly. His defenders detect worthy motives, and find it equally easy to interpret it in their way. But it is a truism that even the simplest human behaviour is often susceptible to a great variety of interpretations. Why did the gentleman raise his hat to the lady? Perhaps out of mere formal politeness; perhaps because he was genuinely pleased to see her; because he hoped to make a favourable impression; or perhaps he was not raising it to her at all, but only settling his hat more comfortably on his head. It is all too easy to find an intepretation that suits us, and assume that it is the only possibility. But even if it is correct, it may not be the only one or the most important. We like to kill as many birds as possible with one stone; and the behaviour which is supported by most motives stands a good chance of being the strongest and therefore of prevailing.

Hearnshaw suggests that Burt's main motive was to reply to attacks upon his position from the environmentalists. These attacks came, he says, in two waves – in 1953–4 and in 1963–4 – and Burt wrote his papers in pique to reply:

His two twin articles of 1955 and 1966 were his rejoinders, as he himself makes clear, and were motivated by a determination to get the better of his critics. They were not, in the proper sense, research reports, written calmly and painstakingly, following the patient collection and cool analysis of the data. They were written in haste and anger.

(Hearnshaw 1979: 241)

It was his emotional involvement, according to Hearnshaw, that was his undoing, for it explains why he did 'such a botched job of deception, and left so many loose ends and contradictions in his reports' (ibid.).

That both articles were, at least in part, intended to reply to environmentalist critics is true enough. But Hearnshaw suggests that Burt's motive in replying was nothing but personal hostility and aggression: he wanted to get the better of his critics. Burt is not permitted to wish to defend a position which he believes to be true, because he believes it to be true; nor is he allowed, as a leading hereditarian, to have any duty to reply to critics in the interests of scientific truth. Of course Burt, being human, might well also feel a personal hostility to his critics; it is notoriously difficult to avoid such animosity creeping in. We can all therefore feel that there may well be an element of truth in Hearnshaw's allegation. But only those with an excessive dose of humbug will imagine that such motives render Burt an exception, a mere self-seeker with no redeeming features, while all the rest of us are free from such crude motives and may sit in judgement on this base fellow. But we must be cautious. Hearnshaw will presumably have his evidence ready. How, then, does he support his allegations? How, in particular, does he support the assertion that Burt wrote these articles in haste and anger?

So far as Burt (1955a) is concerned, Hearnshaw offers no evidence whatsoever. Had he looked for evidence, he would have found that Burt (1955a) is not properly to be described as a 'twin article' at all. It is a general review of ideas and sources of evidence about intelligence, with a small section towards the end summarizing the kinship data, of which the twin data form only part. It does not purport to be a 'research report' at all. It is in fact a calm and thorough piece of work, which treats his critics with scrupulous fairness and detachment. There is no evidence that it was written in 'haste and anger'.

So far as Burt (1966a) is concerned, Hearnshaw again offers no evidence that it was written in anger. He does, however, attempt to show that it was written in haste. He argues that Burt's diaries indicate that he started to write it on 13 May 1964 and finished on 19 May 1964. Hearnshaw regards this as excessively hasty. But everything surely depends upon how well Burt's material was prepared when he started. Having been familiar with the field for at least fifty years, he might be supposed to find it fairly easy; and a simple calculation shows that he must have written about 1,200 words, or two pages, per day – by no means an impossible labour. We also know that the paper underwent considerable revision. Hearnshaw himself notes that it was revised a number of times, while the journal in which it appeared gives 8 September 1965 – fifteen months later – as the date when the manuscript was received. So the diary notes appear to refer simply to the start and finish of Burt's first draft, and really offer no evidence of haste. Banks (1983: 31) comments as follows: 'I have reread these two papers and can find nothing approaching haste and anger; an awful lot of history and scholarly argument, yes, as well as evidence; many references to other work as well as his own; a well-balanced summary in each case.'

The missing evidence

The case against Burt rests primarily upon the absence of any trace of either his research assistants, Howard and Conway, or his original data; but, as we pointed out, the significance of this negative evidence depends upon the likelihood that either could now be found. The absence of such convincing positive evidence permits the critics to accuse Burt of fabricating his data; but the strength of their case depends heavily upon what alternative explanations are available.

The missing assistants

So long as it is supposed that the defence must establish that Howard and Conway were in touch with Burt during the fifties and sixties, the failure to trace them is a strong argument. It is hard to believe that they could have been so recently around, collecting important data, without anyone being aware of it; and even harder to believe that they could both have lived through the publicity of the seventies without coming forward. The position is radically changed when it is realized that the defence is happy to accept that Howard and Conway were not in touch with him after 1950, and probably started to help in the twenties and thirties. Thus Archer (1983: 53) says that Burt told her that Howard and Conway worked for him while he was with the LCC. In this case, they could hardly have been born later than 1900 – a guess consistent with the apparent age of 'Howard' in the Psychological Society photograph of 1937. They would therefore in all probability have been in their late seventies when Gillie wrote his *Sunday Times* article, and in 1987, if still alive, they would be in their late eighties. It is possible they were older: if they were the same age as Burt himself, they would have been in their nineties in 1976.

It is possible, as Archer suggested, that they emigrated in 1950. If they did, they would be very hard to trace now. The Australian High Commission in London does not keep migration records for individuals from as far back as 1950 (letter of 6 February 1984); and the Canadian

Consulate General keeps no records once a person has been legally admitted to Canada (letter of 3 February 1984). In any case, they would probably now be dead.

There are so many imponderables that nothing very definite can be deduced simply from their absence; and we are most unlikely to get much further than the few isolated recollections we already have. The 'missing ladies' were an admirable subject for sensational speculation in the media. They are an unprofitable basis for sober conclusions.

The missing data

If there seems little likelihood that the assistants will now be traced, there seems none whatever that any original records will ever be found. If any material was in existence when Burt died, there is no mystery about what must then have happened to it. The greater part of Burt's papers were destroyed a few months after his death before even an inventory of their contents had been compiled. This extraordinary occurrence deserves a fuller account.

Burt left no instructions for the disposal of his books and papers. The books presented no problem: they were donated to various universities and libraries. But the papers posed difficulties. There was a great quantity to be accommodated: according to Banks, the whole of the top floor of the flat – two attics plus landings – was filled with records and documents which had never been properly filed. Marion Burt, now in her eighties, could not travel from Malvern to take care of so much. Miss Archer wanted to vacate the flat without delay, and in any case it is hardly the duty of a housekeeper to act as a literary executor. What, then, was to happen to this unique record of British psychological history?

It might have been supposed that Hearnshaw, as the accredited biographer, would have been happy to assume responsibility. He certainly visited the flat and removed a few items, including some of Burt's diaries and correspondence, but the great bulk was left. 'Nobody was available to spend weeks sorting through Burt's papers in detail,' he explains (1979: 238). But what was needed was not instant scrutiny; only a telephone call to a removal firm, who would have stored everything cheaply and safely until it could be properly studied. Hearnshaw, however, left everything to Miss Archer, saying, 'Keep as much as possible. If in doubt the best policy is to keep and send to me' (ibid.: 238).

What happened next is described by Miss Archer in a letter of 10 May 1975:

> In the end, I decided to burn all the papers which, as far as I knew, had already been published, but was not quite sure about the material in 2–3 large boxes in the attic. So one evening when Michael Young brought

Liam Hudson along to see me, I took them upstairs, showed them the boxes and told them I don't know anything about statistics, but guess they contain the material he had accumulated for his articles on twins, which were published, but I was still in doubt whether I should destroy it or not. They both thought I could burn the whole material (consisting of bundles of test sheets with name and age of children given at the top, long strips of figures and calculations etc.) if it had already been used for publication.

(See Hearnshaw 1979: 238.)

Cohen has commented as follows:

It is hard to believe that anyone could be so tasteless and so lacking in good faith as to take it upon himself to participate in deciding to destroy the documentation of one who, while he was alive, you treated as your bitter enemy, and on whom, after his death, in a radio discussion, you heaped calumny.

(Cohen 1983: 70)

Hudson himself, in a letter to Archer dated 24 May 1975, gives his point of view:

There was really no point in preserving them: only Professor Burt himself could have reassembled and reworked them, should there ever have been cause to do so. Whether they dealt specifically with his twin studies, or some other project, I do not know.

It was not very long before others wanted to inspect Burt's documents. Jensen writes as follows:

In hopes that some of the original data might be recovered after Burt's sudden death in October 1971, I corresponded with Burt's personal secretary about the possibility and also looked into it further when I was in London the following summer. But by then, alas, nothing remained of Burt's personal possessions save various notes, letters, manuscripts, reprints, and books. I was told that shortly after Burt's death many of the books and journals had to be sold and donated to university libraries, and that many boxes of old data, which Burt had kept for many years, were disposed of in the course of vacating his flat in Hampstead. These boxes, etc., I was informed, were either poorly labelled or not labelled at all, so that their exact contents were not apparent to casual inspection. And so, unfortunately, the original data are lost.

(Jensen 1974: 24–5)

Hearnshaw's conclusion is that 'There is, in fact, no certainty that the material in the boxes did relate to twins, and some reason to think, as we shall see, that most of it at any rate did not' (1979: 238). This is true, but it is not the whole truth. Although there is no certainty that the material related to twins, there is some reason to think that it did, namely, the suggestion made by Miss Archer. Further, it is important to remember that, whether or not there was twin material in those boxes, there must have been twin material somewhere if Burt's data were genuine. Whether these data were in those two boxes, or somewhere else among the papers, is immaterial. What is important is that there is no certainty that Burt's kinship data were *not* somewhere in those attics; and consequently, if Hearnshaw had taken steps to preserve all Burt's papers, he might have found evidence therein that his subsequent accusations were false.

It is important for Hearnshaw to believe that Burt left no twin material behind him. This is consistent with his belief that most of it was destroyed in 1941; it supports his conviction that Burt must have been fabricating twin data in the late fifties and sixties; and it enables him to ignore the possibility that much of the extra data reported after 1955 had been recently found. It also relieves him of any feeling of negligence, however inadvertent, in the loss of the documents which might have cleared Burt's name; for after all, if there were no twin data there, Hearnshaw cannot be blamed for not preserving the material. There is of course no question of accusing Hearnshaw of any desire to destroy Burt's research material. Another explanation for his behaviour is suggested by Cohen's recollection (1983: 68) of a visit from Hearnshaw:

I showed him my high stack of Burtiana, letters, memoranda, etc., and he did not so much as suggest that he might be permitted to have a glimpse of even one of them. These unique documents clearly held no interest for him.

What, then, are Hearnshaw's reasons for supposing that most of the material in the boxes did not relate to twins? There is no specific indication what he has in mind. Presumably one reason is the suggestion (1979: 250) that most of it was destroyed in 1941; but that, as we have seen, is only a possibility and by no means a certainty. Perhaps another reason is that when Burt was asked to give further details, as he was several times, he usually failed to do so (1979: 246-7). This, like so many of Hearnshaw's arguments, employs negative evidence: if Burt had possessed the data, he would have replied; but he does not reply, so he probably did not possess them. Mcloughlin (1983: 6), however, refers to papers by Broad and Wade (1982, 1983) which suggest that it is an erroneous assumption that psychologists are able, or willing, to make raw data available to any colleague who makes a request. For various reasons, roughly half the people asked are likely to ignore the request.

There were two exceptions when Burt did reply to requests for kinship data – from Erlenmeyer-Kimling in 1963, and from Jencks in 1968. It appears that Burt did reply when distinguished scholars approached him: perhaps he grew weary of requests from humbler sources. However, Hearnshaw makes much of the length of time it took Burt to reply in these two cases: over nine weeks and seven weeks respectively. His implication is that the delay indicates Burt's embarrassment. But is this really such bad going for an old gentleman in his eighties? Jencks had asked in 1968 for a table of the IQs and social classes of the separated MZ twins. Hearnshaw (1979: 247) continues:

> According to his diary Burt spent the whole of the week from 2 January 1969 onwards 'calculating data on twins for Jencks'. . . . Had the IQ scores and social class gradings been available they could have been copied out in half an hour at the most. So quite clearly the table of IQ scores and social class gradings was an elaborately constructed piece of work, and we are forced to the conclusion that he simply did not possess detailed data, at any rate for the whole sample of his separated MZ twins.

But without knowing how the data were recorded, it is hard to know what Burt would actually have had to do to collect them. He might have had to look through many sheets of material. It is also to be noted that the table in question was eventually published by Jensen (1974: 15), who reports a comparison of the difference in scores between the members of each twin pair with the similar differences in the data of three other investigators, totalling sixty-nine pairs. The distribution of Burt's twin differences was not significantly different from the distributions in the three other studies (Jensen 1974: 16). This suggests that Burt's data were genuine.

Hearnshaw also notes that, in apologizing for his delay in replying, Burt gave several false reasons, such as being away for Christmas when he had stayed at home. Let everyone who has ever invented excuses beware! It is remarkable that the only deception which Hearnshaw has properly established in this whole string of accusations should concern a number of conventional fibs.

Conclusions

There are a number of respects in which Burt's kinship research differs markedly from the type of inquiry which would usually be undertaken today. The data were collected over a long period of time, as part of a general survey of scholastic capacities, with the help of a number of assistants who had little or no formal training in psychological research, other than that provided by Burt himself. It accordingly reflects many of the drawbacks of pioneering work. But there can be no serious doubt that Burt did collect much kinship data from the time of the First World War onwards, probably completing most of it by about 1950, when he retired.

Two main features of the work have given rise to serious misgivings: the invariant correlations, and the extra twin material reported in the late fifties and sixties. Both factors are hard to assess in view of the dearth of relevant information on crucial points.

The invariant correlations

Many of the correlations reported in 1966 had already been given in 1958 or 1955, though to judge by the Ns they ought to have changed. In these cases Burt was probably repeating previous correlations because he had no fresh data, and has failed to indicate the numbers properly. However, he has nothing to gain by this, for the repeated figures are mainly in the non-intelligence areas; that is, where Burt had least temptation to tamper with the data. What really matters is whether he had altered the new correlations, and there is no evidence that he did; on the contrary, the fact that these are new suggests that they are genuine, while the fact that they predominate in the assessments of intelligence strongly suggests that Burt is not attempting to deceive in the area where he had most interest in so doing.

The extra twin material

The critics agree in supposing that Burt's main offence consisted in claiming to have collected an extra thirty-two pairs of separated MZ twins between 1955 and 1966, with the help of Howard and Conway. But we need not suppose that Burt would have claimed this. Most of these thirty-two extra pairs were probably collected earlier, but had been mislaid during the wartime moves. Burt's papers stress over how long a period he had been collecting his data, rather than how recently.

The evidence here is almost entirely negative: that one would have expected there to be traces of the assistants, records of the data, records in the diary, and so on. But such evidence is not to be found. It seems, however, most unlikely that much evidence would now survive anyway: the assistants are probably long since dead, and all Burt's data were destroyed after his death.

Despite the confidence with which Burt has been accused of dishonesty, the evidence that he committed any major deception in relation to his kinship data is thoroughly inadequate. He may have occasionally indulged in minor transgressions, but the major frauds have not been established. The problem is complicated by two further factors: (1) so many of these events happened so long ago that the trail is cold and we cannot question the chief parties; and (2) Burt was very old when he wrote his 1966 paper – eighty-three years of age – and hence becoming less alert. Burt's own comment to his sister, in 1963, was a warning: 'What I write has to be checked and re-written several times before it is fit for the printer. Most of the mistakes are quite childish' (see Hearnshaw 1979: 242).

It remains true that Burt's kinship papers are open to many legitimate criticisms. Too often there is insufficient information about the data, especially about the subjects, their environmental conditions, and the circumstances under which they were tested. The techniques of intelligence testing are also open to critical scepticism. It would therefore be unwise to place too much confidence in Burt's conclusions.

Chapter eight

Burt's last papers

The most important of the allegations against Burt have now been considered: the historical falsifications, which were the most extensive; and the twin frauds, which were the most spectacular. There remain two further matters which have been widely regarded as confirming Burt's dishonesty. The first concerns a paper entitled 'Intelligence and social mobility' (Burt 1961b) which appeared in the *British Journal of Statistical Psychology*. This dealt with the controversial question of the relation between intelligence and occupational class, and whether any such relation was more plausibly attributed to heredity or environment. The second concerns a paper entitled 'Intelligence and heredity: some common misconceptions' (Burt 1969c) which appeared in the *Irish Journal of Education*. This dealt, among other things, with the almost equally controversial matter of whether there had been changes in educational standards over the previous half-century, and how any such changes were to be explained.

In the final section of his examination of the evidence against Burt, Hearnshaw (1979: 253–9) discusses these two papers and concludes that the 1969 paper provides markedly stronger evidence for Burt's guilt than the 1961 paper. Thus the 1961 paper is said to be 'a dubious exercise, though perhaps "fraud" is too strong a word to use', whereas the 1969 paper was 'much more open to question' (1979: 256). However, the 1961 paper has been the subject of an analysis by Dorfman (1978), who claimed to find convincing evidence of fraud in it. This study came too late for Hearnshaw to use it in his biography, but he has since indicated that he accepts it as strengthening his case (Hearnshaw 1980: 1). Both papers therefore need to be regarded as equally relevant.

'Intelligence and social mobility' (Burt 1961b): Hearnshaw's comments

In this paper, Burt reported data on the distribution of intelligence in the various occupational classes, and compared figures for adults with those for children (see Table 8.1). In the case of adults, there is a marked

Table 8.1 Distribution of intelligence according to occupational class

I Adults

	50–60	60–70	70–80	80–90	90–100	100–110	110–120	120–130	130–140	140+	Total	Mean IQ
I Higher professional									2	1	3	139.7
II Lower professional							2	13	15	1	31	130.6
III Clerical				1	8	16	56	38	3		122	115.9
IV Skilled			2	11	51	101	78	14	1		258	108.2
V Semi-skilled		5	15	31	135	120	17	2			325	97.8
VI Unskilled	1	18	52	117	53	11	9				261	84.9
Total	1	23	69	160	247	248	162	67	21	2	1000	100.0

II Children

	50–60	60–70	70–80	80–90	90–100	100–110	110–120	120–130	130–140	140+	Total	Mean IQ
I Higher professional						1		1	1		3	120.8
II Lower professional				1	2	6	12	8	2		31	114.7
III Clerical			3	8	21	31	35	18	6		122	107.8
IV Skilled		1	12	33	53	70	59	22	7	1	258	104.6
V Semi-skilled	1	6	23	55	99	85	38	13	5		325	98.9
VI Unskilled	1	15	32	62	75	54	16	6			261	92.6
Total	2	22	70	159	250	247	160	68	21	1	1000	100.0

Source: From Burt 1961b: 370.

correlation between occupational class and mean IQ: the mean IQ for the 'higher professional' class is 139.7, and this declines regularly to a figure of 84.9 for the 'unskilled'. In the case of children, a similar decline is evident, but the range is now much smaller, extending only from 120.8 to 92.6. Thus the mean intelligence of the children, in comparison with that of the adults, shows a regression towards the general mean. A further difference is that, within each occupational group, the intelligence of the children varies over a much wider range than does that of the adults. In the 'lower professional' class, for example, the intelligence of the children ranges from 80–90 to 130–140, whereas that of the adults ranges only from 110–120 to 140+. Clearly, if each child retained the same IQ and the same occupational class when it grew up, the distribution of the next generation of adults would differ markedly from that of the present generation. So Burt concluded that, if the distribution of the intelligence of the adults in the various classes was to remain constant over successive generations, there must be considerable 'social mobility' – the brighter children tending to move upwards into higher occupational classes, and the less bright downwards into lower.

After the twin papers, this article probably featured more prominently than any other in the genesis of suspicion. In 1974 the Clarkes remarked that the regression in the children's mean intelligence, which was half-way toward the general mean, appeared to be 'suspiciously perfect' (Clarke and Clarke 1974: 168). Shortly afterwards, Clarke and McAskie (1976: 256) noted that the mean IQ for the 'higher professional' class, which had been given as 153.2 in 1943, had 'miraculously shrunk' to 139.7 by 1961. The simple and innocent explanation is that in 1961 Burt had re-scaled his original assessments of IQ to the conventional mean of 100 and standard deviation of 15, as Hearnshaw (1979: 256) notes. Clarke and McAskie (ibid: 269) also observed that, in contrast with the environmental hypothesis, the polygenic model of inheritance, which Burt had adopted from Fisher, required the children's variance to exceed that of the adults; but only Burt's data showed this feature. However, as we have seen, these doubts did not lead to an explicit accusation of dishonesty, which came only with Gillie in 1976.

Hearnshaw introduces the 1961 paper by describing it as one of Burt's 'contentious' articles (1979: 254). The choice of adjective ('contentious' means quarrelsome: *Concise Oxford Dictionary*) suggests that Burt was deliberately trying to stir up controversy and was indulging in emotional arguments instead of restricting himself to scientific matters. Hearnshaw offers no evidence whatever for this pejorative description, any more than he had offered evidence for describing Burt's 1955 and 1966 papers as written 'in pique'. It illustrates how easily a man's reputation can be unfairly blackened. The paper is in fact written in Burt's usual detached and even-tempered style. Of course, the topic is controversial and likely to arouse strong feelings; but it is precisely on such themes that unbiased and factual argument is needed.

Hearnshaw's discussion of Burt (1961b) relies heavily upon the Hull group, and the nature of the assistance which he received is noteworthy. After a reference to Clarke and McAskie (1976), Hearnshaw (1979: 254) continues as follows:

> This led McAskie and Clarke to look carefully at Burt's data, and they came to the conclusion that not only was his description of the material he had used grossly inadequate, but that there were other anomalies that were hard to account for. As a result of these doubts McAskie carried out a more detailed analysis of Burt's 1961 article and concluded that the data reported were in all probability fraudulent.

This is followed by a brief account of the main grounds on which McAskie reached his conclusion. It is also accompanied by a reference to 'McAskie, M. Burt's 1961 parent–child I.Q. data according to parent occupation: an autopsy (awaiting publication)' (ibid.: 254, footnote). Unable to trace this paper, I wrote to McAskie twice requesting an offprint, but received no reply. Later I met him and asked why he had not replied, and he said he must have run out of offprints. Subsequently he added that the paper had been offered to the *British Journal of Mathematical Psychology* but had been refused; and it had not been published elsewhere. So, in this particular section of his case against Burt, Hearnshaw is relying upon evidence not yet accepted for publication, utlimately refused publication, and not available for inspection.

Burt's methods of assessing adult intelligence have also encountered much criticism. Kamin (1974: 60), for example, made scathing remarks about Burt's reference to the use of 'camouflaged tests'. Doubts about these data were in fact long-standing. While working at the National Institute of Industrial Psychology during the twenties, Burt had published tables of occupational IQ which had roused some uneasiness in one of his assistants, Spielman (see Hearnshaw 1979: 101–2). In fairness to Burt, however, it should be stressed that he had himself said that his figures were rough, as Hearnshaw recognizes. Thus he wrote that 'the figures finally arrived at are to be taken as nothing more than the roughest approximations' (Burt 1926: 15). Hearnshaw (1979: 102), however, also states that in his later articles Burt gave his readers 'little idea of its extreme unreliability'. But this seems not entirely fair. Thus in 1961, Burt described his early study as a 'pilot inquiry' and said that the assessments of adult intelligence were 'less thorough and less reliable' than those of the children (Burt 1961b: 9). Later, in a letter to Professor Beardmore, Burt elaborated this, dividing his parental data into three groups of varying reliability (see Hearnshaw 1979: 255).

The first group consisted of 'just over 100' fathers who had been assessed when, as children, they had attended LCC schools between 1913 and 1920. This, said Burt, was 'the most reliable group I have'.

The second group was one in which 'about 370' fathers were 'roughly assessed' by 'various groups of social workers'. There had been some attempt to equate the standards of the various interviewers, and it was here that Burt had spoken of 'camouflaged tests'.

The third group was one in which 'attendance officers and social visitors' had been asked to make 'rough estimates of fathers' IQs'. These amounted to well over 1,000 cases; and, added Burt, 'the unreliability of the assessments would be very large'.

Hearnshaw describes this material as 'mostly rubbish' (ibid.). It may be that many would agree with him today. But there is little sign that Burt's contemporaries were so sceptical, and the frankness with which Burt mentions these details, and refers to the limitations of the data, seems far removed from deliberate deception.

Burt stated that his data had been transformed to a base of 1,000 (that is, had been expressed as a proportion of 1,000); but he did not indicate what were the actual numbers involved, except in the case of the 'higher professional' class. In this case, he said that the row total of three actually represented 120 adults. Several writers have assumed that, in every category, there would similarly have been forty times as many subjects as the total given. This would give a grand total of about 40,000 subjects, a number which amazed commentators proceed to boggle at. But Burt never said he had tested such a number, or anything like it. It is almost certainly a wild exaggeration, and the correct number is probably much nearer to the 1,500 to 2,000 suggested by Burt's letter to Beardmore. Hearnshaw (ibid.) suggests that Burt expressed his data in this way in order to conceal the actual sample sizes. He gives no reason for supposing this, and the imputation is unjustified since there are plenty of good reasons for Burt's procedure, particularly that it expresses each figure as a percentage of the total, which facilitates immediate interpretation.

Lastly, Burt failed to respond to Beardmore's request for data. Hearnshaw interprets this to mean that Burt no longer had his original data, and was working from summaries of the results. Perhaps it does – but as usual there are plenty of innocent possibilities. In 1968 Burt was eighty-five years old. He might have been unwilling to go up to the attics to look for the data, especially as Ménière's disease made bending down and looking for things very trying (Banks's suggestion – personal communication).

Dorfman's accusations

Dorfman (1978) claimed to demonstrate beyond reasonable doubt, by statistical analysis, that Burt had fabricated his data in the 1961 paper. The general theme of Dorfman's criticism is that Burt did not first collect his data, and then calculate what conclusions could be deduced from them. He first decided what conclusions he wanted to reach, and then worked backwards to produce the data that would be required to give those results. The two most important instances of this, according to Dorfman, concern the totals of the rows and columns in the tables for adults and children. He alleges that Burt first decided what he wanted these to be, in order to conform to his own theoretical preconceptions, and then invented the necessary entries for the various cells. These allegations fall under two separate headings.

1 The marginal frequency distributions

Dorfman expressed Burt's column totals, or marginals, as percentages rounded to whole numbers. At the same time, he reduced Burt's ten classes to eight by combining the two extreme classes, 50–60 and 140+, with their respective adjacent classes, which contained very small proportions. In other words, he gives the frequency distributions, pooled over occupational class. These are as follows, and are identical for both adults and children:

60/70	70/80	80/90	90/100	100/110	110/120	120/130	130/140
2	7	16	25	25	16	7	2

Dorfman also calculated the theoretical normal distribution with mean 100 and standard deviation 15. He found that this was not significantly different from the distributions for adults and children. In short, all three distributions coincided. Dorfman (1978: 1180) described this as 'extraordinarily good'. He also noted that in previous papers Burt had often observed that IQ data regularly departed from the normal curve. At this point, Dorfman gave a lengthy examination of previous findings by other writers to establish that the great majority of IQ distributions are skewed from normal, so that the almost perfect fit of Burt's adult and child distributions to the normal curve suggested that what Burt called his 'actual' distributions were not actual distributions. Dorfman concluded that:

> beyond a reasonable doubt, the frequency distributions of Burt's tables . . . were carefully constructed so as to give column marginals in agreement with the normal curve. The readers were not informed . . . that that had been done.
>
> (Dorfman 1978: 1181–2)

In addition, a regression coefficient can be calculated from Burt's genetic theory which would be 0.50. But this conforms precisely with the regression for each occupational class in Burt's data. Since he had himself described his data as 'crude', so perfect an agreement is highly suspicious, as the Clarkes had suggested.

2 The data reclassified

Burt had next depicted the distribution of intelligence with a different set of IQ intervals or categories. He now employed six categories, one for each occupational class, and so chosen that the row and column totals were almost identical for children and adults. The probability of obtaining such a match was extraordinarily remote, continued Dorfman, so that Burt could not have been reclassifying data as he claimed. He must have constructed the distribution. (The totals in question are the row totals from Burt's Tables I and II).

Finally, Dorfman showed that these row and column totals, supposedly depicting the observed figures reduced to numbers per thousand, could in fact be traced back to figures published by Burt as long ago as 1926. In *A Study in Vocational Guidance*, Burt (1926) described vocational categories in terms very similar to those of 1961, and gave the percentage of male adults estimated for each category. There was so marked a similarity here that it was impossible to doubt that this was where Burt had, in 1961, obtained his row and column totals. Since Burt had supposedly collected his data over a period of fifty years, from 1913 onwards, added Dorfman (1978: 1183), 'the coincidence is bizarre indeed'. Moreover, when he originally compiled these figures, Burt had relied considerably on earlier census returns, especially that of 1921, so that his 'row totals' 'were based upon a census taken nearly forty years before completion of his 1961 study' (Dorfman 1978: 1184).

Dorfman summarized his analysis as follows:

These findings show, beyond reasonable doubt, that Burt fixed the row and column totals of the tables in his . . . 1961 study. Since the totals are completely determined by the cell entries, Burt determined the cell entries. Thus Burt's co-called 'actual' frequency distributions were systematic constructions.

(Dorfman 1978: 1184)

The Dorfman controversy

Dorfman's conclusions were at once attacked by three independent critics – Stigler, Rubin, and Banks – whose arguments were in close agreement.

Stigler (1979) presented the most detailed case. He declared that

Dorfman was in error in two major respects, and that his other assertions were 'sufficiently open to reasonable doubt to call his conclusions into serious question' (p. 242). The two major errors concerned what we have described as Dorfman's two main contentions, and will be considered in order.

The first concerns Burt's row and column totals. Dorfman had said that these totals were simply 'totals per mille', implying that Burt had decided what the totals should be in order to suit his favourite hypotheses. But here, said Stigler, Dorfman had failed to note what Burt actually said. Burt wrote: 'To obtain the figures to be inserted (numbers per mille) we weighted the actual numbers so that the proportions in each class should be equal to the estimated proportions for the total population' (Burt 1961b: 10). In other words, the numbers which Burt had collected in each category did not correspond to the proportions to be expected in the population as a whole. So he went back to his earlier figures, from Spielman and Burt, and used these as a guide in weighting each cell. In Stigler's own words: 'Burt is *saying* he has weighted the counts to get precisely the agreement that Dorfman presents as evidence of fabrication' (Stigler 1979: p. 244).

The second error concerns the close approximation to a normal distribution. Here again Stigler maintains that Burt had said that his figures had been 'rescaled'. Contrary to Dorfman's implication, Burt believed that the distribution of IQs was approximately, though not exactly, normal. He wanted his numbers to conform to such an expectation; and since the figures only represented a 'pilot study', he chose to re-scale using a normal distribution. (And one might add that if Burt had been trying to deceive he might have introduced deviations from a normal distribution just to conceal what he was doing.)

As regards Dorfman's claim that Burt's regression coefficients all work out at exactly 0.50, Stigler argued that Dorfman had used the wrong formula. The figures should have been: 0.52, 0.48, 0.49, 0.56, 0.50 and 0.49.

Thus Stigler answers both Dorfman's points in a similar way. He does not deny that Burt's data possessed the characteristics to which Dorfman drew attention; nor does he deny that Burt deliberately ensured that it possessed those features. His point is that Burt was submitting his data to normal statistical procedures, which he was not trying to hide. There are no grounds, therefore, for supposing that Burt did not possess the raw data.

In summary, Stigler maintains that the fact that Burt determined his row and column totals does not at all imply that he had fabricated the individual entries; and if Burt really did fabricate his data, he chose an extremely difficult way to do it. Stigler (ibid.: 245) concludes:

I do not wish to be interpreted as endorsing either Burt's statistical procedure or his unclear explanation of what he did (and his refusal to present the raw data), but given the standards of Burt's time and his repeated disclaimers (it was merely a 'pilot inquiry', 'data are too crude and limited') the charges of fabrication or fraud would seem, at least in this instance, to be without foundation; the evidence presented is irrelevant to the case.

Rubin (1979) was briefer, but also argued that to fix the marginal totals of a table did not determine the cell entries. It was a useful and accepted tool in many statistical problems.

Finally, Banks (1979: 150) independently put Stigler's two main points in a nutshell:

> Dorfman . . . omitted the crucial paragraph in which Burt explained what he had done. He wrote: 'In constructing the tables the frequencies in the various rows and columns were proportional frequencies and in no way represent the numbers actually examined. . . . To obtain the figures (numbers per mille) we weighted the actual numbers so that the proportions in each class should be equal to the estimated proportions for the total population.' And 'finally . . . we have rescaled our assessments of intelligence so that the mean of the group is 100 and the standard deviation 15.' To anyone who knows Burt's work this rescaling meant scaling to a normal distribution. Professor Dorfman, then, is simply criticising Burt for weighting and rescaling his figures. Dorfman thinks they are empirical, whereas they are empirical results transformed to population estimates. Where, then, is the fraud?

It might have been supposed that Dorfman, faced with this evidence that he had failed to read and understand the crucial passages in Burt's paper, would have been somewhat abashed. But Dorfman was made of sterner stuff. In reply to Banks, he declared that the passage had been 'buried in a sea of deception and disingenuousness' (Dorfman 1979a: 150). He did not explain how it was that others had noticed it easily enough. Nor did he deny the existence of the passage, or explain what he thought Burt had meant by it.

Dorfman (1979b) replied to both Stigler and Rubin, denying that they had demonstrated that Burt told the reader what he had done – an argument difficult to sustain since Banks had quite independently come to the same conclusion as Stigler. He also objected to Burt's failure to give his observed frequencies. Rubin and Stigler (1979) replied that 'using Dorfman's inappropriate statistical techniques to detect fraudulent data would be to condemn a major portion . . . of empirical science as fabrication' (p. 1206). Dorfman (1979c) replied that he had been misunderstood.

It is not possible to summarize the intricate arguments involved both fairly and briefly. Dorfman could not claim to have achieved his goal – that of furnishing solid proof beyond reasonable doubt – for three colleagues had at once doubted him, and there was no sign at the end that any of them was any less sceptical than when they started. My own impression of the argument is that Dorfman claimed that Burt invented his 'data' – he did not have some data which he manipulated illegitimately. He simply had no data, but pretended he had. This seems most unlikely, in view of all that Burt collected over the years. Since Burt did not give his raw data, the question is now insoluble. It is possible to hold that he invented it all; and possible to hold that he was simply applying statistical procedures to actual figures, as he implied. Neither position can be proved, but the Stigler–Rubin–Banks position is more likely. Burt's statistical techniques may well be open to objections, though these are not any clearer at the end than they were at the beginning. Hearnshaw's (1980: 1) assumption that Dorfman had established his case is unjustified, and it is surprising that he fails to mention that Dorfman's conclusions had been challenged by three critics.

'Intelligence and heredity' (Burt 1969c)

The final instance of Burt's alleged duplicity arose in connection with the post-war controversy concerning comprehensive and selective schooling. Some of the more traditional educationists compiled a number of so-called 'Black Papers' in which they criticized not only the comprehensive movement but also many of the newer fashions in teaching method. Burt (1969a) contributed an article called 'The mental differences between children' to *Black Paper II*. This article was concerned among other things with changing levels of attainment over the years in the state schools, and aroused considerable opposition from the 'progressive' camp.

Burt (1969a) began by conceding that there had been a marked improvement in the level of attainment in the basic subjects since the end of the Second World War. But standards then had been at a low ebb owing to wartime disruptions, and a longer view gave a different conclusion. If current standards were compared with those just before the Second World War, or just before the First, then 'the overall trend has shown, not an improvement, but, if anything, a decline' (Burt 1969a: 23); and the average attainments in the basic subjects were now 'appreciably lower' than they had been in 1914. Burt ascribed the decline primarily to 'progressive' methods of teaching, which he saw as encouraging 'self-expression', 'creativity', and 'originality', when the main requirements were, he believed, hard work and discipline.

Burt gave no figures to support his claim in this *Black Paper* article, but referred the reader to a paper in the current issue of the *Journal of the*

Association of Educational Psychologists, and to further references there cited. The paper in question (Burt 1969b) was entitled 'Recent studies of abilities and attainments' and gave a brief review of recent writing on mental inheritance and its practical implications. Here Burt began by mentioning Jensen's article in the *Harvard Educational Review* (Jensen 1969) on school programmes and cultural enrichment, noted their disappointing outcome, and asked how far British experience was similar. After mentioning work by Vernon and others, Burt referred to his own surveys of educational attainments over many years, which would shortly appear, he said, in the *Irish Journal of Education*. Meanwhile, he provided what he called his 'findings for the latest available data, taking the norms for 1914 as 100.0' (Burt 1969b: 8). These findings gave the following figures: for Accuracy of Reading, 95.4; Comprehension, 99.3; Spelling, 91.1; Mechanical Arithmetic, 92.5; and Problem Arithmetic, 96.3. His conclusion was that attempts to improve the academic achievements of 'disadvantaged children' through the new 'compensatory methods' had been 'on the whole disappointing' (ibid.).

It should be noted that Burt ended this article by stressing that innate intelligence was by no means the only factor determining educational progress. Differences in temperament and character played 'an important and often a crucial part', as well as environmental influences both before and during the years of schooling. Finally, Burt remarked that 'our present preoccupation with the problem of intelligence . . . combined with the popularity of . . . "progressive methods" . . . has led us to forget the supreme importance of cultivating habits of self-discipline, effort, and sheer hard work' (ibid.: 9).

The paper referred to in the *Irish Journal* (Burt 1969c) was entitled 'Intelligence and heredity: some common misconceptions'. In it, Burt said that he had asked 'two or three of my former research students to attempt a

Table 8.2 Comparison of school attainments, 1914–65

| Year | Intelligence | Reading | | Spelling | Arithmetic | |
		Accuracy	Comprehension		Mechanical	Problem
1914	100.3	101.4	100.1	102.8	103.2	101.3
1917	100.1	95.3	96.5	94.7	91.1	92.5
1920	100	100	100	100	100	100
1930	98.6	100.7	105.2	100.8	103.4	94.7
1945	99.3	90.8	91.1	89.5	88.9	93.2
1955	99.8	95.1	96.9	93.8	91.4	95.5
1965	99.5	96.7	99.4	94.6	95.5	97.6

Source: From Burt 1969c: p. 89.

systematic comparison of the available data for the last fifty years' (p. 88). In particular, a Miss M. G. O'Connor had made a comparison of school attainments based on tests applied by teachers or research students from 1914 onwards. The results are given in Table 8.2, the figures being medians, and relating to the last year of the primary school (namely, aged ten to eleven). The figures have been based on 1920 as 100.0. The generalizations which Burt had made are in accordance with these figures; but how accurate are the figures?

There are undoubtedly serious grounds for criticizing Burt in his description and presentation of his material. At no point, for instance, does he indicate the numbers from which these various medians were taken; nor does he say where, or by whom, the data were collected. But Hearnshaw is misleading when he states that 'Burt had provided no information about the tests he had used, or about his methods of sampling' (Hearnshaw 1970: 256). As regards the tests, it is true that Burt did not list them; but he refers to the successive editions of his *Mental and Scholastic Tests*, and he was not unjustified in assuming that his work was sufficiently well known to an audience of educational psychologists not to require detailed recapitulation. As regards the methods of sampling, the statement that Burt gave 'no information' is simply false. Burt refers specifically to a method of 'median sampling', which he had been developing, and which was described more fully in the book. In this, a school inspector would be asked to select an average school, and in each the investigator would pick out the median pupil in the age-group under consideration. Burt claimed that this was a reliable as well as an economical method. He wrote as follows:

Actual trial shows that by testing about 20 or 30 children thus selected (often even less) one can get a much better estimate of the average of the general population than if one attempted to test all the children in what was designed to be a genuinely random sample.

(Burt 1969c: 88–9)

Even so, Burt recognized that the comparison of samples collected over a lengthy period presented numerous problems. All such samples, he said, were 'precarious'. He mentioned Vernon's observations on the difficulty of procuring samples which could safely be regarded as comparable, and added that this caution applied equally to his own figures. Burt's conclusion was expressed in moderate terms: he regarded his data as furnishing 'a strong prima facie case against the unverified claims so often advanced for large-scale improvements during the last half-century' (ibid.: 90).

Hearnshaw's main accusation is that some of Burt's figures had in fact been fabricated, and his evidence was regarded by Cronbach (1979) as even more damaging than that concerning the twins. It is especially important, therefore, to examine it.

Hearnshaw does not claim that all Burt's figures have been fabricated. He accepts the data for the middle years, from 1917 to 1945 inclusive, when Burt was working in London with access to schools. It is the remaining data, those for 1914, and for 1955 and 1965, which Hearnshaw questions. So far as the material for 1914 is concerned, Hearnshaw does not deny that Burt had already, by that early date, conducted numerous tests of intelligence, and begun to accumulate data on reading, writing, and arithmetic. His allegation here is that Burt had not yet adequately standardized his tests, or applied them to other than small pilot groups (Hearnshaw 1979: 257). This may be true; but it does not amount to a fabrication of data, only to a use of unreliable data – and in view of Burt's warnings about the 'precarious' nature of his comparisons, this provides no evidence of dishonesty. However, it is the data for the two final years, 1955 and 1965, which Hearnshaw regards as providing the chief evidence for his accusation. We may therefore concentrate upon this material.

Hearnshaw states that Burt was interviewed by a reporter from the *Guardian* about his surveys, and he writes that 'a statement appeared in its issue for 7 November 1969' (1979: 258). He then prints a number of lines which appear in quotation marks, and purport to come from this statement. They include the following sentence:

These tests had been given regularly to a sample of about 200 children, aged 10, in 10 inner London schools between 1914 and 1965.

(Ibid.)

Hearnshaw then argues that an investigation of this kind, which would involve the co-operation of teachers and the testing of 200 children, could not have been carried out without the consent of the education authority. But there is no record of any such consent being given over the whole period from 1952 to 1965. In addition, Burt had no research funds for a programme which must have involved many hours of testing, and which must have been quite expensive to mount. He concludes that 'it seems improbable in the extreme that any testing programme was carried out under Burt's direction either in 1955 or 1965' (1979: 259). This is the central pillar of Hearnshaw's case: what he calls Burt's 'massive operation' conducted in 1955 and 1965 could never have taken place, and accordingly the figures Burt gives for those years must have been fabricated.

One might well agree that, if any such 'massive operation' was needed or claimed in order to provide the figures for 1955 and 1965, then these data could be fraudulent. But the assertion that in both years Burt would have to test, either by himself or with an assistant, some 200 children in ten schools rests entirely upon a newspaper report. There is no mention whatever in Burt (1969c) of 200 children, or ten schools, nor indeed of any number of children or schools. (As already mentioned, it is a weakness of Burt's report that he does not give the actual numbers for *any* year.) On the contrary, as we have seen, the implication in Burt (1969c) is that, because of the use of the method of median sampling, elaborate testing was not required. In addition, Hearnshaw himself quotes a letter which Burt wrote to Mr G. F. Peaker, Inspector of Schools, on 21 November 1969. Peaker had, apparently, queried the method of sampling, and Burt in reply referred to the method of median sampling, stating that

> We selected median schools, i.e., those drawing mainly from classes IV and V in my eight-fold scheme . . . and then took a few median pupils from each of the selected schools. How far this device has been successful I am unable to say. . . . I willingly allow that my figures may well be out by 4 or 5 points on a percentage scale.
>
> (See Hearnshaw 1979: 258)

It seems, then, from such evidence as we have, that Burt was disclaiming, rather than claiming, any 'massive operation'. The figures which he gives for 1955 and 1965 could well have been based upon a far smaller number than 200 pupils, and may have been selected from a very few schools. Burt had in fact retained several contacts among teachers who could have helped (Banks – personal communication); and there is no reason to suppose that permission would be asked for such a small-scale inquiry, or that financial support would be needed. Burt certainly ought to have given a precise indication of the number of subjects upon which his figures were based, and the schools involved. But if any imputation is to be made from his failure to do so, the most likely would be that he was concealing the small number of subjects involved. This – if it really could be established – would certainly be reprehensible; but it is not to fabricate data.

It should also be noted that the actual figures given for 1955 and 1966 (the two years which Hearnshaw thinks were fabricated) are precisely those which have the least tendency to support Burt's argument, among all those given. These figures show a marked improvement over those for 1945, thus reducing considerably the size of the decline since much earlier years. If Burt had been inventing the figures he would surely have chosen numbers which would strengthen his argument rather than weaken it.

Hearnshaw's assertion, then, that Burt claimed a 'massive operation', rests entirely upon the alleged *Guardian* report, and wholly ignores the evidence, both in Burt (1969c) and the letter to Peaker, that the method of sampling had been adopted in order to make such large numbers unnecessary. It might now be suggested, perhaps, that Burt claimed such large numbers, in his *Guardian* interview, in order to cover up the small numbers actually used. Why he should do this when his paper, and his letter to Peaker, were inconsistent with any such claim, would be mysterious. But before we speculate about Burt's motives for making the *Guardian* statement, we should check on this alleged report. Hearnshaw's whole case, as we have seen, rests upon this newspaper article. It provides his sole ground for accusing Burt of fabrication, for if Burt made no such claim Hearnshaw's argument collapses.

A newspaper article is not the most reliable of sources. However honest the journalist, he might easily misunderstand Burt's meaning, and quite unintentionally misrepresent him. Burt, now eighty-six years old, might mishear the questions, or give oversimplified answers for a popular account. Everyone would surely agree that before the published account is accepted in evidence there should at least be some assurance that Burt had seen and approved the report. Where the report is to be used to condemn a man who can no longer defend himself, our standards will presumably be even stricter. So, even if the report turns out to be as Hearnshaw describes it, some scepticism will be in order. In Hearnshaw's account there is no indication that Burt had vouched for its accuracy; Hearnshaw appears to be accepting the reporter's word at second-hand. There is also no specific mention of these numbers applying to the crucial years 1955 and 1966. It would be prudent, before we go further, to examine the report for ourselves.

The search for the report proved long, and the eventual outcome was unexpected. Nottingham University Library does not keep old numbers of the *Guardian*, so I asked Miss S. A. Lander in the Library's inter-library loan department to obtain a copy for me. She approached the British Library and the Newspaper Library in London, but was informed in both cases that their staff were unable to trace any relevant article or statement. The Newspaper Library sent photocopies of several of the most likely pages, but no trace could be found. I myself then wrote twice to the *Guardian* itself, but received no reply. At this point, and unknown to me, Miss Lander wrote direct to Hearnshaw, on 1 October 1984, explaining that she had 'a reader' who was anxious to consult the article, and requesting either a photocopy of it or a confirmation of the reference. Hearnshaw replied to Miss Lander in a letter dated 20 October 1984, in which the relevant passage was as follows:

Unfortunately, I cannot help you in your inquiry. The reference to the Guardian came from a secondary source, but I cannot now remember what it was, and I have dispersed a lot of the rough notes that I collected for my book on Burt. I have checked through my remaining files, but can find nothing relevant.

Hearnshaw's prime evidence for Burt's guilt in this final accusation was a newspaper article which he had not bothered to check. It was not merely second-hand evidence of an obviously unreliable kind. It was third-hand evidence, and he could not even remember where it came from. Yet he had quoted it as if he had seen it himself. If Burt had done this, instead of Hearnshaw, what would the critics have made of it?

Review of conclusions

The major charges of deception brought against Burt have been examined, and the conclusions may be summarized. The charges were made in two main stages. First came the accusations reported by Gillie in 1976, supported by the Clarkes, McAskie, and Tizard, and joined shortly afterwards by Kamin. These critics were inclined to regard Burt's whole career as tainted, but they concentrated their attention upon his work on the inheritance of intelligence, especially in relation to twins. None of them, however, attempted to set out a thorough and complete case, specifically directed towards establishing Burt's guilt. Consequently, psychologists in general suspended judgement. The second stage came with Hearnshaw's biography in 1979. This not only purported to provide confirmation of many of the criticisms already made with regard to the inheritance of intelligence; it also added two other areas of deception not hitherto publicly alleged, concerning factorial history and educational standards. But Hearnshaw regarded the deceptions as restricted to Burt's later life, and remained a staunch admirer of many of his earlier achievements. This, the first attempt to set out a complete and formal case against Burt, rapidly secured general if not universal acceptance. Several of Burt's previous defenders, notably Eysenck, Jensen, and Vernon, now changed their minds and professed themselves ready to accept his guilt. But there remained, and still remain, a considerable number who have been steadfast in their belief that Burt was innocent. Banks and Cohen are the most prominent of these.

Accordingly there are currently three main positions concerning Burt's alleged dishonesty: that he was wholly innocent throughout his life (Banks, Cohen); that he was untrustworthy throughout his life (the Clarkes, McAskie, Kamin); and that he was honest at first, but degenerated from the 1940s onwards (Hearnshaw). Hearnshaw regards his own position as striking a balance between Burt's defenders and his detractors. As an overall estimate of Burt's character and the reliability of his work, that is no doubt true. But on the narrower question of Burt's integrity, it is hardly justified. Hearnshaw not only accepts the main charges, he also makes additional charges concerning the history of factor analysis and concerning educational standards. Hearnshaw's claim would have been more justified if he had argued that Burt was guilty, but on fewer counts or lesser charges.

As the only detailed and comprehensive statement of the case against

Burt, Hearnshaw demands most attention. Hearnshaw's first charge, of historical falsification, has little foundation, as Cronbach (1979) has suggested, as Banks (1983) has demonstrated, and as the present study has substantiated. It would not be unreasonable to hold that Burt's historical account lacks confirmation in certain important respects, and attaches greater importance to the contributions of Pearson and of Burt himself than many would think appropriate. But such differences of interpretation are to be expected in an historical inquiry, and Burt's account is far more knowledgeable, and far more reliably documented, than that of Hearnshaw. In particular, Burt's claims concerning the content of his early papers, though occasionally overdrawn, are fundamentally accurate and reasonable. Hearnshaw's allegation that Burt was conducting a campaign to rob Spearman of his due credit, and install himself in his place, is baseless. In general, Hearnshaw's historical accusations have proved so unreliable that his first charge must be rejected without qualification.

The third charge, of fabricating data on educational standards, is also very poorly supported. Hearnshaw accepts that most of Burt's figures, from 1917 through 1945, were genuine, and concentrates his scepticism on the results for 1955 and 1965. It is remarkable that these two years show an improvement not a decline. Hearnshaw also overlooks Burt's indication that he used a method of median sampling, and assumes he must have surveyed some 200 cases in ten schools. Here, however, Hearnshaw speaks of using a second-hand report, from a source he has forgotten, of a journalist's story which it has so far proved impossible to trace. A further charge that Burt fabricated data on intelligence and occupational class has been alleged by Dorfman, and accepted by Hearnshaw. It has been refuted by Stigler, Rubin, and Banks, which Hearnshaw has ignored.

The central charge, that Burt produced spurious data on the inheritance of intelligence, specifically concerning MZ twins, has more to be said in its favour. The repeated correlations, and the missing research assistants, certainly require explanation, whether or not that explanation entails duplicity. It is absurd to suggest that Burt introduced the repeated correlations deliberately because he thought there was something to be gained by the sheer consistency of identical coefficients. On the contrary, such an anomaly could only arouse suspicion if it was noticed, as indeed happened. We have also shown that the repeated figures are concentrated in the area of physical and educational measures, where Burt had least incentive to give spurious results. This is an important finding, because it leads us to notice that the remaining, new, correlations are concentrated in the crucial areas of intelligence, and hence strongly suggest that the extra data on twins, which were added in 1958 and 1966, were genuine.

It is very likely, as Banks has suggested, that Burt simply repeated old figures where new ones were not available. But it is also necessary to explain why Burt did not clearly indicate the correct numbers involved in every case. This could be interpreted as an unnoticed outcome of the difficulties he encountered in collecting his data. It was probably only because there was a chance repetition of the crucial MZ apart correlation for intelligence that anybody started to look at Burt's figures closely, and noticed the anomalies.

Probably little can be concluded from the missing assistants. It is certainly possible that, as Burt himself said, they helped him to collect most of the data before 1950, probably mainly in the twenties and thirties. Then the increased numbers reported by Burt from 1958 onwards may reasonably be regarded as reflecting the re-discovery of Conway's missing data, as Banks's (1983) recollections have suggested. It is also very possible that by 1976, when the search for them began, Howard and Conway had died long since.

The uncertain state of the evidence permits a variety of different accusations to be made, varying in severity. The most extreme is that which denies that Burt ever had any twin data, and that Howard and Conway ever existed (the Clarkes, and so on). Here Burt fabricates everything. A more moderate view holds that Howard and Conway did once help, and that Burt did have some twin data, but that Burt pretended to go on collecting fresh data long after he had actually stopped (Hearnshaw). The view advocated here is that there has been no reliable indication of fabrication whatever.

The four charges reported by Gillie in 1976 and endorsed by the Clarkes and McAskie may now be considered. The first charge, that Burt guessed parental IQs and then treated his guesses as scientific measures, is unjustified since Burt himself drew attention to the unreliability of his estimates. Hearnshaw's (1979: 256) conclusion here is that it was 'a dubious exercise, though perhaps "fraud" is too strong a word to use'. The second charge, that Howard and Conway probably never existed, has been undermined by Hearnshaw's contrary conclusion, by Cohen's and Stephenson's recollections of Howard, and by other less positive recollections of Conway. The third charge concerned the invariant correlations. These were never a very convincing sign of fraud, and careful examination of their distribution has in fact provided evidence for the genuineness of Burt's additional data. The fourth charge, that Burt fabricated data to fit his favourite genetic theories, is so vaguely formulated that it is open neither to verification nor refutation. As might be expected in a newspaper article, the evidence was most inadequately presented.

On several occasions Burt has failed to give full and accurate information about the numbers of subjects employed. This may suggest a deliberate refusal to give the reader important information, or it may be a simple consequence of the difficulties experienced in collecting the data. But there has been no demonstration, beyond reasonable doubt, that Burt

213

has fabricated data or invented assistants; and many of the allegations have been found to be entirely without foundation.

Some particular impressions may be set out in conclusion. First, the arguments of the critics are frequently negative, relying on the absence of evidence to the contrary; yet this dearth of evidence is readily explicable, since so many of Burt's papers have been destroyed, while his assistants were probably already dead. Second, the critics have not established their case conclusively in a single instance. Third, any delinquencies of which Burt might be at all plausibly accused appear to have been of a minor and relatively common variety, and come nowhere near the sensational frauds which have been so widely alleged.

Further problems

Hearnshaw has described how, when he became convinced that the charges against Burt were valid, the problem became that of explaining how a man of Burt's eminence and exceptional gifts could have succumbed in this way. These explanations did not only serve to explain how Burt succumbed. They necessarily dwelt upon Burt's alleged personal short-comings, portraying his personality as disturbed and flawed, and therefore as providing the natural source of his grave offences. That is to say, he was depicted as the sort of person who might be expected to behave in this way. This in turn made it still more believable that he had committed the offences, and so reinforced the evidence already presented.

Similarly, to become convinced that the charges were not valid again transforms the problem. But now the task is to explain how it was that such false accusations came to be made, and, still more, how they came to be so widely accepted. Is it really plausible, it might be said, that so many different people should all have found such a variety of grounds for suspecting Burt, if there were not some substance in the charges? Further, the difficulty of establishing any single charge is inevitable in view of the time which has elapsed since they were committed, and the cleverness of the man who perpetrated them. A completely innocent man would never have been exposed to such a succession of suspicions. Such arguments cannot be shrugged aside. Only if satisfactory answers can be found to these further doubts can the matter be regarded as settled.

Hearnshaw's account of the Burt affair saw it as the story of a flawed individual, as a matter of personal pathology. In so far as we become doubtful about Burt's guilt, a different series of questions comes to light. Now attention is necessarily focused upon the character of contemporary psychology. Only in so far as valid answers are found to these further questions can our task be regarded as complete. However, if valid answers are found, Burt's innocence will become still more believable, and so once again the evidence already presented will be reinforced.

These reflections indicate that there are two tasks remaining to be performed. First, Hearnshaw's account of Burt's character must be examined. Our conclusion will not be that this account is wholly mistaken, nor that Burt's character and behaviour are irrelevant. They must inevitably play their part, and colour the pattern of events as it unfolds. But they cannot carry the whole burden of explanation as Hearnshaw's standpoint requires. Second, the character of contemporary psychology must be considered. The Burt affair must be seen as a social, not as a merely individual, phenomenon.

Chapter nine

The mad professor

Having decided that Burt was guilty, Hearnshaw faced the question of accounting for his fall: 'the problem became that of explaining how a man of Burt's eminence and exceptional gifts could have succumbed in this way' (Hearnshaw 1979: viii). Hearnshaw sets out his explanation, attempting to do justice both to Burt's achievements and his shortcomings, in a chapter entitled 'The man' (chap. 13). The explanation cannot be accused of oversimplification: it involves a study of major influences extending over the whole of Burt's life; and incorporates a number of principles which have been widely used in modern psychology: 'The psychologist must himself be psychologised' (ibid.: 261). Its central feature is that Burt suffered from a 'psychological disturbance'; specifically, from 'marginal paranoia'.

It has often been held, by both psychologists and psychiatrists, that criminal behaviour and mental disturbance are closely connected, and sometimes even that the former is always to be explained by the latter. In common parlance, those who are bad are held to be mad. Hearnshaw himself comes close to this position: after saying that the problem was to explain how Burt could have succumbed, he at once adds (p. viii), 'The problem became, in fact, a medico-psychological one.' But this is not a connection which can be taken for granted. It may be that those who are 'emotionally disturbed' are more likely to find themselves at odds with the law, if only because their sense of responsibility may be impaired. But the connection is far from universal. Many mental patients have no criminal involvement; and many criminals have no history of mental disturbance – and even where there is such a history, it may well be incidental. There is no necessary connection between mental illness and delinquent behaviour. Thus even if Burt were guilty, it would not follow that we have to seek a 'medico-psychological' solution.

However, from the point of view of a psychologist, there may be advantages in believing that Burt was 'disturbed'. Such explanations tend to exonerate Burt; and they also tend to weaken any notion that psychologists are especially prone to fraudulence, for mental illness is a misfortune which might befall any scientist. But in exonerating Burt, such explanations also tend, paradoxically, to strengthen the belief that he committed fraud. This is because the diagnosis of mental illness carries with it the suggestion that the sense of responsibility is impaired, and therefore that the sufferer is less resistant to temptation. This brings us to another consequence.

Today, a diagnosis of mental illness is often said to carry no stigma. But it is doubtful whether this is, or ever could be, entirely true. There are still highly undesirable consequences for anyone so labelled. It reduces a man's standing in the community by depriving him, to a greater or lesser degree, of the status of an ordinary responsible citizen. There is a tendency to reject, or cast doubt upon, what he says or does as being unworthy of serious consideration. So this diagnosis of Burt is a licence to remove his later work and achievements from credit, just as happens to the Soviet dissident.

From our standpoint, all such explanations of Burt's behaviour are marginal, because the evidence for Burt's guilt is so meagre. What requires explanation, so far as we are concerned, is how it was that Burt was singled out, on such slender grounds, for attack and condemnation. This question is considered in the last two chapters. Here we turn to the view that Burt was 'psychologically disturbed'; for however unnecessary this 'explanation' may be, it tends to undermine confidence in his reliability, and hence to make his alleged misconduct more credible.

Burt's supposed character

There is no record that during his lifetime Burt was ever thought to have been in need of psychiatric treatment, so Hearnshaw's first task is to find some ground for introducing a pathological intepretation. This is supposed to be shown by a contrast between two features of Burt's character. The first feature is a desire for intellectual supremacy in his chosen field of individual psychology. This is described as the 'driving force' of Burt's life (1979: 268); and as a consequence he is said to have become increasingly jealous of rivals such as Spearman, Thurstone, and Eysenck. The second is an alleged 'duality' or contradiction in his character, such that he was capable of arousing both 'rapturous admiration and intense distrust' (ibid.: 261). These two are linked together in the following passage (ibid.: 270):

> It was almost as if he had marked out a certain territory for himself – in this case intellectual territory – within the boundaries of which he was determined to maintain the mastery, lay down the law, and drive off all rivals. To those who presented no challenge – children, women, students of average ability, the maladjusted – he could be both charming and generous. To those who challenged him, directly or indirectly, he

217

presented a very different face – hostile, cantankerous, and, if need be, unscrupulous. Whence came this duality?

These two features are of great importance in Hearnshaw's analysis because they pave the way for an explanation in pathological terms. The first – the desire for supremacy, to lay down the law – foreshadows a prime symptom of paranoia. The second – the duality – suggests some deep-seated conflict which may be expected to disturb mental balance. Thus Hearnshaw's explanation begins by asking how the 'duality' originated, and ends by diagnosing 'marginal paranoia'. These two characteristics, therefore, set the scene for Hearnshaw's explanation. In view of their importance it will be advisable, before we follow the details of the analysis, to examine them more closely.

There could hardly fail to be a considerable measure of truth in the assertion that Burt possessed these two characteristics, at least to some extent. Concerning the first feature, ambition is one of the commonest human motives, and it must be at least as common in universities as anywhere else. Any academic, if he is worth his salt, will surely have some desire to distinguish himself, to excel. There is in consequence a good deal of rivalry and envy to be observed. The important question therefore is not whether Burt was ambitious, whether he sought intellectual supremacy, but whether he was excessively and arrogantly ambitious. Was he really overbearing and domineering, or is this just the description which envious rivals have provided?

The second feature – that of being charming to those who presented no challenge, but hostile to those who did – is also, surely, a very common human trait. If Burt had shown such contrasting attitudes to the same person on different occasions, sometimes friendly and sometimes hostile, with no obvious incident to account for the change, then indeed there would have been something to explain. But is it not an almost universal characteristic to prefer those who agree with us to those who oppose us? Where is the paragon who feels as favourably disposed to those who criticize him as to those who applaud him? The important question again is whether Burt displayed this characteristic in exaggerated form.

It would seem, then, that we are almost certain to be able to find evidence that Burt was ambitious, and evidence also that he preferred to be acknowledged rather than challenged. Further, it is likely, in view of Burt's own success and eminence, that there would be envious critics who, having crossed swords with him, would be anxious to damage his reputation by exaggerating his ambition and intolerance. It will be important to bear these complications in mind in assessing Hearnshaw's view of Burt's character.

Hearnshaw's whole elaborate analysis of Burt's character begins with the question 'Whence came this duality?' He sees it as an intellectual challenge, to be solved by deploying all the resources of modern psychology. But even if Burt possessed this characteristic to a marked degree, it would seem to be capable of a very simple explanation; indeed, Hearnshaw himself seems already to have given it. It comes in the passage quoted above in which the two leading features of Burt's character were linked together. Burt's resentment of those who challenged his supremacy surely sprang from the fact that he sought intellectual supremacy – they frustrated that desire. Similarly, those who presented no threat did not frustrate it. Moreover, the stronger his ambition, the more he would be likely to resent any challenge, and the greater would be the contrast between his behaviour to those who challenged and those who did not.

The contrast in Burt's attitude does not, then, spring from any pathological conflict; it does not reflect some mysterious underlying 'duality'. It springs from the opposite: from the strength of Burt's dominating motive. It is the very integration of Burt's life round this theme which produces the contrast. The cause lies not in any split or conflict between different and incompatible aspects of character, but in the strength of the integration round a central theme. Moreover, the stronger this 'driving force' is believed to be, the greater the contrast is likely to become. So the explanation of Burt's 'duality' is obvious and simple. When Hearnshaw invites us to follow him on an elaborate trawl through Burt's past life, in an attempt to dredge up possible causal factors, he is embarking upon a wild-goose chase. On such a venture, no one must be surprised to encounter some strange sights.

Childhood influences

Hearnshaw begins by admitting that the records of the first nine years of Burt's life are almost non-existent. Accordingly, he writes (1979: 271) that 'we are left with a few bare facts, which have to be supplemented by a good deal of imaginative reconstruction'. There is no need to quarrel with this statement, which is fully illustrated in Hearnshaw's treatment of both hereditary and environmental factors.

So far as *hereditary factors* are concerned, Burt's ancestry is said to be mixed, his father being of 'solid Saxon stock' and his mother a 'more volatile Welsh woman' (ibid.: 271). A number of points lack scientific demonstration: (1) Is there any reliable evidence for racial differences of temperament between the 'Saxon' and the 'Welsh'? (2) If so, does it take the form suggested? (3) If these preliminaries are established, are there grounds for supposing that Burt's father did possess the relatively pure 'Saxon', and his mother the relatively pure 'Welsh', genetic constitution? (4) If so, are there grounds for believing that such a mixture is likely to result in a kind of dual temperatment, of the kind ascribed to Burt, in which the contrasting elements remain in conflict; or is a balanced blend equally likely?

Presumably Hearnshaw derived his suggestions from Burt's autobiographical sketch (Burt 1952a). But Burt ascribes the view to his parents, and is treating it playfully. I do not think Burt imagined for one moment that his readers would take it seriously; and if he could have known that it would one day be solemnly advanced as a partial explanation for his own mental disturbance, it would surely have given him endless amusement. The truth of the matter is that our ignorance of the genetic facts in this case is so complete that our speculations can lend themselves to almost any interpretation we want to make: that this 'mixture' was responsible for an unbalanced temperament; or a balanced one; or a richly diverse one; and so on, according to the manner in which we choose to imagine these imaginary constituents combining.

Another hereditary influence is mentioned later: 'There was in all probability an innate instability in Burt's psychosomatic make-up' (ibid.: 277). In evidence, some reports from Burt's sister, herself a medical practitioner, are mentioned. But actually she only suggests that certain 'physiological functions' were 'no doubt innate'; and she of course had no very reliable grounds for making the suggestion. All that can really be said about these various speculations, whether of Saxon–Welsh ancestry or of psychosomatic instability, is that they may contain some element of truth; and they may not.

So far as *environmental factors* are concerned, Hearnshaw (ibid.: 279) begins by remarking that 'The profound influence of the early years of life on personality development is now an accepted doctrine among psychologists'. That this vague generalization has been exceedingly popular among psychologists and educators we need not dispute. Ever since it was adopted, with sweeping dogmatism, in the early years of the century by such diverse movements as psychoanalysis and behaviourism, it has been treated by some as an article of faith. But not by everyone. More cautious writers have often urged that it is too sweeping – (for example, Allport 1955: 31–3); and Sluckin (1971: 9), to whom Hearnshaw appeals, only says in the passage quoted that early experiences *may* have a profound effect, not that they *must*. More recent writers are still more cautious. Clarke and Clarke (1976: 3–24), after surveying findings, conclude that 'a child's future is far from wholly shaped in the "formative years" of early childhood'. The events in Burt's early life which Hearnshaw lists as exemplifying the principle are not such as might convince even a moderate sceptic.

The first aspect mentioned is the character of Burt's schooling before the family moved to Warwickshire in 1892, when he was nine years old. Before that, while they still lived in London, Burt apparently attended a local elementary school in one of the poorest parts of the town. Exactly which school it was, and how long Burt attended, are unknown; but Hearnshaw

(p. 273) surmises that most of the children must have been 'an obstreperous crowd of little gamins'. Young Cyril had to survive as best he could in what Hearnshaw calls the 'gamin culture'. 'Cyril . . . had to mix with this mob, and somehow survive' (ibid.). Cyril must – this is the suggestion – have picked up all sorts of unspecified bad habits from his unsavoury companions. But then, instead of straightway displaying these habits, they somehow remained submerged for most of his life beneath the conventional behaviour of a middle-class academic. 'He had learned the gamin art of survival, and from that time on there was a gamin component to his own personality, which though overlaid by a polite veneer, persisted, much of the time below the surface, for the remainder of his life' (p. 273). But the component did surface eventually, when Burt was in his sixties.

Hearnshaw makes all those assumptions which are consistent with the interpretation he wants to make, conveniently ignoring any possibility which might conflict. Why, for instance, should we not suppose that Burt, with his middle-class background, was revolted by the 'gamin culture' – always supposing that this was what he encountered? And how convenient it is that the habits he is supposed to have acquired are weak enough to be overlaid for the greater part of his life (enabling him to secure a reputation for sound behaviour in his early and middle life), yet strong enough to persist for more than fifty years (to emerge when required to explain the frauds).

A second alleged influence concerns the move to Warwickshire, when Burt was nine and began to attend a 'middle-class' grammar school. The change in both school and home environment must indeed have been great; Hearnshaw (p. 273) calls it 'incredible'. The reader might imagine that Cyril, fresh from the trials and tribulations of the 'gamin culture', would find all this an enjoyable relief. But this is to forget that there is a 'duality' of personality to be explained: the change must contribute to an underlying weakness of character. Accordingly we find that 'The sharp break . . . was, it may be hypothesised, a major reason for the duality of his own personality, together with a genetic contribution from his mixed stock, part Saxon, part Celtic' (ibid.: 274). Once again, a convenient interpretation is chosen, though there is not the slightest positive evidence that any such effect occurred, but rather the reverse, for apparently 'Burt was quick to adapt himself to his new surroundings, and came to love the country' (ibid.).

Yet another early environmental influence mentioned is Burt's training in the classics. Hearnshaw remarks that the classical scholar was often given the task of writing Greek and Latin prose or verse in the style of one of the ancient authors. This, he suggests, was 'in a subtle way a training in pretence'; the scholar had to produce a perfect 'fake'; and so 'For more than ten years of his early life Burt was subjected to this regular discipline' (ibid.: 263–4). Hearnshaw seems here to have hit upon the explanation of

221

how Great Britain acquired the reputation of 'perfidious Albion': so many of our diplomats used to be trained in the classics.

There is so little positive evidence for any of these suggestions, whether hereditary or environmental, that if there were not supposed to be an eventual deterioration of character to explain, and if we did not also adhere to the prevalent nostrums about early childhood, it would not occur to anyone to mention them. It would not occur to anyone to suggest that, even if they happened, they necessarily had the effects postulated, and not some other, equally plausible, outcome. Indeed, it can be demonstrated in Hearnshaw's case that it was only after he had become convinced of Burt's guilt, and thought he had something to explain, that he mentioned these things at all. The Memorial Address of 1971 refers to Burt as 'fortunate in his birth and in his background' (Hearnshaw 1972: 31); and the early chapters of the biography, describing Burt's childhood, give no hint of pathogenic factors. There is nothing whatever to suggest that a 'duality' is in the making. But these chapters were written before Gillie's accusations, whereas the speculations about genetic and environmental factors were added later, when he was looking for an explanation.

Later shocks

During Burt's middle years, his behaviour was stable and productive. The dual temperament and the *gamin* component were held in check. Why was this? Because Burt was 'finding his métier' and this enabled him to achieve an 'equilibrium' (ibid.: 274). But not indefinitely:

> In the late 1930s things began to go wrong, and over the last thirty years of his life Burt suffered a series of setbacks which gradually upset his inner balance, always somewhat precarious.
>
> (Ibid.)

These setbacks will be examined in turn. They are set out in Table 9.1, where they are accompanied by the dates when Burt's main delinquencies are supposed to have occurred. The table also lists certain successes which Burt enjoyed over the same period.

Some critics, such as Eysenck (1982), have doubted whether these setbacks would be enough to account for Burt's breakdown, and have accordingly placed greater stress on the hereditary elements. But this does not seem to be a very fundamental criticism. Hearnshaw himself does not maintain that the setbacks would be sufficient by themselves, but only in conjunction with a pre-existing weakness. That is why he needed to imagine those early influences. The difference here between Hearnshaw and his critics appears to be a comparatively minor one, consisting in a disagreement about the relative strength of the earlier and later factors – a

Table 9.1 Timetable of crimes, shocks, and successes

Shocks		Alleged crimes	
Date	Incident	Date	Incident
Late 1930s to 1952	Breakdown of marriage	Late 1930s onwards	'Devious' behaviour
1941	Loss of research material		
1941	Onset of Ménière's disease	1947–68	Falsification of factorial history
1950s	Breach with old department		
1953/56 & 1963/64	Two waves of critics	1955–66	Twin frauds
1963	Loss of editorship	1961	Parent–child correlations
1966	Ménière in right ear	1969	Educational standards

Successes	
Date	Incident
1946	Knighthood
1947–63	Editor, *Brit. J. Stat. Psychol.*
1948	Hon. D.Litt., Reading University.
1950	Fellow, British Academy.
	Hon. Fellow, Jesus College, Oxford.
1950s	Several important public lectures.
1954	Organizing Committee, International Congress of Criminology.
1964	Patron, Association of Educational Psychologists.
1971	Thorndike Award.

disagreement which arises because nobody has a reliable, or even an unreliable, way of measuring the strength of any of these factors, and therefore no grounds for any firm conclusion. The position taken here is simply that these later setbacks are as uncertain in their effects as were the earlier influences.

1 The marriage breakdown

Burt married in 1932, when he was already forty-nine years of age. It seems to have been an odd arrangement from the start. He was some twenty-six years older than his wife; and according to Hearnshaw (1979: 131), he was 'strangely unenthusiastic . . . the enterprise seemed fantastic to most of their friends . . . both preferred their own work to each other's company'. If one were looking for signs of instability in Burt's character, it is surely here in this belated gamble that one would begin. But Hearnshaw's hypothesis requires Burt to be still in a stable phase at this point, so the matter is passed over without comment. Instead, the end of the marriage in 1952 is treated as 'a heavy blow to Burt's pride' (ibid.: 275).

Of course, this is perfectly possible; but not a shred of evidence is produced to support it. Hearnshaw (p. 274) himself tells us that 'It is an area of Burt's life veiled in secrecy. Nothing to do with his marriage has been preserved, every scrap of evidence removed from the records.' But in this case it is impossible to reach any reliable conclusions about the effect of the separation. Many men would be only too delighted if their wives would pack up and leave; and for all we know Burt was vastly relieved to see the back of her. He may have been more than content to return to the bachelor life he knew so well. He had a loyal housekeeper, a devoted secretary, a charming friend in Mrs Warde, and a flat on Primrose Hill which he thought one of the best in London. Many men would have settled for this setback.

2 Loss of research material

There can be little doubt that in 1941 Burt did lose much research material which he had collected over the years. Hearnshaw (p. 275), who needs another setback, describes it as 'a disaster of catastrophic dimensions'. But there are several crucial uncertainties. First, nobody knows how much was lost, or what it was. As we have already seen, much of the material may have been dispersed to different places – the college, Wales, or Eton Road – and so the presumption is that *not* everything was lost. In particular, it is not certain that the twin data were lost.

A second uncertainty concerns Burt's reaction to the loss. Hearnshaw (p. 282), assuming that Burt had lost the bulk of his twin material, speaks of his 'gradual realisation during the summer of 1941 of their almost certain loss'. Again, no evidence is given for any such reaction. Such evidence as there is actually seems to suggest the opposite. Thus his housekeeper, Miss Archer, wrote that:

> Whilst at Aberystwyth and then again at University College, Sir Cyril told me he was too busy with lectures, his students and college affairs to miss packed up material. It was only after his retirement, when he revised some of his books and wanted to work on his accumulated material, that he realised that a lot of it had got lost somewhere, and started to ask for it.

Hearnshaw (p. 251) actually quotes this passage without seeming to realize that it strongly suggests that, in April 1941, Burt did not even realize he had lost very much, let alone feel it was a catastrophe. Archer's statement that after his retirement Burt realized that a lot of material had got lost 'somewhere' also suggests that the material had been dispersed to different places, and so it should not be assumed that if anything was lost it must have been lost in the air raid.

Banks (personal communication) suggests that Burt probably left behind in London only research material which he had finished with himself, and was keeping in case it proved useful to research students. So it would not have been a great loss if it were destroyed. But anything of great value to himself, which he had not finished working on, such as the twin material, he probably took to Aberystwyth to work on and to ensure its safety. So Burt was not worried during the war, because he knew it was safe. But some of this was mislaid during the return to London, so it was then he became worried. However, they managed to find some of it among their stores: as Miss Archer says (ibid.), Burt was 'always very glad to find something "useful" upstairs.'

3 Burt's ill health

Here at last is something which is reasonably well documented. The first attack of Ménière's disease in 1941 seems to have been highly unpleasant and at least temporarily incapacitating. By the time the second attack came in 1966 new drugs were available, which eased the problems very considerably, but undoubtedly Burt suffered a great deal of inconvenience, and worse, from this painful disorder. But how far Burt's mental balance was upset is debatable. Many people suffer from illness in their later years without becoming unbalanced. So we require additional evidence that these troubles had the psychological effect Hearnshaw postulates. This might be found in the timing of the attacks: the first attack coming while Burt's 1943 paper was in preparation – the first, according to Hearnshaw, to show signs of deterioration; and the second, less convincingly, coinciding with the 1966 paper. But any such connections require very firm proof, because Burt never suffered a lengthy breakdown in health. There is no evidence that he ever had sick leave from the university, and he maintained in old age a work load which many younger men would have found a heavy strain.

4 The breach with his old department

Burt's whole life had centred on the Galtonian tradition, and there can be little doubt that he most ardently hoped that, when he retired, a successor would be appointed who would continue it, as he had done on Spearman's retirement. He must have been correspondingly disappointed when things turned out differently, and this may well have been among the most unwelcome events of his later life. Of what followed, we have only the account given by others, and little record of Burt's own views. Burt is said to have been permitted to continue with some lecturing in the department, contrary to the university's settled practice, and to have tried to interfere in some of the arrangements which his successor made for the running of the department. If Hearnshaw's account be accepted, then certainly Burt behaved unwisely in certain respects. Such behaviour is not, however, so very unusual among those who have retired from important positions. There are no good grounds here for supposing that his disappointments had upset his mental balance.

5 The loss of the journal

When the *British Journal of Psychology* inaugurated a statistical section in 1947, Burt became joint editor with Godfrey Thomson. After Thomson's death in 1954, he became sole editor, as he had in effect already been for some time. But the society became dissatisfied with his management of the journal, chiefly on account of the costs of producing it, and disagreements about where it should be printed. So Whitfield was appointed joint editor in 1957; but again Burt was soon in sole charge. Finally, in 1963, after renewed complaints, Audley took over and Burt's long association with the journal ended.

Hearnshaw points out, rightly in my opinion, how advantageous the position of editor was to Burt, in providing him with a ready platform for his views, and an established place in the psychological world; and no doubt Burt fought tenaciously to retain it. Perhaps its loss was a 'severe blow' (1979: 195). But perhaps the severity can be exaggerated. It came when Burt was eighty years of age. It is not unreasonable to suppose that a man will by then have acquired some philosophical detachment in face of the inevitable losses of old age. One would be quite as justified in stressing how very fortunate Burt must have felt to be able to retain such a position for so long, as in urging that it must have been a heavy blow to lose it. Further, the loss comes when, according to Hearnshaw, Burt was already far gone in his career of deception; and we can hardly regard as a major cause of deterioration an event which does not occur till a man is eighty. It is to be hoped that retirement from the post of editor will not be too widely quoted as a contributory cause of mental illness.

6 The attack on selective education

Down to about 1950, the year of his retirement, Burt's ideas about intelligence and education enjoyed wide support: he was swimming with the tide. But in the post-war climate the tide began to turn, and during the twenty years of his retirement there was mounting opposition to educational selection, and to the whole complex of ideas about inherited ability. The trend culminated in the Labour government's declared intention of introducing comprehensive education, endorsed by the House of Commons in 1965.

Hearnshaw notes that the attack on selective education came in two waves, in 1953–6 and in 1963–4, and he sees Burt's two main twin papers of 1955 and 1966 as being a reaction to this double onslaught. According to Hearnshaw (1979: 241), these papers 'were his rejoinders, as he himself makes clear, and were motivated by a determination to get the better of his critics'. But this is not the whole of Hearnshaw's explanation. If it were, Burt's reaction might be perfectly sane. He might calculate that he could best win the argument by inventing irrefutable evidence for his standpoint; and therefore invent it. In this case, Burt would be a level-headed villain. This straightforward interpretation of Burt's behaviour has seemed the most likely to some commentators (for example, Mackintosh 1980).

But Hearnshaw goes further than this. He wants to introduce Burt's mental deterioration as an intervening factor. He believes that Burt's 'egotistical and devious behaviour was a reaction to the setbacks he began to suffer in the late 1930s, and that as the setbacks accumulated, so the changes in his personality became more pronounced' (p. 286). So it is not simply that, faced with criticism, Burt invents data; but that the various setbacks – which include these political attacks – increasingly disturb the precarious balance of his personality, until eventually he becomes willing to cheat rather than see his opponents triumph. Thus Hearnshaw's explanation involves both a reaction to the attacks, and a mental deterioration. Here again Hearnshaw is refusing to believe that Burt's behaviour could have been the straightforward reaction of a sane villain. For Hearnshaw, the supposed decay of Burt's integrity, after a lifetime of honesty, requires the hypothesis of psychological disturbance.

Hearnshaw's account of Burt's motives in writing these two papers is unsatisfactory. First, Burt's 1955 paper certainly seems to have been written primarily as a rejoinder to the environmentalists; but in the case of the 1966 paper a more important motive seems to have been the desire to meet Shields's 1962 observation that he had previously given insufficient details about his twins. This is an important difference. It undermines Hearnshaw's argument, because, on his own view, it was the 1955 paper which contained genuine data, whereas it was the 1966 paper which contained the fabrications. So it would be when Burt was *not* primarily concerned to answer the environmentalists that his chief deceit comes: precisely the wrong way round.

Second, Hearnshaw's allegation that Burt's motive was simply 'to get the better of his critics' is yet another of the insinuations which Burt's critics so often produce in place of sound evidence. It might be said of anyone who is engaged in defending his position that he wants 'to get the better of his critics'. Of course he does. No doubt the angels in heaven, if they ever indulge in anything so degraded as an argument, are motivated solely by a pure desire to attain the truth, and have no interest in winning the argument as such. Is Hearnshaw trying to tell us that he himself, and the majority of psychologists, operate on this elevated plane and eschew the vulgar business of wanting to win an argument? What matters is not whether Burt wanted to get the better of his opponents, but whether he wanted to do this to the exclusion of a proper consideration for the truth; whether he really was willing to cheat rather than see his opponents triumph. Hearnshaw has not demonstrated that Burt's motive was indeed limited to wanting to win. He has insinuated it by stating, quite correctly, that Burt wanted to win, and implying that this was all he wanted. He has not argued his point; he has assumed it.

Burt was not, of course, the only psychologist to react to the attacks of the environmentalists. Why, then, should he be selected as especially resenting them? Hearnshaw argues that Burt's papers show signs of hasty and emotional composition. This we have already seen he fails to substantiate. It may be added that, even if this were true, it would not show that Burt had cheated; only that he got angry about it.

In summary, Hearnshaw has provided no adequate demonstration that Burt did react to these various 'setbacks' in the way he postulates, and in several cases there are obvious alternatives.

Triumph and disaster

There is also a more general objection to the argument. Any man's life, especially if it is a long one, is likely to be enormously rich in events of the most varied character, important and trivial, rewarding and punishing, fulfilling and frustrating. Any of these events might in fact be especially influential in the life of a particular person, and the total effect of the whole is only too likely to be extremely difficult, if not impossible, to assess – at least in the present state of psychological knowledge. Moreover, this environmental variety impinges, as Bartlett (1932) long ago emphasized, upon an equally complex variation in the temperaments and characters of the reacting individuals. It follows that it is fatally easy to find events which will give plausibility to a great many hypotheses. The range of materials is so large that there is no difficulty in picking out incidents to support our preconceptions, and overlooking the numerous other incidents which may conflict.

Hearnshaw's treatment of Burt's later life illustrates this danger. He believes that Burt's character declined, and that this was precipitated by setbacks. He duly finds a number of setbacks, and, thinking his hypothesis established, looks no further. But he overlooks at least two additional considerations.

First, there is nothing especially noteworthy or surprising in the circumstance that Burt encounters numerous setbacks in his later years. Most of us do. Of the six 'shocks' mentioned by Hearnshaw, three are very regular accompaniments of that stage of life: his ill health; his loss of control over his old department; his loss of the journal. Perhaps the decline in the popularity of his views, and his estrangement from his wife, also border on that category, for they must surely often be experienced by the elderly. Only the loss of the research material is clearly unconnected with advancing years. Thus it is likely that one could find similar incidents in most people's later life. If such common events have any reliable tendency to elicit a deterioration in personality, this ought to be a frequent accompaniment of later years. The number of persons whose mental balance is precarious cannot be small, judging by the incidence of neurotic and psychotic disorders, and so a deterioration in personality in response to 'setbacks' should be fairly predictable. Hearnshaw quotes no evidence that anything like this actually happens, which reveals that his assertions are not founded on any scientifically established system of generalizations. They are merely plausible guesses designed to support his preconceptions. But many people certainly do manage to meet and master the 'slings and arrows of outrageous fortune', and so it is not surprising that Hearnshaw could produce so little evidence that Burt really did react in the way he imagines.

A special aspect of Hearnshaw's argument is, of course, that in Burt's case the deterioration was accompanied by delinquent behaviour. This certainly does not find an echo in established generalizations. It is well known that all criminal statistics tend to agree strongly in suggesting that the incidence of crime is highest in adolescence, and declines steadily throughout life, not excepting old age. In extreme old age, indeed, we appear to recapture the innocence of the infant, along with so many other childhood traits. In believing that Burt became a delinquent in later life, Hearnshaw has certainly given himself a hard nut to crack, and perhaps it is not surprising that he falls back on mental imbalance.

Second, one ought to consider whether the troubles Burt encountered may not have been counter-balanced by successes. Is it accurate to concentrate attention so exclusively upon the failures? The period in Burt's life from 1940 onwards, which Hearnshaw depicts as a time of troubles, could also be described as a success story. Table 9.1 lists the main possibilities open to us, of which the knighthood was the highlight. This, the first ever awarded to a British psychologist, brought him a most gratifying correspondence from friends and colleagues eager to express their goodwill. At the same time he had the satisfaction of returning at last from his exile in Aberystwyth to resume the headship of his department, and the chance of developing it in the directions he wanted. He is popular among his many research students: they raise a petition to allow him to continue longer in the department. And so in 1950, lucky enough to be rid of an unsuitable wife – we are still supposing a selection of the possibilities which suit us – he is free of his departmental responsibilities and can settle down happily in his Primrose Hill flat, his reputation assured, and his time his own. And so the story continues – editor of his journal, lecturer in great demand, author of a flood of papers, recipient of the Thorndike Award. This is the happy warrior.

To have concentrated exclusively on these successes would have involved no greater selectivity than Hearnshaw's concentration on the setbacks. Certainly they might sensibly be regarded as providing some counter to the setbacks, and therefore as factors promoting mental balance. They are passed over in total silence: they do not fit the required pattern.

Mention of Burt's successes suggests another possible hypothesis to explain his misbehaviour – if misbehaviour there was. Instead of treating the deterioration as a reaction to setbacks, we could regard it as arising from the opposite cause: as a reaction to too much success. Perhaps, it might be hypothesized, Burt's head is turned by his triumphs, making him arrogant, intolerant, and self-important. Hence he resents all opposition and criticism, and cheats rather than allow others to defeat him. That pride goes before a fall is a story with a respectable pedigree. The point of raising this possibility is not to advocate it, but simply to illustrate how easily one can invent plausible stories and find evidence to support them. There is yet another possibility of course: that Burt was not unduly affected by either his triumphs or his disasters, but knew how to 'treat those two imposters just the same'.

Marginal paranoia

As we have just seen in the case of the attack on selective education, the explanation we are examining does not suppose that the various setbacks led directly to Burt's eventual delinquencies. They first produced a paranoid condition. Hearnshaw's (1979: 290–1) theory is

> that Burt suffered, in the final phase of his life, from a marginally paranoid condition; that this condition was a reaction to the setbacks which he experienced from the late 1930s onwards; and that it led to a regressive reactivation of behaviour patterns he had acquired in the London period of his boyhood, and from the 'gamin' sub-culture in which he had been immersed. This, we suggest, is the basic explanation of the deceptions and subterfuges which marred his work in its later stages. In the end he chose to cheat rather than see his opponents triumph.

In short, the setbacks provoke paranoia, and the paranoia provokes regression. The regression is the immediate origin of the deceptions.

It is widely recognized that psychiatric diagnosis is a somewhat unreliable business at the best of times. Even when it is conducted under the most favourable conditions, where the patient is readily available for daily observation and examination by experienced psychiatrists, mistakes can very easily be made. How reliable is this diagnosis of 'a marginally paranoid condition'? There is detailed medical documentation on Burt available from 1940 onwards (Hearnshaw 1979: 278), but there is no record that Burt was ever examined by a psychiatrist or psychological consultant; nor that any medical practitioner – or anybody else for that matter – ever suggested that he ought to be. Nor has any psychiatrist, since Burt died, examined the evidence and confirmed the diagnosis. The main attempts to assert seriously that Burt did suffer from a pathological condition have come from Hearnshaw, and also from Eysenck. But neither is medically qualified and neither has based his assertions on daily clinical observation. Again, neither breathed a word of his suspicions until after Burt's delinquencies had been alleged, and when some explanation was required. Not surprisingly, they give different diagnoses: for Hearnshaw, marginal paranoia; for Eysenck, a psychopathic state.

The evidence which Hearnshaw offers in support of his diagnosis consists primarily in the personality characteristics which Burt is alleged to have shown in his later years, which are examined in the next chapter. His conclusion (1979: 289–90) is as follows:

> Characteristic features of such marginal forms are self-aggrandisement and inflated egocentricity, oversensitiveness and suspiciousness, queru-lousness, secretiveness, compulsive drive . . . and hypochondria. Such a condition is . . . reactive, that is primed by external events, usually of a repeated nature, in a personality with some basic peculiarity or weakness. . . . The picture is concordant with the known facts about Burt.

Just as it is possible, in the great variety of events in a person's life, to pick out those which are concordant with your preferred hypothesis and ignore those which are not, so in the varied traits of character which are displayed even in a 'simple' personality, one may choose to emphasize a particular group to the exclusion of the remainder. When Hearnshaw wishes to show that Burt possessed the traits supposedly typical of a Ménière patient, he has no difficulty in discovering 'Obsessional, perfec-tionist characteristics and marked psychosomatic lability' (1979: 281 – see Chapter 10); and now he has no trouble in finding paranoid characteristics.

It is no answer to say that Hearnshaw has in fact recognized the existence of other features also, especially in his references to 'duality'; because it is also well known that much of the time the paranoid may appear rational and amiable. It is essentially a matter of the balance of contrasting traits.

Even a perfectly sound character may occasionally be secretive, sensitive, and querulous. The question becomes just how far these characteristics were developed in Burt. Were they so blatant that we are justified in calling him paranoid? Or so minor that we have to say they are well within the normal? It is significant that Hearnshaw's diagnosis is in fact 'marginal' or 'incipient' paranoia. Whether a critic wants to deny Burt's paranoia, or assert it, Hearnshaw can reply in the same way: that he said it was only marginal. Wherever he thinks the evidence is sufficient, or where he needs the explanation, Burt becomes paranoid; when the evidence is lacking, or he wants to stress Burt's sanity and balance, it is only marginal.

There is another fallacy in Hearnshaw's argument. In the various examples given of Burt's personality characteristics Hearnshaw mixes up two aspects which his theory requires him to keep separate. These two aspects are (1) items which demonstrate Burt's dishonesty, and (2) items which demonstrate his (marginal) paranoia. These should be kept distinct because the paranoia is supposed to account for the dishonesty. An instance of this tendency to combine the two is shown when he refers to 'the exaggeratedly egotistical and somewhat devious behaviour which became more and more prominent as the years went by' (p. 284). Hearnshaw uses the same incidents to justify his assertion that Burt was 'devious', 'unscrupulous', and 'dishonest' and that he was 'suspicious', 'self-aggrandising', and 'querulous'. The mode of argument is circular. If we ask how Burt's unscrupulous behaviour is to be explained, the answer is that he was paranoid. If we ask how we know he was paranoid, the answer is to point to his unscrupulous behaviour. But it is essential, where mental disorder is used to account for or excuse criminal behaviour, that the two should be established independently, as Flew (1973) has argued with force and wit in his exposure of the fallacies of psychiatric diagnosis in criminal cases. At one point, while purporting to establish Burt's paranoia, Hearnshaw breaks off to explain why we should not suppose that Burt had always been dishonest (1979: 285–6). The two questions, 'Was he mad?' and 'Was he bad?' are not clearly distinguished and separately established. Samelson (1980: 624, note 9) puts the point neatly when he remarks that 'Hearnshaw's explanation of Burt's actions as due to "pathology" does not seem very satisfactory. Except for Burt's physical afflictions, the diagnosis is almost exclusively derived from the behaviors it tries to explain.'

A type of symptom which, if found, would go far to establish a pathological condition, would be the delusion. The other traits – the egocentricity, the secretiveness, and so on – may well be encountered in persons who are sane enough. But delusions indicate a degree of remoteness from reality strongly suggestive of the psychotic. Hearnshaw remarks that 'paranoia in its fully developed form is generally classed as a delusional psychosis', but he adds that in the marginal form 'the delusional element is fairly inconspicuous' (p. 289). Did Burt suffer from delusions?

Hearnshaw's answer is a masterly blend of 'yes' and 'no'. 'It is difficult to say with certainty, but perhaps in the end he became a victim of his own delusions' (p. 178). 'Whether actual delusions were involved is harder to determine. . . . Was Burt himself deceived by his own deceptions? . . . of this we cannot be certain' (p. 290). Perhaps Burt suffered from 'marginal delusions'.

Here we may recall that one of Hearnshaw's main reasons for supposing that Burt suffered from delusions was derived from Burt's historical claims: Burt's 'apparently total blindness to the implausibility of his story suggests that a delusional system had taken over' (Hearnshaw 1979: 179). It was the attempt to check this point, and the discovery that Burt's story was accurate, which sparked off this whole inquiry.

The question of regression

The final step in Hearnshaw's (1979: 290–1) explanation is that the paranoia induced a regression to delinquent modes of behaviour acquired in childhood:

> a regressive reactivation of behaviour patterns he had acquired in the London period of his boyhood, and from the 'gamin' sub-culture in which he had been immersed. This, we suggest, is the basic explanation of the deceptions and subterfuges which marred his work in its later stages.

This is not the place to consider the general validity of the principle of regression, one of the most familiar hypotheses of the Freudian system. We need only ask how appropriate it is in the present case. From this point of view, two questions may be raised. Does it, in this instance, conform to the known facts? Does it, in this instance, explain what it is required to explain?

As regards known facts, we may repeat that Hearnshaw has provided no positive evidence that Burt was ever immersed in anything like a 'gamin' sub-culture. Burt was present in his London school for only a short time, and, even if they were an 'obstreperous crowd', there is no ground for thinking that Burt conformed and not the opposite. Of course there is equally no evidence that this was not so. But this merely shows that Hearnshaw's postulate may be true. It does nothing to show that it is. Reliable conclusions cannot be based upon the absence of evidence that they are false. Nor can one appeal to Popper's principle that a scientific hypothesis is tenable until it is refuted, because here there is no possibility of ever refuting it, for the evidence is unobtainable.

Suppose, however, that Burt did acquire those *gamin* behaviour patterns. Would this explain his eventual 'deceptions and subterfuges'? If any one thing can be said with some confidence in this whole business, it is surely that a 'reactivation of behaviour patterns he had acquired in the London period of his boyhood' would not explain his later lapses. These delinquencies are supposed to consist of a falsification of the early history of factorial analysis; of the fraudulent invention of data on separated identical twins; and of the pretence that educational standards had declined since 1914. Which of these behaviour patterns does Hearnshaw consider was part of the *gamin* sub-culture?

It may be said that this is a mere quibble: of course Hearnshaw did not mean that Burt learned those particular habits in his childhood. He meant only that it was then that he learned to rely on cheating, on underhand methods in general, and it was this to which he eventually returned. But if this was all that was intended, he should not have spoken of 'behaviour patterns'. This phrase suggests something specific to the observable behaviour of those *gamins* – a definite habit which might be acquired. But 'cheating' is an abstract concept, which might be exemplified in a great range of different behaviour patterns. If this was intended, why was it necessary to postulate regression to a *gamin* culture? Is cheating unknown at grammar schools? Or at universities? Why indeed is it necessary for a man to regress to any period in his past life before he can produce deceitful behaviour? Was not Burt, in his later life, sufficiently intelligent to appreciate what he might gain by dishonesty, without having to go back to any previous instance? Why should it not occur to anybody, at any stage of life, that this is a possibly advantageous thing to do? Hearnshaw is providing an absurdly complicated and dubious mechanism to account for something which, if it ever happened, could most simply be explained in far more ordinary terms. In short, what purports to be reliable scientific explanation proves on examination to be unverifiable speculation about superfluous absurdities.

The 'relentless onslaught' on Philpott

Hearnshaw also draws conclusions about the 'deterioration' in Burt's character from his relations with some of his colleagues, notably Dr S. J. F. Philpott. Philpott had been appointed by Spearman in 1920, and remained in the department until his death in 1952 at the age of sixty-four. He was from all accounts a tower of strength: he was 'a man whom to know was to respect and love', wrote his colleague Flugel (1954: 29). His main research interest lay in the study of 'work curves' and oscillations in mental output, and he claimed to have discovered certain constants which marked a revolutionary advance in the conception of mental work (Philpott 1932). A discussion of his ideas appeared in the *British Journal of Psychology* (1952, 43: 169–99) shortly before his death.

For Philpott's last twenty years, Burt was the head of the department;

and Hearnshaw accuses Burt of grossly ill-treating him. Hearnshaw (1979: 142–4) alleges that Burt regarded Philpott's research work with 'pulverising disdain', and subjected him to a 'barrage of memoranda and letters which poured scorn on it'. There is much more in the same vein, culminating in the assertion that 'Burt consistently blocked any promotion for Philpott, and, beneath his bland exterior, never relented'. Philpott, apparently, could be 'wholly ignored'; and 'it was this kind of conduct, even more than his opinions, that brought upon Burt in his later years so much distrust and hostility' (ibid.). Later Hearnshaw (ibid.: 286) writes that 'The relentless onslaught on Philpott and his researchers was certainly pathological in its intensity.'

The only definite evidence which Hearnshaw mentions in support of these sweeping allegations is some letters and memoranda which Burt wrote to Philpott between 7 and 27 January 1944, when the department was at Aberystwyth. The letters alone totalled some 16,000 words, exclaims Hearnshaw (ibid.: 143) incredulously:

> On the peak day, January 10th, no less than 8,000 words were typed. The longest letter was commenced just before midnight. What demonic force drove Burt to such extravagant and absurd lengths? Why did he think it necessary to spend hour upon hour of his time . . . to make this devastating attack on someone with whom a chat would have been easy and far more appropriate?

Those who read the letters will have no great difficulty in finding the answers to these questions. Some eight letters from Burt to Philpott have survived from this period. Two of them are entirely concerned with departmental business, and most of the remainder contain some reference to departmental business. In all, some 4,000 of the 16,000 words deal with such matters. As to whether the remaining 12,000 words, concerning Philpott's research, were excessive – a complaint which sits oddly with the other complaint that Philpott could be 'wholly ignored' – we should remember that Burt belonged to a generation which was used to writing letters far longer than most of us would dream of writing today. It has been calculated that Bernard Shaw's letters would fill thirty volumes of 1,000 pages – a total of something like 10 million words. Shaw wrote about ten letters a day, and was quite capable of ending a fifty-pager with apologies for haste. 'What demonic force', one might ask, 'drove Shaw to such extravagant and absurd lengths?' Burt's efforts seem to have been modest by comparison: of his letters dealing with Philpott's research, only two are of any length – those for 7 January, eight pages, and for 10 January, ten pages.

But why these 'lengthy screeds' as Hearnshaw calls them 'when a chat would have been easy and far more appropriate?' Part of the answer is that a letter does not preclude a chat; and Burt's first letter refers to 'what you said when you called this evening' (7 January 1944), and his second to a 'long discussion' (10 January 1944). Again, a chat was not always possible: 'So far I have had no luck in trying to get you on the telephone' (27 January 1944). But the main answer lies in the simple fact that Philpott had written to Burt. Philpott's letters have unfortunately not survived; but, as Burt makes clear, his own long letter of 7 January was in answer to *two* letters which Philpott had written to him on 3 and 4 January, and his long letter of 10 January was in answer to *two further* letters which Philpott had written on 7 and 8 January. The 'demonic force' in question, therefore, was the normal obligation to deal with one's correspondence. Philpott's letters must have been substantial, because Burt's two letters consisted of numbered points in reply to what Philpott had said, the first containing fifteen such points, and the second thirteen. Burt could hardly have been sure of being able to deal with all these points adequately in a 'chat'. As he said, 'I find it difficult to think out mathematical problems on the spur of the moment, especially if someone else is present. Further, when I have thought them out at leisure . . . I forget them if I do not put them down' (Burt to Philpott, 10 January 1944).

There is a remarkable contrast between Hearnshaw's attitude to Burt's letter-writing when he wants to suggest that Burt displayed a pathological ill will towards Philpott, and his attitude elsewhere when he has no such aim. Now lengthy letter-writing becomes a characteristic, and admirable, feature of Burt's behaviour. For instance,

> Burt must have been one of the most assiduous and remarkable letter-writers of his time! . . . many of his letters were of extraordinary length, at times amounting to a dozen, or even twenty pages. The time he devoted to correspondence must have been prodigious.
>
> (1979: 199)

Again, referring to letters written to his research students while he was at Aberystwyth, Hearnshaw (ibid.: 218) writes:

> These letters from Burt bring out both his critical powers and also the richness of the knowledge he had at his disposal. Often his letters, which might easily run to 5,000 words or more, are masterpieces replete with information and ideas, and they were poured out in profusion.

There is no good reason, in my opinion, why Burt's letters to Philpott should not be described in equally flattering terms. But Hearnshaw's desire to put Burt in the wrong on this occasion leads him astray. Thus he claims that the 'tone' of the material was 'infuriating', and gives three examples:

First, Burt had referred to the views of 'Dr Philpott'; and he apologizes for writing in this style, saying 'I find it easier to write about other people in the third person. It must sound very stilted and pugnacious' (Burt to Philpott, 10 January 1944). Hearnshaw refuses to accept that Burt's apology could have been sincere, and asserts that Philpott must have found it infuriating. No evidence is given that this was Philpott's reaction.

Second, Burt, commenting upon the difficulty of following some of Philpott's arguments, suggested that this difficulty was due, not to any shortcomings on Philpott's part, but to 'the fact that where mathematical arguments are concerned we are nearly all Goddam idiots' (Burt to Philpott, 12 January 1944). Hearnshaw describes this as 'snide humility' (ibid.). In my opinion, Hearnshaw has misunderstood the context in which Burt makes his remark. Earlier in the letter, Burt has referred to himself as the 'Goddam Idiot' as though Philpott had used this phrase to describe those who misunderstood him; so that Burt only seems to be picking up a phrase used by Philpott and using it in a way which he thought would smooth Philpott's ruffled feelings.

The final example concerned a visit by the Provost to the department, after which Burt said that 'The Provost noted that there was a good deal of work going on in connection with work curves, and I think he rather wondered how that helped the war effort' (Burt to Philpott, 27 January 1944). Hearnshaw says this was said 'just to be nasty' (ibid.), but again the context suggests a different interpretation. Burt had been reminding Philpott of the university's current policy, that only research which helped the war effort was to be encouraged. But he also went on to say that he did not think that need any longer be taken too seriously because 'I should be inclined to say that now we are nearing the end of the war . . . there would be more freedom . . . to select purely theoretical problems of scientific interest regardless of their immediate practical importance' (Burt to Philpott, 27 January 1944).

Hearnshaw appears to have gone through these letters looking for anything which could be made to bear an interpretation harmful to Burt. It would have been much easier, and far less misleading, to have listed some of the friendly and appreciative comments which Burt made. For example: 'After working off a few official letters, I have turned to what interests me very much more, namely, your own two recent notes' (Burt to Philpott, 7 January 1944); 'I think most people think you have hit upon something really valuable and original' (ibid.); 'I found that you threw a flood of light on my own problems' (10 January 1944); 'Your "theoretical curve" interests me enormously for its ingenuity' (12 January 1944); and so on.

It is also true that Burt's letters contain much pungent criticism of Philpott's research work; but his motive for embarking upon this must be weighed carefully. Philpott wanted to be promoted to a Readership, a position of greater academic prestige, though no greater salary, than his existing post of Senior Lecturer. The primary requirement for a Readership is eminence in research; but, as Hearnshaw (1979: 143) himself says, Philpott's work 'has not proved either as revolutionary or as fruitful as he himself supposed'. Banks (personal communication), who was working in his department at this period, describes the position as follows:

> Burt was very worried about all this, because he thought Philpott would not be accepted, and that this would be a dreadful blow. On the other hand, if he did not put Philpott forward he would be accused of prejudice against him. . . . In his letters to Philpott about 'work curves' Burt was trying to spur Philpott on to read more and to put his work into proper statistical setting, as well as to regularize his formulae and set the whole thing out more clearly and exactly. I don't think P. could do this. He was a marvellous undergraduate teacher, and a very good senior lecturer, but Hearnshaw's description of his research strikes me as hitting the nail on the head.

This interpretation seems to be borne out by the internal evidence of the letters, especially where Burt remarks that, in making his criticism, he is acting as 'devil's advocate' (Burt to Philpott, 7 January 1944). He was trying, for Philpott's benefit, to say all he could against his ideas. This is, after all, what a good research supervisor does all the time; and it would be far more appropriate to note how much time Burt gave up to try to help Philpott, than to accuse him of conducting a 'relentless onslaught'.

Even if Burt decided against supporting Philpott for a Readership, this does not in the least demonstrate that Burt was biased. Senior Lectureships are usually awarded for outstanding teaching and administrative work: this it would seem Philpott fully deserved – and received. Readerships are usually awarded for distinguished contributions to research. Hearnshaw gives no reason whatever for thinking he deserved this; the best he can say for it is that 'it was honest work, patient work, and perfectly harmless' (ibid.: 143). Surely this suggests that Burt's judgement was found.

Hearnshaw completes his account with a number of unattributed comments. 'After all this the two men were not on speaking terms; in fact one Aberystwyth student said that she never saw them speak to each other during their last two years there' (ibid.: 144). (The 1944 letters, as we have just seen, show how unreliable this assertion is.) 'Philpott in weary resignation came eventually to the conclusion that Burt was mentally unbalanced' (ibid.). No doubt Hearnshaw heard this gossip somewhere, but he should have given his sources. He ought also to have balanced the hostile remarks with the contrasting recollections which are also available. John Cohen, Emeritus Professor at Manchester, took his first and higher degrees at University College immediately before the war, and he remained in close and friendly contact with Burt for nearly forty years. He writes (Cohen 1983: 68):

Hearnshaw makes much of the alleged hostility between Burt and Philpott and of the ill-treatment of the latter by the former. I never saw the slightest sign of this, and for years I used to see them almost daily together. On the contrary, I always saw Burt treat Philpott in the friendliest way, and vice versa. Each held the other in high regard.

In reply to this, Hearnshaw (1984a: 6) writes that 'Cohen is . . . blind to facts about Burt that were obvious to others. He states that he never saw the slightest sign of the hostility between Burt and Philpott, even though this hostility was notorious.' But Hearnshaw provides no evidence that it was 'notorious', though if it were it should be easy enough for him to provide.

Banks was at Aberystwyth throughout the war, and remarks that Hearnshaw never asked her about anything which took place there. She continues (personal communication):

> I knew quite a bit about the relations between them, as I used to go to tea with the Philpotts in Aber. It was Mrs Philpott who had a pathological hatred of Burt, who she thought had ruined Philpott's career. This notion was accentuated during the war, because when Burt developed Ménière's disease he couldn't go to War Office meetings in London and sent Philpott instead, which Mrs P hugely resented. Some of this rubbed off on Philpott, who, to his credit, never said anything in the Department, and I don't think he was really unhappy, but in a ghastly position. Mrs P went on about Burt vitriolically at tea, even when I was there.

It must be remembered, of course, that both Cohen and Banks are favourably disposed towards Burt, and their recollections are no more to be relied upon without question after forty years than are anyone else's. But this does not justify brushing them aside, and attending only to the opinions of other, unnamed, persons who for all we know might have strong prejudices against Burt. If, for example, Hearnshaw happened to be relying upon what Mrs Philpott had told him, or upon what some third party told him that they had been told by Mrs Philpott, he could hardly claim to have established with any certainty that Burt had indeed conducted a 'relentless onslaught'.

Conclusion

Examination of the explanation proffered by Hearnshaw shows that it is little more than an invention and selection of causes and consequences which, if true, would be highly convenient for psychology. But it only serves to indicate how far psychology is from being able to cope with so complex a problem in a manner that deserves to be called scientific.

If psychologists had not been looking for an explanation for Burt's supposed frauds, it is highly unlikely that anyone would have attached much importance to the traits and events which now figure so prominently. It was not until after Gillie's accusations that the suggestion of mental imbalance made its appearance. It may be that some oddities of personality would have attracted attention. Thus his obituary in *The Times* mentioned a tendency to resent those who challenged his pre-eminence. But any such traits would probably have been seen as relatively unimportant quirks, a not uncommon accompaniment of advancing years.

If it is unlikely that Burt's 'psychological disturbances' would have figured prominently in his biography, how much more unlikely it is that the various factors which are supposed to have produced them would have been mentioned. Indeed, we know that they would not, for Hearnshaw did not mention them in the early chapters of the biography. Or let us suppose that Burt's delinquencies had never been 'discovered' – as might very easily have been the case – would anyone studying his life have listed all Hearnshaw's pathogenic factors and then asked why they did *not* result in delinquent behaviour? Would he have described Burt's early life in terms of a dual temperament, an innate psychosomatic lability, and a *gamin* sub-culture? Would he have explained how this unstable personality was held in abeyance during Burt's middle years by the satisfactions of a successful career? Would he have listed the setbacks of those later years, and described the paranoid characteristics which they induced? Would he have considered a regression to those *gamin* habits likely? And would he, finally, have asked how it was that all these causal agents failed to induce some flagrant fraud?

But if, peradventure, Hearnshaw had found himself asking these questions, there can be little doubt that he would have had not the slightest difficulty in accounting for Burt's unexpected honesty. It would have been because the rich compensations of his later years – the knighthood, the honorary degrees, the public recognition, the comfortable bachelor life – all combined to maintain his precarious stability.

Chapter ten

Burt's character

If a pathological explanation does not seem to meet the case, it remains important to assess Burt's character, especially with a view to determining its role in the Burt affair. Hearnshaw's analysis of Burt 'The man' (1979: chap. 13) is largely given over to a detailed examination of the origins and development of Burt's supposed pathology, whereas the task of providing a general description of his character is given much less specific attention. It is scattered in many different places throughout the book, and is only briefly referred to again in chap. 13. It is, of course, important to obtain as accurate a description of Burt's character as possible, otherwise any explanations are likely to be misconceived.

Although Hearnshaw's descriptive material is scattered in various places, it plays a most important part in his presentation of the case against Burt. According to Hearnshaw (1979: 284, 286), Burt displayed 'exaggeratedly egotistical and somewhat devious behaviour which became more and more prominent as the years went by', and was also 'self-aggrandising, suspicious, cantankerous and devious'. These assertions are supported by numerous alleged incidents reported by persons who were in contact with Burt – incidents which are generally much less reprehensible than the major charges of fraudulence, but which tend, in so far as we believe them, to render the major charges more plausible. If we are convinced that Burt was often underhand in small matters, we are more inclined to suppose him capable of deception in serious affairs.

This point is especially important because of the way in which Hearnshaw introduces his evidence about Burt's character. He does not first examine the major charges and then, having concluded that Burt was guilty, turn to the question of Burt's character. On the contrary, many of the allegations about Burt's devious and egotistical behaviour are introduced at an earlier stage, well before the main charges have been broached. This is particularly evident in chap. 8 concerning Burt's time at University College, which contains numerous highly damaging allegations (see especially pp.130, 142–4, 147–8, 152–3). It can hardly be denied that these preliminary attacks prejudice the reader. It is tantamount to the members of a jury reading hostile comment in the press before considering their verdict. Plainly, in elementary fairness to Burt, this material needs critical examination. But even if we agree with Hearnshaw's account, it remains essential to try to ensure that our judgement concerning the main charges is not biased by prior suggestions about character in general. Burt might have been cantankerous and self-aggrandising without falsifying the early history of factorial analysis or inventing research assistants and twin data.

Methodological requirements

The main source of information for Burt's character must lie in the observations and impressions of those who knew him. Numerous examples are to be found in Hearnshaw's book, and also in other places, notably in the centenary issue of the *Journal of the Association of Educational Psychologists*, entitled 'Sir Cyril Burt: the essential man' (Mcloughlin 1983). It should be noted, first of all, that Hearnshaw's conclusions are not based upon his own recollections, at least not in any obvious way. His only personal observations are given in the preface, and refer to the opinion he held immediately after Burt's death. He writes (1979: vii-viii):

> At this time my assessment of Burt and his work was almost wholly favourable. . . . I knew from my contacts with Burt as examiner and committee member that he could be difficult and prickly in business matters, but I regarded this as the justifiable prerogative of a great man in his dealings with lesser mortals. When approached for information I had always found him, as others did too, exceedingly generous in his response. It never occurred to me to suspect his integrity.

These remarks indicate that Hearnshaw, though admittedly not closely acquainted with Burt, had not only observed nothing to rouse his suspicions during Burt's lifetime, he had also heard nothing from others. His conclusions in the biography, therefore, are based chiefly on what others alleged subsequently, mostly after Gillie's charges in 1976.

Although personal recollections may be very useful to a biographer, they have to be treated with caution. It is only too obvious that a man's acquaintances may like or dislike him, and that their testimony may be coloured accordingly. There is a particular risk of bias when, as in the present case, a man stands accused of nefarious practices; and if he is also unable to defend himself, it becomes a prime duty of his biographer, certainly not to gloss over his faults, but to see that justice is done. So he must examine what he hears with critical detachment, carefully weighing and sifting his material to ensure that it deserves to be taken seriously. In particular he must ensure that the material used is representative of those who admired Burt, as well as of those who disliked him.

A further important requirement is that observations should be recorded as close as possible in time to the occasion. The longer the interval which elapses between the behaviour alleged and the recording of it, the less reliable the report becomes. However, the greater part of the material used by Hearnshaw was not written until after Gillie's accusations in October 1976. Thus, even if the behaviour alleged took place in the last year of Burt's life, at least five years must have elapsed before a record was made. Frequently, and this includes several of the most important reports, a much longer period, sometimes as much as forty years, must have elapsed before they were written down. Hearnshaw does not once mention this potential source of unreliability.

There are many further important requirements, which may be listed briefly. Second-hand observations and comments are to be avoided; the time and place of the observation should be recorded; any emotional involvement of the observer in the subject or the incident should be noted, whether tending to a favourable or unfavourable opinion; every effort should be made to ensure that the witnesses form a representative selection of those who knew the subject; and finally material should be checked and verified from other sources wherever possible.

To insist that nothing which breaks any of these rules should ever be used would be a counsel of perfection. But it will be found that they are repeatedly broken in much of the material to be examined, sometimes in the most blatant form, and that Hearnshaw entirely overlooks it. In so far as such defects are present, and especially in so far as the biographer himself ignores them, we are in danger of sinking to the level of the gossip column.

We begin with five letters written to Hearnshaw by academics who had contacts with Burt at some time between about 1935 and 1955. The first, from Professor Clarke, is dated 23 September 1976 and is the only one written before Gillie's article of 24 October 1976. The next three, from Professors Harding, Russell, and Stephenson, were all written shortly after this. The last, from Eysenck, came a year later. In no case does Hearnshaw indicate why the letters were written, whether spontaneously or in response to some request from himself.

Letter from Alan Clarke (23 September 1976)

Clarke's letter is of outstanding interest for a number of reasons. It is the first occasion on which an explicit accusation of dishonesty is made against Burt in writing. Several other persons have, of course, claimed that they knew or suspected that Burt was dishonest long before this; and Clarke himself makes such a claim in his letter. But all the other claims lack a

verifiable contemporary record. The first occasion when we can be sure
that Burt is suspected is 23 September 1976, almost exactly five years after
his death.

It may be argued that such claims can sometimes be verified by other
witnesses. In the present case, for instance, Ann Clarke would presumably
confirm her husband's story, for it concerned her as well as him. But such a
confirmation could hardly be regarded as independent. She and her
husband have obviously had so many opportunities of talking over the
alleged events that agreement between them is inevitable, especially
bearing in mind the strong interest they would have in presenting a united
front. In the remaining cases either no witnesses are quoted, or they are
only quoted at second hand. The first occasion when it can be asserted,
without possibility of contradiction, that Burt has been suspected of
dishonesty seems to be 23 September 1976. It is also the first occasion of
which we have record when such suspicions were brought to Hearnshaw's
attention.

Clarke's letter refers to incidents which are said to have occurred in
1950, some twenty-six years previously, and according to Hearnshaw
(1979: 148) these incidents 'sowed the seeds for their later role as
instigators of doubts as to Burt's integrity'. Hearnshaw shows no signs of
appreciating that Clarke's memory might be somewhat imperfect after
more than a quarter of a century.

Hearnshaw's account (1979: 148) begins with a couple of introductory
sentences:

The Clarkes after graduating at Reading enrolled as Ph.D. students with
Eysenck at the Maudsley Hospital. Since Eysenck was not then a
recognised teacher of the University they had formally to register with
Burt, who was one of the examiners for their theses.

He then quotes a lengthy passage from Clarke's letter which will repay
study:

After the Ph.D. vivas [writes Clarke] Burt said that we were both to
glance at some brief summaries he had made of our theses and approve
them, because 'I like to publish some of the more promising results'.
These summaries proved to be a little inaccurate. We corrected them,
and almost forgot about the incident. In the autumn, to our astonish-
ment, we found two articles under our authorship in the *British Journal
of Educational Psychology* implicitly attacking Eysenck. We did not
recognise them as the same summaries (of which of course we had no
copies) we had corrected at University College. Our theses had indeed
been critical of the 'dimensions of personality' approach [i.e., the
approach favoured by Eysenck] – but the whole emphasis of 'our'

articles was slanted. We went personally to Eysenck to apologise, who, hearing our disclaimer, was exceedingly generous, saying that this sort of play was typical of the old man. When I asked him for advice he suggested that I should let the matter drop. Nevertheless I wrote an angry letter to Burt, and was told that he thought we were out of the country and hadn't therefore sent galley proofs. By this stage we had become quite clear that Burt was dishonest, and predictably he later quoted 'our' two articles as independent support for his attack upon Eysenck.

The circumstance that the Clarkes had not retained copies of the corrected summaries makes it impossible, of course, for anyone to check these directly against either Burt's original uncorrected summaries (which are also unavailable), or against the 'articles' which eventually appeared. Thus the story depends entirely upon the accuracy of Clarke's memory. However, it is possible to examine the Clarkes' own summaries, which appeared in their two theses, lodged at University College, and compare them with the published 'articles'. If Clarke's story is accurate there ought to be very considerable differences, corresponding to the changes which Burt allegedly introduced into the conclusions they had reached. Hearnshaw makes no attempt to make this check, but simply accepts Clarke's letter at its face value, as evidence of Burt's devious ways. Yet there are a number of points which need to be checked.

First, Clarke's statement that the journal contained two 'articles' under their authorship is misleading. In fact, these publications comprise two out of three items appearing under the heading 'Summaries of research theses', a section which appears routinely in this journal. And this is all they are. That by Alan Clarke (1950b) is entitled 'The measurement of emotional instability by means of objective tests' and is one-and-a-half pages in length. That by Ann Clarke (Gravely 1950b – her maiden name) is entitled 'An investigation of perceptual tests as measures of temperament' and is one page only in length. Both summaries are comparable in length to the summaries frequently required of Ph.D. candidates, and neither would normally be referred to as an 'article', which suggests a more elaborate piece of work. By calling them 'articles' Clarke implies that Burt introduced extensive alterations and increased their significance as a critique of Eysenck. This may be thought a small point; but it is through the accumulation of small inaccuracies that a great inaccuracy is built up, and those who wish to accuse others of dishonesty should take pains to be strictly accurate themselves.

In order to support the very serious allegations which he is making against Burt, Clarke ought also to have given some examples of the kind of alterations which he thinks Burt introduced, contrasting these with the conclusions actually reached in the theses. But he only states that the theses had been 'critical' of the 'dimensions of personality' approach, whereas the 'articles' were 'implicitly attacking Eysenck' and that their whole emphasis was 'slanted'. No evidence is given. I have myself examined the two original theses, and the two published summaries, and I have been quite unable to find any justification for Clarke's charges. On the contrary, both of the published summaries appear to me to be accurate and well-balanced accounts of the main points contained in the theses. Evidence for this statement follows.

Alan Clarke's *thesis* (Clarke 1950a) states at the outset that 'several of the tests herein are based on Dr Eysenck's previous work' (see preface). Then, in a section headed 'Summary and evaluation' (chap. vii), Clarke gives the inter-correlations of the three best tests (Table 46, p. 166). His conclusion is that 'The coefficient of multiple correlation of these tests with neuroticism was .384, which clearly confirms that even when taken in combination and given appropriate weighting, these tests do not correlate sufficiently highly with the criterion to be of any practical value' (p. 166). The last sentence of the thesis is 'Finally, in the writer's opinion, of the tests employed in this research, only the motor-association techniques appear to warrant further development.' The allegedly 'slanted' *summary* has the following conclusion: 'None of the tests proposed has a sufficiently high validity coefficient to claim any practical value for purposes of screening or diagnosis. Moreover, being individual tests, and requiring somewhat elaborate apparatus, they would, in their present form, consume as much time, and need as much expert control, as would be required for an ordinary psychiatric interview. However, these defects might no doubt be overcome by farther research; and the detailed findings of the present investigation suggest the more promising lines for improvement' (Clarke 1950b: 202). There seem to be no grounds here for serious complaint; indeed, the final sentence of the summary appears, if anything, rather more favourably inclined towards Eysenck's tests than does the thesis – the reverse of Clarke's allegation.

Ann Clarke's *thesis* (Gravely 1950a), under the heading 'Summary and conclusions' (chap. xii), states that 'The conclusion is therefore reached that although it may be possible to discriminate between two groups such as those employed in this research at a fairly high level of statistical significance, it is improbable that any of the tests investigated could be usefully used for screening purposes' (p. 222). Specifically comparing her own results with those of Eysenck, she writes: 'The present results on the whole show far smaller discrimination between the groups tested than did the previous work' (p. 223). Her final sentence is: 'In the opinion of the present writer, a great deal of further research would be necessary before any of the measures could have any useful clinical application' (p. 224). The allegedly 'slanted' *summary* has the following conclusion: 'Although with several of the tests there are small positive correlations between the results of the test and the subject's neurotic condition, these correlations (with the possible exception of the questionnaire on symptoms) are far too low for the methods to be of any practical value. There is little evidence for the suggestion that non-verbal or perceptual tests might yield better indications of temperamental differences than verbal, at any rate in their present condition' (Gravely 1950b: 204).

Such evidence as we possess indicates that there are no grounds for Clarke's allegations in either case, and if he wishes to maintain his charges, he must offer something better than unsupported twenty-year-old memories.

Even if it were shown that Burt did make substantial changes in the published summaries, it would still remain to show that he was wrong to do so. Much must depend upon Burt's official position in relation to these two research students. It is generally accepted that a supervisor has certain legitimate interests and rights in the work which his student does, and especially in any publications which result from the work. The supervisor will probably have given the student much help in the form of ideas, hypotheses, methods, and so on. So it is usually accepted that the supervisor's name may legitimately appear, as the senior author, on any paper reporting the research. Under these circumstances, it must frequently happen that the supervisor has the last word on what goes into the paper. If, then, Burt was the supervisor for these two theses, very little objection could reasonably be raised if he did try to influence the reports – provided, of course, he did not falsify the outcome; indeed, it might be thought generous of Burt to permit the summaries to appear without insisting that his own name was included, thus giving his students full credit. It becomes important therefore to determine exactly what Burt's position was.

In the acknowledgements at the beginning of his thesis, Alan Clarke refers to Burt as the 'Supervising Teacher' and states that he 'has at all times been ready, both in correspondence and in personal discussion, to offer advice when difficulties arose; such advice has proved invaluable' (Clarke 1950a, preface). In the acknowledgements at the beginning of her thesis, Ann Clarke states that 'The writer wishes to thank her supervisory teacher, Professor Sir Cyril Burt, for the generous way in which he has put his time at her disposal, and for the valuable advice he has given during the course of the work' (Gravely 1950a, preface). In marked contrast to these comments, neither thesis acknowledges any assistance from Eysenck whatever.

One subsequent elaboration of Clarke's allegation is worth mentioning, because it illustrates how easily the gossip grows. Burt has been accused of altering the articles of contributors to the *British Journal of Statistical Psychology*, of which he was editor, without their permission and often at the proof stage. Gibson, in his biography of Eysenck, repeats this charge, and illustrates it by referring to Clarke's story about the Ph.D. theses (Gibson 1981: 34), thus transferring the whole incident to the wrong journal. Clearly Gibson cannot have consulted either of the journals in question to check the story, but he has managed to add another piece of 'evidence' to the allegations about Burt's behaviour as editor of the statistical journal.

Three letters

Professor D. W. Harding became Professor of Psychology at Bedford College, a constituent of London University, in 1945, and so was a colleague of Burt during the last five years of the latter's time at University College. Harding's letter (29 October 1976) was written only five days after Gillie's article. It does not date the events which it describes; but they must have taken place – if they took place at all – in the late 1940s. Harding first describes how, when his acquaintance with Burt began in 1945, he had 'nothing but respect and liking' for Burt; but gradually, as he got to know him better, he 'began to disapprove of what he did', until eventually he came to the conclusion that in some respects Burt 'just had a bad character' (Letter from Harding to Hearnshaw, 29 October 1976; see Hearnshaw 1979: p. 147).

The only instance of Burt's 'unscrupulous' (ibid.) behaviour which Hearnshaw quotes from Harding concerned a committee which was considering whether to establish a clinical diploma in Eysenck's department at the Maudsley Hospital. Harding describes what happened as follows:

> Burt was the most determined opponent of the Diploma, and Aubrey Lewis the main supporter. Finally there came a meeting at which it was definitely agreed that the diploma should be established with Eysenck's proposals accepted in outline. Philpott was secretary of the Board, and when his minutes came round before the next meeting this very definite decision had been changed into an agreement that the discussion should be continued. Aubrey Lewis arrived at the meeting in a state of controlled seething, and of course objected to the minutes of the previous meeting. Burt blandly expressed his impression that we had not actually made a decision, but everyone else had to say that the minutes were wrong, and the item was altered as Lewis wanted. When I spoke to Philpott afterwards he said rather sheepishly that, of course, he knew it was wrong, but Burt had absolutely insisted on his phrasing it as he did.

Harding does not present his colleagues to any great advantage: Sir Cyril tries to deceive the committee in order to get his own way; Aubrey Lewis, Professor of Psychiatry at the Maudsley – he is described by Gibson (1981:

39) as possessing a 'reputation for ferocity and over-bearing manners'; he was knighted in 1959 – arrives spoiling for a fight; while Philpott, a senior lecturer in Burt's department, and President of the British Psychological Society in 1948, falsifies the minutes.

Harding's account of what Philpott said to him – namely, that Burt insisted he phrase the minutes as he did – is second-hand. All that Harding can vouch for from his own experience is a series of very ordinary events: Philpott's minutes said the decision had been postponed; Burt says he thinks that is correct; the other members disagree and alter them. Harding's statement that he recalls Burt expressing his opinion 'blandly' – which implies, presumably, that one could tell from Burt's manner that he was insincere – is hardly convincing. Even if Burt did insist that Philpott phrase the minutes in a certain way, it is not at all clear why this shows that Burt was being 'unscrupulous' or 'devious'. Why, after all, did Philpott allow Burt to interfere? Perhaps Burt sincerely thought that Philpott had made a mistake. As evidence to be used in condemning Burt twenty-five years later, all this is hard to take seriously.

The measurement of individual differences had been a major concern at University College ever since Galton and Pearson inaugurated the biometric approach in the late nineteenth century, and more especially since Spearman had arrived in 1907. When Burt retired in 1950, the tradition had lasted for half a century; and to many members of the 'London School', as it was sometimes called, this was one of the most valuable and distinctive features of British psychology, to be cherished and defended against all comers. But Burt's successor, Roger Russell, was an animal psychologist from Pittsburgh, and a very different proposition from anything that University College had so far experienced.

Russell was not by any means unsympathetic to the established traditions. In fact, at the time of his appointment, he was working at the Maudsley Hospital exploring connections between animal behaviour and personality differences; and he invited Burt to continue working in the department for a time, lecturing on statistics and supervising his remaining research students. But this gave rise to considerable strain, as so often happens when a retiring head remains on the scene of his former glories. Such difficulties are widely recognized. It is a condition of appointment at some boarding schools that a retiring head shall not continue to reside in the same county; and a bishop is often expected to leave his diocese when his time is up. Similarly, it was a long-standing custom at University College that retiring professors should not continue to lecture in their old departments. Russell generously sought, and was granted, an exception for Burt; but it would have been wiser to let the custom take its course.

In his letter to Hearnshaw, written three weeks after Gillie's article, Russell (15 November 1976) describes the difficulties which arose, culminating in Burt being requested to retire fully in the ordinary way. From what little Russell says, it appears that Burt unwisely opposed changes which Russell wished to introduce, and of course had every right to introduce. But there is nothing to suggest that Burt was unscrupulous or dishonest; until, that is, we reach the last few sentences, which give a very damaging impression.

> I think it is a pity that Burt could not have retired as gracefully as Flugel did. In my experience he was intolerant of those who held different views than his own and of those he thought might be challenging his pre-eminence. I believe that your search will uncover instances which suggest he was egocentric to a degree which led him to protect his position at almost any cost.

The open-ended insinuation contained in the last sentence is grossly damaging. Burt is not accused, it will be seen, of any particular crime; he is simply alleged to be capable of almost unlimited misbehaviour in defence of his own interests. No evidence whatever is provided for this assertion. Russell has not furnished a single instance in which Burt did anything unscrupulous or devious. He says, 'I believe that your search will uncover instances . . .'. Either he knew of such instances – in which case it was his plain duty to list them in order to justify his imputations; or he did not – in which case he had no right to make them. Hearnshaw is equally at fault. He should either have asked for evidence to justify the allegation; or he should have omitted it.

The publication of Russell's letter was especially harmful to Burt, because by this time Russell had become the Vice-Chancellor of Flinders University, South Australia, as Hearnshaw reminds his readers. But no man should be damned on the say-so of another, however eminent that person may be.

William Stephenson, a distinguished figure in the factorial world, enjoyed contacts with both Spearman and Burt extending back before the war. He had embarked upon a Ph.D. with Spearman as long ago as 1926, and remained at University College with Burt in the thirties. After the war, he was at Oxford for a time, before emigrating to America. Few people have been in a better position to judge both men, at least so far as the period down to 1950 is concerned.

Hearnshaw seizes upon a phrase in Stephenson's letter (dated 1 December 1976) in which Stephenson says that, before the war, Burt several times dropped hints in lectures that 'he, Burt, was the initiator of factorial methods' (see Hearnshaw 1979: 130). Hearnshaw returns to this twice (pp. 177 and 269) and seems to regard it as an early example of Burt's deviousness. He continues by saying that 'while Spearman was alive Burt did not dare to do more than "drop hints"'.

It is not at all clear to me why 'dropping hints' should be regarded as reprehensible. When Burt arrived at University College in 1933, Spearman was a figure of enormous prestige. Might it not be that over the years an altogether too reverential attitude towards Spearman had grown up in the department, and that Burt felt it his duty to introduce a little fresh air? A newly appointed professor, even when as in this case he is expected to continue the established traditions, might still wish to introduce some new points of view. What this incident really illustrates is that Burt did not rush in like a bull in a china shop, loudly criticizing his predecessor. He tactfully began by 'dropping hints'.

We do not, of course, know what Burt actually said, so that our justification for drawing any very definite conclusion is flimsy. Since he was only 'dropping hints' presumably whatever he said was rather vaguely phrased. But even if Burt was claiming to be the initiator of factorial methods – and Burt's writings on this matter usually give the credit to Pearson – and even if all such claims were unfounded, Burt himself might still have believed that the claim was valid. And if Burt believed the claim was valid, why should he not make it? Hearnshaw too often writes as if any criticism of Spearman, and any suggestion that others might have been involved in the origins of factorial analysis, is a sign of moral turpitude. There is nothing sacrosanct about particular interpretations of psychological history, however long and however widely they may have been believed.

Whether Stephenson himself wished to be allied with such imputations against Burt's honesty seems doubtful. He adopted a restrained and cautious attitude to Burt's alleged misdoings, which is well illustrated in his account (Stephenson 1983: 52) of his contact with the media in 1976:

> When the story of Burt's malefactions broke, Mike Wallace, an American news reporter, invited me to New York to be interviewed for the CBS television news program, *Sixty Minutes*. In the course of a lengthy interview, I refused to blacken Burt in any way, much I felt to Wallace's chagrin. . . . The program on Burt duly appeared on *Sixty Minutes*, with Liam Hudson against Burt. My own interview with Wallace did not appear.

In this case, then, Hearnshaw appears to be extracting evidence against Burt which is neither justified, nor, apparently, intended by Stephenson. Every suspicion, every insinuation gradually contributes its quota to the impression that Burt was a 'bad character', capable of practically anything; and as each piece of mud sticks, it provides an adhesive surface which helps each subsequent piece to stick more readily.

Letter of H. J. Eysenck (16 November 1977)

Eysenck's reactions to the Burt affair have shown a curious reversal. Immediately after Gillie's article, Eysenck was among the first to spring to Burt's defence, denouncing the attack as a political smear campaign and an attempt at character assassination (Letter to *The Times*, 12 November 1976). Shortly afterwards, he was assuring Burt's sister that 'the future will uphold the honour and integrity of Sir Cyril without any question' (Letter to Dr. Burt, 16 November 1976). Exactly a year later he was writing to Hearnshaw to add his own nail to Burt's coffin.

Eysenck was born in Germany in 1916, and came to England in the thirties to escape the Nazis, eventually graduating in Burt's department in 1938. After taking a research degree, also with Burt, Eysenck was able to establish his own department at the Maudsley Hospital, which he has made one of the most prolific centres of psychological research in Britain. With Burt's retirement in 1950, Eysenck became the dominant figure in psychometrics in Britain. The relations between prominent psychologists and their more independent pupils or followers have often been marked by initial enthusiasm followed by eventual estrangement. The story of Freud and Jung is well known, and Burt and Eysenck, as we shall see, seem to have followed a not dissimilar pattern.

Eysenck's letter to Hearnshaw, which came more than a year after Gillie's article, recounts an incident from the thirties. This is one of the earliest examples of Burt's 'deviousness' which Hearnshaw accepts. In 1938 Thurstone had published his monograph on 'Primary mental abilities', which was something of a turning point in factorial history, since it firmly rejected Spearman's notion of the general factor. According to Eysenck, Burt suggested to him that they should jointly review Thurstone's contribution, Burt writing the text and Eysenck carrying out some calculations. Eysenck continues:

> Burt then showed me the paper he had written under our joint names, and I thought it was very good. I was rather surprised when it finally appeared in the *British Journal of Educational Psychology* in 1939 with only my name at the top, and with many changes in the text praising Cyril Burt.

Eysenck describes this as 'rather unscrupulous', and Hearnshaw (1979: 285) adds that 'This high-handed practice of altering material supplied by others and slanting it to enhance his own achievements and reputation became, of course, almost standard practice with Burt, carried out brazenly and without compunction.'

We have already seen how inadequately Hearnshaw has established this allegation, and Eysenck's example is no better. Eysenck states in his letter that Burt's offer occurred 'I think, in my first year at University College in his department.' This can hardly be accurate. Burt's offer can not have been made earlier than the year in which Thurstone published his monograph, 1938, but this was the year in which Eysenck graduated. In any case, Burt would surely be unlikely to make such a flattering offer to a first-year student! Eysenck makes no effort to prove his allegations, whether by reference to the original version of the review – presumably this has long since disappeared – or by quoting the published text. But anyone who reads the review (Eysenck 1939) will find that there is little or nothing in it which could be described as praising Burt. Eysenck has forgotten his own very pertinent remark that 'As psychologists will know better than anyone, memory unrefreshed by reference to printed material can play strange tricks' (Eysenck 1977c: 258). Hearnshaw accepts Eysenck's story without question.

This story is also repeated by Gibson (1981: 36), but with a significant difference. Burt again alters the text to flatter himself; but this time it is Eysenck, not Burt, who drafts the original version, as well as performing the calculations. Such a material difference does not encourage confidence. The review as published certainly adopts a very Burtian stance; but it would be surprising if, at that time, Eysenck did much more than echo his professor's views. After all this, it seems a little unfair that Burt should be accused of the high-handed practice of slanting material.

The uneasy relations which developed between Burt and Eysenck underline the need for caution. It is hardly even-handed to assume that Eysenck must invariably be reliable, dispassionate, fair-minded and self-deprecating; and that Burt is always an unprincipled liar. But Hearnshaw's account is one-sided in presenting Burt as invariably a villain. For instance, Burt was '. . . deeply suspicious of rivals, particularly his own most able students, like Cattell and Eysenck' (1979: 290); and Eysenck's 'promotion and advancement Burt did everything in his power to stop . . .' (1979: 270). Hearnshaw provides not the slightest ground for including Cattell in this category, and he seems to have forgotten that only a few pages earlier he had included Eysenck's name in a list of students who '. . . paid glowing tribute to the help they received from Burt' (1979: 265–6). The allegation that Burt did 'everything in his power' to stop Eysenck's promotion is strongly worded. Everything? And if Burt did oppose it, are we expected to assume that this necessarily puts Burt in the wrong? Any such opposition must have occurred primarily before Burt's retirement in 1950, when Eysenck was 34 years old. Burt appears to have had doubts about the wisdom of promoting Eysenck too rapidly; and it was, of course, perfectly legitimate for someone in Burt's position to be cautious. Subsequent events certainly suggested that his caution was not unreasonable, and if Hearnshaw had mentioned these events a rather different impression would have been given.

During the forties and early fifties, Aubrey Lewis, the head of the Institute of Psychiatry, regarded Eysenck as something of a 'spiritual son' (Gibson 1981: 66) and backed his advancement strongly, Eysenck becoming Reader in 1950 and Professor in 1955. His promotion, so Gibson (ibid.: chap. 4) assures us, met with considerable hostility from a number of psychiatrists, who disapproved of Eysenck's approach to mental disorder and its treatment, and who 'may well have felt resentful against Lewis for advancing a man like Eysenck to a position of such power at the Maudsley' (ibid.: 66). It was not very long before the relations between Eysenck and Lewis himself, at first so cordial, became increasingly uneasy. Eventually there was a 'momentous clash' (ibid.: 70), followed by an unbridgeable gulf, the disagreement centring on Eysenck's contention that psychologists should practice behaviour therapy.

I do not wish to suggest that we should simply adopt the opposite view, and regard Burt as always in the right. It would not be at all surprising if Burt did sometimes resent the challenge of the younger generation. This surely is a common enough attitude among the established, and not a rarity whose mere existence is sufficient to condemn Burt. It is also common enough to find the younger generation suspicious and hostile towards their elders, whom they see as standing in the path of their advancement. Hearnshaw seems simply to adopt whatever interpretation will discredit Burt. When Burt is in the position of the younger generation, as in his relations with Spearman, Burt is assumed to be trying to steal his credit and take his place. Spearman is never seen as overbearing or domineering. But when Burt is in the position of the older generation, he at once becomes resentful and repressive. In personal disagreements, there may surely be faults on both sides. Since none of the allegations against Burt in this matter have been adequately supported, and since Burt had no opportunity of putting his own side of things, we have no good grounds for condemning him.

In addition to any personal grounds for tension, it ought not to be forgotten that there were genuine and important intellectual differences between Burt and Eysenck. Both were committed to psychometric tests; but where Burt wished to moderate these with clinical judgement (as we have seen), Eysenck was strongly critical of much clinical work, and preferred behavioural assessment. Behind this disagreement lay the oldest of psychology's rifts – between the behaviouristic Eysenck and the introspective Burt.

Eysenck's reminiscences

The examples so far considered were all used by Hearnshaw in his biography; but the most striking example of a posthumous attack on Burt's character comes in a later article by Eysenck (1983) entitled 'Sir Cyril Burt: polymath and psychopath'. It is remarkable for the dramatic volte-face which it reveals, from Eysenck's original vigorous defence of Burt in 1976, to this unrestrained personal attack seven years later. It consists largely of vague and unsubstantiated anecdotes about things which he claims to recall, sometimes at second hand, from up to forty years earlier, or even longer. A selection follows.

First, referring to Burt's pre-war lectures, which he had attended as an undergraduate, Eysenck (1983: 58) writes that Burt

> kept arguing against Spearman's conceptions, and emphasising his own approach and even priority. When I looked at the original writings of these two men, I could find no support for Burt's claims, and this again diminished his image in my eyes.

Eysenck does not detail Burt's claims, Spearman's conceptions, the original writings he consulted, nor how these refute Burt's claims; nor does he appeal to any written record made at the time, some forty-five years previously. Presumably he is referring to Burt's historical claims, so that his own claim is that he was aware of Burt's alleged tendency to falsify the historical record about forty years before Hearnshaw made it public, while he himself was still an undergraduate. If Eysenck wishes this to be believed, he must explain why, some years later, he wrote that 'we owe the original formulation of factor analysis to Pearson, and not, as is often believed, to Spearman' (Eysenck 1952: 45). It is abundantly obvious that in 1952 Eysenck is simply echoing Burt's then recent historical account, which he now claims to have rumbled as an undergraduate.

Second, Eysenck (1983: 59) alleges that Thurstone told him in 1950 that Burt was 'devious and untrustworthy' and he 'would never take anything published by Burt seriously or believe anything he said'. This is recounted after more than thirty years, with no original record, and with no indication of what had aroused Thurstone's scepticism, or how he justified it; nor is the reader reminded of the rivalry between Burt and Thurstone over priority for the formula for multiple analysis.

Third, Eysenck (ibid.) recounts a story about a 'well-known statistician' (unnamed) who was asked by Burt (date unstated) to review a book by Eysenck (unspecified). The review (no reference) was 'extremely hostile and critical' (no details). Ten years later (date unstated) Eysenck meets the statistician in a queue (place unstated) and the latter informs Eysenck that actually the review had been quite favourable, but Burt, as editor, had changed it (still no reference and, of course, no evidence about what the original review contained). Here Eysenck is relying on what an unnamed witness claimed to have recalled ten years after the event. There is no explanation of why a 'well-known statistician' was so unconcerned about false material appearing over his signature, that he allowed ten years to elapse before he told Eysenck what had happened.

Fourth, the perennial subject of Burt's alleged opposition to Eysenck's promotion elicits the following story: 'His [Burt's] opposition (at a meeting of the University Selection Committee) became so emotional and exaggerated that the Vice-Chancellor told him sharply that she would be no party to a cabal!' (ibid.: 60). Clearly Eysenck himself was not present at this meeting. Presumably, then, the incident was retailed to Eysenck by someone else (unnamed). Eysenck is therefore asking us to believe something to Burt's discredit which he claims to be able to recall accurately after some thirty years, which was told him at second-hand by an unnamed person for whose accuracy he cannot vouch. That person was, of course, abusing the confidence of the meeting, and thereby demonstrating his unreliability.

This tells us nothing reliable about Burt. It does suggest that academic life revolves around backbiting, innuendo, second-hand gossip, and abuse of confidence; and that people form their opinions of others without regard for evidence and fact. In such an environment, Burt would indeed have needed at least as much craft to survive as in any '*gamin* culture'.

Eysenck (ibid.: 60) concludes, oddly enough, by saying that 'Burt entirely lacked the temperament and training of an experimental scientist'.

Finally, the contrast between Eysenck's attitude in 1976 and later naturally excites comment. As he says (Eysenck 1982: 3), it may be asked why he, and others, were at first 'so reluctant to believe in his guilt'. His reply (ibid.: 3) is worth examining:

> The answer, of course, is that most people are guilty of small dishonesties, but few are found to commit a serious crime. The psychopathic kinds of behaviour that Burt had shown towards me, for instance, while seriously affecting the prospects of a young student, were hardly 'crimes' in the sense that his later fraudulence was. Furthermore, of course, a serious accusation like that of Oliver Gillie demands evidence. . . . That evidence simply was not available until Hearnshaw's book was published.

Eysenck is, of course, quite right to suggest that the misdemeanours he has alleged are trivial compared to the later 'crimes'; but he is not justified in suggesting that these misdemeanours are comparable to the 'small dishonesties' which 'most people are guilty of'. He is, after all, using this behaviour of Burt to suggest that he was psychopathic; he cannot now suggest that it is comparable to 'small dishonesties' – unless of course he wants to imply that everyone is psychopathic. Eysenck's whole catalogue of misdemeanours is intended to suggest that Burt's behaviour was abnormal; it is intended to imply that it foreshadowed his later, and worse, 'crimes'. He cannot now claim that he originally defended Burt because these things were so trivial that his suspicions were not aroused. Anyone who thought Burt was psychopathic should immediately have been highly suspicious.

Eysenck is correct in saying that, until the evidence was available, judgement should be suspended about the later 'crimes'. Accordingly Eysenck was right not to accept the charges at once. But it does not follow that he was right to defend Burt so confidently. If he knew or believed that Burt had been psychopathic, he should have suspended judgement, not defended him. What he has to explain is how, if he believed Burt to have been psychopathic, he could have expressed such assurance about his innocence, when he must have known that Burt was perfectly capable of it, however much the particular incidents still required proof.

Miscellaneous cases

There were also a number of further exchanges between Burt and his colleagues from which Hearnshaw deduces that he became increasingly devious, high-handed, cantankerous, and unscrupulous. These are derived from (1) Burt's behaviour as editor (see especially 1979: 287–8), and (2); from his behaviour when disagreements arose in various matters (see especially 1979: 204–6). These instances will be only briefly considered, since the evidence advanced by Hearnshaw is sketchy.

As editor

In his treatment of material submitted to his *Journal of Statistical Psychology*, Burt is alleged to have displayed 'a high-handedness which frequently passed the bounds of propriety' – altering texts, and preventing the author from saying what he wanted (1979: 287). This was also alleged, of course, by Alan Clarke and by Eysenck, although as we have seen the evidence to support these instances was non-existent. Hearnshaw subsequently refers to two further instances, neither of which is any more convincing.

The first example arose out of a review which Burt wrote in 1960 of some experiments on telepathy by Soal. Hansel wrote a letter, for publication in the journal, in reply to this review. He gives his account of what happened next in a letter to Hearnshaw (20 April 1978), which Hearnshaw (1979: 287) summarizes as follows:

> Burt as editor altered Hansel's reply to this review. Hansel restored his original version in the proof, which was finally altered again by Burt. The published version, therefore, did not represent Hansel's intention, but Hansel was dissuaded by the British Psychological Society from taking the matter further.

Hearnshaw regards this incident as displaying Burt's high-handedness; as reflecting badly upon Burt's standards as editor. But clearly he can only believe this if he also believes that the British Psychological Society, at that time, held this same view – that is, that they too supposed at that time that Hansel's complaint was justified. Hearnshaw must believe this because if he did not he would necessarily recognize the possibility that they simply rejected Hansel's complaint. After all, if they rejected his complaint, and if that was why they dissuaded him from taking it further, Hearnshaw's case would dissolve; for if they exonerated Burt at the time, we have no good grounds for resurrecting the case now.

But if Hearnshaw thinks that the society dissuaded Hansel from taking the matter further, even though they thought his objection justified – even though they thought Burt in the wrong – one has to ask what motive Hearnshaw is ascribing to the society. It must be the desire to avoid trouble: they feared the scandal or controversy which might arise if there were any public rebuke of so eminent a figure as Burt. So they try – successfully – to dissuade Hansel from taking it further. And Hansel, not wanting to make himself unpopular with the society, agrees to drop it. It is only on this interpretation that the incident can be regarded as reflecting badly on Burt, for only so can we assume that the society thought he was wrong. But in this case there seems little to choose among Burt, deliberately suppressing other people's opinions; the society, deliberately letting him get away with it; and Hansel, in conniving at the whole improper behaviour. Hansel is not entitled to complain later if he did not stand up for himself when it mattered.

The second example comes from 1958. Dr C. Wrigley had indicated, in a letter to D. F. Vincent, that a footnote in a paper he had published in the statistical journal had been added by Burt, and not by himself. Wrigley then mentioned that Burt, as editor, made more changes in his manuscripts than might generally be expected; but he took this to be a continuation of Burt's tutorial role (Burt had been Wrigley's tutor at University College). He then said: 'Mostly I don't mind. He does not ever change the main arguments, and most of the incidental changes he introduces do seem to me to improve the paper' (Letter from Wrigley to Vincent, 23 September 1958).

Wrigley's own comments hardly justify any conclusion – except perhaps that Burt, as editor, often made changes which improved papers, but was scrupulous to avoid distorting the main arguments of a paper. In my own experience, editors vary greatly in the changes they introduce: some are chary of making any, and hesitant and apologetic about them; others alter freely, and take it for granted that they are entitled to do so – or that, if you want to object, you will do so (though they are often pressed for time, and give the minimum, if any, opportunity for objecting before publication). So Burt's behaviour here does not seem very extraordinary. However,

Hearnshaw then quotes from Vincent's reply to Wrigley (23 October 1958), in which Vincent says that he personally would mind very much, and he thinks the changes very extensive and highly excessive. Thus Hearnshaw is simply accepting the interpretation which Vincent placed upon the matter, not that of the supposed victim of Burt's misbehaviour. We shall have to return to Vincent in the final chapter.

As controversialist

Hearnshaw (1979: 204–5) takes two examples from Burt's correspondence in the sixties which illustrate, so he says, that Burt was 'extremely sensitive to those who in any way seemed to challenge his authority in his own areas of competence, and promptly jumped in to the attack'. The first example concerns an exchange of letters with McLeish, who had published a book containing, in Hearnshaw's words (1979: 205), 'remarks on intelligence and intelligence testing, written from a left-wing standpoint [which] provoked Burt, and he immediately counter-attacked'. Hearnshaw admits that McLeish originated the controversy, in a widely publicized book, and admits too that he introduced political considerations into a supposedly scientific debate. This behaviour, however, escapes criticism, while Burt is attacked for defending his own standpoint in private correspondence.

The second example concerns correspondence with Hudson, in which Hudson complains, 'in some exasperation', of 'frightful misrepresentation' (1979: 205–6). Hearnshaw quotes at length from Hudson, and concludes that 'in controversies of this kind Burt could be both slippery and unscrupulous'. But Hearnshaw quotes nothing from Burt's letters to support this judgement. He merely takes Hudson's side of the story without question. There may well have been a good deal of truth in Hudson's complaints. But when people argue there are often faults on both sides, and one is unlikely to reach a fair assessment by listening to one side only.

Burt's defenders

Hearnshaw does not maintain that Burt's behaviour had always been devious and unscrupulous. He believes that before about 1940 it was sound enough, and only subsequently underwent a deterioration. Thus he writes (1979: 285) that 'Those who knew him in the 1920s and early 1930s had a high regard for him, and any suggestion that his work was not entirely above board was regarded by them as unbelievable.' He quotes in support the opinions of Thouless and Cattell, both of whom knew Burt well during those earlier years. Thouless said, 'I find it quite unthinkable that he knowingly fudged his results.' Cattell wrote that 'If I had to base a judgement of Burt purely on my own interactions with him over the years

1924 (when I first met him) to his death, the fact is that it would record many instances of generosity, no instances of "cheating".' The many complimentary remarks which were addressed to Burt on the occasion of his knighthood in 1946 were also clearly based mainly upon those years (Hearnshaw 1979: 260). On the other hand, the adverse comments which we have been examining come predominantly from the post-1940 period. This distribution of opinion is, of course, consistent with Hearnshaw's view about the marked alteration which he supposes took place in Burt's character after about 1940. But are the opinions quoted by Hearnshaw a fair and unbiased sample, which accurately reflects a real change? Or has Hearnshaw inadvertently selected material which favours his own views, and would a more thorough search reveal more hostile opinions before 1940, more favourable opinions after 1940?

So far as the earlier period is concerned, some have of course maintained that Burt was always a devious character, notably the Clarkes. We have seen that they have provided no very convincing evidence for their view, but this failure does not demonstrate that Hearnshaw is correct. After this lapse of time, it is hardly surprising if very little has survived. One shred of evidence, perhaps hardly worth mentioning, concerns the neatly worded sobriquet 'the Old Delinquent'. According to Harding (personal communication), this was employed by May Smith, who had known Burt since his undergraduate days at Oxford; and Harding was prepared to believe that Burt's misbehaviour was of long standing. In my opinion, the evidence from these earlier years is insufficient for any confident conclusion to be drawn; but such evidence as we possess, from persons who knew him well at that time (Cattell, Thouless), is in Burt's favour.

So far as the post-1940 period is concerned, there is undoubtedly far more favourable opinion available than Hearnshaw mentions. The number of those who have expressed faith in Burt's probity is now very considerable. Even after the biography appeared, many have continued to express varying degrees of scepticism about the charges. Most refer to the period after 1940, and have appeared mainly either in the *Bulletin of the British Psychological Society*, or in the centenary issue of the *Journal of the Association of Educational Psychologists* (Mcloughlin 1983). It is surprising that Burt's biographer, who apparently had so little difficulty in finding persons willing to undermine Burt's reputation, should not have found more of these favourable comments to redress the balance, especially since they all have connections with University College or the world of education which would make them natural targets for enquiry.

Some of their observations are very brief, for example: Terence Moore, Emeritus Professor of Clinical Psychology, University of Aarhus, Denmark – 'a charlatan, a scheming fraud – never when I knew him, if there is any validity at all in personal impressions' (Moore 1983: 42); Grete Archer, Burt's housekeeper and eventual secretary from 1950 to 1971 – 'His whole character would have been incapable of any such thing' (Archer 1983: 54); Professor James Tanner, of the Institute of Child Health, University of London – 'The whole journalistic-political chicanery makes one retch' (Letter to Cohen, 10 November 1976; see Cohen 1983: 72); Babington Smith, a statistician and experimental psychologist at Oxford – 'I find the idea of deliberate falsification inconceivable in the man I knew' (Letter to Cohen, 11 November 1976; see Cohen 1983: 73). This publication also contains three longer expressions of support. That by Banks (1983) has already been mentioned frequently, but those by Wall and Cohen are also especially notable.

W. D. Wall, now Emeritus Professor of Educational Psychology at the University of London, has been a distinguished figure in post-war education. He studied for a Ph.D. with Burt during the war, and remained in contact with him until Burt's death. The opinion of the Clarkes (1980: 18) that Burt was 'a poor applied psychologist' may be compared with Wall's remark (1983: 43) that 'Burt set for me the high and ideal standard of the professional psychologist'. Wall's (1983: 45) comments on the evidence against Burt are pointed:

The flurry about Burt's later work and its political overtones, leaves me puzzled still and not a little incredulous, in spite of Hearnshaw's patient scholarship. It seems incomprehensible that someone as intelligent as Burt could have committed deliberately, the simple statistical gaffe of reproducing the identical coefficients of correlation a second time and claim that they were based on further data. Burt would be the first to know that an increase in sample size would almost certainly change, if only slightly, the value of correlation coefficients. Indeed, oversight is a more plausible explanation for such a slip than deliberate intent. Many of the other 'charges' – for example that his parental IQs were not based on specific testing, reflect more upon beliefs and methodologies current in his day than upon Burt's integrity. After all he never claimed them to be more than estimates. One wonders too about the 'invented' collaborators and particularly what bearing the destroyed boxes of data and papers might have had upon this mystery.

In the light of the evidence collected here, Wall's comments seem wholly justified.

John Cohen, Emeritus Professor of Psychology at Manchester, has from the beginning been one of the most uncompromising and caustic opponents of those he calls the 'detractors' (Cohen 1977). He begins his contribution by saying, 'I recall Cyril Burt with profound admiration, esteem and affection. For 38 years I had a continuous, most amicable relation with him, for seven of these years as his student' (Cohen 1983: 64). Cohen furnishes one of the most detailed and knowledgeable accounts of

Burt's character which has appeared. It is an essential corrective to the views of Hearnshaw, who lacked Cohen's long and close association with Burt.

In the context of the attacks on Burt's probity, a number of the personal characteristics stressed by Cohen are especially noteworthy. First, Burt's invariable insistence on meticulous accuracy, which he demanded from himself as much as from his students. Second, that though Burt held himself aloof and distant, 'anyone not too bashful or nervous could call in to see him in his office at any time without an appointment, and he could chat, offer cigarettes, and give advice without limit' (ibid.: 66). Third, Cohen notes that when he himself left the factorial field after the war Burt showed no sign of petulance or rejection, but continued to show a keen interest in his work. Fourth, Cohen criticizes the frequent assertion that Burt was primarily an applied psychologist, pointing out that Burt always displayed the widest and deepest theoretical interests. Finally, Cohen refers to the statement by Connolly (1980: i), in his introduction to the 'Balance sheet on Burt', that 'there now seems no reasonable doubt that Sir Cyril Burt perpetuated a fraud in that he fabricated data'. Cohen regards it as 'shocking that the President of the British Psychological Society, in an official BPS document, should be guilty of making such an outrageous and, in my opinion, unsubstantiated allegation' (Cohen 1983: 72).

There have also been numerous further expressions of support for Burt, from a remarkable variety of different people. Some of these, made in response to the British Psychological Society's endorsement of Hearnshaw's verdict, are mentioned in the final chapter. Some others, which have seemed to the writer to be especially memorable, are as follows. From Fraser Roberts, FRS, of Guy's Hospital Medical School: 'I should like to condemn most strongly the idea that he cooked his data' (Letter to *The Times*, 25 November 1976). From R. B. Cattell (1978: 18), Research Professor Emeritus, University of Illinois: 'I personally find it revolting that the insinuations against a man who so completely dedicated his life to our science, who made some of the main contributions on which we proceed today, and who is no longer here to defend himself, should evoke so little indignation as the present generation of psychologists apparently has the courage to show.' From Sir Halford Cook, a postgraduate student with Burt in 1939, and sometime President of the Australian Branch of the British Psychological Society: 'Burt will be remembered long after *all* his detractors will be forgotten' (personal communication; see Appendix D). From Moyra Williams (1984: 101): 'As a former student of the late Sir Cyril Burt at UCL, I was disturbed and disgusted by the presentation of him in [the BBC Horizon] programme. Far from being the bigoted, humourless, self-centred man depicted, most of his students found him, as I did, an extremely helpful, encouraging person, always ready to listen to original ideas. . . . It is remarkable that the programme did not include a single interview with one of his British students or research assistants.'

Most of these comments were written after the publication of Hearnshaw's biography, and so these particular documents were not available to Hearnshaw when he was writing. Later, in responding to them, Hearnshaw (1984a: 5) wrote that:

> it is valuable to have the testimony of those who personally knew Burt, often over a long span of years, and who worked with him closely. The main attackers (Kamin, the Clarkes, Gillie, McAskie, Dorfman, Gould), it should be pointed out had, on the contrary, no personal acquaintance with Burt, or in the case of the Clarkes, only the most tenuous formal contacts . . . surely some weight must be given, and I am sure ultimately will be given, to so much first-hand testimony from those who knew him closely over a period of time.

But it would have been perfectly possible for Hearnshaw to have obtained a similar collection before he published the biography; indeed, it is one of the primary tasks of a biographer to obtain 'the testimony of those who personally knew' his subject. Hearnshaw had only to circularize those well-known people who had been closely connected with Burt, and ask for their opinions. But he chose to restrict his pro-Burt statements to the pre-war years, and for the later period relied mainly on those who, for whatever reason, were hostile to Burt.

In Hearnshaw's view (1979: 284), the signs that Burt's character was deteriorating 'became more and more prominent as the years went by'. If this is correct, from the early 1940s onwards hostile comment should gradually increase as the deterioration developed, while favourable comment should gradually decrease. There are two weaknesses in the evidence which undermine it. First, Hearnshaw has not demonstrated the required gradual increase in hostile comment as the years go by. If the reader studies the dates of the misbehaviour alleged by Hearnshaw's witnesses, he will find that they belong predominantly to the decade from the early 1940s to the early 1950s. To this period belong the allegations made by Clarke, Harding, Russell, and Eysenck; and also the 'relentless onslaught' on Philpott. The main incidents which belong to a later time are those involving Hansel, Wrigley, McLeish, and Hudson; and I think it must be agreed that these are less serious matters than those alleged earlier. It might be said that this is because, after his retirement, Burt has less opportunity of displaying his degeneration. But this defence does not provide evidence for Hearnshaw's theory; it only offers to explain why the evidence is absent. Second, it has not been shown that favourable comments become sparser and weaker. Many of the complimentary references come from a later period than do many of the hostile comments.

Conclusions

Hearnshaw's account of Burt's character is unsatisfactory for several reasons. His selection of evidence is one-sided. The favourable views which he quotes belong mainly to those who knew Burt in his earlier years, while the unfavourable are drawn mainly from the later years. This naturally gives a strong impression that Burt's character deteriorated in his later years, in accordance with Hearnshaw's hypothesis. He also fails to treat the evidence critically, too often accepting the hostile comments of Burt's enemies without examination. When we add in the favourable comments, the conclusion must be that it is a matter of dispute whether Burt's character deteriorated. Many who knew him well – far better than some of the critics – would deny it.

The dramatic contrast between the views of Burt's character presented by his enemies and his friends certainly makes it very hard to reach a fair and accurate assessment. Hearnshaw (1979: 262) takes the contrast very much at its face value, as a reflection of 'startling contradictions' in Burt's character. It is an illustration of the 'duality' which he sets out to explain. But it is arguable that the contrast throws as much light upon the differing bias of the observers as it does on Burt himself. Friends and enemies will always tend to give discrepant accounts, especially where the subject is a controversial figure. It does not follow that the contrasting accounts have no basis in fact. As we argued, it is a common human trait to prefer those who approve of us to those who do not, and accordingly to present a more attractive face to the one than to the other.

But Burt's character is not irrelevant to 'the Burt affair'. It seems not unlikely that, especially when thwarted, Burt was capable of fighting his corner as hard as the next man, and that in the process he could be thoroughly awkward, and would exploit any advantage he possessed. But I have seen no adequate justification for singling Burt out as less scrupulous than those he crossed swords with, or for treating him as a moral pariah. No one can afford to be censorious in such matters. I can also well believe that Burt was in some ways an odd-ball; that his long and often solitary life left him lacking in some of the conventional habits and sympathies of the gregarious. 'He lacked ordinary social feeling,' remarked Harding (personal communication), meaning that he sometimes seemed unaware of the impression he was creating. But I do not think we should try to encapsulate him in any of the conventional psychiatric categories, whether as a creative psychopath, an incipient paranoid, or a common-or-garden obsessional. Burt was not only a student of individual psychology; he was also highly individual himself. If he belongs anywhere it is among those quintessential individualists, the English eccentrics.

Psychology has shown itself peculiarly incapable of judging Burt dispassionately and accurately. He was always something of an outsider, and became more so with advancing years. His less attractive traits acquired in some minds an altogether disproportionate importance, and his unpopular views provided an admirable excuse for vilification. Nature and circumstance combined to make him an enticing scapegoat. We must turn to consider the world around him.

Chapter eleven

How it happened: the accusation

For those who believe that Burt was guilty, 'the Burt affair' is the story of a personal failure. The precise interpretation of that failure varies. If Burt is believed to have been sane and healthy, the failure was a deliberate wickedness; if unbalanced or senile, an excusable weakness. But whatever the pathology, it remains an individual pathology; and as such it is the tragedy of an individual, which might have occurred in any science, and which bears no essential relation to psychology itself. From this point of view, a study of the affair can teach us much about Burt but little about psychology. It would follow also that Burt was accused because good reasons were found for suspecting him, and that the accusation was accepted because numerous competent persons found conclusive grounds for endorsing it.

But if Burt was innocent, the affair takes on a different, more problematic, meaning. We must ask how the mistake came to be made, and why so many made it. It may be that Burt's character was a contributory factor, but this can no longer be given pride of place. 'The Burt affair' ceases to be the story of a personal failure, and becomes a collective mistake. It is to be understood, less by probing into the secret life of the victim, more by observing the public life of his colleagues.

Social psychology has been suggesting, at least since the time of the 'culture pattern' theorists in the 1930s, that traditional or mainstream psychology places the burden of explanation too exclusively on the psychology of the individual and his biological inheritance, neglecting the social context. This has often been a criticism of the explanations offered by the psychometric movement itself; and however much particular writers such as Burt may at times have sought to recognize the influence of social life, their central concern remains, and must remain, the supposedly inherent talents and traits of the individual. It is this same objection which we are now making to Hearnshaw's way of explaining the Burt affair. Certainly he mentions the social context – the drive towards comprehensive education, the opposition which Burt encountered from his colleagues –

but Burt's reaction to these pressures is seen as determined primarily by his personal quirks and failings, and these in turn are traced to his individual history and his individual biological background.

In recent years, social psychologists have, unsurprisingly, turned increasingly to the social context. Thus Sarason (1981) in *Psychology Misdirected* argues that psychology has been a study of the individual organism unrelated to the history, structure, and unverbalized world views of the social order (see also *inter alia* Gergen 1973; Semin 1986; and review by Handy 1987). Such writers argue that this limitation applies also to psychology itself, the academic discipline: that psychologists have been wrongly assuming that their theories and practices are unrelated to, and independent of, their own relationship to the social order. So long as psychology was mainly a laboratory-based, university discipline these limitations could be overlooked; but the immense growth of applied psychology forces the psychologist increasingly to see his work in the contemporary social context, and to realize the extent to which he is often unwittingly influenced by the 'unverbalized world views' which he absorbs from his surroundings (Sarason 1981).

It is not suggested here that the Burt affair is to be explained entirely in terms of social factors, and that the individual psychology of Burt, and his colleagues too, can be neglected. These remain very important; but they are to be seen in a social context which is itself highly complex. The key to understanding is to be sought in the nature of psychological inquiry as it has grown up over the past hundred years, in the ambitions and personal relations of its practitioners, and above all in the relations between this psychological inquiry and the human world which it sets out to understand. Seen in this context, the Burt affair takes on a certain fatal inevitability.

The destruction of Burt's reputation was the outcome of a lengthy series of events. They may conveniently be considered in two parts. The first part, to be discussed in this chapter, concerns everything which led up to the original accusation in the *Sunday Times*. The second part, to be dealt with in the final chapter, concerns the publication of the biography and the general endorsement of its verdict.

Twentieth-century schools

We must begin with the character of the psychological world in which Burt worked. In the first decade of the century, when Burt was McDougall's pupil at Oxford, psychology was on the threshold of its quest for scientific status. Many of the early pioneers set out with high hopes, eager to become the Galileo or the Darwin of the new science. But things did not work out as smoothly as many expected. A major feature of the new psychology, at least down to mid-century, was a proliferation of different 'schools' or movements, each advocating a distinctive approach to the task ahead. As Woodworth (1949: 3) wrote in his *Contemporary Schools of Psychology*:

> a 'school' is a group of psychologists who put forward a certain system of ideas designed to point the way that all must follow if psychology is ever to be made a genuine, productive science of both theoretical and practical value. We have several such schools pointing in different directions.

Behaviourism, Gestalt Theory, Psychoanalysis, and Factor Analysis are perhaps the best-known of these schools. They originated in the first decade of the century, or a little earlier, and it is an intriguing historical question why so many should have arisen just at this period. Certainly, none of the schools sprang out of the blue. There were almost always antecedent influences and premonitory trends. However, the existence of competing recipes for a scientific psychology was an unmistakable indication that psychology had a long way to go before it deserved comparison with the established natural sciences.

Each school arose in connection with a special field of inquiry. Thus Behaviourism was associated with Watson's studies of animal behaviour; Gestalt Psychology with Wertheimer's experiments on perceived movement; Psychoanalysis with Freud's clinical practice; and Factor Analysis with Spearman's enquiries into intelligence. Under these circumstances it is hardly surprising if there were marked differences in theory and method, and it might be supposed that this provides a satisfactory explanation for their diversity. To an extent the suggestion is reasonable, but it cannot account for everything.

Although each school had its headquarters in a particular research area, none was content to remain there. Each regarded its chosen field as providing the key to the understanding of a much wider territory; and each was inclined to speak and act as if it alone was entitled 'to point the way which all must follow'. Factor analysis, declared Spearman, was 'a school to end schools'. In short, each claimed to find in its own field the pattern of scientific thought and method which it believed to be appropriate for psychology in general. Consequently, no school was content to remain quietly cultivating its own garden. Each proceeded to apply its principles over a wide area. So Freud regarded the principles he had devised for the understanding of neurotic behaviour as furnishing a guide to normal personality; Watson believed that animal learning was the prototype of human acquisition; and so on. And as each school extended its scope, they inevitably came into conflict.

It might have been hoped that the use of scientific methods would settle the differences among the schools, and show how far each was acceptable. But unfortunately their arguments often cannot be settled by reference to scientific method precisely because they are so often arguments about what is the correct scientific method in psychology. This is a problem of great complexity and no simple answer can possibly meet it, as James recognized when he said that psychology was concerned with the relations of the knower and the known, which physics leaves aside. Too often psychologists have tried to get away with that 'genial, whole-hearted, popular-science way' of formulating their problems which James (1892: 333) warned would not suffice.

But, however chequered the progress of psychology in the twentieth century may have been, and however ill-founded particular claims, this cannot be taken to mean that the whole venture is mistaken. James (ibid.: 335), in warning of the dangers ahead, said of the long-awaited Galileo or Lavoisier of psychology that 'come they some day surely will'. Perhaps the most illuminating standpoint from which to look at schools is that of the historian of science, Thomas Kuhn (1962). His analysis of the progress of science offers a corrective to undue pessimism. Kuhn suggests that, in the emergence of a new science, a long period may elapse before its practitioners manage to establish successful 'paradigms', that is, accepted patterns of scientific activity, which bring steady and productive progress. Before that happy state is reached, a science usually experiences a lengthy 'pre-paradigm' period, marked by the presence of competing schools of thought, but possessing no accepted means of deciding among the rivals. Kuhn indicated that in his opinion psychology, like some other social sciences, was still at the pre-paradigm stage.

If Kuhn is right, the rivalries of the schools and their successors do not necessarily mean that psychology can never achieve its goals. It may one day emerge from its pre-paradigmatic stage to confound its critics. But if it does, it may well look very different from anything which we envisage today. However, our purpose here is to draw attention to the character of psychology as it existed in Burt's lifetime, and especially during the period of his active career, from his arrival at Oxford in 1902 until his retirement in 1950. This was the period during which the conflicts of the schools were at their height, and this was the stage on which he had to play his part.

The existence of rival schools goes far towards explaining a number of the characteristics of the psychology of the period which are particularly relevant to the Burt affair. One is the degree of competition which it stimulated, and the consequent tendency to overstate claims and achievements. This readily leads to the suspicion that others are being unscrupulous, and to accusations of disingenuousness or worse. Thus Freud has frequently been labelled a charlatan. In the psychometric field, Spearman was accused of 'bad faith' by the French (Oléron 1957: vii). This arose because Spearman claimed – on the most slender grounds – that Binet's conception of a single measure of intelligence in 1905 was inspired by his own advocacy of the general factor the previous year. The French resented 'l'annexation de Binet'. Such suspicions are fanned by the absence of an accepted scientific method of deciding claims, and by conflicting views about how things ought to be settled.

Post-war trends

Many would say that schools in psychology are things of the past, and need no longer worry us. There is a good deal of truth in this suggestion. In every case the original doctrines and techniques have undergone extensive modifications, and often the changes serve to reconcile differences and underline similarities. Moreover, the original leaders have long since passed on: Watson, the last survivor of the founding figures, died in 1955; and with their departure, much of the early rivalry and contention has gone. But we should probably be unwise to assume that we have seen the last of them. Woodworth (1949: 5) wrote that

> If we could suppress them all for a couple of decades, very likely they would emerge again with the same vitality as before. It must be that they represent points of view that are almost inevitable till some higher synthesis is found capable of combining them all.

An example of the persistence of these points of view, even today, is to be found in a widely used text on personality by Mischel (1981). Recognizing the lack of a single perspective from which to organize his material, Mischel employs four successive perspectives, each with a distinctive set of hypotheses and methods. These he calls 'social behavioural', 'phenomenological', 'dynamic', and 'psychometric'. They are not hard to recognize as the contemporary versions of the four main schools – Behaviourism, Gestalt, Psychoanalysis, and Factorial Analysis – now much modified and up-dated, but still at heart unreconciled. They provide an admirable illustration of the remark with which Woodworth (Woodworth and Sheehan 1964: 390) concluded his last review of 'contemporary schools': 'Perhaps we might describe the living, growing record of psychology as a palimpsest underneath which has been engraved the now somewhat obscured but ever enduring history of the schools.'

The dominant school in Britain in the earlier part of the century was the psychometric or factorial, centred at University College. When Burt was in his heyday, in the 1930s and 1940s, British psychology was far smaller than it is today. In consequence, University College occupied a relatively more important position, rivalled only by Cambridge and Edinburgh. So the psychometric approach loomed large on the psychological scene, acquiring prestige from the eminence of Spearman and Burt.

After the war, it was inevitable that great changes would occur. When Burt retired in 1950 the Galtonian tradition had enjoyed a long innings. Rumblings of dissent were becoming increasingly insistent, and soon all the major tenets of traditional psychometrics were under attack. The accepted tests of intelligence were criticized as too narrow in scope – ironically, the criticism with which Burt himself had entered the field fifty years earlier. It was argued in particular that such tests failed to assess the more creative and imaginative aspects of intellect, and there was a vogue for appraising 'creativity' with 'new-type' tests (for example, Guilford 1950; Getzels and Jackson 1962; Hudson 1966). At the same time, there was growing support for the belief that the role of environment in cognitive growth had been underestimated (Hebb 1949), and that test scores were far more affected by the environment than the traditional testers had been willing to admit (Hunt 1961). If the critics were right, and the conventional scales could no longer be taken as a reliable guide to man's natural endowment of general ability – a powerful tool for selection and guidance in education and industry – many professional psychologists faced some uncomfortable re-thinking.

These doubts were reinforced by more general scepticism about the statistical and factorial foundations of psychometrics. Before the war, Bartlett expressed marked hostility: 'Once he plainly told an international audience in Cambridge that he never let statisticians loose in his laboratory' (Adiseshiah 1978: 133). Cambridge psychologists continued to be prominent in voicing opposition (Chambers 1943; Heim 1954); and many of the rising generation were influenced by the persuasive polemics of Zangwill (1950), who described intellectual testing as 'a technology whose theoretical foundations are distinctly insecure' (p. 141), and factorial analysis as 'a brilliant but misguided departure from the central path of empirical psychology' (p. 160).*

The rapid expansion of British psychology after the war hastened the decline of the London tradition. Most of the new universities, and many of the new polytechnics established their own departments; and their teaching and research interests were centred for the most part in experimental and comparative psychology, or in social and developmental areas, rather than in differential psychology. They also often turned for their inspiration to American sources rather than to home-grown ideas. It was a sign of the times when, on Burt's retirement in 1950, the chair at University College was filled by an American animal psychologist (Russell). This, as we have seen, marked the effective break with the long-established Galtonian tradition.

But however widespread the attack on psychometrics, these issues can still not be regarded as settled, any more than can the more general differences among the schools. The psychometric approach retains numerous supporters, as Mischel's survey of personality illustrates (Mischel 1981). So far as England is concerned, Eysenck remains its most powerful exponent, and he regards the traditional techniques for the measurement of intelligence

* For one view of 'the central path of empirical psychology' see Liam Hudson's *The Cult of the Fact* (1972).

as a paradigm which has proved its worth. His discussion of 'The paradigm and its critics' reviews the main objections which have been brought forward in recent years, and concludes by claiming that 'in the measurement of intelligence we have made a good beginning' (Eysenck 1973a, Part 10: 487).

The significance for the Burt affair of these post-war intellectual trends is certainly not to suggest that they were in any way directly responsible for the accusations eventually made against Burt. But it is clear that the climate of opinion in which the accusations were made, in the 1970s, was very different from that which had prevailed when Burt's reputation was unchallenged, in the 1930s and 1940s; and this must have affected, at least to some extent, the way in which the accusations were received. In 1946, for example, such charges would have concerned an approach still widely regarded as of central importance, to which a great many psychologists were committed. Moreover, Burt himself would have been a familiar figure in the profession. Thirty years later, a very different scene prevailed. Now the approach was widely regarded as outdated, and a man would have to be about fifty to recall Burt as a working psychologist. It was inevitable that, by the 1970s, many psychologists would feel relatively indifferent to the fate of a man they had never known, whose work they had perhaps never studied, and who had belonged to a tradition many believed to be outmoded. It is not hard to appreciate that thirty years earlier those same charges would have met a far better informed and committed audience, who would have been far more likely to insist upon the most thorough examination of the evidence.

Applied psychology

If these fundamental disagreements had been confined to academic psychologists in the universities, there would be no great cause for concern. It might be thought that they could spend their time in better ways; but in itself their work would be harmless, and one day it might even prove valuable. But there have always been psychologists who have been willing to tackle the contemporary problems of society, from such pioneers as Binet (intelligence), Stanley Hall (adolescence), Lombroso (crime), Munsterberg (industrial efficiency), and Sully (childhood) onwards. Indeed, the two psychological movements which have made most impact on the modern imagination – psychoanalysis and intelligence testing – have both been especially concerned with application. This practical involvement makes all the difference. In so far as the advice of the psychologist is followed, the validity of his new science becomes a matter of public concern; and the more widely it is applied, the more legitimate that concern becomes.

It should be noted that the psychologist's involvement in social and individual problems is by no means to be traced wholly to the eagerness of the psychologist to press his expertise upon an indifferent public. Not infrequently the impetus has come at least in part from the layman. Binet devised his scales in response to a request from the French government for assistance in identifying backward children. Freud began to explore new clinical techniques because he found orthodox procedures ineffective, and his patients urgently needed help. Again, the expansion of departments of psychology at the universities, as students flock to study a popular new subject, also stimulates a demand for professional careers when training is completed. But, however the involvement begins, it brings with it many troublesome questions.

Two major problems may be mentioned here. The first concerns the psychologist's professional competence. Practical problems are only too likely to involve a complexity of conditions which are beyond the range of available methods. However much the psychologist may emphasize that his advice is tentative, his willingness to attempt the task at all, and to accept financial reward, must suggest that he has something more to offer than untutored common sense. This may prove to be a dangerous position, especially since he will often be under pressure to produce answers without undue delay, and therefore without the time he might have liked in which to conduct appropriate research. It is arguable that a psychologist should refuse to undertake practical tasks unless he has well-established methods and findings to hand whose efficacy has been demonstrated by appropriate trials in some closely related field, as would occur in the introduction of a new drug. In so far as the psychologist fails to do this, he runs a grave risk of being labelled a charlatan – a quack who pretends to a knowledge he does not possess. It is no defence to protest that the layman insisted on being helped. He who cannot help should say so.

But the problem is not easily resolved. To a considerable extent it is only by tackling practical issues that the investigator can acquire the experience and develop the methods which are needed. Hearnshaw (1979: 35) quotes a letter written by Burt in 1914 in which he put the point forcefully:

> the educational investigator cannot merely carry over the conclusions of academic psychology into the classroom. He has to work out almost every problem afresh, profiting by, but not simply relying on, his previous psychological training. He has to make short cuts to practical solutions, which, for the time being, leave theory or pure science far behind.

The question is how far pure science is to be left behind, and how long we shall go on making short cuts; and the danger is that we shall forget that they are short cuts, and one day, when they have become established practice, we shall discover how inadequate they are.

These difficulties have been compounded by the existence of the schools of psychology. The major movements all had their distinctive contributions to make to applied psychology, and their preferred interpretations to defend. So the conflicts of the schools have spilled over into the applications, painfully exposing the limitations of the new science. We do not have to wait for the layman to accuse the psychologist of sharp practice. The devotee of one school is indignant when the exponent of a different system lays claim to an expertise, and a public recognition, which he regards as unfounded, and which ignores his own supposedly superior claims. Thus Watson (1930: 297; his italics) said of psychoanalysis:

> I venture to predict that 20 years from now an analyst using Freudian concepts . . . will be placed upon the same plane as a phrenologist. *And yet analysis based upon behaviouristic principles is here to stay and is a necessary profession in society – to be placed upon a par with internal medicine and surgery.*

Today, more than fifty years later, the controversy between psychotherapy and behaviour therapy still flourishes.

A second danger, perhaps in the long run even more serious, is that many of these applications have political, social, or religious overtones, and consequently may arouse prejudices or preconceptions, whether in the public or the psychologist. The psychotherapist may find himself regarded as trespassing on the professional territory of the priest; the occupational psychologist may be accused of preferring the interests of the employer to those of the employee; the educational psychologist has to avoid becoming embroiled in arguments between egalitarians and elitists. Any science may find itself in such political deep water, but the human sciences are probably more prone to it, simply because their problems are so directly related to the human condition.

Either of these two features of much applied psychology – its uncertain foundations, and its potential social involvement – would be hard to cope with alone. In combination they make an explosive mixture. Psychologists, whether academic or applied, are under great pressure to live up to the expectations which are aroused by the claim to scientific expertise. It sometimes seems that too much – research grants, promotions, publicity – depends upon the successful projection of unrealistic pretensions. The term 'confidence-trickster' becomes an easy, but a dangerous, one for psychologists to apply to their colleagues. It is hard to know, among the varied applications of psychology, where a reasonable confidence ends and an irresponsible pretence begins; and however honest they may be, no two psychologists are likely to draw the line in exactly the same place.

It is not, then, surprising that psychologists have sometimes been warned in trenchant terms of the dangers they are courting. Zangwill (1950: 215–

18), then Professor of Experimental Psychology at Cambridge, was among the most outspoken:

> Despite all that psychology has to gain from closer contact with the world of affairs, real and dangerous problems arise if we accept the contemporary challenge in full measure. May not our research workers develop into mere technicians who bring their ingenuity and knowledge to bear on problems whose relation to fundamental theory is tenuous in the extreme? May they not on occasion be saddled with problems whose ethical implications are suspect? Shall not those of us who are university teachers run the risk of educating a generation of psychologists whose scientific aims can be disentangled only with difficulty from their political aspirations? These are serious dangers which cannot be lightly dismissed.
>
> . . . psychology at the present day is quite incapable of solving the vast majority of human social problems. The mere fact that most, if not all, of the major problems of the present day are, at bottom, psychological does not mean that an individual who calls himself a psychologist is in any position to solve them. . . . Let us, therefore, firmly reject all such exalted aspirations and limit ourselves to the systematic study of problems within the reach of our present methods of inquiry. . . . It may be that scientific knowledge makes possible rational control. It is certain that bogus science spells disaster.

Since those words were written, there has been a great expansion in the application of psychology; and some prominent scientists have expressed misgivings. Professor Sir George Porter, referring to psychologists and others, recently criticized those who were, he believed, damaging science by giving false importance to unproven claims. He said:

> They are sometimes far too eager to put unsubstantiated assertions into practice on the public. There are experts who will make assertions such as they understand why this man is a criminal and what to do about it, when in fact we don't know.
>
> (Report in *The Times*, 31 August 1985)

He added that

> In the field of psychology progress has been very significant. But it is still probably at about the leeches stage in terms of comparison with medical development. With some limited exceptions, leeches are not a good thing.

Zangwill's fears have, in fact, been illustrated only too clearly, over the last thirty years, in the field of intelligence testing. Here the two features of so much applied psychology are both present – its uncertain foundations and its potential social involvement; and they have given rise, as we shall next see, to a sequence of events which have made a mockery of scientific inquiry. The Burt affair is to be seen as a dramatic episode in this sequence, and not as an isolated incident unrelated to contemporary psychology.

Political complications

Cronbach (1975), in a paper on 'Five decades of public controversy over mental testing', has reminded us that psychometrics has repeatedly aroused public concern since its early days. In the earlier part of the century, Burt and some other educational psychologists had regarded their work as providing one of the means by which greater equality of opportunity could be achieved: the bright children of poor parents, whose talents might otherwise be wasted, could be selected for a 'free place' at a grammar school. In short, these psychologists had been in tune with the 'progressive' thinking of the day, and found natural allies among contemporary liberals. But after the Second World War there were further developments in the political climate which hastened the dangers foreseen by Zangwill.

After the war, radical opinion began to take a different view of these questions, as Hearnshaw (1979, chap. 7) has described. Now selection was increasingly regarded, not as a step towards a more egalitarian society, but as a means of preserving an elitist regime. Simon (1953) attacked testing as leading to a selective and graded system which served the needs of a class-ridden society. Other investigators suggested that in fact middle-class children benefited disproportionately from the system. Thus Douglas (1964) claimed that middle-class children aged between eight and eleven were three times as likely to be selected for grammar school places as working-class children of equivalent IQ: while Floud, Halsey, and Martin (1956) showed that when the middle-class children reached grammar school they were likely to make better use of their chances. Burt, of course, believed that such middle-class advantages reflected, at least in considerable part, a genuine correlation between natural ability and occupational class; but the critics were more inclined to trace the effect to environment. Their thinking helped to create the climate of opinion in which a Labour government introduced comprehensive education in 1965, and Burt now found himself on the conservative side of the fence. The Plowden Report of 1967 carried these trends a step further when it recommended that 'equality of opportunity' should give way to 'positive discrimination', this being the only way in which the 'under-privileged' were ever likely to overcome the environmental handicaps which were held to be responsible for their plight.

When politics and social science thus became mixed up together, it was not long before tempers rose and suspicions flourished. Eysenck experienced this soon after the war. In 1950, when hostility to fascism was especially strong, often in association with left-wing views, a group of American social psychologists published *The Authoritarian Personality* (Adorno *et al.* 1950), which attributed certain undesirable personality characteristics to fascists, and ascribed these in part to their social background. In his own book, *The Psychology of Politics*, Eysenck (1954) concluded that these characteristics were in fact typical of extremes of the left as well as of the right, of communists as well as fascists – an anticipation of the 'fascism of the left' which Shirley Williams attacked in the 1970s. Eysenck soon found that he had stirred up something more than scientific interest. Gibson's (1981: 224–5) account of the reaction which the book encountered in some quarters is instructive:

> Christie revealed the pains to which he had gone in order to find some discreditable evidence of fraud. . . . He found that there was a reference to 'Melvin (1954)' in the text, but in the bibliography Melvin was cited as having a Ph.D. thesis dated 1953. He therefore wrote to the librarian of the University of London library to inquire about this mysterious discrepancy, and the librarian replied that he had no such thesis on file. So we are left to assume that Eysenck invented it! In fact, Melvin finished his thesis in 1953, presented it in 1954, and it was filed in the library in 1955, but instead of writing to Melvin or Eysenck to establish the facts, Christie chose to make a mystery of it.

The behaviour of these critics foreshadowed the treatment which Burt was shortly to receive. Towards the end of the 1960s there appeared a number of so-called 'Black Papers' (Cox and Dyson 1969a, 1969b, 1970) which expressed a reaction in Britain against the educational philosophy of the left. Burt, who retained his life-long belief in selection, was among those who contributed, and it was here that he made his allegations about a decline in educational standards. Burt was strongly criticized as an extremist in the *Sunday Times* and elsewhere. Eysenck (1977b: 20) protested about what he considered to be the unfairness of some of these attacks, and described the behaviour of the *Sunday Times* in the following passage:

> In 1969 the *Sunday Times* published what I can only call a direct lie concerning him. Sir Cyril . . . had mentioned that an article giving certain relevant statistics had been written by him for the *Irish Journal of Education*. The *Sunday Times* report said that the Editor of the *Irish Journal* had been contacted, and he had said that he had 'never heard' of the article. The Editor in question wrote in straight away to say that

the article did in fact exist and was indeed already being prepared for the printer. After about a month the *Sunday Times* was forced to publish a letter by Professor C. B. Cox, correcting the grievous imputation of lying, and an apology was received from the personal assistant of the *Sunday Times* editor.

It should be noted that Gillie himself was not involved in this incident (see Gillie 1978a: 199). Nor does he seem to have been involved in another incident, involving the same newspaper, which took place a little later. On this second occasion Eysenck was the target, as he describes:

> When my book on *Race, Intelligence and Education* (1971) appeared, I was interviewed by three representatives of the paper, who then produced a whole page of mis-statements about my position, accusations of a grossly libellous nature, and conclusions completely at variance with my own views as I had communicated them to the interviewers
>
> (Eysenck, ibid.)

It is clear from these incidents that, well before Gillie's involvement, the *Sunday Times* had shown much interest in the controversy, though the paper seemed to have difficulty in giving an accurate account.

But there was much worse to come. The reaction to Jensen's *Harvard Educational Review* article of 1969 revealed the depths of irrational emotion which could be released by discussion of the heredity–environment issue. Jensen had argued that 'Project Headstart', designed to provide compensatory education for the under-privileged in the United States, was doomed to failure because genetic factors were so strongly implicated. Jensen believed that the reported black–white differences in average intelligence were largely genetic. He can hardly have been prepared for the extraordinary reaction which his views provoked, not simply among the media, but among some students and even faculty.

> He was burned in effigy by campus radicals, threatened in person on the telephone, condemned as a fascist and racist by liberals and Negroes, ostracised by professional colleagues and, most bitter of all, lauded by segregationalists. As observed by Professor Christopher Jencks, Jensen became the 'most publicized (and vilified) figure in psychology today'.
>
> (Gibson 1981: 230)

Eysenck soon found himself subjected to similar treatment. In 1973 he was assaulted at the London School of Economics, and his invited lecture disrupted, apparently by hooligans from Birmingham University. Shortly afterwards the National Union of Students in Britain issued an edict to prevent Eysenck from speaking, on any topic whatever, at any meeting sponsored by them. Similar behaviour later appeared in Australia, when in 1977 both Eysenck and Jensen were forcibly prevented from speaking at a number of universities. Eysenck (1972) describes the dangers of the 'New Zealots'.

It will be seen that Gillie's posthumous attack on Burt did not spring unheralded out of the blue. It came against a background of many years of heated controversy about the inheritance of intelligence, and the place of selection in education. Others besides Burt had already been the target of vilification, and forcible attempts had already been made to prevent those who stressed heredity from even expressing their views. Several, including Burt, had already been accused of deception; indeed, the accusation had been made in the *Sunday Times* itself. All these events are, of course, perfectly compatible with the possibility that Burt was guilty as charged. But they also indicate that leading hereditarians were highly likely to be the target for such charges, however flimsy the evidence, and, further, that there was an audience ready and willing to believe accusations of dishonesty, even in the universities themselves. However, even if political bias is established, it must not be assumed that this is the only factor involved, or even the chief. There are many other forms of bias – personal, intellectual, religious, and so on – which have been reviewed by Jensen (1980) in his *Bias in Mental Testing*.

The role of Kamin

It is in this context that we must consider Kamin's book *The Science and Politics of IQ* (1974), which was the immediate stimulus to Gillie's accusation two years later. The book was primarily an attack on the hereditarian standpoint in psychology in general, and although Burt figured prominently, he was by no means the only target. Kamin was chiefly concerned to criticize American hereditarians and the practical implications which had been drawn from their conclusions. Thus earlier writers such as Brigham, and contemporaries such as Jensen and Herrnstein, were his major concern, while British writers escaped more lightly. Eysenck, for instance, was not mentioned at this stage. Kamin argued that the whole mental testing movement, with its strong belief in the measurement of innate ability, had been fostered by men with strong right-wing political and social convictions and values, who had misused it for political purposes. Testing, for example, had been an extremely useful means of excluding from entry into the United States persons with racial backgrounds other than those of the dominant North European immigrants. The methods and the conclusions of the testers were not justified in their own right, on objective empirical evidence, but were adopted because they supported those values. Pseudo-science, he concluded, was being used to justify political opinions.

In an exceptionally fair and penetrating review, Mackintosh (1975: 685) wrote that Kamin had performed 'a notable service by subjecting the evidence on the heritability of intelligence to searching and critical analysis', and said that 'both in quality and quantity the evidence for the heritability of IQ is very much less than had generally been suggested. The data are sparse rather than plentiful, and at best persuasive rather than decisive.' But Mackintosh added that Kamin did not show the same critical acumen when environmentalist evidence was in question. Fulker (1975) was less favourable, and said the book 'lacks balanced judgement and presents a travesty of the empirical evidence in the field'.

There is, in my opinion, a great deal of truth in Kamin's contention that political values had often been allowed to influence psychometric work, and he has performed a most important critical task in drawing attention to it. It seems that many psychologists had accepted the innate component in intelligence far too readily, together with the capacity of existing tests to assess it, and that some of them had done this at least in part because it suited their values. Yet there are a number of respects in which Kamin has spoiled a good case.

Kamin greatly exaggerates the extent to which mental testing, and belief in heredity, were fostered exclusively by persons of right-wing conviction. As we have seen, early socialists had frequently acknowledged the importance of heredity and eugenics; and Burt and other pioneers had often been inspired by a liberal desire to help the disadvantaged (above, page 24). But while the possession of liberal motives absolves Burt from the charge of right-wing political bias, at least during the earlier part of his career, it does not necessarily demonstrate that he, or others, were therefore free from all political prejudice. The psychologist is as prone to left-wing as to right-wing bias. Kamin never considers this possibility.

Further, Kamin always seems to assume that bias must be deliberate. It seems far more likely that, at least in very many cases, the influence of political conviction or social value is something of which the culprit is unaware, which he would wish to deny if it were alleged, and which he would honestly want to avoid if he became convinced that the charge was true. It operates primarily through unquestioned assumptions and pre-conceptions. It is an habitual mode of thinking which can only with difficulty be broken, rather than a deliberate act undertaken with malice aforethought.

But Kamin is not prepared to recognize such relatively innocent, if dangerous, possibilities. At the very outset he makes a sweeping insinuation against the whole hereditarian movement: 'Patriotism, we have been told, is the last refuge of scoundrels. Psychologists and biologists might consider the possibility that heritability is the first' (Kamin 1974, 1st edn: 3).

Such an open invitation to the reader to approach the whole matter in the belief that the writers to be examined are villains, is unlikely to ensure that the discussion remains on a reasoned, scientific plane. Rather, it appears likely to implant the strongest possible prejudice before a single scrap of evidence has been produced. In the remainder of the book, Kamin does not scruple to make similar innuendoes against particular individuals. Thus Jensen is twice alleged to be 'disingenuous' (ibid.: 181ff.), and on the second occasion this is said to be the 'kindest characterisation' that can be made. Yet these accusations of double-dealing are never supported by any adequately argued case. Eysenck is not similarly vilified in 1974, but Kamin's tactics are by no means restricted to his 1974 publication. On a later occasion, after attacking Eysenck for such relatively routine failings as 'slipshod references', 'misleading claims', and 'fictitious matching', Kamin (1981: 153) once more implies dishonesty: 'The scientist, given half a chance, seems as likely as the used car salesman to try to slip one over.'

Since Kamin so often imputes dishonesty to hereditarians, it would not be surprising if he made the same imputations against Burt; indeed, it would be surprising if he did not. It is in fact hard to find any unambiguous and explicit accusation of fraud or dishonesty concerning Burt in Kamin (1974). This conclusion seems to be confirmed by the remarks which Gillie makes when he is discussing his own inference, from reading Kamin, that Burt's work must be fraudulent. He writes that 'Kamin did not use the word fraud in his book nor do I recall him doing so in August 1976 when I talked to him on the telephone' (Gillie 1980: 9). However, it seems very likely that Kamin did in fact intend to imply fraud in 1974. Thus Gillie goes on at once to say: 'However he went as far towards saying it as is usually regarded as decent in academic circles' (ibid.). A further reason for supposing that such was Kamin's intention is provided by the claim which he himself makes in 1981. Referring to the conclusion he had drawn in 1974 – that 'The numbers left behind by Professor Burt are simply not worthy of our current scientific attention' – Kamin wrote that 'The clear implication – that Burt had invented the data in order to support his ideas about social and educational policy – was left for the reader to make' (Kamin 1981: 102). Whether or not we think that this was a 'clear implication', we may well accept that it was in Kamin's mind, not only because he says it was, but also because it is his regular accusation.

But if Kamin really was making this 'clear implication' in 1974, why did not his book make the same sensational impact that Gillie's article achieved two years later? Alternatively expressed, if Kamin, a psychologist of standing, had already made the accusation in 1974, how was it possible that an article by Gillie, a journalist, should create such a *furore* two years later? The answer, I think, is complex. In 1974 Kamin made the charge less openly than did Gillie in 1976. The charge was not 'clearly implied' but it would nevertheless be likely to be inferred. This restraint inevitably reduced the impact of Kamin's criticism. It was further muted by the circumstance that he had also made similar charges against others. Few readers could seriously believe that all the hereditarians were as unscrupulous as Kamin was suggesting, so the impact of his accusations against any one of them was correspondingly reduced. There was no reason why the reader should be particularly struck by the clear implication against Burt when so many others were equally, if not more, exposed. Finally, of course, Gillie's charge was made publicly in the press, with all its powers of publicity. Thus for Kamin to have made the same impact in 1974, which Gillie made in 1976, he would have had to accuse Burt in plain language, accuse him alone, and secure the same publicity for his views.

In addition, there are a number of occasions in his book where Kamin seems to espouse carelessness or old age as the explanation of the anomalies in Burt's papers. Thus after referring to systematic over- and under-estimations in Burt's data, Kamin comments that 'it is of course not necessary to assume that any such systematic effects are consciously produced' (Kamin 1974: 68). Elsewhere he seems to prefer senility as a possible explanation, as when he says that Burt's first serious paper on twins (1955) was the work of a seventy-two-year-old gentleman with strong opinions. The majority of the cases described in his final report, Kamin added, were collected between that time and his eighty-third year. 'The revised lists of IQs and social-class ratings were being dispatched around the globe in his eighty-eighth year' (ibid.: 71).

Kamin's fundamental criticism – that the hereditarian standpoint may sometimes be adopted in part for political rather than empirical reasons – is both true and important. But his own conclusions can hardly be regarded as free from prejudice themselves. Hearnshaw (1979: 232) remarks:

> It is hard for an unprejudiced reader not to feel that a great many of Kamin's criticisms are distinctly captious, and unfortunately he did not subject the studies supporting the environmentalist case to the same rigorous scrutiny. So his work must be regarded as biased.

A strong confirmation of this conclusion is to be found in Kamin's claim (1979: 30) that 'When I first read Burt's research reports in 1972, it was at once obvious that I was reading the words of a liar and a fraud'. This may be taken to indicate, not that Burt's papers were obviously unsatisfactory, or that Kamin was particularly perspicacious, but that he was altogether too ready to find what he was looking for. Since Kamin was so certain that Burt was dishonest, he accepted the explanation which suited him: 'The speculations about Burt's personal motivations seem to me to miss the point entirely. The "data" invented by Burt were, very simply, a conscious (and successful) effort to influence social and educational policy' (ibid.: 31). Finally, a possible source of Kamin's bias is not far to seek. In a later work (Rose *et al.* 1984: ix) he declares: 'We share a commitment to the prospect of the creation of a more socially just – a socialist – society'.

Kamin is hoist with his own petard; but he is by no means alone in permitting his political loyalties to colour his supposed science. We have already referred to earlier incidents, in which Kamin had not been involved, where Burt and Eysenck had been the targets of unsuccessful attempts to label them dishonest. Numerous other instances might be given, but two must suffice. Evans and Waites (1981: 178) refer to 'a huge quantity of secondary literature, dominated by hereditarians, who have systematically misrepresented and misinterpreted the original research literature . . . in an intellectually dishonest effort to convince people that hereditary differences are of overwhelming importance.' It is hardly necessary to add that they provide no remotely adequate evidence for this sweeping accusation. With an equal lack of evidence, Vetta (1980: 241) talks about 'a question mark concerning the integrity of Jensen'. Eysenck's comment is entirely justified: 'It is intolerable that aspersions of this kind should be thrown out in this irresponsible manner, without proof, without discussion, and without details' (Eysenck 1980a: 361). By the 1970s, to be accused of dishonesty had become an occupational hazard for anyone who believed in the influence of heredity, and the more prominent the exponent the more likely he was to be accused.

Investigative journalism

It was the activities of Gillie which ensured that 'the Burt affair' would hit the headlines. As Kamin later remarked, 'The argument about Burt's data . . . might have tiptoed around the question of Burt's fraudulence were it not for Oliver Gillie' (Kamin 1981: 102). Gillie's account (1980) of how his *Sunday Times* article came to be written was given as a lecture at the annual conference of the British Psychological Society at Aberdeen in 1980, and subsequently published in the 'Balance sheet on Burt' (Beloff 1980b). Gillie's interest in genetics was longstanding. He had been trained in the subject at Edinburgh in the late 1950s, and had recently published a book entitled *Who Do You Think You Are?* (Gillie 1976a). It was only after he had completed this that Gillie read Kamin's *Science and Politics of IQ* (1974), which first aroused his suspicions about the authenticity of Burt's work. Accordingly, Gillie's book provides an indication of his frame of mind immediately before he embarked upon his charges against Burt.

Who Do You Think You Are? is a spirited work, as its chapter headings suggest: for example, 'Dr Frankenstein and the "Y" men'; and 'The great brain robbery'. Gillie's theme is similar to that of Kamin: he argues that genetics has often been misused for political ends, not only by politicians, but also by geneticists who have allowed their political enthusiasms to

283

cloud their scientific judgement. He hits the nail on the head in the following passage:

> When people look for certain guidance in the face of explosive social issues, science is sometimes used to give authority to what people want to believe anyway. Experts are consulted, and when hard evidence is scarce, the experts who can produce answers in the spirit of the times are most readily believed.
>
> (Gillie 1976a: 42)

Unfortunately Gillie, like Kamin, can detect bias readily enough when hereditarians display it, but not when environmentalists are at fault. His own standpoint is heavily environmental, and this is made a vehicle for his own political enthusiasms. He offers 'the prospect of a new social engineering that seeks to improve people through improving their environment' (ibid.: 16), and attacks all the standard bogies of the radical – racists, sexists, and elitists. His own article in the *Sunday Times* is a prime example of the selectivity he professes to deplore. As he himself says, his story needed 'someone in authority' to tell it; and he selected just those 'experts' who would endorse his own views, ignoring all those who might have contradicted him.

Who Do You Think You Are? says little about Burt; and it was only after his suspicions had been aroused by reading Kamin that Gillie decided to investigate Burt's work. We have already described his attempts to locate Howard and Conway, and how this brought him into touch first with Tizard, and then with the Clarkes. Only a few weeks elapsed between Gillie's first active steps to substantiate his suspicions in August, and his publication of the accusations on 24 October 1976.

It is not unreasonable to suppose that Gillie, as a journalist, was interested in the prospect of a 'big story' (Gillie's phrase; see Gillie, 1980: 9–10; and above page 32) and hoped to be the first to tell it. But he was also aware that he must be careful. The task was of course made much easier by the fact that Burt was now dead, and would not be able to defend himself. But Burt had been a much-admired figure in many quarters, and there was an obvious risk that old friends would spring to his defence. The case must be made as strong as possible if it was to be made at all.

Acting on a suggestion from Tizard, Gillie went to Hull to talk to the Clarkes, presumably in August or September 1976. This visit clearly played a crucial part in paving the way for Gillie's article. Neither Gillie nor the Clarkes have given any very detailed account of what passed between them at Hull, but Gillie's account of his frame of mind at the outset is illuminating:

> When I travelled up to Hull to see them I did not know exactly what

their evidence would be. I believed that fraud was involved from Kamin's work and from what they had told me on the telephone – but the story needed someone in authority to say it.

(Ibid.: 10)

Clearly, Gillie went to Hull looking for 'someone in authority' to tell the story of fraud which he believed to be true. He must have been well aware that, if he published the story on his own authority, he might find himself in grave difficulties. Such extraordinary charges, directed against so eminent a man, and alleged only by an outsider, would be disbelieved and resented by many psychologists. It would not be possible, in the space available in a newspaper, to provide the detailed analysis which would be needed to convince the experts – even if he was capable of supplying it, and even if the readership of the *Sunday Times*, relaxing in hostelry or golf club, would find it entertaining. The only effective way to ensure that the story was taken seriously was to find 'someone in authority to say it'. That someone must be a psychologist, and a psychologist of standing whose word would carry weight. At Hull, Gillie found what he was looking for; in fact, he found three such persons. As we shall shortly see, the Clarkes had not, prior to Gillie's visit, yet reached the definite conclusion that Burt's data were fraudulent. 'We spent a long time', writes Gillie (1981: 10), 'discussing Burt's work and how certain we could be that fraud was involved.' Plainly, they eventually decided that it was sufficiently certain to go ahead with publication; and, though they have not recounted this aspect of their discussions, they must also have reached certain agreed decisions about how publication was to be effected, and what part each would play.

The Hull group must have assured Gillie that, if he published, he could count on their support, otherwise he would never have included their confirmatory statements in his article. Gillie presented the whole story as an account of what 'leading scientists' were saying, and he would have been finished if they had promptly denied it. It is also clear that Tizard must have been involved. The article mentioning him, and indicating that he too accepted the charges, appeared in *The Times* on the day after Gillie's article appeared. It would be absurd to suppose that this was a coincidence. In short, Gillie had managed to find four reputable psychologists (Tizard, the two Clarkes, and McAskie) who were prepared to endorse his story.

There is no reason to doubt that the four psychologists who were thus associated with the charges had already entertained suspicions of Burt before Gillie appeared on the scene. But it also seems that, until Gillie appeared, none of them had yet been certain of Burt's guilt; none had yet prepared a detailed written statement intended to give a complete account of the grounds on which they accused him of dishonesty; and none had yet contemplated an unequivocal public exposure.

The evidence, especially as it could be set out in the articles, was far from conclusive. The chief charge – that the ladies 'may never have existed' – originated with Tizard, Hetherington, and Partridge. Gillie had given further substance to these doubts with his own enquiries, and was the first to publish them and to place them in the centre of the case against Burt. But there was no attempt to indicate what claims Burt himself had made about them, when he said they had collected data for him, or whether it was at all likely that it would now be possible to trace them. There was a suggestion from the Clarkes that Burt, knowing his data were inadequate, wrote the papers alone, then added the names for credibility; but other explanations were not considered.

The second charge – concerning the repeated correlations – had originated with Kamin. There was no attempt to explain why such an expert as Burt should make such a transparent error, or what he had to gain by it. There was no indication that Jensen had discussed these correlations without suggesting fraud, and would probably continue to deny it now. Nor does Gillie record that he made any attempt, though unsuccessfully, to contact Jensen to ask his opinion of the charges.

The third charge, about guessing parental IQs, was presumably derived from Kamin, but its basis was not given in full. There was no mention that Burt himself had drawn attention to the limitations of his data here.

The final charge was the most loosely formulated of all. It alleged that Burt had worked backwards from his conclusions to invent data which would support them. It was not elaborated in sufficient detail to permit fully-informed assessment, and it is still not clear to me what this allegation was supposed to refer to.

The second and third charges had both been published before, without giving rise to open accusations of dishonesty. If they had composed the whole case, the impact would have been drastically reduced, and the Clarkes would have had to explain why these well-known facts must now be interpreted afresh. But the missing assistants had not been previously publicized. They were the essential justification for making the accusation. So long as they could not be traced, it was arguable that they had never existed, and possible therefore that Burt had invented them. The greatest danger which faced Burt's accusers was that, when Gillie drew attention to the missing people, they might emerge unexpectedly to refute the story. The advertisement placed in *The Times* (16 October 1976) was a precaution against any such mishap. When this produced no reply, it was considered safe, a week later, to go ahead.

It could not seriously be claimed that the article provided a properly documented and argued case for Burt's guilt. Except for the follow-up of the missing assistants, the article was heavily reliant on the Clarkes. Plainly, if the Hull group had not been prepared to back the accusation, Gillie would have been in an impossible situation. He would have been challenged to provide the evidence, and would have had to make out the case on his own. The support of the Clarkes was crucial: they provided the authority which Gillie knew the story needed. Gillie's reaction when he was shortly challenged by Eysenck illustrates his appreciation of their importance.

Eysenck (*The Times*, 12 November 1976) accused Gillie of a political smear campaign, and argued that the evidence justified no charge stronger than that of carelessness. Eysenck was on strong ground here, but it was a mistake for him to concentrate so exclusively on Gillie, as if he thought that Gillie, having written the article, must be seen as the prime target. This gave Gillie the opportunity for a neat counter-attack:

> Eysenck has presented the argument over Burt as if a challenge were being made by a newspaper to a respected profession, namely psychologists. This is a disgraceful ploy. Eysenck must know that the case he has to answer is first of all to his colleagues. My own contribution . . . was original only in so far as I described my attempts to trace Howard and Conway. The allegations of fraud were new but Eysenck is in error again in suggesting that I personally made them. The suggestion that some fraud was involved was made by Dr Ann Clarke and Professor Alan Clarke and a quotation from them agreeing appeared in the story. The Clarkes said: 'Scientifically, Burt's results were a fraud.'
>
> (Gillie 1977: 257; and he added that the quotation had been omitted from certain editions of the paper because of technical problems)

There is considerable substance in Gillie's defence. The article does convey a strong impression that Gillie thought of himself as primarily a reporter of what 'leading scientists' were saying. Clearly, if the Clarkes had not given their endorsement to the article, it is most unlikely that it would have appeared. It does not purport to give a detailed and documented account of the evidence, such as would satisfy an expert audience; it only purports to be informing its lay readership of what the experts were saying. As the principal experts endorsing the story, the Clarkes were electing to allow the story to be told on their authority. As such, it was for them to provide the primary justification for the allegations. Gillie was entitled to say that Eysenck had first of all to answer his own colleagues, not the newspaper which acted as their mouthpiece.

But if Gillie was entitled to say that the primary responsibility lay with the experts, he was not also entitled to imply that he himself had acted merely as the bearer of messages, which originated with others. His own role had been more active, and more influential, than he was suggesting. It was a consequence of Eysenck's exaggeration of Gillie's role, that Gillie was able, in correcting that mistake, to ignore the less important, but still crucial, part which he had played. This may be seen in two main ways.

First, Gillie's denial that he had alleged fraud, and his assertion that the allegation came from the Clarkes, could no doubt be justified so far as the article was concerned. But it did not follow, as an uncritical reader might very easily suppose, that Gillie held no views on the subject, and was merely the indifferent purveyor of the views of others. The suggestion of fraud had in fact originated with Gillie himself. As we have just seen, he went to Hull convinced that Burt had been fraudulent, and looking for an 'authority'. At that time, the Clarkes were not yet convinced. As we shall shortly see, the news which Gillie brought, that he could not trace the assistants, was for them the 'turning-point'. Thus it was actually Gillie who produced the crucial piece of evidence which persuaded the Clarkes. He went to Hull to persuade them that his story was true and to secure their endorsement when it was published. Kamin's remark, that psychologists would have tiptoed round the problem if it had not been for Gillie, was correct: it was Gillie who persuaded them that Burt had been fraudulent, and persuaded them also to endorse the story publicly. This by no means rules out the possibility that they were very ready to be persuaded. But it was Gillie who first embarked upon a systematic search for the assistants he called 'Burt's missing ladies', who first conceived the notion of a public accusation in the Sunday press, and who set about arranging it with great energy and dispatch. The picture of Gillie as the mere reporter of what the experts were saying was, to say the least, incomplete, since those experts had only reached their conclusion when Gillie encouraged them to do so.

A second weakness of Gillie's defence was that even someone merely acting as a reporter was surely under an obligation to satisfy himself, so far as lay within his power, that the story was accurate and fair, especially where it concerned the reputation of a man who could not defend himself. But Gillie must have known that his story omitted to mention many points whose inclusion would have weakened its impact considerably and which we listed above. The failure to give as much attention to all that might be said in Burt's defence is especially striking – for example, in the failure to mention Jensen's well-known views on some of the crucial features. Morever, Gillie purported to be more than a bread-and-butter reporter: he was a 'medical correspondent'. This was an implicit claim that he was not just a layman in these matters; he was something of an expert himself, who could be taken to be well informed. Under these circumstances, it is not easy to avoid the conclusion that the story was intended to make things look as bad as possible for Burt. This indeed was what made it a sensation.

Someone in authority

None of the psychologists involved has given any very detailed account of their discussions with Gillie. Neither Tizard nor McAskie has said anything at all, while the Clarkes have given only the briefest indication (Clarke and Clarke 1980a). The Clarkes' account is nevertheless important, because it shows when they made up their minds.

The Clarkes state that they did not suspect Burt of fraud at the time of their first critical remarks in 1974. They add: 'this came slowly, as one of us collaborated with Michael McAskie in a detailed analysis of several papers (McAskie and Clarke, 1976). The turning point came when Dr Gillie revealed that neither Howard nor Conway could be accounted for' (Clarke and Clarke 1980a: 17). According to this account, Gillie's news converted whatever previous suspicions they had entertained into a conviction that fraud must have been involved. This confirms the point already made, which Gillie's article omitted to mention, that the 'leading scientists' only became convinced of Burt's fraudulence in consequence of Gillie's news. This was for them the 'turning point'. In short, it was Gillie who crucially persuaded the Clarkes that Burt had been fraudulent. Without Gillie's stimulus, it is unlikely that their suspicions would have become certainties, and most unlikely that they would have made the accusation publicly. As Kamin so aptly observed, without Gillie psychologists would have 'tip-toed' around the question. Thus it was not that Gillie simply heard and reported, and then followed up, what 'leading scientists' were already saying. Rather, Gillie converted their suspicions into certainty by providing, in the missing assistants, a crucial reason for believing it. He did not report what he discovered they were saying; he persuaded them to say what he was already saying himself, so that he could report them as saying it.

If the Clarkes' account thus reveals something about the genesis of the accusation which we might otherwise not have appreciated, there are also two important matters which it omits. The first concerns certain additional events which occurred in the weeks immediately before the article appeared in October 1976, and the second concerns events which had occurred long before. The remainder of this section will deal with the former matter, reserving the latter for the following section.

The Clarkes' account does not mention certain other steps which were taken at this time, which must have also influenced their decision to support Gillie. Before they could safely proceed with the public accusation, there was one danger which they had to guard against with particular care. The crucial piece of evidence, and the one piece not previously published, was that concerning the missing assistants. But there was no positive proof that they were fictitious; only negative evidence that they could not be traced. The publicity that would inevitably accompany publication might easily bring the assistants to light, discrediting the whole story. It can hardly be a coincidence that it was just at this time (on 23 September 1976) that Alan Clarke wrote to Hearnshaw.

We have in fact already referred to this letter in an earlier chapter. It is that in which Alan Clarke alleges that Burt deliberately distorted the conclusions of his own and his future wife's Ph.D.s in order to discredit Eysenck – an allegation which we have seen was unfounded. Hearnshaw (1979: 148) refers to this letter in the context of Burt's behaviour while he was at University College, using it uncritically to suggest that Burt's character was already deteriorating before he retired. But he does not refer to it again when he comes to describe the events which lead up to Gillie's article, though it is here that its true significance lies. Whether or not Clarke asked for information about the missing assistants, it is plain, from the date of his letter, that it was written during, or shortly after, Gillie's visit to Hull, and while the discussion of Burt's fraudulence was fresh in their minds. The letter therefore demonstrates that Burt's alleged distortion of their Ph.D. summaries was also in their minds at this time, which recalls Hearnshaw's (1979: 148) remark that 'The incident . . . was of particular importance, as it sowed the seeds for their later role as instigators of doubts as to Burt's integrity'. We have shown that Burt did not in fact distort the summaries; however, the Clarkes' allegation suggests that their suspicions now played a significant part in their accusations, in addition to other evidence they possessed such as Gillie's inability to trace the assistants. This will be examined more fully below.

Perhaps it also occurred to them that it was important to the success of their venture that Hearnshaw should accept their view of Burt's dishonesty. His forthcoming 'official' biography might well be highly influential, and the more evidence they could give him the more likely it was that he could be persuaded to take their point of view. The danger that they might find themselves isolated and condemned would be very much reduced if a man of Hearnshaw's detachment and probity accepted their conclusions. The Clarkes' communications with Hearnshaw clearly had some effect in helping to convince him that Burt had misbehaved, as shown by Hearnshaw's quotations from the letter of 23 September; and although Hearnshaw did not go the whole way with them, as the following passage indicates, he was strongly influenced:

> although I disagree, and disagree strongly, with Kamin, the Clarkes and Gillie in the virulence and extent of their denigration of Burt I believe that they all performed a most valuable service in exposing his delinquencies, and I must thank Dr Ann Clarke in particular for the continued and generous assistance she has given me.
>
> (Hearnshaw 1980: 1)

Any reply to Clarke's letter must have been reassuring, for although Hearnshaw has expressed a belief that the research assistants were real enough, he has never been able to furnish incontrovertible proof of this.

Thus the accusation of October 1976 was the immediate outcome of, first, a journalist's conviction that Burt had been fraudulent in a matter of bitter current political controversy – a controversy in which that journalist had already shown himself to be strongly committed to one side; and, second, the readiness of a group of psychologists to furnish him with further evidence to strengthen his case, together with the promise of support if he published.

Shortly after the accusation, Hearnshaw (1977: 22) expressed regret at the manner in which it was published:

> it is a great pity that the controversy about Cyril Burt and his alleged malpractices has been ventilated in the first place in the public press rather than among psychologists themselves. Several of the charges . . . are quite unfair, and could easily have been put straight by psychologists with some knowledge of the background.

Some delay at this point would certainly have given Burt's critics time to examine Gillie's allegations more thoroughly, and prepare a complete statement of their case, suitable for academic publication.

But Gillie had not only managed to secure the support of psychologists with some claim to expertise in the field of Burt's alleged deceptions. Alan Clarke and Tizard might also be described as people 'in authority', in another and perhaps even more important sense. It happened that both Clarke and Tizard occupied at this time positions of major influence in the British Psychological Society, the professional organization of British psychologists.

The Council of the British Psychological Society consists of both officers and ordinary members. The most important officers are the President-Elect, the President, and the Vice-President. This is a progressive appointment. The President-Elect is chosen to serve for twelve months, from April to April; at the end of this period he automatically becomes President for the next twelve months, and then Vice-President for a final twelve months. In the year 1976/77, the year in which Gillie published the accusation, the Vice-President was Tizard, and the President-Elect was Alan Clarke. So Clarke became President in the following year, 1977/78, and Vice-President in the year after that, 1978/79. In 1979/80, the year when the biography was published, Clarke was no longer an officer of the society, but continued as an ordinary member of the council. It is the council which, more than any other body or person, is entitled to speak as the representative of British psychologists. Gillie had indeed found 'someone in authority'.

The Maudsley connection

That Gillie's visit was the turning-point in convincing the Clarkes does not rule out the possibility that they were very ready to be convinced. Indeed, if they were not ready, it is hard to see how they could have accepted Gillie's arguments so speedily. This brings us to the second omission, mentioned above, in the Clarkes' account of how they had reached their conclusions, namely, events which had occurred long before.

The Clarkes' account leaves it to be supposed that their belief in Burt's fraudulence sprang entirely from their own study of his post-war papers, combined with Gillie's news about the missing assistants. But when we study their background, and especially the people to whose influence they had been exposed, we find that there are grounds for supposing that the reasons which they give, though genuine enough, also gave them an opportunity for expressing an antipathy to Burt which they had entertained for a long time. The reasons which they give did indeed precipitate their accusations but predisposing conditions had been established long before.

Jack Tizard and Alan Clarke were old friends whose careers had followed very similar paths. Both had returned from the war to take degrees in psychology; and after graduating in 1948, both had gone to the Institute of Psychiatry at the Maudsley Hospital. Here Alan Clarke worked for his Ph.D. as did his future wife Ann, while Tizard joined the Unit for Research on Occupational Adaptation (since re-named the Social Psychiatry Research Unit). Both men married colleagues who were to collaborate with them in their academic work; and both specialized in developmental psychology and mental deficiency. Eventually, in 1962, Clarke became professor at Hull, and in 1964 Tizard became Professor of Child Development at the London University Institute of Education.

Thus three of the four psychologists who supported Gillie – Tizard and the two Clarkes – had worked at the Maudsley Hospital at the same time, many years ago. But we already know, from Alan Clarke's letter of 23 September 1976, that the Clarkes themselves have traced their distrust of Burt back to this period, to his supposed distortion of their Ph.D. summaries. In fact this accusation, as we have seen, is without foundation; and it follows that their suspicions could not have originated in this alleged incident, whatever they may have thought twenty-five years later. Where then did their mistrust come from? One possibility has been mentioned – in another context – by Clarke himself. In an autobiographical sketch, he recounts an incident which occurred just before the Ph.D. theses were examined by Burt, and therefore shortly before the alleged distortion of the summaries. He states that: 'Sir Aubrey Lewis took the precaution of alerting us to the possibility that our Ph.D.s might be dealt with unfairly' (Clarke 1978: 484). Some may be prepared to interpret this warning by Lewis as furnishing yet another confirmation of the view that Burt was psychopathic and untrustworthy. But Clarke gives no indication of what grounds, if any, Lewis provided to justify his attack on Burt's integrity. In fact, nothing happened to justify it; on the contrary, as Clarke himself says, 'in the event there were no problems' (ibid.). Thus, once again, we are presented with gossip about long past incidents, entirely unsupported by any adequate evidence. Indeed, although events themselves refuted the charge, Clarke repeats it without hesitation. However, we now know that suspicions of Burt were planted in the Clarkes' minds by Lewis before the examination, and this prompts us to look more closely at Lewis's role in the whole affair.

Sir Aubrey Lewis (1900–75) was an Australian psychiatrist who joined the Maudsley Hospital in 1929. He succeeded to the chair of Psychiatry there in 1946, and was knighted in 1959. As head of the Institute of Psychiatry, it was he who gave Eysenck his first appointment in 1942, and backed him strongly thereafter. In his biography of Eysenck, Gibson has an illuminating chapter on the relations between Lewis and Eysenck, whom he calls 'The Allies' (Gibson 1981, chap. 4). According to Gibson, Lewis regarded Eysenck as a 'spiritual son', supporting his promotion to a Readership in 1950, and to a Professorship in 1955, and also favouring his plans to introduce a Diploma in Abnormal Psychology. Burt, however, was not happy with these developments and opposed them. His opposition did not please either Eysenck or Lewis, and the disagreement seems to have been a major source of the ill feeling which developed. The arguments about the Diploma mentioned by Harding in his letter of 29 October 1976, when he described Lewis as arriving at a meeting in a state of 'controlled seething', were part of this hostility between the two parties.

There is no good reason why all the blame for these quarrels should be laid at Burt's door. Gibson describes Lewis as a man with a 'somewhat ferocious manner' (Gibson 1981: 64). Perhaps Lewis regarded what happened in the Institute of Psychiatry as his business and nobody else's, and deeply resented what he saw as Burt's interference; though since these matters had to be decided at meetings of the appropriate committees, Burt was entitled to express his views, as were others also. But whatever the rights and wrongs of the quarrel, Clarke's story about the warning they received from Lewis reveals the lengths to which Lewis was prepared to go in his hostility to Burt. Indeed, Clarke's story throws such a revealing light upon Lewis's character that we may look at it more closely.

Clarke tells his tale as if it was simply one more piece of evidence to damn Burt, but when we examine it critically we find that it is not Burt who is damaged by it, but Lewis. As Clarke tells the story, Lewis provides no justification for his allegation that Burt may treat the Ph.D.s unfairly. He simply puts this suspicion to the Clarkes – who apparently swallow it without question. It is bad enough that Lewis should spread such suspicions without evidence. But his conduct is made very much worse by the circumstance that he was making the allegation about one of his own colleagues, a fellow member of the University of London Senate, and making the allegation, behind that colleague's back, to junior research students. If the Clarkes had in fact been dissatisfied with their examination, and had then made an official complaint, the matter would have been brought before the Senate, where Lewis could have voted on the issue without revealing the part he had played. Clarke recounts Lewis's behaviour without showing the least inclination to question it. Perhaps he imagines that Lewis is justified in view of Burt's supposed dishonesty. But even if Lewis had been right in this supposition, his behaviour would still have been improper. He should either have taken his suspicions to the appropriate authority, or remained silent. Instead, he chose to bias the minds of the candidates, giving Burt no opportunity to defend himself.

When we recall Eysenck's own reminiscences about Burt, we cannot doubt that in the late 1940s and early 1950s Lewis and Eysenck, working together at the Maudsley, were united in their distrust of Burt, and permitted their juniors to see this. We have just seen that Lewis did this immediately before the Ph.D. examinations in 1950. A little later Eysenck behaved similarly: when the Clarkes told him that Burt had altered their summaries, Eysenck said (according to Clarke, Letter of 23 September 1976 to Hearnshaw) that 'this sort of ploy was typical of the old man'. These allegations have never been properly substantiated; but they must have made a strong impression upon the young research students.

We have now traced no less than five of Burt's most virulent critics to a common source in the late 1940s at the Maudsley Hospital: Lewis and Eysenck; the Clarkes; and Tizard. But this is not the end of the 'Maudsley connection'. Russell, also much relied upon by Hearnshaw, worked in Eysenck's department before he was appointed to Burt's old chair in 1950. It may be that while he was there Russell heard nothing of these suspicions and hostilities; on the other hand, it may be that he did – and that this contributed to the difficulties which arose when he took up his new appointment at University College.

It seems likely, then, that several of Burt's chief critics acquired some at least of their suspicions from their common association with the Maudsley. But we cannot rule out the possibility that this suspicion originated in part in professional conflicts and rivalries, rather than in sound evidence, and hence that the later accusations were, to some unknown extent, biased. So the position taken here is that the accusations were not based solely on relevant evidence. But nor were they based solely on prior bias. The behaviour of Burt's critics is only to be explained as a combination of both factors. They were prejudiced, in the sense that they had acquired a frame of mind which made them ready to accept as conclusive, evidence which, without that predisposition, they might well have regarded with a more detached and critical caution, as did so many others.

We must next ask how far political convictions also contributed to this predisposition.

Political affiliations

We have already seen that, in the late 1960s, there were strong left-wing protests against those who emphasized heredity, and especially against Eysenck and Jensen. In view of this background it is not surprising that some psychologists immediately saw political motivation in Gillie's attack in 1976, especially since Gillie himself placed the political implications at the forefront. Eysenck, in a letter to Burt's sister (Eysenck to Dr Marion Burt, 16 November 1976), wrote, 'I think the whole affair is just a determined effort on the part of some very left-wing environmentalists to play a political game with scientific facts'. He also wrote (*The Times*, 8 November 1976) that the environmentalist attacks were 'based on ideological preconceptions rather than on scientific evidence'. Environmentalists made the same charge in reverse, Rose referring to 'the ideological foundations of the hereditarian position' (*The Times*, 9 November 1976). Heim had already remarked that 'the pre-occupation of the left-wing with extreme environmentalism and of the right-wing with heritability is never stated – both sides claiming to be interactionists – but this pre-occupation largely accounts for the axe-grinding dogmatism of the protagonists' (*The Times*, 1 November 1976).

The following year Sir Andrew Huxley, in his presidential address to the British Association, was reported as saying that:

There was now a body of scientists who regarded the assumption of equal inherited ability as something which does not require experimental evidence to establish – and which it is politically wicked to question, because the conclusion might disagree with their social and political preconceptions. . . . There is a taboo on open-minded investigation of these topics at least as strong as the resistance in Darwin's day to questioning the authority of the Bible. (Reported in the *Times Educational Supplement*, 2 September 1977, p. 5.)

Serious charges require adequate evidence, whether the bias comes from the left or the right. It is not enough to show that a particular writer has political affiliations. Simply on a chance basis, some 50 per cent of environmentalists might be expected to have left-wing sympathies, and a similar proportion of hereditarians to have right-wing sympathies. So additional positive grounds should always be sought before concluding that political views have actually influenced scientific conclusions. The following criteria are suggested as tending to show this. Neither singly nor in combination do they conclusively demonstrate bias; but the more of these signs are present, the more likely it becomes: (1) explicit support for a political position in a supposedly scientific work; (2) use of violent and inflammatory language; (3) presentation of contrasting positions in black and white terms, such that extreme judgements are favoured; (4) the rapidity with which conclusions are reached, pointing to a desire to reach preconceived conclusions; (5) intolerance of differing opinion, such that there is a desire to suppress opposed points of view. With these points in mind, we shall next ask how far political prejudice was in fact at work, whether of the right or the left.

A left-wing political connection was present among at least some of the Maudsley group, as in the other troubles of the period, mentioned earlier. Gibson (1981: 91, 109, and 222) gives much background information. He alleges that the staff included several communists at that time: Shapiro is said to have been a member of the Communist Party, and he married Alan Clarke's sister. Barbara Tizard, in a memoir of her husband, describes him as a 'passionate egalitarian' who was 'for several years a member of the Communist Party'. However, from the mid-fifties onwards he took no active part in politics 'believing that he could most effectively help to improve society through his research' (see Tizard and Clarke 1983: 2–3). He also opposed Jensen's hereditarian views. Kamin's socialist convictions and Gillie's left-wing sympathies have already been noted. Thus the three people who took the initiative in publicizing the case against Burt (Kamin, Gillie, and Tizard), all were on the left politically, and all betray their motivation by displaying one or more of the characteristics listed above. The other three participants – McAskie and the Clarkes – do not appear to have given any public expression to any political convictions they might possess, and it is proposed here to respect the privacy of those who prefer to keep any political opinion to themselves.

However, in reaching the conclusion that some political bias was at work, certain disclaimers must at once be made. First, this does not seem to be the only potential source of prejudice. In the case of Eysenck himself, for instance, it was apparently intellectual differences and personal frustration which sparked his hostility, not political conviction. It may be that political prejudice simply provided a rallying point to which numerous other possible sources of prejudice were recruited. Second, there is no reason whatever for jumping to the conclusion that the opposition to Burt was dishonest in the sense that they did not believe him to be guilty, but nevertheless went ahead with their accusations. We need not doubt their integrity; only their impartiality. Third, it would be monstrous to suppose that, in general, those who hold left-wing views are particularly prone to such bias, or that extremists of the right may not be equally prejudiced.

One of the most striking features of the Burt affair is that no fewer than four psychologists were willing to co-operate with a journalist in attacking the reputation of one of their most eminent colleagues. They ought surely to have reflected that Gillie's article could not provide a statement of the evidence sufficiently detailed to establish the charges; and that the public sensation which would be caused would be highly detrimental to a calm and rational discussion of Burt's alleged guilt. They surely should have appreciated that a thorough discussion in the academic journals would have served the interests of psychology better, as Hearnshaw (1977) and Eysenck (1977a) soon observed.

Summary

'Shall not those of us who are university teachers run the risk of educating a generation of psychologists whose scientific aims can be disentangled only with difficulty from their political aspirations?' Zangwill's (1950: 216) warning has unfortunately proved all too relevant. The controversy between hereditarians and environmentalists has given rise to repeated accusations of political bias, both from the right and the left, over the past thirty years; and there are substantial grounds for thinking that bias is sometimes present. In this heated atmosphere, the suspicion that opponents are deliberately and fraudulently twisting and inventing evidence flourishes only too easily; but it is suggested here that the bias is far more likely to be the product of habitual attitude than deliberate deception. It is against this background that the accusations against Burt must be judged.

Burt himself, after a liberal start, found himself on the conservative side of the fence in later life, and his involvement in the 'Black Papers' of the late 1960s made him vulnerable – whether justifiably or not – to accusations of political extremism. We have also found, however, that there are good grounds for concluding that left-wing sentiment was involved in Gillie's accusation of fraudulence and in the support which he received from Kamin and Tizard. Those who alleged at the time that the accusations against Burt were politically motivated were to that extent justified.

However, though political bias is real and important, it is certainly not the only factor involved, and it is probably not the most important factor in many cases. Several other influences are also evident, without which the political might have been far less potent. Three may be singled out. First, there were other sources of hostility besides the political. Both Eysenck and Lewis at the Maudsley Hospital resented Burt's opposition to their plans for the development of psychology there and for Eysenck's promotion, and a connection with the Maudsley can be traced in several of Burt's initial accusers. Simple academic rivalry and jealousy can account for a good deal. Second, we must not lose sight of Burt himself. His quirks of character did not help his cause, and his failure to include many important details in some of his later papers rendered him open to suspicion. Third, psychology is still in numerous respects a controversial inquiry, in which deep divisions of opinion exist concerning the validity of its methods and explanations. Consequently it is often hard to find acceptable scientific criteria to judge disputed points, which is especially

297

important in matters of current political and social concern, and leads to suspicion and distrust.

It seems reasonable to conclude that the accusations of fraud were not made, as might have been expected, because certain psychologists, having conducted a full and thorough investigation into Burt's guilt, had independently concluded that there was decisive evidence against him and had then prepared a detailed scientific paper, whose implications they released to the press. Rather, it was a journalist who took the initiative. He conceived the idea of a newspaper exposure; brought the crucial evidence to the attention of the psychologists, thereby persuading them that Burt had been fraudulent; and then obtained their co-operation in the accusation. It is true that the suspicions of the psychologists had already been raised by their own previous studies of Burt's papers. Even so the evidence was by no means conclusive, and we cannot exclude the possibility that they also had additional motives for attacking Burt. There is, indeed, good reason to think that most of the accusers were to some extent biased, either through their previous associations at the Maudsley, or through their political convictions, or both. The reasons given for the accusation undoubtedly provided prima facie grounds for investigation. But this was not how Burt's accusers treated them. They took them as furnishing an adequate basis for a conclusive public condemnation. It would have been prudent to examine the evidence more thoroughly before committing themselves to so drastic a step. It is not surprising that the accusation was not at first universally accepted. It remains to ask how it came to be endorsed.

Chapter twelve

How it happened: the endorsement

Gillie's article was not enough to secure general acceptance of Burt's guilt, even with the support it received. Burt still had many defenders, and there were a number of indications that the outcome remained undecided. Notable pointers were Wade's (1976) conclusion that the facts so far available did not permit a decision, and Hearnshaw's (1977: 23) suggestion that 'the proper course . . . is to suspend judgement until all the evidence can be fully and fairly assessed'. It was also significant that both McAskie (1978) and Dorfman (1978), in offering further evidence against Burt, began their papers by remarking that the case had not yet been established. So it was that for nearly three years – from Gillie's accusation of October 1976 until the publication of Hearnshaw's biography in July 1979 – Burt's reputation hung in the balance.

But if the controversy rumbled on indecisively while Hearnshaw was completing his biography, it does not follow that nothing was happening. Hearnshaw himself was gradually reaching his conclusions as the evidence accumulated, and a number of psychologists played some part in this process. It is instructive to ask how the main actors were occupying themselves, beginning with the small group of British psychologists who, with Gillie, were the prime movers in the accusation.

The accusers

'Throughout our long collaboration Dr Gillie has proved to be a responsible and trustworthy colleague,' declared the Clarkes (1980a: 17) when they looked back on their part in the affair. They had spent many hours in discussion with him; they had advised him on material to include in his article; and they had publicly supported his charges. They had been helped by Tizard and McAskie. These four psychologists together had made Gillie's accusation possible.

In October 1976, when they associated themselves with the charges, none of them had yet provided the kind of detailed account of their reasons which an adequate justification would require. The brief criticisms of Burt previously made by the Clarkes and by McAskie made no explicit charge of dishonesty, so that it was impossible to tell which of their published criticisms were supposed to be relevant. Their comments were in any case so brief that they formed an entirely inadequate basis for such serious allegations. Similar considerations apply to Tizard's contribution. Gillie's article, also, provided none of the documentation or detailed argument necessary to establish the case, and Gillie himself has made it plain that he was primarily expressing their views. Yet these were the most serious and damaging charges which could have been made; and having associated themselves so publicly with them, it might have been supposed that they would all take the earliest opportunity of justifying their position. They had made the accusation possible, by lending their names to it. They owed it to everyone, not least to the dead man, to explain and justify their position. Their actions will be examined in turn.

The following May, Tizard (1977) published a short review of some of the arguments which had so far been advanced. This was remarkable chiefly because it made so little reference to his own previous reported allegations, which were neither amplified nor justified. The review simply summarized what others had said. It was magnanimous about Burt's motives; but it took for granted that Burt was guilty as charged. In short, Tizard behaved as if he personally was not involved, and Burt was obviously guilty. Tizard died in 1978, and so we shall now never know in any detail what evidence he actually possessed when he took part in the original attack.

McAskie did not publish again with the Clarkes after their *Times* letter of November 1976. But he did produce, some eighteen months later, a three-page paper entitled 'Carelessness or fraud in Sir Cyril Burt's kinship data?' (McAskie 1978). Brief as it was, this paper is revealing because McAskie began by admitting that 'as yet, no clear evidence for fraud has been presented, and . . . all that has been reported are claims and strong suspicions' (ibid.: 496). If this was so, it was strange that four academics should have endorsed them in public. McAskie hastened to add that 'it does not necessarily make these claims mere speculation' (ibid.). Perhaps not, but it surely implied that the charges had not yet been established 'beyond reasonable doubt', and made it urgent that 'clear evidence' should be given without delay. This was what McAskie now attempted to do.

McAskie's main purpose is to argue that Jensen's suggestion of carelessness is an unconvincing explanation for the anomalies in Burt's kinship correlations. McAskie claims to demonstrate number preferences in Burt's figures. Some digits are over-represented, and some under-represented, providing grounds for concluding that Burt was inventing his figures, and inadvertently choosing his preferred digits. McAskie also referred to a further paper on 'Burt's parent–child IQ data' which he said was 'in preparation' and would provide further evidence (see McAskie 1978: 496).

Jensen (1978) replied. He first noted with satisfaction McAskie's admission that the charges had been accompanied by 'no real substantiation'; and observed that 'Now, over a year later, McAskie serves up the first bit of seemingly intrinsic evidence for the indictment of Burt that supposedly amounts to more than just "claims and suspicions"' (Jensen 1978: 499). He also pointed out, correctly, that the evidence now produced by McAskie 'was never even so much as hinted at' in previous writings. This underlines the admission that the case so far lacked 'real substantiation'; and echoes Tizard's failure a year before to provide any evidence for his own charges.

Jensen then admitted that 'carelessness' did indeed seem to be an 'incongruous' explanation for the invariant correlations in view of Burt's statistical sophistication. 'I confess I am deeply puzzled by it', he wrote (Jensen 1978: 500). He added that he could find no evidence for any systematic bias in the results such as one might expect if the figures were intentionally slanted. Burt's figures seemed altogether comparable with those of others: Rimland and Munsinger (1977: 248) had pointed out that 'the deletion of Burt's data would have no appreciable effect on the overall picture'. Jensen (ibid.: 501) also found the idea that Burt might have invented all his twin and kinship data 'bizarre, to say the least'. He also stated (ibid.) that Shields had informed him in personal correspondence, long before the recent charges of fraud, that he had 'come across a number of twins who said they had been tested by Burt'. (In a letter to Jensen, dated 15 June 1973, Shields said, 'I have come across an occasional pair of twins reared together who were once tested by Burt'.)

Jensen's (1978: 502) answer to McAskie's specific charge is uncompromising: 'McAskie's method of attacking Burt's integrity, by showing non-random distributions of terminal digits and other "digital preferences", is not only half-baked, as presented, but it is, in principle, incapable of standing up as evidence of fraud in Burt's (or anyone else's) data.' He gives a number of reasons, of which the two most important are, first, that it is always possible, among the numerous possible preferences which might be considered, to find a few statistically non-random features, and second, that some such statistically non-random features would be likely to occur even when simply copying data as Burt was often doing. 'Thus it seems evident that the nefarious deeds of which McAskie accuses Burt are in reality the result of a human frailty found universally in all of us, no doubt including McAskie himself. I trust that we shall not hear from McAskie again on this matter until he has carefully reviewed his own work and can assure us that he himself is more immune to digital preferences and is a more accurate recorder of final digits than was Burt' (ibid.: 502).

It is striking that, having said nothing more about the evidence they were supposed to possess when they supported Gillie – other than admitting that 'as yet no clear evidence for fraud has been presented' – this fresh evidence should prove so inadequate. It is equally striking that McAskie has published nothing more to justify his part in the accusations, and that the promised further paper has never materialized.

Like Tizard and McAskie, the Clarkes have done little to substantiate their charges. Apart from some reviews of the biography, they have written only a few words to *The Times* in November 1976 declaring their conviction that Burt was a fraud; a letter to the *Bulletin of the British Psychological Society* (March 1977); and a brief contribution to the 'Balance sheet on Burt' (Clarke and Clarke 1980). It is remarkable that they should have been the principal supporters of the original charges, and yet have done so little to justify them. The letter of March 1977 has already been considered: it is that in which they offer some 'minimal documentation' about Conway, and say, quite correctly, that there is no evidence that she collected data for Burt after 1950. This is largely a repeat of what Gillie had already said, and makes no mention of Howard, though her name had been equally prominent in the original charges. Hearnshaw's later argument in the biography follows this line closely, adding mainly that the diaries make no mention of either assistant in the 1950s.

The Clarkes' brief comments in 1980 are mainly concerned to contradict Hearnshaw's belief that Burt only embarked upon his delinquencies in later life. The only positive evidence they offer for delinquency before 1940 concerns Burt's 1921 Report on Backward Children, and his letter to Miss Spielman of 1925. These large claims need much more elaboration to be convincing. They counter Hearnshaw's argument that nobody suspected Burt before the war by stating that 'the hallmark of a *successful* confidence trickster is precisely that people are persuaded of his honesty' (ibid.: 18). If this strange argument is accepted, everyone who is trusted must be regarded as a successful confidence-trickster.

In short, all that the Clarkes have provided in justification for their attacks on Burt's honesty, has been a superficial documentation of some of Gillie's claims about the missing assistants, and a flimsy attempt to extend Burt's guilt back into his earlier life. They left it to Gillie to publicize the original charges, and to Hearnshaw to draw up the detailed case. This does not mean, however, that they played little further part in the affair. As they themselves said, 'After our public association, in October 1976, with the charge of fraud, we worked mostly privately, our only other public statement being in the *Bulletin* in early 1977' (Clarke and Clarke 1980: 17). This prompts a number of questions.

Why did they decide to 'work privately'? Did they lack confidence that they could justify their behaviour to the satisfaction of their colleagues?

The piece of evidence they found most convincing, and which had swayed their minds (the 'turning-point'), was the failure to find the two assistants. But this was primarily the contribution of Tizard and Gillie. All they could do was 'document' it. They had nothing much to add to that. They could not claim to have found out anything else important, because they had not. So any paper would have had to be largely an expansion of Gillie's findings. But Gillie had presented the Clarkes as having reached their conclusions independently. The inconsistency would be revealed.

Eysenck also urged that it would have been better to thrash it out in the scientific journals. In other words, before they committed themselves to endorsing Gillie's accusations, they should have prepared an adequate academic paper, setting out the precise charges they were making, and the grounds on which they made them. Then everyone could have seen and assessed the soundness of their case. Whatever excuses or explanations might be given, the upshot was to avoid an adequate presentation of the case; and to secure maximum publicity and damage.

A further question is why the British Psychological Society did not institute an inquiry. It would surely have been natural for Council, bearing in mind Burt's eminence and the significance of the charges, to invite the Clarkes and Tizard to produce their evidence, especially when Eysenck did in fact ask for such an inquiry. But his request was refused. We have already seen that Clarke and Tizard occupied influential positions on Council, and we shall later examine the role of the council in more detail. No one should jump to the conclusion that either abused his position to sway the decision of Council against Burt. The point is simply that their presence on the deciding body inevitably arouses a reasonable doubt whether Burt received fair treatment.

The pressures on Hearnshaw

Since the biography was so decisive in tilting opinion against Burt, it becomes important to ask what factors influenced Hearnshaw in reaching his conclusions. His views certainly seem to have undergone a drastic change. When he embarked upon the task, in late 1971, his assessment of Burt was 'almost wholly favourable', and it 'never occurred to me to suspect his integrity' (Hearnshaw 1979: vii–viii). By April 1978, his conversion was complete, for it was then that he felt he must tell Burt's sister of his conclusions: 'It was painful for me to have to inform her that the evidence had finally forced me to accept the accusations' (ibid.: ix–x). So his change of mind took place sometime before early 1978. It also seems to have been a slow process with several contributing factors: 'Gradually, as evidence accumulated from a variety of sources, I became convinced that the charges against Burt were, in their essentials, valid' (ibid.: viii). What, then, were these sources, and how and when did they operate?

Gillie's article (24 October 1976) clearly made a strong impression on him. He writes that

> Though it did not seem to me that Gillie had convincingly proved his charge of fraud, the problems he pointed to were undoubtedly genuine problems, which could not be dismissed outright, and these, together with the anomalies noted by Kamin, and confirmed by Jensen, rendered my task both unexpectedly different, and far more difficult than I had anticipated when I undertook it.
>
> (Ibid.: viii)

This involved, he says, a good deal of extra research, and it was this which gradually convinced him that the charges were valid. It is clear from this passage that Gillie's article did not immediately convince Hearnshaw that Burt was guilty; and this is confirmed by Hearnshaw's letter of January 1977 suggesting that until he had finished his research no one was in a position to reach a final conclusion (Hearnshaw 1977).

It is further confirmed, and other influences added, by Hearnshaw's later statement in the 'Balance sheet on Burt' where he writes:

> For me the most important outcome of Burt's exposure was that it encouraged witnesses to talk frankly about matters of which they had previously been reluctant to speak. Several witnesses in whom I placed complete trust, Professor D. W. Harding, Professor R. W. Russell and Dr C. B. Frisby, to name three of the most important, satisfied me that at any rate in the late 1940s and 1950s Burt could be high-handed, devious and corrupt.
>
> (Hearnshaw 1980: p. 1)

We know that Harding and Russell wrote to Hearnshaw on 29 October and 15 November 1976 respectively, because Hearnshaw quotes from these letters. He nowhere quotes any correspondence with Frisby, but we may conclude that Frisby was in touch with him about the same time, because on 21 November he wrote to D. F. Vincent to say that 'Clifford Frisby tells me that you have material on Cyril Burt. . . . If you have any material or recollections which would assist to unravel some of the mysteries I should be most grateful if I could see it' (Letter to Vincent, 21 November 1976). This was the start of a fairly lengthy correspondence between Hearnshaw and Vincent, which provided Hearnshaw with considerable material.

From this account, we might jump to the conclusion that Gillie's article was the first thing to raise Hearnshaw's suspicions about Burt's honesty. But this would be to overlook the letter which Hearnshaw received from Alan Clarke on 23 September 1976, a clear month before the article appeared. We have already noted that Clarke's letter contains the earliest written accusation of dishonesty. Hearnshaw refers to this letter simply as giving evidence for Burt's supposed distortion of the research theses (Hearnshaw 1979: 148); but the letter was written when Gillie had recently been consulting the Clarkes in Hull about the missing assistants, and they must above all have been afraid that they might be located. Hearnshaw was the obvious person to consult. However this may be, Clarke's letter of 23 September 1976 is the earliest written evidence we possess of serious doubts about Burt's integrity coming to Hearnshaw's attention. It is also clear that this letter was by no means the end of the influence which the Clarkes exerted on Hearnshaw's conclusions. Hearnshaw (1980: 1) writes that 'I must thank Dr Ann Clarke in particular for the continued and generous assistance she has given me'.

The upshot is that serious doubts about Burt's integrity seem to have been brought to Hearnshaw's attention initially by a number of events which occurred in quick succession, beginning with Clarke's letter of 23 September 1976. This was followed by Gillie's article on 24 October; and then by the three communications from Harding (29 October), Russell (15 November), and Frisby (sometime before 21 November). Hearnshaw quickly realized that a good deal of extra research was going to be needed, and he wrote to Burt's sister in November 1976 to let her know (Hearnshaw 1979: viii).

These events, accompanied as they were by the public attack on Burt, must have come as a considerable shock to Hearnshaw. He had been collecting material on Burt for some five years. He had already embarked upon the actual writing of his book (Hearnshaw 1979: viii). He might have been forgiven for supposing, at this stage, that he knew as much as anyone about Burt. To be confronted at this late hour with such far-reaching suspicions, which if true must involve him in much extra research and a radical reassessment of his subject, must have been unsettling, to say the least. In addition, to find that so many people who had known Burt had apparently long ago entertained suspicions must have been a most unwelcome experience. It must be rare for a biographer, supposedly an authority on his subject, to find his long-standing views so dramatically challenged, just as he supposed he was entering upon the final phase of his work. It would be no disgrace to Hearnshaw if these unexpected events somewhat unsettled his judgement, and made him less critical than he might have been in calmer times.

There was also considerable pressure on Hearnshaw to complete his enquiries without undue delay. The longer it took him to finish, the longer the contentious controversy was likely to continue, with all its attendant unwelcome publicity. Hearnshaw in fact completed the book with remarkable speed. Between his decision to extend the research in the autumn of 1976, and the date of his preface (25 July 1978 – about twelve months before the publication date), less than two years elapsed. Yet in this time there were three major tasks to be conducted: the evidence concerning the charges had to be investigated; and explanation for Burt's lapse had to be devised; and the remainder of the biography had to be completed. Perhaps a more leisurely timetable would have been wise.

The origin of the historical allegations

Whether or not Hearnshaw, if left undisturbed, would eventually have made any charges against Burt himself, it is clear that several of the main accusations were suggested initially by others, and only subsequently endorsed by him. Most of the charges relating to the kinship data originated with others: the repeated coefficients, and the complaint of inadequate information, came primarily from Kamin and Jensen; the missing assistants, with the implication that Burt had invented much of his twin data, came from Tizard and Gillie, with help from the Clarkes. Hearnshaw's main contribution here was to document the absence of evidence in Burt's diaries for any contact with Howard and Conway in the 1950s and 1960s – negative evidence which in any case is irrelevant. The charges concerning the relation between intelligence and class came from the Hull group, and were then extended by Dorfman. The final accusations about declining standards in schools had been made by the *Sunday Times* while Burt was still alive. In all these cases, the various deceptions were alleged first by others, and Hearnshaw's role was primarily to provide supporting evidence – or not to provide it, as in the matter of the Clarkes' allegations of lifelong trickery. It may be that, left to himself, Hearnshaw would eventually have reported some, even all, of these alleged delinquencies. But the fact is that he had already been engaged upon collecting his material for five years without so doing; nor did he, in the remaining two years, unearth any fresh misbehaviour of importance in these areas.

However, the historical allegations may appear to be in a different category. Hearnshaw was the first to publish the opinion that Burt's historical views were a deliberate invention; and his account of the matter (1979, chap. 9, especially pp. 169–80) is almost complete (p. 177) before there is any indication that others had held similar views before him. Even then, the reader receives the impression that any such prior doubts and suspicions were of secondary importance in the genesis of Hearnshaw's views. The conclusion the reader is likely to carry away is that Hearnshaw, through his own historical research, has uncovered a fresh field of Burt's deceptions; and, since he is accepted as a detached and objective writer, this provides a powerful reinforcement for the allegations of other, perhaps less unbiased, writers in other fields. Thus it may seem that there is indeed a different category of evidence here – one in which Hearnshaw himself was largely responsible for originating the accusations.

It may well be that Hearnshaw himself was the source of a good many of the instances of historical falsification which he alleges; but there is evidence that, here too, others played a major role in rousing Hearnshaw's suspicions, and in directing him towards certain conclusions. Hearnshaw mentions three British writers as having been dissatisfied with Burt's historical views: Godfrey Thomson, who is said to have been 'uneasy', and D. F. Vincent and C. B. Frisby, both of the National Institute of Industrial Psychology (NIIP), who 'thought it prudent to remain silent' (Hearnshaw 1979: 180). We shall begin with Vincent, who figures most prominently in the biography.

D. F. Vincent, who died in August 1984, worked in the tests section of the NIIP for many years. He was interested in factor analysis, writing popular articles for the NIIP's 'house journal', *Psychology at Work*, followed by two academic papers elsewhere (Vincent 1953, 1954). One of the popular articles traced the origin of factor analysis to Spearman in the conventional manner; and Vincent then received a letter from Burt questioning this ascription, and saying that it began in 1901 with 'two important contributions published by Karl Pearson describing the method of principal axes' (Letter from Burt to Vincent, 3 October 1951). This was the start of a correspondence between the two men which continued, off and on, for at least a year.

Hearnshaw's account of this correspondence is brief and misleading (1979: 177–8). He makes three main statements. First, he begins by giving Burt's letter of 3 October as an example of the way in which Burt 'picked on' younger psychologists who had innocently adhered to the orthodox account, and 'castigated them for crediting Spearman with factor analysis'. This is intended to support and exemplify Hearnshaw's assertion that Burt conducted a 'campaign' against Spearman, and that he suffered from 'a blind and warping compulsion' (ibid.). Second, he states that 'Vincent made a critical study of Burt's published articles and analysed their misrepresentations, contradictions and evasions'. Third, he states that it was Vincent who broke off the correspondence, because, in Vincent's words, 'I should not get a simple answer to a simple question. I should get half-a-dozen foolscap sheets of typescript, all very polite and cordial, raising half a dozen subsidiary issues in which I was not particularly interested . . . and after the first letter my problem has been how to terminate the correspondence without being discourteous' (Letter from Vincent to C. F. Wrigley, 23 October 1958; see Hearnshaw 1979: 178).

Examination of the documents suggests otherwise. First, Burt's letter of 3 October 1951 is as far removed from 'castigation' as it could well be. There is no suggestion whatever that Vincent is being blamed or attacked for the views he had expressed; indeed, Burt recognizes that 'alternative views' are likely to be held, and writes in the mildest and most tentative manner: 'it is possible that I have missed some early work to which you are referring and that my memory is at fault.' He concludes: 'Forgive me for troubling you. May I say how much I admired the skill and lucidity of your own exposition? It was a remarkable feat to have made the underlying principles so plain to the non-statistical reader.' Nor does Vincent seem to have shared Hearnshaw's view of Burt's letters. In the passage quoted in the previous paragraph, he described Burt's letters as 'all very polite and cordial'; and in a letter to Hearnshaw he described Burt's letter as 'very polite and courteous' (Vincent to Hearnshaw, 28 November 1976). I should myself describe Burt's letter of 3 October as a mild and reasonable expression of his point of view, together with a number of polite requests for information about various remarks Vincent had made in his article.

Second, Vincent's supposed 'critical study of Burt's published articles' consists of some forty numbered points, running to ten foolscap pages in all. Each consists of a quotation from Burt (taken mainly from *Brit. J. Stat. Psychol.*, vols 1 and 2) on some abstruse statistical issue, followed by a brief comment from Vincent stating why he disagrees – usually because he thinks Spearman has been misrepresented. A number of these points (for instance, No. 26 – concerning Spearman's use of the term 'factors'; and No. 32 – concerning the 'proportionality criterion') are closely followed in the biography, though there is no indication there that they had been derived from Vincent. When Hearnshaw declares that Vincent had analysed Burt's 'misrepresentations, contradictions and evasions', he makes no attempt to show that Vincent was right; indeed, he does not even give an example. Thus he takes for granted that Vincent's strictures were correct, and so provide further evidence against Burt, when in fact those strictures have never been published, and nobody has been given an opportunity of seeing them. Hearnshaw adds (1979: 177): 'This analysis was never published because Vincent believed that no publisher or journal would agree to accept it, such was Burt's reputation at the time.' This is an inadequate excuse. If Vincent had offered the paper for publication, and had it rejected, he would be entitled to say so. But in failing to submit his paper for publication, he avoided giving Burt, or anyone else, the opportunity of examining his case; and permitted Burt to continue his supposed misbehaviour. He is not entitled subsequently, once Burt is safely out of the way, to accuse editors and publishers of being overawed by reputation (though they might have been); nor is he entitled to imply that, if it had been published, Burt would have had difficulty in demolishing it (though he might have had). Actually, it is not in the least surprising that this 'critical study' was never published, for in its existing form it is quite unsuitable for publication. It makes no coherent case against Burt, such as might form a continuous argument. It is simply a string of separate comments on particular points, of very varying degrees of importance, most requiring much fuller exposition before publication would be appropriate. I should have expected an editor to refuse it until it was thoroughly revised and amplified. It might be more accurately described, not as a 'critical study', but as 'notes in preparation for a critical study'; and it would require much more work before anything solid could emerge from it. Hearnshaw is not entitled to treat such unpublished notes as providing further grounds for allegations against Burt, especially when he has shown no sign of having examined them critically himself.

Third, in order to judge this point, we need first to note that Hearnshaw's statement that Vincent provided him with copies of his correspondence with Burt (Hearnshaw 1979: 177, note) is a half-truth. Vincent provided only the first three of Burt's letters (dated 3, 15, and 27 October 1951) with his own replies (dated 11 and 22 October, and 2 November 1951), together with an odd letter from Burt written a year later and dated 24 October 1952. Vincent said, 'I have some later correspondence with Burt, but by that time Burt had a fair idea of how much I knew and he was considerably more cautious about what he said' (Letter to Hearnshaw, 10 December 1976). In short, Vincent simply selected those letters which he thought most damaging to Burt, concealing the remainder which, for all we know, may have contained convincing rebuttals of Vincent's allegations. But those he did send contained nothing to support his assertion that, after the first letter, his problem was how to terminate the correspondence. Thus Vincent's reply to Burt's first letter described it as 'very interesting' (11 October); to Burt's second letter, he said 'Thank you very much for your long and interesting letter . . . I feel that I have had a peep behind the scenes', and finished with two requests for further information (22 October); and to Burt's third letter, 'I have found what you have told me of the inside history of these early years more than merely interesting. It presents the genesis of factor theory in an entirely new light' (2 November). It may be that the later letters told a different story – but we have been given no opportunity of judging. Vincent's remarks to Wrigley could have been an excuse for not taking up points with Burt: perhaps he had already tried in the later letters, and found himself worsted.

Finally, as regards the origin of the allegations of historical falsification, it should be noted that Hearnshaw wrote to Vincent on 21 November 1976, asking to see the correspondence with Burt, and that Vincent, in his reply dated 28 November 1976, made the following general accusation: that Burt 'was trying to discredit Spearman and steal the credit for the development of factor analysis'. He concluded as follows:

> I hate credit thieves and I have always had a considerable admiration for Spearman. If anyone starts a campagne [sic] to de-bunk Burt that will discredit his belittling of Spearman, I think that I should co-operate. The evidence that I have would be valuable ammunition.

But Vincent never himself made use of this 'evidence' and wanted someone else to take the initiative. This hardly suggests that he really had much confidence in it. Indeed, in a letter to William Brown, dated 5 February 1952, he wrote, apropos his examination of Burt's papers: 'Out of the hundred or more pages I have combed through I have found surprisingly few misstatements that it is possible to pin down as deliberate and intentional.' Only someone with a presupposition that Burt was dishonest could be surprised at finding little evidence for it.

Vincent's statement that Burt was trying to steal Spearman's credit is, of course, the main burden of Hearnshaw's allegation, too. However, we must not jump to the conclusion that this is where Hearnshaw derived his notion. In his reply to Vincent, Hearnshaw said that he agreed totally on this point, and added that he already had a good deal of documentation on it, instancing the manuscript for the revised edition of *Factors of the Mind*. He added that he would like to see Vincent's correspondence with Burt because 'it would serve to complete the picture I already have' (Hearnshaw to Vincent; undated, but it must have been written between Vincent's two letters of 28 November and 4 December 1976). Thus Hearnshaw was already, apparently, familiar with the charge before he received Vincent's letter of 28 November 1976. But this does not prove that the charge originated with Hearnshaw. We must also ask why he wrote to Vincent. This brings us to Frisby.

C. B. Frisby, who died on 21 May 1982, joined the NIIP in 1928, and was its Director from 1939 to 1967, when he retired at the age of sixty-five. There is a brief obituary by Blain (1982: 319). Frisby is one of the witnesses in whom Hearnshaw placed 'complete trust' and who satisfied him that 'at any rate in the 1940s and 1950s Burt could be high-handed, devious and corrupt' (Hearnshaw 1980: 1). He appears in the biography as a 'critic', and as one who 'distrusted Burt personally' (1979: 180 and 229). But nowhere does Hearnshaw give any indication why Frisby held these views, nor why 'complete trust' is justified. In such a serious matter, no witness should be given 'complete trust'. Once more, Burt is condemned on the arbitrary say-so of prominent names.

It was in fact Frisby who suggested that Hearnshaw get in touch with Vincent. Hearnshaw's first letter to Vincent began by saying that 'Clifford Frisby tells me that you have material on Cyril Burt. . . . I should be most grateful if I could see it' (Hearnshaw to Vincent, 21 November 1976). In his reply, Vincent explained how Frisby came into it. He said that 'Dr Frisby was very angry about Burt's claims. As you probably know, Spearman had been a personal friend of his' (Vincent to Hearnshaw, 28 November 1976). Later, Vincent stated that Frisby had asked him in the early 1950s to go through back issues of the *British Journal of Statistical Psychology*, note any attacks on Spearman's reputation, and let him have comments (Vincent to Hearnshaw, 10 December 1976). If this statement is correct, it appears that Frisby must have been one of the first to suspect Burt's historical claims, and that it was he who suggested that Vincent should investigate, long before Hearnshaw eventually published the charge. But Frisby does not seem to have been prepared to do anything himself.

Later, after Gillie's article, Frisby again tried to stir others to action. Thus Vincent also told Hearnshaw that 'Regarding the correspondence with Burt that I have, Dr Frisby has suggested to participants in the *Times* fracas that they should contact me and I have just had a letter from him saying that he wants to have another look at it' (Vincent to Hearnshaw, 4 December 1976). So Hearnshaw was one of those to whom Frisby wrote, and it may be that this was the first occasion when Hearnshaw's suspicions were aroused concerning Burt's historical claims. But again Frisby himself did nothing more than write to others. There is no evidence that he himself ever unearthed anything to justify his suspicions: his forte seems to have consisted in trying to persuade others to attack Burt. As for himself, he 'thought it prudent to remain silent' (Hearnshaw 1979: 180). He liked to lead from the rear.

The third person concerned, Godfrey Thomson, is the most important, since he was a recognized authority on factorial analysis. In the biography, Hearnshaw asks why Burt's falsifications were not exposed by his colleagues at the time; and then writes:

> Godfrey Thomson, Burt's joint editor, should perhaps have spoken up before his death in 1954. It appeared that he was uneasy, but deferred to Burt's superior historical knowledge, and, as joint editor, he probably hesitated to rock a boat that was in some danger of foundering altogether. His friendship with Burt moreover was of long standing. So Thomson did not openly protest.
>
> (Hearnshaw 1979: 180)

There is a plain implication here that Thomson suspected Burt's honesty in this matter. But no reference is given to justify the assertion, though Thomson's evidence would be of the first importance. What, then, is the origin of it? The only possible source that I have come across concerns an exchange of letters between Vincent and Thomson in 1952. Vincent wrote to Thomson to ask his opinion of Burt's claim that factor analysis had originated with Pearson (Vincent to Thomson, 5 August 1952). Thomson replied briefly as follows:

> I am pleased that you think my writings show no bias. But I am loth to become in any way involved in the controversy you say has arisen over a

claim that Karl Pearson was the originator of factor analysis. I have the greatest admiration for K.P. and he was very kind to me many years ago. I have known his 'closest fit' paper nearly all my life and have an offprint of it. True, it did not occur to me that it originated factor analysis; but I do not wish to take sides in any more controversies, and would not in any case do so without studying again the original paper, for which my present engagements leave no time.

(Letter from Thomson to Vincent, 7 August 1952)

In my view, this letter is a clear indication that Thomson did not want to express an opinion on Vincent's question, and would not do so without looking at the papers again, which he did not propose to do. But Vincent treats it as endorsing his own position. Thus after saying that Pearson's 'closest fit' paper had nothing to do with factorial analysis, he added: 'This was the opinion of Godfrey Thomson, who knew far more than Burt about factor analysis' (Letter from Vincent to Frisby, 3 January 1978).

In short, it seems that even in the case of the alleged historical falsifications Hearnshaw was far from first in the field, and there is reason to suppose that his suspicions were first aroused here by Frisby, who had long ago set Vincent to work on it, but had never himself unearthed anything to justify it. Thus we reach the striking conclusion that none of the main charges which Hearnshaw brought against Burt had actually originated in his own research. In every case, the suspicion first came from others. It is an instructive reflection that, if Hearnshaw had been left in peace to complete his work in his own time and his own way, it is unlikely that he would ever have accused Burt of dishonesty at all.

The reviewers

An important factor in securing acceptance of Hearnshaw's verdict was the example set by reviewers. Most academics have little time to follow developments in fields outside their immediate interests, and rely heavily upon reviewers to keep them informed. Hearnshaw's biography was very widely reported, in the professional journals and beyond, but one may safely guess that only a minority of psychologists would read the book, and fewer still would attempt a thorough study of it. Most would take their opinions, either from one or two reviews which had come their way, or from conversation with colleagues whose experience was little wider than their own. There is nothing reprehensible in this. It would be a waste of time to drop all other interests on such an occasion in order to form a personal opinion; and reviewers are chosen, or should be, for their knowledge and reliability in the relevant field. One of their functions is to provide expert opinion to keep the rest informed.

But a biography of Burt presented rather unusual problems for reviewers. Most books are primarily concerned with fairly precise fields of research, and with the recent literature. There are usually several people whose knowledge of the area is on a par with the author's, and who can provide what deserves to be called an 'expert assessment'. They are already familiar with much of the literature on which the book is based, and have acquired a special skill in judging work in the area. If one reviewer misjudges a book, there are plenty of others to correct him – not least, the author himself.

But a biography of Burt was not a run-of-the-mill piece of research. Burt's interests were remarkably wide, and while some reviewers might have equally wide interests, it was most unlikely that they would coincide with those of Burt. Taking only the most salient matters, a reviewer would need more than a smattering of knowledge and interest in: the history of psychology at the turn of the century; the origins of psychometric and factorial work; the contributions of Spearman and Thurstone; the growth of applied psychology in Britain; not to mention genetics, parapsychology, the philosophy of mind, and so on. The majority of reviewers would probably have to do much work to become knowledgeable about such a variety of topics. When we consider the reviewers, they almost all were especially well qualified to judge in *some* respect: perhaps for a knowledge of heredity, or an interest in psychometrics, in educational psychology, in scientific method. Virtually none were skilled in all, while many would know little of the early history of factorial analysis, though this plays so vital a part in Hearnshaw's verdict. Even a considerable interest in the history of psychology is most unlikely to guarantee more than a nodding acquaintance with many of the relevant early papers.

It follows that in this case, reviewers have to be taken with more than ordinary caution. They would be given a deadline and a limited number of words. What would most of them do except assume that Hearnshaw had done his homework, and knew what he was talking about? How many would now make the kind of study of Burt's contributions – most of them published many years earlier – that they would already have made of work in their own specialized field? How many of them checked a selection of Burt's early papers to see if Hearnshaw's allegations were accurate? How many looked again at his post-war twin papers? Thus even if the reviewers were chosen fairly and without bias, we should have to take what they said with more caution than usual. In the case of the biography of Burt, a review was less an expert critical study by an exceptionally well-informed person, and more an echo of what Hearnshaw said, by someone who simply took it for granted that he could be relied upon. There is little sign, among the large number of reviewers, that any were prepared to remind their readers that their knowledge of the area was limited, and their judgements tentative. Certainly I have not myself come across any review of the biography which for thorough, critical assessment could stand comparison with Mackintosh's review of Kamin.

But were the reviewers an unbiased selection? Looking first at the notices which appeared in the media, one can only suggest that it is hard to sustain a case that Burt was fairly treated. The experience of Stephenson is not reassuring. He records that when interviewed by CBS television he refused to blacken Burt's name in any way, much to the interviewer's chagrin. The interview never appeared. But an interview with Hudson, who was strongly critical of Burt, was shown in its place (see above, p. 251). It can hardly be denied that the media sometimes give the impression of believing that the public wants to see the names of the eminent in the mud, and the media try to oblige.

Nor does the weekly press seem to have been over-concerned to secure fair treatment. Those who were hostile to Burt, or to the positions which he had defended, had little difficulty in expressing their agreement with the verdict. Halsey, well-known as a left-wing critic of selective education, asked whether Hearnshaw had yet revealed the full extent of Burt's dishonesty – contriving to suggest that there was much more to be found without giving any reason for supposing so (*Times Higher Education Supplement*, 3 November 1979). Kamin expressed his satisfaction that Hearnshaw had accepted that Burt cooked his results (*Education Guardian*, 6 November 1979). Stephen Rose, another socialist and anti-hereditarian, referred to 'the biggest scientific scandal since the Piltdown hoax' (*New Statesman*, 28 September 1979). Such writers were far from subjecting the book to the kind of critical analysis they would have given without question to an hereditarian treatise, and took it as an opportunity to gloat over Burt's exposure and suggest that we didn't know the half of it. The Clarkes reviewed it twice, in *Nature* (8 November 1979), and in the *British Journal of Psychology* (1980, 71: 172–3), each review consisting largely of all the most damaging charges against Burt, together with their customary suggestion that there was more to be uncovered.

There can be no objection whatever to critics of Burt acting as reviewers, except in so far as their ill-concealed pleasure at the outcome outweighed their capacity for critical appraisal. But their views were not balanced by the opinions of those who were favourably inclined. None of the following, for instance, figures among the reviewers, at least in the most widely circulated journals: Audley, Banks, Cattell, Cohen, Jensen, Summerfield, Wall. Jensen (1983: 13) supposes that his initial defence of Burt precluded such invitations, editors preferring to follow the popular line of condemnation. It should be stressed that there were also reviewers who showed a detached attitude to the issues at stake, such as Chown (1980), Hawkes (1979), Mackintosh (1980), and O'Neil (1980); but all these accepted Hearnshaw's verdict without serious question. Of those I have seen, only Cronbach (1979) expressed reservations.

Probably the general impression most people would carry away from reading one or two reviews was that Hearnshaw had done a thorough job and that Burt's guilt had now been established beyond reasonable doubt. Few of the reviews were very lengthy, or showed much critical insight, or made any very penetrating analysis of the book's strengths and weaknesses. It is striking, and not perhaps surprising, that reviewers concentrated almost entirely on the issue of Burt's guilt, and passed over other aspects of Burt's contribution. My own opinion is that the historical allegations played a specially important part in persuading readers that Burt was guilty. Here was a lengthy series of additional deceptions, previously unpublicized, which they were in no position to assess without investing a prohibitive amount of time in studying old journals, and where Hearnshaw was assumed to be expert. After this, almost anything was believable. Thus the consensus of the reviewers, in accepting the verdict, meant little more than that Hearnshaw had made out a superficially convincing case, which none of them had the time or inclination to investigate.

It may be thought that the above remarks are grossly unfair, and that most reviewers would certainly have made the necessary study of the appropriate literature. However, it seems not unlikely that there is a fairly widespread tendency to avoid reading papers. Hudson (1977), when dealing with the initial question of why Burt was so long undetected, suggested that it was because few people read papers very carefully. Precisely the same point might be made about why his supposed exposure was so readily accepted. McCullough (1983) sounds a much-needed warning about the mistakes and misrepresentations which arise from reliance on secondary sources, and the uncritical acceptance of evidence that suits us. But he then adds that 'It would be too easy . . . to recommend that writers should always carefully check their primary sources: most have neither the time nor the stomach for such a dull and usually (one would hope) redundant task' (ibid.: 4). Certainly it would be 'grossly hypocritical', as McCullough suggests, to pretend that one invariably reads primary sources, and reads them carefully. But everything we have found in our study of the Burt affair strongly suggests that this can certainly not be assumed to be a redundant task, and that it may well be far too widely neglected, even in those instances where it is most obviously desirable. As Schwieso (1983: 89) observes, 'If we have no time, then we are surely doing too much . . . perhaps [psychology] can do without indifferent scholarship.' When Kamin claimed that he knew at once that Burt was fraudulent, and when Gould (1981) added that 'anyone could have exposed Burt's story as fiction after an hour's effort', they only illustrate how superficial their own efforts were, and how much they wanted to believe Burt guilty. As Hudson (ibid.: 13) remarks, we need to 'relearn the discipline of reading scientific papers before holding forth about what they contain'.

A particularly important group of commentators consisted of those who had a special claim to knowledge in the most relevant fields, who had defended Burt initially, and who altered their opinions when the biography appeared. Eysenck, Jensen, and Vernon were the three chief writers in this group. If these three had continued to defend Burt, and had offered a critical dissection of Hearnshaw's arguments, there can be little doubt that the controversy would never have subsided so quickly. The dissatisfaction of such authorities would have kept the issues open. When they now accepted the main charges, many would feel that the battle must be over.

Undoubtedly their defection seems a strong argument for Hearnshaw's verdict. But perhaps it is less powerful than it looks. Throughout the affair, writers have repeatedly asked how it was that they had failed to detect Burt's errors and deceptions long before. Why was it left to the environmentalists to discover the weaknesses in the evidence? The question was asked by Kamin (1977a), by Mackintosh (1980), and by many others. The implication was that they tended to accept without critical examination what suited their convictions. We have already agreed that 'hereditarians' had indeed accepted the 'evidence' too readily – just as the 'environmentalists' accept what suits them with equal agility. But if they were so negligent before, why should their conversion be regarded as so impressive now? Why should we suppose that they have learned their lesson, and now read the relevant papers with care before they pronounce? Why should so much reliance once more be placed upon the judgement of those who, supposedly, had so recently demonstrated their fallibility?

Did they now read Burt's early papers to satisfy themselves that Hearnshaw's statements were correct? Did they read his post-war papers to satisfy themselves that Burt's claims were as alleged? Unless they did, their opinion is worth little more than that of anyone else who read the biography. Vernon, in a review (an exception to the usual failure to ask Burt's supporters for comments), wrote that Hearnshaw had a reputation as a psychological historian of the utmost integrity and objectivity, and said that his book 'stills all doubts that . . . Burt did commit fraud' (Vernon 1980: 325). Does not this suggest that Vernon was so impressed by Hearnshaw's reputation that he thought it unnecessary to check? Jensen seems similarly to have been impressed, while Eysenck has since revealed the extent of his opposition to Burt.

The Council of the British Psychological Society

It is arguable that the public endorsement of Hearnshaw's verdict, by the council in February 1980, was among the more important influences leading to the general acceptance of Burt's guilt. In so far as British psychology could be said to have an official view, this was it. It is not unreasonable, therefore, to suppose that Council's announcement would have a powerful effect in persuading many psychologists that the whole controversy could now be regarded as closed, and that Burt's guilt could henceforth be assumed. Everyone would suppose that so important a decision, concerning so eminent a figure, by such an authoritative body, would have been taken only after careful examination of the evidence.

No reader need be told that, in reaching its decision, Council had a duty to be mindful of the need for a scrupulous adherence to considerations of justice and fair dealing. There are two main reasons for this. The first is simply that, even if Burt were guilty, he was still entitled to fair treatment; indeed, since he was unable to defend himself, the need for fair treatment was so much the stronger. The second reason is that if by any chance it should one day appear that Council's decision was mistaken, it would be of great importance to be able to demonstrate that the decision had been taken with due care. This would be in part in order to protect the reputation of the members of Council who had been responsible, but even more to protect the good name of psychology itself. If it transpired that the decision had been taken lightly, or hurriedly, or under the influence or possible influence of prejudice or personal ill will to Burt, the implications would be unfortunate.

There seems to have been a number of occasions on which Council considered the Burt affair, and made decisions about it. One such was reported in February 1980, in a statement which said that, when Gillie's charges became public, it had been decided that 'because Professor Leslie Hearnshaw was engaged on a biographical study of Burt, it seemed best to await his judgement on the issues raised rather than, for example, to set up a special inquiry' (see *Bull. Brit. Psychol. Soc.*, 1980, 33: 71). Obviously this decision had been taken some years earlier, presumably in late 1976 or early 1977. I have not been able to find any record of it in the minutes of Council for 1976 and 1977. However, there is a minute from a meeting of Council on 12 February 1977 which concerns Burt. This is of interest as showing the opinion which prevailed in Council at that time, and it may be this which Council had in mind in 1980.

On 12 February 1977, Council discussed a Report from the Finance and General Purposes Committee, a body which consists of the officers of Council, and whose function it is to prepare the business for full meetings of Council. Since Clarke and Tizard were both at that time officers of the society, they were members of the Finance Committee as well as Council, and were therefore in a powerful position to influence decisions. Item 1196, sub-section 6, reads as follows:

Letter from Professor H J Eysenck: re the late Sir Cyril Burt.

NOTED A letter from Professor Eysenck expressing concern about the behaviour of certain journalists in reporting views about the work of the late Sir Cyril Burt, and suggesting the setting up of an expert Committee to consider the matter.

RESOLVED: That the Standing Committee on Publications be asked to review existing editorial and refereeing procedures in order to ensure that inadequate papers do not in future appear in the Society's journals; and that the President be asked to write to Professor Eysenck informing him of this decision.

The issue raised by Eysenck concerned primarily the alleged frauds, not the wider question of errors in general. In his letter to the *Bulletin* of January 1977, Eysenck had regretted that the controversy about Burt's fraudulence had not been thrashed out in the appropriate scientific journals, which, he said, 'operate a proper refereeing system which guarantees as far as humanly possible absurd and nonsensical allegations do not pass this screening' (Eysenck 1977: 22); and he had also urged that the British Psychological Society should set up a committee of experts to look into the whole question of 'Burt's alleged misdemeanours' (ibid.).

The statement of February 1980 gave the impression that, from the time when the question of Burt's honesty was first raised (namely, 'when Gillie's charges became public') Council had scrupulously avoided taking sides in the matter or reaching a decision; it had decided to 'await Hearnshaw's judgement' rather than for example to set up a special inquiry. The minute of February 1977 certainly confirms that Council had decided not to agree to Eysenck's request for a special inquiry 'on the issues raised'. But there is no indication that Council resolved to maintain a neutral stance until Hearnshaw's verdict became available, nor that it decided to await Hearnshaw's judgement. Rather, it acted from the beginning as if Burt was at least to some extent already shown to be guilty. So far was Council from attempting to see that there was a fair inquiry that it took up a critical position without holding any inquiry.

If a special inquiry had been held at this time, it is plain that one of its first actions would have been to request those psychologists who had supported the charges to explain their reasons and provide their evidence. It would have been improper for Clarke and Tizard to serve on such an inquiry themselves, and instead of being judges in the matter, they would have found themselves being judged. Moreover, it would have been essential if an inquiry had been set up that the membership should be fairly constituted to ensure that justice was done – and who knows what such a committee of inquiry might have concluded? Since the evidence was at that time quite inconclusive, and since neither Clarke nor Tizard had much fresh evidence to add to what had already been published, it is very possible that any inquiry would have declared the charges unproved.

Thus it came about that the principal accusers were not required to justify themselves in public. The accusation, validated by their authority, hung unanswered in the air. Suspicion did duty for evidence. During the crucial months – from October 1976 until April 1978 – that Hearnshaw was making up his mind, two of Burt's principal accusers were occupying in succession the most influential positions in the British Psychological Society. One of them was at the same time in touch with Hearnshaw, through his wife (whom Hearnshaw thanked for her continued valuable assistance), and able to influence Hearnshaw's conclusions himself, as in his letter of 23 September 1976.

Council seems not to have taken any further action, after its decision of February 1977, until its meeting of 20 October 1979, held some three months after the publication of the biography in July 1979. Its decisions were announced the following February, 1980, when the Monthly Report in the *Bulletin* (1980, vol. 33: 71) stated that Council had discussed the Burt affair in the light of the biography. After listing the three main charges made by Hearnshaw, the Report continued as follows:

> With the evidence of fraud before it, the Council at its meeting on 20 October decided to take five further steps:
> (1) That at the Annual Meeting in Aberdeen in March 1980 Professor Hearnshaw should be invited to give a paper assessing the impact of Burt's falsifications.
> (2) That a symposium should be organised in which Burt's deceptions should be seen in the wider context of scientific method in psychology, and that in this symposium, Dr Gillie should be invited to speak.
> (3) That the Standing Committee on Publications should consider the preparation of a list of those of Burt's publications which should be considered unreliable.
> (4) That the Professional Affairs Board should consider the possibility of producing a statement of the effect of Burt's work on public policy.
> (5) That Dr Ann Clarke, who with Professor Alan Clarke had been instrumental in establishing Burt's fraud should be asked to consider the feasibility of establishing whether there were any further misdemeanours to which attention should be drawn over and above those already documented in Professor Hearnshaw's book.

It will be seen that the statement accepts without question that Hearnshaw's verdict was justified, and concerns itself simply with the further action deemed necessary in the light of his conclusion. A number of questions arise:

1 How long before the meeting of Council were its members informed

that they were going to be asked to consider the matter, and how many of them had in fact read the biography when they took their decision?

2 The Report claims that Council had 'the evidence of fraud before it'. Presumably this means that they possessed copies of the biography. But it should be clear that the book contains none of the evidence whatever. The evidence is to be found in the various books, papers, letters, and other documents to which the book refers – and of course other material not referred to by the book at all. The book contains only Hearnshaw's account of the evidence, not the evidence itself. The vital need was for someone to find out whether Hearnshaw had given an accurate and trustworthy account.

3 Was it proper that Dr Ann Clarke, known to have played a leading role in the accusations, should be invited to consider the possibility of 'further misdemeanours' – especially since the Clarkes had so often expressed the view that Burt had always been a 'confidence-trickster'?

4 The Monthly Report makes it plain that the symposium was not suggested with any view to holding an open discussion of Hearnshaw's conclusions, at which all shades of opinion would be able to find expression; nor to test the feeling in the society before reaching any decision; nor to give anyone an opportunity of replying to Hearnshaw's charges. It was to be held in order that 'Burt's deceptions should be seen in the wider context of scientific method in psychology'. In other words, it was intended to take Burt's guilt for granted. This conclusion is confirmed by the title given to the symposium at Aberdeen: 'The Burt scandal: what lessons can we learn?'

5 Although the decision had been taken in October 1979, the announcement of it was not made until February 1980, nearly four months later and only a few weeks before the conference was due to begin on 27 March. Whether or not this delay was intentional, its effect is obvious. Only those invited to take part in the symposium would have more than brief notice of what was to happen. Others would be left with little time to prepare anything, and no assurance that it could be used if they did. In particular, any member who wanted to protest about what was to be done would be unable to publish his protest before the symposium. Thus a letter from Audley, the first to object, did not appear until after the conference (Audley 1980). Others appeared still later.

Because the delay in announcing the symposium had these effects, we cannot assume that the effects were intended – that there was a deliberate attempt to bias the proceedings. But first no potential supporter of Burt was invited to take part. Banks writes (personal communication): 'No-one was asked. I only heard at the last moment . . . so I rang the President, and he almost begged me not to go, as Gillie was to be there, and they – the BPS – had had great trouble with him, he kept ringing up the Society!'

Second, Gillie, though neither a psychologist nor a member of the society, was invited to speak. In his introduction to the 'Balance sheet on Burt', the President of the society said that Council had arranged 'for an open discussion of the matter at the Annual Conference' (Connolly 1980: i). It is not easy to see how this claim can be justified.

It is not surprising that there were a number of forceful protests. Professor Audley, writing from University College, considered that it was 'more in the spirit of Gilbert and Sullivan than of respect for either justice or the pursuit of truth to pronounce a sentence on the basis of a book, no matter how great the known probity of the author', and that if it was thought desirable 'to pronounce and administer a sentence as severe as this on a deceased distinguished Fellow, then surely there was need for the special inquiry that was hinted at' (Audley 1980: 135). He added that 'at stake was the honour of a man, great in his day, and yet no sense of this, nor of sensitivity to judicial rectitude is apparent . . . if it is thought that the man should be judged, let the judging be fair and be seen to be fair' (ibid.).

Audley's letter appeared in April. It was followed in May by further objections from Summerfield (1980: 222) and from Norton (1980: 222); while subsequently both Parry (1980: 260) and McKellar (1980: 294–5) expressed their concern, the latter saying, 'May I ask for a more balanced perspective by the Council of the Society in assessing the many-sidedness of a very important figure in the history of British Psychology?'

Council took no further action in the matter, and left Dr Halla Beloff, who had edited the publication, to face the music. She argued that many psychologists had no reasonable doubt that Burt had used spurious data, and accordingly 'More in sorrow than in anger, some of us believe that as a discipline and as a profession, we have to acknowledge this, and acknowledge it publicly. Scientific probity demands it' (Beloff 1980a: 294). But the objection which the critics were making was not that Council had concluded publicly that Burt was guilty; it was that Council, in reaching its decision, had not shown a proper concern for ensuring that its procedures were adequate and fair.

An individual who brings charges of dishonesty against another has a duty to ensure that his evidence is soundly based. But how much greater was the obligation of Council to ensure that its decisions were beyond suspicion. All that we have found about the way in which Council conducted its affairs – especially the prominent part taken by those who had been his foremost accusers – and all we have discovered about the inadequate evidence on which the accusations were based, makes it hard to believe that Burt was treated fairly. Indeed, it is not easy to see how we can avoid Franglen's (1980: 222–3) severe judgement: 'Council's behaviour is totally unworthy of a learned society' (ibid.: 222–3).

The chain of events

Those who believe that Burt was innocent need feel no great difficulty in explaining how the accusations came to be made, nor in understanding why they were eventually so widely accepted.

The accusations arose in a field which had been the centre of political controversy for a long period, and which had recently become especially heated. Burt was only one among many accused of dishonesty; but in his case matters went further, not least because being recently dead he could no longer defend himself. But there were many motives for supporting the accusations besides the political: intellectual disagreements; academic conflicts; and also those personal characteristics of Burt which aroused antipathy in some.

The endorsement of the accusations was the almost inevitable outcome of a sequence of prejudicial events. First, publication in the media secured the maximum publicity for the charges with the minimum possibility of serious or sustained examination of them.

Second, Hearnshaw was under pressure from both the 'anti-Burters' and 'pro-Burters'. He hit upon the idea of striking a compromise between the two, which inevitably meant a verdict of guilty – not as guilty as the anti-Burters alleged, but not as innocent as the pro-Burters maintained.

Third, reviewers generally believed Hearnshaw's account without hesitation, apparently making little attempt to check it. Their unanimity gave the impression that 'the experts' agreed with Hearnshaw, whereas those who disagreed got little say.

Fourth, a final factor was the action of the Council of the British Psychological Society in approving the verdict. The bias of the council, of which Alan Clarke was still a member, was evident in several ways, especially in accepting a one-man inquiry as sufficient, in arranging a symposium which was to take his guilt for granted, and in allotting to Ann Clarke the task of looking for further evidence.

There were however two major indications that the verdict might prove premature. The first came immediately in the form of numerous letters of protest. The second was delayed until 1983 when the *Journal of the Association of Educational Psychologists* produced its series of papers at Burt's centenary. It was unfortunate that this appeared in a journal whose circulation is small and specialized. The accusations had been blazoned across the media. The defence had to be content with relative obscurity.

Burt's work was more detached than that of Kamin, more self-critical than that of Eysenck, more firmly based in experience than that of the Clarkes, more accurate than that of Hearnshaw, and more knowledgeable than that of all of them combined. But all was to no avail once he was dead. Then he could be attacked with impunity.

Lessons of the Burt affair

Jensen (1974: 26–7) lists the information which kinship studies ought ideally to contain. Thoday (1981: 517) is more directly concerned with avoiding fraud, and suggests: (1) that 'editors of professional journals should be more inclined to publish basic data, and require careful accounts of how raw data have been treated'; and (2) that 'editors should be required to submit their own papers to external referees, nominated by someone other than the editor, for many of Burt's papers were not refereed'. (The second recommendation had already been adopted by the British Psychological Society in 1977. Burt's major paper, 1966a, was not in fact published in his own journal, and so was refereed as Thoday suggests.) Perhaps we may add that for psychology the most effective requirements would be, first, certain minimum information about the subjects employed, such as name and address, date of birth, sex; and second, photocopies of raw data sheets, including date and place of examination, and person conducting inquiry; this information to be retained by the journal in question for a minimum length of time, and to be available for inspection by interested colleagues. Such precautions would not overcome the possibility of an author excluding unwanted results; but at least it would enable someone else to repeat the experiment exactly, and compare his own results with those reported. Rennie (1981) discusses several further possibilities.

These suggestions can be supported as strongly by those who think Burt innocent as by those who think him guilty, because they would be as powerful a protection against false accusation as against fraud itself. The charges against Burt could in all probability have been answered immediately, one way or the other, if such precautions were routine. However, most of those who have sought 'lessons' have been preoccupied with ways of eliminating false data. It is equally important to eliminate false accusations. As we have seen, several authors have scattered their insinuations with a minimal regard for evidence, and editors have often published their allegations thoughtlessly. Yet this is highly damaging and irresponsible, and frequently grossly unfair to their victims. We have seen so many examples of this in recent years that its elimination ought to be considered as urgent as the elimination of fraud itself.

The last thing to prevent is criticism; but it must be informed criticism, and those who accuse should produce their evidence before their charges are published. They should not be permitted to sit in judgement on others without themselves being required to justify their behaviour. It may be objected that, while a man is still alive, he is already too well protected by the laws of libel, and further protection will make criticism still harder. But if authors are required to submit raw data, most criticism may effectively take the form of pointing to deficiencies in what has been provided. One of the most marked features of the accusations against Burt has been the failure of the original accusers to provide adequate evidence, even though Burt was then already dead; and this failure is the more striking in that one of their principal criticisms of Burt has always concerned a lack of information.

But whether all this would be enough may be doubted; indeed, there may be a danger of supposing that the sheer mechanical application of rules will solve our problems. Blackman (1980) doubts whether there are fixed rules which provide even experimentalists, at the 'hard' end of psychology, 'with security and safety from making false or inappropriate inductive inferences about their data'. He points cogently to our 'failure to recognize the nature of the *judgements* that we must make about the reliability, generality and importance of psychological data. . . . Any systematic insensitivity to these issues could even perhaps lead to a situation which might be described by others as fraudulent.' He illustrates his point with a quotation from Hudson's *Cult of the Fact* (1972: 125), which expresses the matter so well that it may be repeated here:

the search for meaning in data is bound to involve all of us in distortion to greater or lesser degree. Psychology should be pictured not as a society of good men and true, harbouring the occasional malefactor, but rather, as one in which everyone is searching for sense; in which differences are largely those of temperament, tradition, allegiance and style; and in which transgression consists not so much in a clean break with professional ethics, as in an unusually high-handed, extreme or self-deceptive attempt to promote one particular view of reality at the expense of all others.

Although I agree entirely with these remarks, there is one extremely important aspect which needs to be given greater weight: the social dimension. It is easy to slip into the belief that the 'judgement' involved is entirely individual, and that the prejudice and bias which that judgement may display also belong solely to the individual. This leads us to imagine that more attention by that offending individual to the orthodox rules will put matters right. But the difficulty which is involved presents us with a much tougher nut to crack. As Samelson (1980: 623) argues:

Our search for understanding must go beyond a call for more attentive reading and replication. We must admit that our model of science . . . fails to take into account all the shared social effects impinging on real scientists enmeshed in their society. (The impersonal style imposed on our scientific accounts – and leading to the misrepresentation of actual practice – is symbolic of and contributes to this mystifying oversight.)

These points all find clear illustration in the Burt affair. Again and again, individual judgements are being swayed by social pressures. It is most obvious, perhaps, in relation to political conviction and public policy. Between the wars, questions of selection and the inheritance of ability seem to have been relatively uncontroversial. There was a consensus, which was shared by the psychologists themselves, and their findings – or rather, the interpretations which they placed upon their findings – were taken as giving scientific respectability to that consensus. Supposedly, scientific psychology was endorsing what seemed plain common sense. Burt, as a leading figure, was honoured by his grateful countrymen, and his knighthood symbolized psychology's position as 'the glass of fashion'.

When in the 1950s and 1960s the consensus broke, the limitations of psychology's pretensions were exposed. Now it became clear that more than one interpretation was possible, and weaknesses became evident in the previous 'findings', which had been obscure before. Now Burt and other hereditarians found themselves exposed to criticism, which was the more virulent in that the consensus had disappeared. He is even accused of the most sensational scientific fraud of the century. It is impossible to imagine that Burt would ever have been so accused while his ideas were popular. He was admired as long as his views were in accordance with the accepted wisdom: he was rejected when that wisdom was questioned.

So long as the Burt affair is seen as the story of a flawed individual, there is little to be learned from it that need disturb us unduly. A pathological condition can hardly be foreseen, and might occur in any scientist; accordingly, we may be thankful that it strikes infrequently. Indeed, if there are any lessons at all to be learned on this interpretation, they are rather of a flattering order. Those critics who first detected Burt's iniquities are to be congratulated on their vigilance; his biographer is to be praised for providing such a brilliant analysis of the weaknesses of his character; and the psychological establishment is to be honoured for accepting the outcome so openly and unreservedly. The whole matter may be put behind us while we resume our scientific progress.

The Burt affair must never be forgotten. It must be kept always before us, because whatever Burt did or failed to do, and whatever his critics did or failed to do is what we are all doing all the time. It is a paradigm of the corruption of scientific judgement by the common sense, the values, and the controversies of the everyday world. When psychology can assure us that its judgements are genuinely detached, it will have made a giant step towards mature science.

A disputed priority

There has been some dispute whether Kamin or Jensen originated the posthumous criticism of Burt. The importance of the question – at least to the participants – is obvious. Environmentalists have frequently taunted hereditarians with uncritical acceptance of Burt's 'data'. If Kamin, an environmentalist, was the first to mention Burt's faults, it can be suggested that, left to themselves, the hereditarians would never have noticed them. But if Jensen was the first, the hereditarian preserves some dignity.

Eysenck (1977a) described Jensen as discovering Burt's errors and miscalculations. Vetta (1977) countered that Kamin's talks had preceded Jensen's paper. Eysenck (1977c) replied that in priority disputes only published evidence is usually considered. Kamin (1977a) stated that he had 'pointed out some of Burt's ambiguities and contradictions' in a correspondence with Jensen which he had initiated on 18 April 1972, and added that Jensen (1974: 12, footnote) had acknowledged one of his 1972 talks which had covered the same material. Gillie (1977) also mentioned this point. Mcloughlin (1983: 9, footnote 7) added some further details.

Letter from Thorndike to Spearman, 17 October 1904

[I am grateful to Dr Banks for supplying this letter.]

Teachers College
Columbia University
New York.

Mr. Charles Spearman,
  Haydnstrasse 4, 1,
    Leipzig, Germany.   October 17th, 1904.

Dear Mr. Spearman,

I am afraid I am not quite keen enough yet to fully answer your arguments. I can't even be perfectly sure whether I totally agree with you or totally disagree. My vacation has perhaps been a little too much for me.

I see that my expectation of getting the general accident rate down to one per cent is vain. At the same time I feel a decided preference for working with as accurate original measurements as may be in correlation. I misunderstood, I think, your view of the meaning of the correlation you got between sensory activities and intelligence. I thought you meant that if we had perfectly accurate measures of, say, discrimination of length, they would correlate perfectly with such an accurate measure of general capacity as we arrive at by getting the general sense of, say, a thousand competent independent observers. As I understand you now, your view is that if we got an accurate measure of the common element in all varieties of sense discrimination, it would correlate perfectly with intelligence, the fact being that the different varieties of sensory activity agree together only in a general core or kernel of intellect itself. If this were the case, I should interpret it as follows: that in measuring any sensory activity we measured a complex of the mere sensory capacity and of the capacity to understand instructions, to be attentive and ambitious, to use all the clues that might be available in making the sensory judgement. These latter factors would be practically identical with the factors involved in what we call intellect. The correlation then between sensory activities as measured and general intelligence would be due to the fact that the sensory activity as measured is not a function of the mere reception of stimuli but involves the so-called higher powers. It would seem to me that this shows precisely that what the psychology books mean by accuracy of discrimination does *not* correlate at all with general intelligence. *It* is just the thing which lessens the correlations and which you eliminate by your method of correlation. Of course, this is only verbal, but every one whom I have talked with about your second article seemed to think that you believed that if we got a measure of mere discriminative power uninfluenced by steadiness of attention, comprehension of instruction, zeal, and the like, we would get a high correlation of it with general intelligence. You also give the impression, though I see now that this is due to our stupidity, of believing that if you got a perfectly accurate measure of, say, discrimination alone, it would correlate perfectly with a perfectly accurate measure of general intelligence. As I understand your letter, this is the farthest possible from your view, as it is, of course, from mine.

The data to which I alluded about the sensory faculties of scientific men are not yet, I think, in print. Three or four years ago we tested fifty members of the American Association for the Advancement of Science with the ordinary laboratory tests in sense discrimination, memory, accuracy of movement, and the like. They did not do as well as ordinary college students.

I shall wait a little longer for my encyclopedia letter of questions and facts. Very likely the book you speak of writing on mathematical means of psychological study will answer some of them, if it comes out soon. I have myself written a very elementary introduction to the theory of mental measurements, which I am sending you by this mail. I am afraid there may be some gross blunders in it, though I hope not. It may very likely be such a thing as will serve as a useful preface to your book. I hope you will let me know sometime what you think about the chapter on Relationships in it, at least.

Yours faithfully,

Edward L. Thorndike.

Appendix C

Note from Burt (1917: 53) on the statistical methods he was using

The figures for Tables XVIII. (hypothetical general factor), XIX. and XX. are obtained by employing the usual formula for 'multiple correlation' –

$$r_{12 \cdot 3} = \frac{r_{12} - r_{13} \cdot r_{23}}{(1 - r_{13}^2)^{\frac{1}{2}} (1 - r_{23}^2)^{\frac{1}{2}}} \; \ldots \text{(i.)}$$

Thus, if the h.g.f. be the sole origin of correlations, the theoretical coefficients (Table XIX.) can be found at once by the following equation, which follows directly from (i.), –

$$r_{12} = r_{13} \cdot r_{23} \; \ldots \text{(ii.)}$$

where $r_{13} \cdot r_{23}$ = h.g.f. coefficients, 1 and 2 indicating any tests and 3 the h.g.f.

Again, if the specific correlations be treated as, in the long run, negligible, the h.g.f. coefficients (Table XVIII.) can be found by the following equation, which follows directly from (ii.), –

$$= \frac{a_1}{\sqrt{A}} \; \ldots \text{(iii.)}$$

where a_1 = total (or average) of the entire row of observed coefficients for any test, 1, and A = total (or average) of the coefficients in the whole table. In the case of the reliability coefficients, and certain other tests pairs (cf. Table XX.), the specific factors are not negligible. I have, therefore, assumed that the latter group neutralise each other on taking the table as a whole, and have omitted the reliability coefficients. This omission necessitates a slight, but obvious, complication in applying formula (iii.).

The specific correlations (Table XX.) merely require the use of equation (i.) in its original form.

The whole series of calculations is, of course, but provisional and tentative; and the results but first approximations.

Letter from Sir Halford Cook,
30 August 1984

11 Boisdale Street,
Surrey Hills,
Victoria,
Australia.

30 August 1984

Dear Dr Joynson,

I have been saddened during my visit to Britain to learn from Dr Charlotte Banks that the life and work of Sir Cyril Burt are still being the subject of denigration by lesser mortals. I am now stirred to put pen to paper to say a few things that don't seem to have been sufficiently emphasised. I write as one who was a post-graduate student during 1939, while working on a Ph.D. with Professor Burt as my supervisor and mentor at large.

(1) Great men and women, and for that matter those not so great, should be assessed in the context and by the standards of their times. This applies just as much to Burt as it does say to Darwin or Freud, neither of whom have or will escape the criticism of later generations. Burt was certainly a product of the late 19th and early 20th centuries, without the Tools and well-paid Staff resources of present day research and academic psychologists with their newly acquired scientific methodologies. Burt will be remembered long after *all* his detractors will be forgotten.

(2) Burt's early work with children and his publications 'The Young Delinquent' and 'The Backward Child' may seem 'old hat' now but at the time represented a significant break-through, the first serious attempt by a social scientist (even if Burt may not have described himself in those terms) to study, with a humane and practical concern, these neglected subject areas. It was for this reason alone that I chose to study under Burt at University College, and in this I was not alone. I was not disappointed.

(3) Unfortunately World War II cut short my personal association with Burt, but my impressions of him as a man and a psychologist remain with me. As an Australian in what was for me a strange environment I found Burt warmly sympathetic and understanding, always ready to advise if

331

advice was needed, without any suggestion of wishing to intrude or instruct. In the post-graduate colloquia he revealed an erudition, breadth and depth of knowledge and wisdom with a modesty the like of which I have never since experienced. Methodological weaknesses, human frailty, then or later, one of the truly great men of the period, a giant in psychology.

I treasure that totally unnecessary personal letter he wrote to me when I had to discontinue my post-graduate work because of the war. This is one document, at least, that was not actually destroyed and is some evidence that we both did in fact exist!

You may do with this note as you will.

Yours sincerely,

Halford Cook.
(Sometime President of the Australian Branch of the BPS)

Bibliography

Adiseshiah, W. (1978) Correspondence. *Bulletin of the British Psychological Society* 31: 133.

Adorno, T. W., Frenkel-Brunswik, E., Levinson, D. J., and Sanford, R. N. (1950) *The Authoritarian Personality*, New York: Harper.

Allport, G. W. (1955) *Becoming: Basic Considerations for a Psychology of Personality*, New Haven, Conn.: Yale University Press.

Archer, Grete (1983) 'Reflections on Sir Cyril Burt', *Journal of the Association of Educational Psychologists* 6: 53–5.

Audley, R. J. (1980) Correspondence. *Bulletin of the British Psychological Society* 33: 135.

Banks, C. (1979) Correspondence. *New Statesman*, 2 Feb. 1979: 150.

Banks, C. (1983) 'Professor Sir Cyril Burt: selected reminiscences', *Journal of the Association of Educational Psychologists* 6: 21–42.

Banks, C. and Broadhurst, P. L. (1965) *Stephanos: Studies in Psychology presented to Cyril Burt*, London: University of London Press.

Bartlett, F. C. (1932) *Remembering*, Cambridge: Cambridge University Press.

Beloff, H. (1980a) Correspondence. *Bulletin of the British Psychological Society* 33: 294.

Beloff, H. (ed.) (1980b) 'A balance sheet on Burt', Supplement to *Bulletin of the British Psychological Society* 33.

Blackman, D. E. (1980) 'On data and experimental psychology', in H. Beloff, (1980b: 24–31).

Blain, Isobel (1982) Obituary of Dr C B Frisby, *Bulletin of the British Psychological Society* 35: 319.

Boring, E. G. (1950) *A History of Experimental Psychology*, 2nd edn, New York: Appleton.

Bouchard, T. J. and McGue, M. (1981) 'Familial studies of intelligence: a review', *Science*, 212: 1055–9.

Broad, W. J. and Wade, N. (1982) 'Science's faulty fraud detectors', *Psychology Today* 16: 50–4, 57.

Broad, W. J. and Wade, N. (1983) *Betrayers of the Truth*, New York: Simon & Schuster.

Brown, W. (1911) *The Essentials of Mental Measurement*, Cambridge: Cambridge University Press; 1st edn (2nd edn, 1921, 3rd edn, 1925, by W. Brown and G. H. Thomson).

Burt, C. L. (1909) 'Experimental tests of general intelligence'. *British Journal of Psychology* 3: 94–177.

Burt, C. L. (1911a) 'Experimental tests of general intelligence', Report of the British Association for Advancement of Science 79: 804.

Burt, C. L. (1911b) 'The experimental study of general intelligence', *Child Study* 4: 33–45 and 92–101.

Burt, C. L. (1911c) 'Experimental tests of higher mental processes and their relation to general intelligence', *Journal of Experimental Pedagogy* 1, (2): 93–107.

Burt, C. L. (1912) 'The inheritance of mental characters', *Eugenics Review* 4: 168–200.

Burt, C. L. (1915) 'General and specific factors underlying the primary emotions', Report of the British Association for the Advancement of Science LXXXIV: 694–6.

Burt, C. L. (1917) 'The distribution and relations of educational abilities', London County Council.

Burt, C. L. (1921) *Mental and Scholastic Tests*. London: King & Son; 1st edn.

Burt, C. L. (1923a) 'The causal factors of juvenile crime' *British Journal of Medical Psychology* 3: 1–33.

Burt, C. L. (1923b) *Handbook of Tests for Use in Schools*, London: King & Son; 2nd edn 1948.

Burt, C. L. (1924) 'Historical sketch of the development of psychological tests', in *Psychological Tests of Educable Capacity*: 1–61. Board of Education: HMSO.

Burt, C. L. (1925) *The Young Delinquent*, London: University of London Press.

Burt, C. L. (1926) *A Study in Vocational Guidance*, with co-authors F. Gaw, L. Ramsey, M. Smith, and W. Spielman, Industrial Fatigue Research Board, Report 33, HMSO.

Burt, C. L. (1937a) *The Backward Child*, London: University of London Press; 1st edn.

Burt, C. L. (1937b) 'Methods of factor-analysis with and without successive approximation', *British Journal of Educational Psychology* 7: 172–95.

Burt, C. L. (1938) 'The analysis of temperament', *British Journal of Medical Psychology* 17: 158–78.

Burt, C. L. (1939a) 'William McDougall: an appreciation', *British Journal of Educational Psychology* 9: 1–7.

Burt, C. L. (1939b) 'The factorial analysis of emotional traits', *Character and Personality* 7: 238–54 and 285–99.

Burt, C. L. (1940) *The Factors of the Mind*, London: University of London Press.

Burt, C. L. (1943) 'Ability and income', *British Journal of Educational Psychology* 13: 83–98.

Burt, C. L. (1945) 'The assessment of personality', *British Journal of Educational Psychology* 15: 107–21.

Burt, C. L. (1947a) 'Factor analysis: its aims and results', *Miscellanea Psychologia, Albert Michotte*: 49–75. Louvain: Institut Supérieur de Philosophie.

Burt, C. L. (1947b) 'A comparison of factor analysis and analysis of variance', *British Journal of Psychology (Statistical Section)* 1: 3–26.

Burt, C. L. (1947c) Review of Thurstone (1947), *British Journal of Psychology (Statistical Section)* 1: 70–1.

Burt, C. L. (1947d) Critical Notice of Thurstone (1947), *British Journal of Educational Psychology* 17: 163–9.

Burt, C. L. (1948a) 'Factor analysis and canonical correlation', *British Journal of Psychology (Statistical Section)* 1: 95–106.

Burt, C. L. (1948b) 'The factorial study of temperamental traits', *British Journal of Psychology (Statistical Section)* 1: 178–203.

Burt, C. L. (1949a) 'Alternative methods of factor analysis and their relation to

Pearson's method of "principal axes"', *British Journal of Psychology (Statistical Section)* 2: 98–121.

Burt, C. L. (1949b) 'The two-factor theory', *British Journal of Psychology (Statistical Section)* 2: 151–78.

Burt, C. L. (1949c) 'An autobiographical sketch', *Occupational Psychology* 23: 1–12.

Burt, C. L. (1949d) 'The structure of the mind: a review of the results of factor analysis', *British Journal of Educational Psychology* 19: 100–11 and 176–99.

Burt, C. L. (1950a) 'Factorial study of the emotions', in M. L. Reymert (ed.) *Feelings and Emotions*, New York: McGraw-Hill, 531–51.

Burt, C. L. (1950b) Review of *Human Ability (1950)*, by C. Spearman and L. Wynn Jones, *British Journal of Psychology (Statistical Section)* 3: 191.

Burt, C. L. (1952a) 'An autobiographical study', in *History of Psychology in Autobiography*, vol. IV: 53–73. Edited by E. G. Boring, H. S. Langfeld, H. Werner and R. M. Yerkes, Worcester, Mass.: Clark University Press.

Burt, C. L. (1952b) Introduction to W. McDougall, *Psychology*, 2nd edn, Oxford: Oxford University Press, v–xix.

Burt, C. L. (1955a) 'The evidence for the concept of intelligence', *British Journal of Educational Psychology* 25: 158–77.

Burt, C. L. (1955b) 'L'analyse factorielle: méthodes et résultats', *Colloques Internationaux de Centre National de la Recherche Scientifique*, Paris: 79–92.

Burt, C. L. (1958) 'The inheritance of mental ability', Bingham Lecture, 1957, *American Psychologist* 13: 1–15.

Burt, C. L. (1961a) 'Galton's contributions to psychology', *Bulletin of the British Psychological Society* 45: 10–21.

Burt, C. L. (1961b) 'Intelligence and social mobility', *British Journal of Statistical Psychology* 14: 3–24.

Burt, C. L. (1962a) 'Francis Galton and his contribution to psychology', *British Journal of Statistical Psychology* 15: 1–49.

Burt, C. L. (1962b) 'The concept of consciousness', *British Journal of Psychology* 53: 229–42.

Burt, C. L. (1966a) 'The genetic determination of differences in intelligence: a study of monozygotic twins reared together and apart', *British Journal of Psychology* 57: 137–53.

Burt, C. L. (1966b) 'The early history of multivariate techniques in psychological research', *Multivariate Behavioural Research* 1: 24–42.

Burt, C. L. (1967a) 'The evidence for the concept of intelligence', abridged and revised by the author from Burt (1955a), in *Intelligence and Ability: Selected Readings*, pp. 260–81; ed. by Stephen Wiseman; Harmondsworth: Penguin Books, 1967.

Burt, C. L. (1967b) 'The genetic determination of intelligence: a reply', *British Journal of Psychology* 58: 153–62.

Burt, C. L. (1967c) 'The structure of the mind', abridged and revised by the author from Burt (1949d). In *Intelligence and Ability: Selected Readings*, pp. 193–217. Edited by Stephen Wiseman; Harmondsworth: Penguin Books, 1967. [In revising this paper for Wiseman's collection, Burt added a short section on 'Emotional Factors' (pp. 215–16) not present in the original; and this is the section quoted in the present text.]

Burt, C. L. (1968) 'An illustration of factor analysis', appendix to chap. 2 of Butcher (1968): 66–71.

Burt, C. L. (1969a) 'The mental differences between children', in C. B. Cox and A. E. Dyson (eds) *Black Paper II*, pp. 16–25. London: The Critical Quarterly Society.

Burt, C. L. (1969b) 'Recent studies of abilities and attainments', *Journal of the Association of Educational Psychologists* 2: 4–9.

Burt, C. L. (1969c) 'Intelligence and heredity: some common misconceptions', *Irish Journal of Education* 3: 75–94.

Burt, C. L. (1969d) Toronto Symposium on Intelligence, London: Methuen.

Burt, C. L. (1971) 'Quantitative genetics in Psychology', *British Journal of Mathematical Statistical Psychology* 24: 1–21.

Burt, C. L. (1972) 'The inheritance of general intelligence', (the Thorndike Lecture), *American Psychologist* 27: 175–90.

Burt, C. L. (1975) *The Gifted Child*, London: Hodder & Stoughton.

Burt, C. L. and Banks, C. (1947) 'A factor analysis of body measurements for adult British males', *Annals of Eugenics* 13: 238–56.

Burt, C. L. and Howard, M. (1956) 'The multifactorial theory of inheritance and its application to intelligence', *British Journal of Statistical Psychology* 9: 95–131.

Burt, C. L. and Howard, M. (1957) 'Heredity and intelligence: a reply to criticisms', *British Journal of Statistical Psychology* 10: 33–63.

Burt, C. L. and Moore, R. C. (1912) 'The mental differences between the sexes', *Journal of Experimental Pedagogy* 1(4): 273–84; and 1(5): 355–88.

Butcher, H. J. (1968) *Human Intelligence*, London: Methuen.

Cattell, R. B. (1978) Correspondence. *Bulletin of the British Psychological Society* 1: 18–19.

Cattell, R. B. and Molteno, E. V. (1940) 'Contributions concerning mental inheritance', *Journal of Genetic Psychology* 57: 31-47.

Chambers, E. G. (1943) 'Statistics in psychology and the limitations of the test method', *British Journal of Psychology* 33: 185–92.

Chown, S. (1980) Review of Hearnshaw (1979), *British Journal of Psychology* 71: 171.

Clarke, A. D. B. (1950a) 'The measurement of emotional instability by means of objective tests: an experimental inquiry', Ph.D. thesis: University of London Library.

Clarke, A. D. B. (1950b) 'The measurement of emotional instability by means of objective tests: an experimental inquiry', *British Journal of Educational Psychology* 20: 202.

Clarke, A. D. B. (1978) Autobiographical note. *Bulletin of the British Psychological Society* 31: 249.

Clarke, Ann M. (1980) 'Comments on heritability', in H. Beloff (1980b: 37–8).

Clarke, A. D. B. and Clarke, Ann M. (1974) *Mental Deficiency*, 3rd edn, London: Methuen.

Clarke, A. D. B. and Clarke, Ann M. (1976) *Early Experience: Myth and Evidence*, London: Open Books.

Clarke, Ann M. and Clarke, A. D. B. (1977) Correspondence, *Bulletin of the British Psychological Society* 30: 83–4.

Clarke, Ann M. and Clarke, A. D. B. (1979) 'The cardinal sin', Review of Hearnshaw (1979), *Nature* 282: 150–1.

Clarke, Ann M. and Clarke, A. D. B. (1980a) 'Comments on Professor Hearnshaw's *Balance sheet on Burt*', in H. Beloff (1980b: 17–19).

Clarke, Ann M. and Clarke, A. D. B. (1980b) Review of Hearnshaw (1979), *British Journal of Psychology* 71: 172–3.

Clarke, Ann M. and McAskie, M. (1976). 'Parent–offspring resemblances in intelligence: theories and evidence', *British Journal of Psychology* 67: 243–73.

Cohen, J. (1977) 'The Detractors', *Encounter*, March 1977: 86–90.

Cohen, J. (1983). 'Sir Cyril Burt: a brief note', *Journal of the Association of Educational Psychologists*, 6: 64–77.

Connolly, Kevin (1980) 'Introduction' to H. Beloff (1980b).

Conway, J. (1958) 'The inheritance of intelligence and its social implications', *British Journal of Statistical Psychology* 11: 171–90.

Conway, J. (1959) 'Class differences in general intelligence', *British Journal of Statistical Psychology* 12: 5–14.

Cox, C. B. and Dyson, A. E. (eds) (1969a; 1969b; 1970) *Black Paper I, II and III*, London: The Critical Quarterly Society.

Cronbach, L. J. (1975) 'Five decades of public controversy over mental testing', *American Psychologist* 30: 1–14.

Cronbach, L. J. (1979) Review of Hearnshaw (1979), *Science* 206: 1392–4.

Darlington, C. D. (1962) 'Introduction' to Galton's *Hereditary Genius*, London: Fontana Library.

Dorfman, D. D. (1978) 'The Cyril Burt question: new findings', *Science* 201: 1177–86.

Dorfman, D. D. (1979a) Correspondence, *New Statesman*, 2 Feb. 1979: 150.

Dorfman, D. D. (1979b) Correspondence, *Science* 204: 246–54.

Dorfman, D. D. (1979c) Correspondence, *Science* 206: 142–4.

Douglas, J. W. B. (1964) *The Home and the School* London: MacGibbon & Kee.

Duncan, D. C. (1986) Correspondence. *Bulletin of the British Psychological Society* 39: 378–9.

Evans, B. and Waites, B. (1981) *IQ and Mental Testing: an Unnatural Science and its Social History*, London: Macmillan.

Eysenck, H. J. (1939) 'Primary mental abilities', *British Journal of Educational Psychology* 9: 270–6.

Eysenck, H. J. (1952) 'Uses and abuses of factor analysis', *Applied Statistics* 1: 45–9.

Eysenck, H. J. (1954) *The Psychology of Politics*, London: Routledge & Kegan Paul.

Eysenck, H. J. (1971) *Race, Intelligence and Education*, London: Temple Smith.

Eysenck, H. J. (1972) 'The dangers of the New Zealots', *Encounter* 39: 79–91.

Eysenck, H. J. (ed.) (1973a) *The Measurement of Intelligence*, Lancaster: MTP.

Eysenck, H. J. (1973b) *The Inequality of Man*, London: Temple Smith.

Eysenck, H. J. (1977a) Correspondence, *Bulletin of the British Psychological Society* 30: 22.

Eysenck, H. J. (1977b) 'The case of Sir Cyril Burt', *Encounter* 47: 19–24.

Eysenck, H. J. (1977c) Correspondence, *Bulletin of the British Psychological Society* 30: 258.

Eysenck, H. J. (1980a) Correspondence, *Bulletin of the British Psychological Society* 33: 361–2.

Eysenck, H. J. (1980b) 'Psychology of the scientist: XLIV. Sir Cyril Burt: prominence versus personality', *Psychological Reports*, 46: 893–4.

Eysenck, H. J. (1982) 'Burt's warped personality led inevitably to fraud', *The Listener*, 29 April 1982: 2–3.

Eysenck, H. J. (1983) 'Sir Cyril Burt: polymath and psychopath', *Journal of the Association of Educational Psychologists* 6: 57–63.

Farr, R. M. (1980) 'Some observations on the nature of probity in science: the case of Sir Cyril Burt', in H. Beloff (1980b; 32–6).

Flew, Antony (1973) *Crime or Disease?* London: Macmillan.

Floud, J. E., Halsey, A. H., and Martin, J. M. (1956) *Social Class and Educational Opportunity* London: Heinemann.

Flugel, J. C. (1933) *A Hundred Years of Psychology*, London: Duckworth.

Flugel, J. C. (1954), 'A hundred years or so of psychology at University College', *Bulletin of the British Psychological Society* 23: 21–31.

Franglen, S. (1980) Correspondence, *Bulletin of the British Psychological Society* 33: 222–3.

Fraser Roberts, D. J. A. (1976) Letter to *The Times*, 29 Nov. 1976.

Freeden, M. (1979) 'Eugenics and progressive thought: a study in ideological affinity', *Historical Journal*, 22(3): 645–7.

Fulker, D. (1975) Review of Kamin (1974), *American Journal of Psychology* 88: 505–19.

Galton, F. (1869) *Hereditary Genius*, London: Macmillan (2nd edn, 1892).

Galton, F. (1875) 'The history of twins as a criterion of the relative powers of nature and nurture', *Fraser's Magazine* 12: 566–76.

Galton, F. (1883) *Inquiries into Human Faculty and its Development*, London: Macmillan.

Galton, F. (1888–9) 'Co-relations and their measurements chiefly from anthropometric data', *Proceedings of the Royal Society* xlv: 135–45.

Galton, F. (1889) *Natural Inheritance*, London: Macmillan.

Gergen, K. J. (1973) 'Social psychology as history', *Journal of Personality and Social Psychology* 26: 309–20.

Getzels, J. W. and Jackson, P. W. (1962) *Creativity and Intelligence*, New York: Wiley.

Gibson, H. B. (1981) *Hans Eysenck: the man and his work*, London: Peter Owen.

Gillie, O. (1976a) *Who Do You Think You Are?* London: Hart Davis/MacGibbon.

Gillie, O. (1976b) 'Crucial data was faked by eminent psychologist', London: *Sunday Times*, 24 Oct. 1976.

Gillie, O. (1977) Correspondence, *Bulletin of the British Psychological Society* 30: 257–8.

Gillie, O. (1978a) Correspondence, *Bulletin of the British Psychological Society* 31: 199.

Gillie, O. (1978b) 'Sir Cyril Burt and the great IQ fraud', *New Statesman*, 24 Nov. 1978: 688–94.

Gillie, O. (1979) 'Burt's missing ladies', *Science* 204: 1035–8.

Gillie, O. (1980) 'Burt: the scandal and the cover-up', in H. Beloff (1980b: 9–16).

Gould, S. J. (1981) *The Mismeasure of Man*, New York and London: Norton.

Gravely, Ann M. (1950a) 'An investigation of perceptual tests as measures of temperament', Ph.D. thesis; University of London Library.

Gravely, Ann. M. (1950b) 'An investigation of perceptual tests as measures of temperament', *British Journal of Educational Psychology* 20: 203–4.

Guilford, J. P. (1936) *Psychometric Methods*, New York: McGraw-Hill.

Guilford, J. P. (1950) 'Creativity', *American Psychologist* 5: 444–54.

Guilford, J. P. (1967) *The Nature of Human Intelligence*, New York: McGraw-Hill.

Halsey, A. H. (1979) Review of Hearnshaw (1979), *Times Higher Educational Supplement* 30 Nov. 1979: 18.

Handy, J. A. (1987) 'Psychology and social context', *Bulletin of the British Psychological Society* 40: 161–7.

Harman, H. H. (1967) *Modern Factor Analysis*, Chicago: University of Chicago Press, 2nd edn, revised.

Hawkes, N. (1979) 'Tracing Burt's descent to scientific fraud', *Science* 205: 673–5.

Hearnshaw, L. S. (1964) *A Short History of British Psychology*, London: Methuen.

Hearnshaw, L. S. (1972) 'Emeritus Professor Sir Cyril Burt (1883–1971)', *Bulletin of the British Psychological Society* 25: 31–3.

Hearnshaw, L. S. (1977) Correspondence, *Bulletin of the British Psychological Society* 30: 22–3.

Hearnshaw, L. S. (1979) *Cyril Burt: Psychologist*, London: Hodder & Stoughton.

Hearnshaw, L. S. (1980) 'Balance sheet on Burt', in H. Beloff (1980b; 1–8).

Hearnshaw, L. S. (1984a) 'Commentary on the Burt symposium', *Journal of the Association of Educational Psychologists* 6: 5–6.

Hearnshaw, L. S. (1984b) Letter to Miss S. A. Lander, 20 Oct. 1984.

Hebb, D. O. (1949) *The Organization of Behavior*, New York: John Wiley.

Heider, F. (1958) *The Psychology of Interpersonal Relations*, New York: John Wiley.

Heim, Alice (1954) *The Appraisal of Intelligence*, London: Methuen.

Herrman, L. and Hogben, L. (1933) 'The intellectual resemblance of twins', *Proceedings of the Royal Society of Edinburgh* 53: 105–29.

Hinchcliffe, R. (1967) 'Personality profile in Ménière's disease', *Reports of the Institute of Laryngology and Otology* 17: 152–5.

Hudson, L. (1966) *Contrary Imaginations*, London: Methuen.

Hudson, L. (1972) *The Cult of the Fact*, London: Cape.

Hudson, L. (1977) 'Foreword' to L. J. Kamin (1974) *The Science and Politics of I.Q.*, published in *Penguin Education* 1977.

Hunt, J. McV. (1961) *Intelligence and Experience*, New York: Ronald Press.

James, W. (1889) 'The congress of physiological psychology at Paris', *Mind* 14: 614–16.

James, W. (1890) *Principles of Psychology*, vol. 1. New York: Henry Holt.

James, W. (1892) *Psychology: Briefer Course*, New York: Henry Holt.

Jensen, A. R. (1969) 'How much can we boost IQ and scholastic achievement?' *Harvard Educational Review* 39: 1–123.

Jensen, A. R. (1970) 'IQs of identical twins reared apart', *Behavior Genetics* 1: 133–46.

Jensen, A. R. (1972) Sir Cyril Burt: Obituary, *Psychometrika* 37: 115–17.

Jensen, A. R. (1974) 'Kinship correlations reported by Sir Cyril Burt', *Behavior Genetics* 4: 1–28.

Jensen, A. R. (1978) 'Sir Cyril Burt in perspective', *American Psychologist* 33: 499–503.

Jensen, A. R. (1980) *Bias in Mental Testing*, London: Methuen.

Jensen, A. R. (1981) *Straight Talk about Mental Tests*, New York: Free Press.

Jensen, A. R. (1983) 'Sir Cyril Burt: a personal recollection', *Journal of the Association of Educational Psychologists* 6: 13–20.

Kamin, L. J. (1974) *The Science and Politics of IQ*, New York and London: John Wiley & Sons. (Page references in the text are from the Penguin 1977 edition.)

Kamin, L. J. (1976) 'The hole in heredity', *New Statesman*, 2 Dec. 1976.

Kamin, L. J. (1977a) Correspondence, *Bulletin of the British Psychological Society* 30: 259.

Kamin, L. J. (1977b) 'Burt's IQ data', *Science* 195: 246–8.

Kamin, L. J. (1979) Review of Hearnshaw (1979), *The New Republic*, 20 Oct. 1979: 30–2.

Kamin, L. J. (1981) *Intelligence: the Battle for the Mind*, (H. J. Eysenck versus Leon Kamin), London: Macmillan.

Kelley, T. L. (1923) *Statistical Method*, New York: Macmillan.

Kline, P. (1980) 'Burt's false results and modern psychometrics: a comparison', in H. Beloff (1980b: 20–3).

Kuhn, T. S. (1962) *The Structure of Scientific Revolutions*, Chicago: University of Chicago Press.

Lawley, D. N. and Maxwell, A. E. (1963) *Factor Analysis as a Statistical Method*, London: Butterworth.

Lewis, D. G. (1966) Commentary on 'The genetic determination of differences in intelligence' by Cyril Burt, *British Journal of Psychology* 57: 431–3.

Lovie, A. D. (ed.) (1985) 'The 1909 Spearman–Burt correspondence on general intelligence and the origins of single factor analysis', *Teorie and Modelli* 2: 85–99.

Luria, A. R. (1979) *The Making of Mind*, Cambridge, Mass.: Harvard University Press.

McAskie, M. (1978) 'Carelessness or fraud in Sir Cyril Burt's kinship data? A critique of Jensen's analysis', *American Psychologist* 33: 496–8.

McAskie, M. and Clarke, A. *see* Clarke, A. and McAskie, M. (1976).

McCullough, M. L. (1983) 'A testing time for the test of time', *Bulletin of the British Psychological Society* 36: 1–5.

Macdonell, W. R. (1901). 'On criminal anthropometry and the identification of criminals', *Biometrika* 1: 177–227.

McKellar, P. (1980) Correspondence, *Bulletin of the British Psychological Society* 33: 294–5.

Mackintosh, N. J. (1975) Review of Kamin (1974), *Quarterly Journal of Experimental Psychology* 27: 672–86.

Mackintosh, N. J. (1980) Review of Hearnshaw (1979) *British Journal of Psychology* 71: 74–5.

Mcloughlin, C. S. (ed.) (1983) 'Sir Cyril Burt: the essential man', special issue; *Journal of the Association of Educational Psychologists* 6(1).

MacRae, D. G. (1978) Correspondence, *New Statesman* 96: 820.

Mischel, W. (1981) *Introduction to Personality*, 3rd edn, New York: Holt, Rinehart & Winston.

Moore, T. (1983) 'Thoughts on the integrity of Sir Cyril Burt', in Mcloughlin (1983: p. 42).

Newman, H. H., Freeman, F. N., and Holzinger, K. J. (1937) *Twins: a Study of Heredity and Environment*, Chicago: Chicago University Press.

Norton, M. (1980) Correspondence, *Bulletin of the British Psychological Society* 33: 222.

Oléron, P. (1957). *Les Composantes de l'intelligence d'après les recherches factorielles*, Paris: Presses Universitaires de France.

O'Neill, W. M. (1980) Review of Hearnshaw (1979), *British Journal of Psychology* 71: 175–6.

Parry, J. (1980) Correspondence, *Bulletin of the British Psychological Society* 33: 260.

Paul, D. (1984) 'Eugenics and the Left', *Journal of the History of Ideas*, 45(4): 567–90.

Pearson, Karl (1900) *The Grammar of Science*, 2nd edn, London: Black.

Pearson, Karl (1901a) 'On the systematic fitting of curves to observations and measurements', *Biometrika* 1: 265–303.

Pearson, Karl (1901b) 'On lines and planes of closest fit to systems of points in space', *Philosophical Magazine* 2: 559–72.

Pearson, Karl (1904) 'On the laws of inheritance in man', *Biometrika* 3: 132–62.

Pearson, Karl (1914–30) *Life, Letters and Labours of Francis Galton*, 4 vols, Cambridge: Cambridge University Press.

Peters, R. S. (1962) *Brett's History of Psychology*, ed. and abridged by R. S. Peters, 1953; rev. edn 1962, Cambridge, Mass.: MIT Press.

Philpott, S. J. F. (1932) 'Fluctuations in human output', *British Journal of Psychology, Monograph Supplement*, no. 17.

Rawles, R. E. (1977) Correspondence, *Bulletin of the British Psychological Society* 30: 354.

Rennie, E. F. N. (1981) 'Avoiding scandal: some thoughts', *Bulletin of the British Psychological Society* 34: 127–8.

Rimland, B. and Munsinger, H. (1977) 'Burt's IQ data', *Science* 195: 248.

Rose, S. (1979) Review of Hearnshaw (1979), *New Statesman*, 28 Sept. 1979: 469–70.

Rose, S., Kamin, L. J., and Lewontin, R. C. (1984) *Not in our Genes*, London: Penguin Books.

Rowe, D. and Plomin, R. (1978) 'The Burt controversy: a comparison of Burt's data with data from other studies', *Behavior Genetics* 8: 81–3.

Rubin, D. B. (1979) Correspondence, *Science* 204: 245–6.

Rubin, D. B. and Stigler, S. M. (1979) Correspondence, *Science* 205: 1204–6.

Samelson, F. (1980) 'J. B. Watson's Little Albert, Cyril Burt's twins and the need for a critical science', *American Psychologist* 35: 619–25.

Sarason, S. B. (1981) *Psychology Misdirected*, New York: The Free Press.

Schwieso, J. (1983) Correspondence, *Bulletin of the British Psychological Society* 36: 89.

Semin, G. (1986) 'The individual, the social, and the social individual', *British Journal of Social Psychology* 25: 177–80.

Shackel, B. (1978) Correspondence, *Bulletin of the British Psychological Society* 31: 200.

Schultz, D. (1975) *A History of Modern Psychology*, New York: Academic Press.

Sharp, S. E. (1899) 'Individual psychology: a study in psychological method', *American Journal of Psychology* 10: 329–91.

Shields, J. (1962) *Monozygotic Twins: Brought Up Apart and Brought Up Together*, Oxford: Oxford University Press.

Simon, B. (1953) *Intelligence Testing and the Comprehensive School*, London: Lawrence & Wishart.

Skanes, G. R. (1978) Correspondence, *Bulletin of the British Psychological Society* 31: 201.

Sluckin, W. (1971) (ed.) *Early Learning and Early Experience*, Harmondsworth: Penguin Modern Psychology Readings.

Spearman, C. E. (1904a) 'The proof and measurement of association between two things', *American Journal of Psychology* 15: 72–101.

Spearman, C. E. (1904b) 'General intelligence: objectively measured and determined', *American Journal of Psychology* 15: 201–99.

Spearman, C. E. (1927) *The Abilities of Man* London: Macmillan.

Spearman, C. E. (1946) 'Theory of the general factor', *British Journal of Psychology* 36: 117–31.

Spearman, C. E. and Hart, B. (1912) 'General ability, its existence and nature', *British Journal of Psychology* 5: 51–84.

Spearman, C. E. and Holzinger, K. (1924) 'The sampling error in the theory of two factors', *British Journal of Psychology* 15: 17–19.

Spearman, C. E. and Wynn Jones, L. (1950) *Human Ability*, London: Macmillan.

Stephenson, W. (1979) 'Observations on Sir Cyril Burt and the "Burt affair"', *Operant Subjectivity* 2: 110–23.

Stephenson, W. (1980) 'Professor Kamin, Sir Cyril Burt, and hyperbole', *American Psychologist* 35: 1144–6.

Stephenson, W. (1981) Correspondence, *Bulletin of the British Psychological Society* 34: 284.

Stephenson, W. (1983) 'Cyril Burt and the special place examination', *Journal of the Association of Educational Psychologists* 6: 46–53.

Stigler, S. M. (1979) Correspondence, *Science* 204: 242–5.

Stott, D. H. (1966) Commentary on 'The genetic determination of differences in intelligence' by Cyril Burt, *British Journal of Psychology* 57: 423–9.

Stout, G. F. (1896) *Analytic Psychology*, vol. I, London: Sonnenschein.

Summerfield, A. (1980) Correspondence, *Bulletin of the British Psychological Society* 33: 222.

Sutherland, G. and Sharp, S. (1980) 'The fust official psychologist in the wurrld: aspects of the professionalization of psychology in early twentieth-century Britain', *History of Science* 18: 181–208.

Thoday, J. M. (1981) 'Probity in science: the case of Cyril Burt', Review of Beloff (1980b), *Nature* 291: 517–18.

Thomson, G. H. (1939) *Factorial Analysis of Human Ability*, London: University of London Press.

Thorndike, E. L., Lay, W., and Dean, P. R. (1909) 'The relation of accuracy of sensory discrimination to general intelligence', *American Journal of Psychology* 20: 364–9.

Thurstone, L. L. (1938) 'Primary mental abilities', *Psychometric Monographs*, no. 1.

Thurstone, L. L. (1947) *Multiple Factor Analysis*, Chicago: Chicago University Press.

Tizard, B. and Clarke, A. D. B. (1983) *Child Development and Social Policy: the Life and Work of Jack Tizard*, Leicester: The British Psychological Society.

Tizard, J. (1977) 'The Burt affair', *University of London Bulletin* 41: 4–7.

Vernon, P. E. (1950) *The Structure of Human Abilities*, London: Methuen.

Vernon, P. E. (1980) Review of Hearnshaw (1979), *Bulletin of the British Psychological Society* 33: 325.

Vetta, A. (1977) Correspondence, *Bulletin of the British Psychological Society* 30: 115.

Vetta, A. (1980) 'Concepts and issues in the IQ debate', *Bulletin of the British Psychological Society* 33: 241–3.

Vincent, D. F. (1953) 'The origin and development of factor analysis', *Applied Statistics* 2: 107–17.

Vincent, D. F. (1954) 'The earliest formulae used in factor analysis', *American Journal of Psychology* 67: 155–63.

Wade, N. (1976) 'IQ and heredity: suspicion of fraud beclouds classic experiment', *Science* 194: 916–19.

Wall, W. D. (1983) 'Sir Cyril Burt – a personal note', in Mcloughlin (1983: 43–5).

Ward, J. (1886) Article on 'Psychology' in the *Encyclopedia Britannica*, 9th edn.

Watson, J. B. (1930) *Behaviorism*, Chicago: University of Chicago Press; rev. edn.

Williams, Moyra (1984) Correspondence, *Bulletin of the British Psychological Society* 37: 101.

Wolfle, D. (1940) 'Factor analysis to 1940', *Psychometric Monographs* 3: 69.

Woodworth, R. S. (1949) *Contemporary Schools of Psychology*, 2nd edn, London: Methuen.

Woodworth, R. S. and Sheehan, M. R. (1964) *Contemporary Schools of Psychology*, 3rd edn, New York: Ronald Press.

Wrigley, C. and Neuhaus, J. O. (1952) 'A re-factorization of the Burt–Pearson matrix with the Odvac electronic computer', *British Journal of Psychology (Stat)* 5: 105–8.

Zangwill, O. L. (1950) *An Introduction to Modern Psychology*, London: Methuen.

Index